THE MYSTIC M

The Mystic Mind is the result of a fascinating collaboration between a medieval historian and a professor of psychiatry, applying modern biological and psychological research findings to the lives of medieval mystics and ascetics. This illuminating study examines the relationship between medieval mystical experiences, and the religious practices of mortification of the body.

Laceration of the flesh, sleep deprivation, and extreme starvation, while undoubtedly related to cultural and religious motivations, directly produced dramatic effects upon the body and brain functioning of the heroic ascetics, that in turn brought about altered states of consciousness. Applying modern understandings of physiology, the authors demonstrate how heroic asceticism could be used to obtain a desired mystical state, as well as examining and disputing much contemporary writing about the political and gender motivations in the medieval quest for closeness with God.

Drawing upon a database of 1,462 medieval holy persons as well as in-depth studies of individual saints, *The Mystic Mind* is essential reading for all those with an interest in medieval religion or the effects of self-injurious behavior on the mind.

Jerome Kroll is Professor of Psychiatry at the University of Minnesota Medical School. He is the author of *The Challenge of the Borderline Patient* (1988), *PTSD/Borderlines in Therapy* (1993) and co-author, with Sir Martin Roth, of *The Reality of Mental Illness* (1986). He is the current president of the Association for the Advancement of Philosophy and Psychiatry.

Bernard Bachrach is Professor of History at the University of Minnesota. He has written or edited fifteen books and over one hundred articles on medieval history, including several studies on medieval mental illness in collaboration with Jerome Kroll.

THE MYSTIC MIND

The Psychology of Medieval
Mystics and Ascetics

*Jerome Kroll
and
Bernard Bachrach*

Routledge
Taylor & Francis Group
NEW YORK AND LONDON

First published 2005
by Routledge
270 Madison Ave, New York, NY 10016

Simultaneously published in the UK
by Routledge
2 Park Square, Milton Park, Abingdon, Oxon OX14 4RN

Routledge is an imprint of the Taylor & Francis Group

© 2005 Jerome Kroll and Bernard Bachrach

Typeset in Galliard by
Keystroke, Jacaranda Lodge, Wolverhampton
Printed and bound in Great Britain by
MPG Books Ltd, Bodmin

All rights reserved. No part of this book may be reprinted or
reproduced or utilized in any form or by any electronic,
mechanical, or other means, now known or hereafter
invented, including photocopying and recording, or in any
information storage or retrieval system, without permission in
writing from the publishers.

Library of Congress Cataloging in Publication Data
Kroll, Jerome.
The mystic mind : the psychology of medieval mystics and ascetics /
Jerome Kroll and Bernard Bachrach.
p. cm.
Includes bibliographical references.
Mysticism–Psychology. 2. Asceticism–Psychology. 3. Mystics–
Psychology. 4. Ascetics–Psychology. 5. Church history–Middle
Ages, 600–1500. 6. Psychology, Religious. I. Bachrach, Bernard S., 1939–
II. Title.
BL625.K76 2005
248.2'2'019–dc22
2004020258

British Library Cataloguing in Publication Data
A catalogue record for this book is available from the British Library

ISBN 0–415–34050–0 (hbk)
ISBN 0–415–34051–9 (pbk)

To the hidden Kathleen
Who sees the unseen

To Deborah for her support
Over the many years

CONTENTS

Preface ix
Acknowledgments xi

1 Introduction 1

PART I
Psychology and biology **15**

2 Heroic asceticism and self-injurious behavior 17
3 Mysticism and altered states of consciousness 37
4 Pain and laceration of the flesh 66
5 Sleep deprivation 75
6 Fasting and starvation 83

PART II
History **89**

7 Historical methods: selecting a database 91
8 Pathways to holiness 105
9 Radegund 129
10 Beatrice of Nazareth 146
11 Beatrice of Ornacieux 161
12 Henry Suso 165

13 Mental illness, hysteria, and mysticism	182
14 Conclusion	203
Appendix: statistical analyses	209
Notes	219
Bibliography	248
Index	264

PREFACE

This book has been an interdisciplinary endeavor and, as such, the authors have benefited from many rich discussions, insights, and critiques of colleagues and friends. In particular, we would like to thank the late Roger De Ganck, Chaplain to Our Lady of the Redwoods Monastery for his close friendship, support, and loving conversations. We also thank the late former Abbess Myriam Dardennes and the Cistercian community of Our Lady of the Redwoods Monastery for opening their hearts and their community to us. We have been enriched by discussions with Professor Noel Dermot O'Donoghue of Edinburgh University, Professor Columba Stewart of St. Johns University in Collegeville, Minnesota, Dara Malloy and Tess Harper of the Aran Islands, and the Reverend Marcus Losack of Ceile De in Glendalough, Ireland. Mary Schaffer, Curator of the Arca Artium Research Collection of St. John's University, Collegeville, was most generous of her time and expertise in locating medieval illustrations and supplying textual background for the images that grace this book.

Discussions with professors Luke Demaitre and Stanley Jackson provided us with insight and clarity into the history of medicine in the Middle Ages. At the University of Minnesota, our colleagues gave us their expertise in various physiological and psychological areas: absorption and altered states of consciousness (Auke Tellegen), pain (Donald Simone), sleep (Mark Mahowald and Tom Hurwitz), and fasting and starvation (James Mitchell). Paul Thuras and Joel Hechtner provided the statistical analyses for our studies. We thank our editors in the history section at Routledge, Vicky Peters and Jane Blackwell, for their help and insights in keeping the project on track, as well as Professor Ursula King of the University of Bristol, England and an anonymous reviewer for their thoughtful critiques of earlier drafts of the manuscript that propelled us into more judicious revisions.

We especially appreciate the computer expertise and patience of John Hopwood at the University of Minnesota, who convinced us that there were system solutions other than throwing the equipment (and, with it, the electronic manuscript) out the window. We also thank Jennifer Summer Armstrong for unstinting data entry services and Mary DeWitt, Janet Holland, Janet Bockenstedt and Gloria Wolf for clerical and administrative support.

PREFACE

Finally, JK wishes to express his deep thanks to Kathleen Carey for her continuous support, encouragement, and critical and perceptive readings of the manuscript.

ACKNOWLEDGMENTS

Excerpts from Henry Suso: *The Exemplar, with Two German Sermons*, translated and edited and introduced by Frank Tobin; preface by Bernard McGinn; from The Classics of Western Spirituality, Copyright © 1989 by Frank Tobin, Paulist Press, Inc., New York/Mahwah, NJ. Used with permission of Paulist Press. <www.paulistpress.com>

An earlier version of Chapter 13 appeared in *Mental Health, Religion and Culture* (5: 83–98, 2002), reprinted with permission of Taylor and Francis Ltd. <www.tandf.co.uk>

Reproductions of the engravings, woodblock prints, and manuscript illuminations are courtesy of the Saint John's Rare Book Library and the Kacmarcik Collection of Arca Artium Rare Book Library, Saint John's University, Collegeville, Minnesota.

Reproductions of Dominicus Loricatus, Guthlacum, and Zoerarde are from the *Sylvae sacre*. Images by Marten de Vos; engravings by Johann and Raphael Sadeler. Munich?: 1594. Kacmarcik Collection of Arca Artium.

Reproduction of Cometa et Nicosa is from *Solitudo, sive vitae foeminarum anachoreticum*. Images by Marten de Vos; engravings by Adrian Collaert. Antwerp: Adrian Collaert, *c.*1593. Kacmarcik Collection of Arca Artium.

Reproductions of Amelberge, Bathilde, Odile, and Radegund are from *Images de Saints et Saintes de la famille de l'empereur Maximilien I*. Images by Hans Burgkmaier; woodcuts by H. Frank, C. Liefrink, A. Lindt, J. de Negker, W. Resch, H. Taberith, G. Taberith. Vienna: F.X. Stockl, 1799. The images were printed from woodblocks cut between 1517–1519.

Reproduction of Colette and Marguerite de Cortonne are from *Les vies des SS. Peres des deserts, et des saintes solitaires d'Orient et d'Occident. Avec des Figures qui représentent l'austérité de leur vie, leurs principales occupations*. Book two [of four]. (Printed) Antwerp; (Sold) Amsterdam, Pierre Brunel, 1714.

Miraculous Mass (f.133v) is from the *Book of Hours*. Sarum use. France (Rouen), end fifteenth century. Manuscript on vellum.

1

INTRODUCTION

Defining the questions[1]

Recurring figures throughout medieval history, ones that attracted and still attract more attention than the actual numbers would justify, are the religious mystic and heroic ascetic. Capturing local and, at times, national and international notoriety, mystics such as Hildegard of Bingen (1098–1179), Francis of Assisi (1181–1226), and Julian of Norwich (1342–1416) and heroic ascetics such as Simeon Stylites the elder (c.388–459) and younger (521–597), Peter of Luxembourg (1369–1387), and Catherine of Siena (1347–1380) served as exemplars of Christian pursuit of the divine and rejection of worldly values.

Simultaneously, some of these holy persons also became objects of suspicion and ridicule because of their public displays of excessive holiness and self-injurious practices. Benedict of Aniane (c.745–821), who in his later years was Charlemagne's architect of monastic reform, was criticized for the ferociousness of his earlier self-inflicted injuries. Christina Mirabilis (1150–1224) was considered mad because of her excessive asceticism, and Juliana of Mont Cornillon (1193–1258) drew the ire of her sister nuns for her debilitating fasts. Francis of Assisi was considered a half-wit because of his uncompromising voluntary poverty and Brother Giles of Assisi (d.1262), who went into trance states at the mere mention of the word "Paradise," was taunted by children who shouted "paradise" over and over again. Flora of Beaulieu (1309–1347) was not only ridiculed as a hypocrite by the sisters of her priory for her religious devotions, but was further humiliated when outsiders were invited to the priory to stare at and mimic her.

The high visibility of such mystics and ascetics has made it difficult to gain an accurate estimate and sober appraisal of their prevalence and influence in medieval expressions of piety. Questions about the psychology of intense mysticism and heroic asceticism have similarly been affected by the religious partisanship and emotionality that arise when one considers in detail the other-worldliness of the mystics and the mortifications and physical damage some ascetics have inflicted upon themselves.

The religious quest for a mystical experience can be seen as one special category within an elemental human tendency to escape or transcend the ordinary state of consciousness. If consciousness is a fundamental and defining characteristic of the human condition, then the drive to escape or move beyond the cluttered and often unpleasant day-to-day state of consciousness to a variety of altered states, including mystical states, is an equally basic human trait. All societies recognize and bestow elevated status upon religious and mystical forms of altered states of consciousness and their immediate and long-term after-effects.

Each society determines the specific conditions, induction techniques, rules, and particular types of altered states that constitute legitimate religious ritual and ceremony. Among these methods, sometimes used in combination, are various forms of meditation and prayer, chanting, whirling and dancing, drumming, fasting, social isolation, sleep deprivation, ingestion of alcohol and other drugs, and self-injurious behaviors. Societies also instruct and prepare novices and initiates regarding what types of experiences to expect when in different altered states of consciousness, and provide a rich vocabulary, usually metaphorical, to describe these experiences. In medieval Europe, altered states of consciousness, characterized as pathways to mystical union with God, were the ultimate goal of spiritually oriented persons. This generalization must be refined by the understanding that what was entailed in union with God changed from the intellectualized Platonic notion held in the early Middle Ages to the personalized and emotional notion of mystical union with Jesus held in the later Middle Ages.

Some medieval holy persons appear to have been able to achieve, through techniques of prayer and meditation, those forms of altered states that constitute a mystical experience. Many others were not, especially since Western Christianity during much of the Middle Ages did not have available, despite John Cassian's (d.435) early influence, as strong a tradition of meditative practices as those found in Eastern religions (Hinduism and Buddhism), or even Eastern Orthodoxy, that could be methodically taught to novices and initiates. We are referring here to the absence of a body of prescriptive knowledge and techniques that could be formally taught as an orderly sequence of prayer and meditation that permits and guides practitioners progressively to clear their minds of worldly concerns and to focus, most usually, on the presence of Christ that resides within. Such techniques, when present, were relatively underdeveloped in the West prior to the eleventh century, when the major concerns of the ecclesiastical and governing segments of society were the ongoing conversion of the population to Christianity and the inculcation of a Christian world view into secular society.

Given these limitations in the transmission of meditative techniques, some spiritually driven persons employed harsh self-injurious practices as a method of inducing altered states of consciousness. Mild to moderate self-denying and self-injurious behaviors as a form of ascetic discipline had the sanction of being compatible with and even expressive of the larger Christian world view of *contemptus mundi*. However, there was fairly uniform official disapproval, although ambivalent popular responses, of the extreme measures which some heroic ascetics undertook.

In addition to broad socio-cultural influences that affect attainment of altered states, individuals differ greatly in their ability, propensity, and motivation to experience altered states. As with all other human traits and dispositions that are distributed as dimensional properties across a population, variation among individuals in proneness to experience altered states of consciousness (such as absorption, transcendence, ease of entering into trance states, and suggestibility) most likely reflects differences in genetic disposition as well as differences in life experiences.

For some individuals, altered states are achieved relatively easily. Others, however, including some who express strong desire to experience transcendental states, have great difficulty, if they are able at all, in reaching even moderate levels of altered states that a few gifted persons seem to achieve so effortlessly. To be "earthbound" when the premier value of one's group, such as a fourteenth-century Rhineland monastic community, is literally to soar with the angels, is to be placed at great psychological and moral disadvantage, both introspectively and socially. The thick-boundaried person, one who cannot easily shift into other levels of reality but who nevertheless desires and is encouraged to experience an altered (mystical) state, has several options. One is to help the process along by whatever means are culturally and personally available (such as sleep deprivation, severe fasting, or mortification of the flesh). Alternatively, one may pursue several other patterns, including outright faking such states, or imitating the behaviors of genuine mystics until one can talk oneself into believing that one is really experiencing ecstatic states, or accepting the fact that one's pathway to holiness is not the mystical journey, but rather some combination of moderate asceticism and charitable and administrative works. The role of God's grace as the critical factor in achieving a mystical state, such that human endeavor and merit are irrelevant, inserts itself into these discussions, but in practical terms, the very notion of holiness in later medieval society usually entailed, whatever the theoretical role of grace, an intense personal pursuit of closeness with Christ.

Critics, both medieval and modern, of heroic asceticism have asserted that altered states achieved via self-injury are not bona fide mystical states, and that the heroic ascetic mistakes perversity for holiness. This controversy is part of the larger question of the role of any trance-inducing technique other than prayer and meditation in the formation of a mystical state. We are not here suggesting that self-injurious behaviors are a particularly effective or doctrinally correct way to achieve a mystical state, or that what is achieved is similar to mystical states reached through other methods, but only that religiously committed individuals have in fact used such ascetic behaviors as a method of trance induction. As a corollary observation, use of alcohol and plant medicinals to produce an altered state of consciousness, a legitimate method of religious trance induction in cultures worldwide with minimal political stratification, was criticized and discouraged in medieval Europe, and any altered states thus achieved were not considered authentic mystical states.

In present Western society, alcohol and drugs have been the statistically preferred and socially acceptable methods of altering one's waking state of consciousness for secular purposes. But ingestion of these substances remains, as in medieval times, generally devalued and proscribed as methods of trance induction in mainstream

INTRODUCTION

Christian religious contexts, despite some attempts in the 1960s to experiment with hallucinogens as inducers of transcendental states. Heroic asceticism too is considered, by both religious and professional consensus, a suspect and relatively deviant method of legitimate mystical quest. Prayer and meditation are the preferred routes to pursuit of closeness to God in present Western society, but this has created an awkward situation because knowledge and teaching of meditative techniques, such as were developed in medieval Europe and by the sixteenth-century Spanish mystics, notably Ignatius Loyola (1491–1556) and John of the Cross (1542–1591), have languished in the face of the scientific revolution and the Protestant Reformation. Reflecting the relative poverty of a tradition of meditative practices in the Western world up to the present time, there has been increased attention recently to Eastern forms and techniques of meditation as means of achieving a more "genuine" altered state of consciousness, one that depends neither upon alcohol and drugs nor self-injurious behaviors.

Interestingly enough, the field of psychiatry/psychotherapy has developed a very recent, but intense interest in one category of altered state of consciousness known as dissociative episodes and its extreme expression, multiple personality. One school of modern psychological theory links the propensity to develop dissociative states to experiences of sexual abuse in childhood, although the validity and significance of these findings are fiercely debated. It appears that, in many cases, dissociative episodes with rich and non-credible imagery have been induced in patients by overly zealous therapists, a finding that speaks to the suggestibility and imagination of many persons who readily dissociate. Childhood sexual abuse is also strongly associated in most studies with self-injurious behaviors in adulthood. Thus, the conjunction of self-injurious behaviors and altered states of consciousness, seen prominently in some medieval mystics, appears in some twentieth-century young adults, but, in keeping with the predominantly secular approach to understanding behaviors considered deviant, the convergence is explained in modern times in terms of altered states of consciousness as post-traumatic stress responses to childhood sexual abuse rather than as spiritually directed behavior in search of union with God.

Explicitly, we are not suggesting that there is any relationship between asceticism and mysticism in medieval Europe and the experience of childhood sexual abuse. There are other reasons, nevertheless, for comparing the apparent increase in self-injurious behaviors and its conjunction with altered states of consciousness in the later Middle Ages and in the latter half of the twentieth century. First, we have an opportunity to study directly the physiology and psychology of modern self-injurers, which we obviously cannot do with medieval persons. Although the psychology might turn out, or be postulated, as very different between medieval and modern experiences, the opposite would be true for the physiology. Human physiology, and the major effects of physiological changes caused by self-injurious practices upon psychological functioning, has not changed much if at all in one millennium. It is possible, however, that motivation and a positive emotional state when engaged in self-injurious behaviors might in turn influence the physiological effects of these behaviors in medieval practitioners as compared to modern self-injurers.

Further, there may be similarities in the formal characteristics of the pattern of social diffusion of such self-injurious behaviors within susceptible populations. In both medieval and modern times, there appears to be a contagiousness in how the phenomena of self-injurious behaviors and altered states of consciousness spread among culturally primed or susceptible groups, and in how society, at times, reinforces self-injurious behaviors by providing and endorsing meaningful explanations and responses to such behaviors.

The significance of social support for self-injurious behavior and altered states of consciousness in both periods is noteworthy. This is especially important because there has also been, in each society, considerable opposition to the practice of self-injurious behaviors and suspiciousness about the development of dramatic forms of altered states of consciousness. Critics of the practice of self-injurious behaviors and the development of altered states in medieval and modern times have perceived these behaviors as either outright manipulations of public sentiment or as evidence of deep psychological disturbances. At the same time, social institutions have encouraged in various ways the very actions that they claim to condemn. For example, special status in terms of exemption from work productivity and acknowledgment that temporary caretaking may be required are found in medieval monastic and modern secular institutions for those who display altered states of consciousness and self-injurious behaviors. In addition, in some circles, there has been a certain cachet or mystique in those modern self-injurers labeled Borderline Personality Disorder or, in the case of anorexia nervosa, Hunger Artists.

Attempts to apply modern psychological understanding to the behaviors of the major heroic ascetic figures, and to the hundreds of lesser known ascetics who have earned either their own religious biographies or occasional mention in other medieval source material, are exceptionally controversial. Criticism and defense of the use of the methods and insights of behavioral sciences in regard to medieval patterns of behavior have been colored by the basic attitudes of belief or skepticism with which historians and others have approached the topic. Levels of explanation concerning why certain medieval persons injured themselves have ranged from psychoanalytic investigations, which predictably consider extreme asceticism as examples of psychopathology, to hagiographically tinged studies that perceive ascetic excesses as understandable responses of intensely God-driven individuals.

Historians have traditionally examined and explained the phenomena of excessive self-injurious behaviors among religiously committed individuals in terms of culturally shaped spiritual motivations. These include the attempt of ascetics to make themselves worthy of sustaining a personal relationship with God, although discussion of the intellectual framework within which God might appreciate such behavior is highly problematic. Further, an enduring body of thought, both medieval and modern, identifies efforts to mortify the flesh with the purpose of subduing its demands, particularly in areas of sexual desire, gluttony, and creature comforts. We emphasize here that the traditional notion of moderate asceticism as a form of self-discipline which places body and soul in moral balance is a somewhat different species of behavior than the heroic asceticism to which we refer. Recently, a new generation of social-minded scholars have described and explained aspects of female asceticism, especially that which appears related to an asceticism of food refusal (anorexia), in terms of feminine protest against a male-dominated ecclesiastical hierarchy that tried to constrict the forms by which deep spiritual sentiments may be expressed.

There are other models of explanation of various sorts of human behavior available that traditionally have not formed part of the working apparatus of those who study and write about medieval religious persons. Despite the widely recognized fact that the condition of the body affects the working of the mind, a large body of scholarly thought dismisses out of hand the value of modern medical and biological research as important tools in helping us to understand medieval spiritual phenomena and, in particular, self-injurious behaviors. This stance is very curious in light of extensive modern medical research and clinical experience in regard to human and non-human self-injurious behaviors. At the present time, behavioral scientists have amassed considerable data about the physiological and psychological antecedents and effects of self-injurious behaviors, the personality characteristics of self-injurers, and the personal and social circumstances under which such behaviors proliferate and find social meaning and coherence.

In a similar manner, there has been considerable study during the past few decades into the psychological and neurophysiological characteristics of trance states and other altered states of consciousness. This information too is available for use in an examination of the conditions under which mystical experiences occur in the social context of the modern world and, by extension, of medieval European as well as non-Western societies.

The primary questions that we wish to consider in this book relate to the connections between mysticism and heroic asceticism. How are we to understand the intentional and harsh self-injurious behaviors of some religiously committed individuals during the Middle Ages? How do self-injurious behaviors relate, if at all, to experiences that, during the Middle Ages, were considered mystical in nature? Were they separate phenomena that reflected an underlying unity of personality and intense religious drive, or were the two expressions also linked by some causal interaction between asceticism and the occurrence of mystical states?

In order to approach this topic, two preliminary questions about the population of medieval self-injurers and mystics must first be addressed. The first, simply, is "Who were they?" What are the identifying and defining characteristics of this population? Are they primarily male or female, young or old, early or late medieval, religious or lay persons? The second question asks, "What types of self-injurious behaviors did the medieval ascetics engage in?" What methods were used?

Meaningful answers to these broad questions must take into account the strong likelihood that the heroic self-injurers do not form a homogeneous group, either psychologically or by reason of the temporal, cultural, and regional differences in the thousand-year period designated as the Middle Ages. There is no single "typical" medieval self-injurer. We will address throughout this book the historiographical concerns about the definition of concepts such as consciousness, the problems of identification and case-finding of heroic ascetics and mystics from the larger body of medieval holy persons, the question of exaggeration or suppression of reports of asceticism, and the limitations upon making generalizations about the Middle Ages.

Once the population of medieval self-injurers and mystics is identified and important methodological concerns are addressed, we can proceed toward inquiries about explanation and understanding. One major thesis of this book is that an explication of the physiological effects of self-injurious behaviors will help us to understand why heroic asceticism was practiced by some religiously motivated persons in the Middle Ages. This is certainly not to claim that the key to an understanding of medieval asceticism and its relationship to mysticism lies exclusively in an examination of physiological mechanisms leading to and resulting from the effects of habitual self-injurious behaviors. Nor is it even to claim that the physiological level of inquiry and hypothesis is more important causally than social, psychological, religious, or spiritual factors. This is not a contest or a competition. Understandings and explanations that we develop from modern biological studies are meant to be complementary to the traditional social, cultural, and religious levels of explanation of why medieval ascetics engaged in self-injurious practices and why asceticism was, for some, the pathway to mysticism.

The three categories of self-injurious behaviors most commonly mentioned in hagiographical accounts of medieval ascetics are laceration of the flesh, starvation, and sleep deprivation. Each of these categories of self-injurious behaviors separately brings about a predictable sequence of physiological and psychological consequences. The effects of these separate ascetic practices are cumulative when practiced by the same individual, especially over an extended period of time. More importantly for a consideration of the relationship of asceticism to mysticism, one generalized effect of heroic self-injurious behavior is to bring about an altered state of consciousness that, in a religious setting, can be either the entrance into or the full development of a mental state that is subjectively apprehended as a mystical experience.

Part of the task in examining phenomena from one discipline utilizing the methodology of another is to develop a vocabulary of exchange. It is important that this not be done as a sleight of hand, for in redefining objects and events under scrutiny, one may opportunistically strengthen the basis of an otherwise weak argument. For example, since self-injurious behaviors (SIB) are considered in most secular circles today prima facie evidence of some sort of mental illness, our very use of this modern term or, worse yet, its medical acronym SIB, with its clear pathological connotations, might be seen as both betraying our bias and even as an attempt to prejudice the reader into assuming certain attitudes toward medieval asceticism. Therefore, we take mental and moral pains to point out that, in examining for the moment asceticism and mysticism from a biological framework, ascetic practices are labeled self-injurious behaviors and mystical experiences become altered states of consciousness, but that these terms are used only descriptively, not prescriptively or pejoratively. Of course, the postmodern critical reader will already know that our Western scientific world view must influence our definitions, perceptions, and research methodology, and that our assertion that we use our terms descriptively is disingenuous, since it is assumed that no description can be value-free. We can merely acknowledge in advance this postmodern bias and proceed, letting the readers apply their own judgment regarding the putative hidden agenda behind our declared assumptions.

Throughout this book, we will shift back and forth between scientific and religious vocabularies. To use certain terms interchangeably does suggest that they refer to identical or closely similar processes or phenomena, or to different levels of description of the same phenomena, or that they belong to the same categories. Nevertheless, they certainly do not, as mentioned above, carry the same connotations. The terms asceticism and mysticism carry with them a rich collection of meanings and associations that are not part of the terms self-injurious behaviors and altered state of consciousness, which carry their own modern medical and psychological connotations. Behaviorally, however, ascetic practices of the heroic variety can reasonably be located as a subset of self-injurious behaviors, and mystical experiences, whatever else they may be, are experienced by the mystic as an altered state of consciousness.

There are risks to such transformations of vocabulary. The major ones stem from using the same word but meaning different things by it in different sections of the book, or using different terms interchangeably as if they have the same meaning, or using specialized terms as if there is a presupposed shared agreement by all parties about their meanings. These dangers show up most clearly in transposing technical scientific terms, such as energy, which has a precise operational meaning in physics, into other disciplines that use these terms metaphorically, such as the psychoanalytic adoption of the energy concept. There are also many terms that have specific denotations in psychiatry and psychology, but which have entered into ordinary language (or reentered after an initial appropriation from ordinary language and a secondary transformation into a technical meaning) and therefore have broader meanings in our common vocabulary. The term depression may designate a state of sadness in the vernacular, but refer to an illness condition when used in a medical sense. The whole problem of parallel vocabularies (visions versus hallucinations or perceptual illusions; religious delusions versus idiosyncratic religious beliefs) may come into play here, and must be acknowledged when present.

There are also gains that can be derived from cross-disciplinary work. In the particular area under consideration, we have available a considerable body of scientific knowledge (in this context, information that is testable and replicable) about altered states of consciousness and self-injurious behaviors. By recognizing that one group of behaviors has features in common with another group of behaviors, we can transfer some of our knowledge back and forth between groups.

We would stress the two-way transfer of knowledge. Most modern studies of self-injurious behaviors consider them as a subclass of psychologically abnormal behaviors and, from a psychiatric perspective, as symptoms of mental illness. It is important that psychiatry also considers self-injurious behaviors from non-medical perspectives, such as those of culture-specific ritual, religious sacrifice, and spiritual values. The phenomena of altered states of consciousness, other than sleep and dreams, often suffer similarly from such a pejorative medical perspective, since psychiatry is usually concerned with states of pathological depersonalization and dissociation. It is our thought that psychiatry has much to learn from the study of normal forms of altered states of consciousness, a prime example of which is most likely represented by mystical states.

Just as it is important to recognize what is known scientifically about altered states of consciousness, it is also important to recognize how very much about consciousness in general is not known. There is little philosophical or empirical clarity about the delineation, classification, or full description of the domain of altered states. In fact, the very existence as well as the nature of consciousness itself is fiercely debated. There is no single definition of consciousness upon which all workers in related disciplines can agree. Nevertheless, consciousness, however defined and explained, seems to be a fundamental attribute of the human condition. The capacity for self-consciousness is often vaunted as the single trait, the sine qua non, distinguishing humans from other mammals (although the behavior of non-human hominids and cetaceans pose major problems for such humanoid chauvinists).

At the same time that consciousness is so highly valued, it appears that humans are forever trying to alter and/or escape their ordinary states of consciousness. There seems to be something inherently unpleasant in paying too much attention to the ticker-tape of thoughts and images that constitute our moment-to-moment stream of consciousness, such that altering this type of conscious state becomes a pastime or even a preoccupation of much of humankind much of the time. All societies, apparently in recognition both of the universality of this preoccupation and the diversity of methods by which an altered state of consciousness can be achieved, take an active role in determining legitimate and illegitimate methods of induction into altered states of consciousness. In Western society, as we well know, several different multi-billion dollar industries, legal and illegal, are dedicated to providing chemical substances which will rapidly induce an altered state of consciousness in the consumer. Despite well-known socially and physically deleterious consequences of substance abuse and dependence, the usually unsuccessful attempts by governments and special interest groups to interfere with access to and consumption of consciousness and mood-altering drugs provide telling evidence for the tenacity of this human drive.

Our fundamental hypothesis is that one major and heretofore overlooked motivation for medieval heroic ascetic behaviors is the effectiveness of self-injurious behaviors in bringing about an altered state of consciousness. Such altered states of consciousness in some religiously committed persons in medieval Europe had many of the same physiological and psychological characteristics as a mystical state achieved through meditation and contemplation.

Our understanding of the physiological mechanisms by which mortification of the flesh, sleep deprivation, and extreme fasting may bring about an altered state of consciousness can be applied, although with great caution, to a consideration of medieval ascetics and mystics. The traditional explanations that medieval ascetics injured themselves only for symbolic goals relating to *imitatio Christi* and *contemptus mundi* are too limited. However, postulating symbolic ideals as part of a matrix of motives is fully compatible with the thesis concerning a causal linkage between self-injurious behaviors and altered states of consciousness of a mystical nature. The broader the explanatory spectrum, the more likely we are to grasp the great complexity of human motivation and behavior.

A second hypothesis, one open to empirical verification, is that self-injurious behaviors increased coincidentally with the widespread religious renewal in the late Middle Ages that emphasized the individual's personal relationship to God. If this is found to be the case, then the question is raised, What is the relationship between the increase in heroic asceticism and the sharper focus on closeness to and, ultimately, union with God? One possibility is that both phenomena are independent reflections of a religious renewal initiated in the High Middle Ages. But this leaves unanswered why heroic asceticism in particular should have increased along with increased religious fervor. Many other forms of pious expression were available, such as, for example, increased charitable activities and missionary work. The present religious revival in America is not accompanied by a focus on asceticism, nor was the religious revival of the 1840s.

Our third hypothesis postulates a causal relationship between the increase in heroic asceticism and mystical experiences in late medieval Western Europe, as follows. The Western Christian tradition did not have a sufficiently available series of meditative practices that a religiously committed person could learn and utilize to bring about a heightened sense of closeness to God. For some individuals who were highly motivated but unable to achieve such a mystical state through those contemplative and devotional practices that were regularly available, asceticism offered a socially supported alternative mechanism by which to approximate an altered state that had transcendental characteristics. The heroic ascetics were those individuals who carried socially supported moderate ascetic practices to an extreme, arguably because their drive to experience closeness and union with God either was not matched by a constitutional ability to experience ecstatic states of consciousness or the heightened states that they did experience were not felt to be sufficient.

Our theses require examination of two domains of information. The first consists of modern studies of the physiological and psychological effects of self-injurious behaviors, especially in the production of altered states of consciousness. We review and discuss the relevance of such studies to the practitioners of heroic asceticism in the Middle Ages. This of course necessitates an examination of the nature of consciousness and altered states of consciousness, including material gleaned from studies of dissociative disorders.

The second domain relates to how we use the medieval source material. If we do not spell out the major methodological concerns in using historical sources each time they arise, it may appear to some that we are unaware of them. If we place warnings at every other sentence, such as a reminder that our information may be derived from a male hagiographer writing about a female holy person thirty years after her death, or that the only extant *vita* may be an obviously altered copy of an original manuscript (e.g. the copy contains references to events that we know had occurred after the writing of the original manuscript) that is no longer available, our narrative becomes repetitive. To address these very important concerns, we include a chapter detailing the major methodological problems that permeate all medieval hagiographical research. In addition, we direct attention in the notes to limitations in particular source materials and in the basis for some generalizations. Throughout, we strive for a balance between relevance and repetitiveness, but the reader should keep in mind the derivative nature of much of even the primary source material.

Another methodological problem relates to the very concept of the Middle Ages, which is a construct developed by modern historians. Persons living in the Middle Ages did not consider themselves as living in the Middle Ages (i.e. the centuries between classical Rome and a Renaissance that had not yet occurred). We have chosen to study the behaviors of persons who lived within a thousand-year time span and across broad geographic and political areas. It is difficult to think of any generalization that would not require a discussion of serious exceptions, qualifications, nuances, and limitations.

To anticipate one particular difficulty with generalizations, we can consider, for example, the problem of assessing sleep deprivation in the "average" monk's daily routine. It immediately becomes clear that there is no "average" monk. We need to know, and often the detailed information is not available, what monastery under what religious order under what abbot's and bishop's influence during what years in what region of Western Europe and in what season of the year. We may know the general outline given by the Rule of Benedict or the Augustinians, but not know whether that rule was applied strictly or loosely in each particular case. Nevertheless, despite these limitations, we can outline what we know from modern studies of sleep physiology, and apply this knowledge of the outer limits of sleep requirements and the known consequences of sleep loss and sleep fragmentation beyond these limits, to an examination of the adequacy of sleep patterns for medieval religious persons.

One partial remedy to the problem of generalization is the use of statistical studies. Statistics allows us to see broad patterns among large numbers of individuals and to correct generalizations that may be founded upon the purposeful selection of a few dramatic examples recruited to support a favored thesis, but which may prove not to be representative of the group as a whole. In this book, we employ both techniques, examining the results of data derived from a large number of saints' lives, and then selecting a few lives to scrutinize in detail by way of illustrating or limiting the generalizations based upon large numbers.

We have selected the Thurston and Attwater 1956 revision of *Butler's Lives of the Saints* as a database. We devote much of Chapter 7 on historiography to the methodological problems of selecting a database of saints and our choice of Butler. We have identified 1,462 saints in the Thurston and Attwater revised edition whose death date fell between the years AD 450 and 1500. Out of this cohort of medieval holy persons, we identified those individuals who met descriptive criteria for heroic ascetic behaviors and/or mystical experiences. We present at relevant places in each chapter the problems in studying saints' lives and the limitations of the special uses to which the genre of hagiography lends itself.

The organization of the book follows the major points outlined in the discussions above. Part I, the psychology and biology of asceticism and mysticism, begins with two chapters examining in depth the constructs that form the major points of interest: self-injurious behaviors (heroic asceticism) (Chapter 2) and altered states of consciousness (mysticism) (Chapter 3). Definitions and their many limitations are presented both broadly and within the special contexts that comprised medieval Christendom. We introduce philosophical, anthropological, and psychiatric studies as we inch our way toward understanding the interplay of medieval culture and the pursuit of asceticism and mysticism. The final three chapters of Part I examine the physical and psychological effects on states of consciousness of the three most common forms of self-injurious behaviors among medieval religious persons: laceration of the flesh (Chapter 4), sleep deprivation (Chapter 5), and extreme fasting (Chapter 6).

Part II examines the lives of medieval holy persons in historical context. We are as interested in how we come to know what we think we know as we are in what we know. Chapter 7 provides detailed discussions about theoretical and methodological problems in figuring out how holy persons came to be considered holy, the reliability and limits of source material, and the various pressures that modern scholarship imposes upon how we view and revise our views about the Middle Ages. Chapter 8 discusses the various pathways to holiness, since a study of a large body of medieval saints makes it clear that most saints were best recognized for their administrative skills (bishops, royalty) on behalf of the church and for charitable works on behalf of the populace (and ecclesiastical institutions) rather than for their mystical pursuits and ascetic behaviors. Statistical analysis of the temporal and gender patterns of heroic asceticism and mysticism provide the basis for questioning several generally accepted assumptions about medieval asceticism and offering our own perspective on the complex phenomena of intense medieval religiosity.

These two chapters are followed by studies of four medieval saints. We chose these particular saints to illustrate different combinations of asceticism and mysticism, but there is no ultimate justification of why these four rather than four others. The basis for our selection was affection for these particular saints along with the existence of a fairly rich saint's *vita*, as well as our wish not to rehash the most well-known ones, such as Francis of Assisi or Catherine of Siena. There was not much focus on mysticism in the early Middle Ages. Radegund's (Chapter 9) life is both representative in some ways and atypical in other respects of Merovingian royalty. Her asceticism was ferocious and encompassed a combination of personal anguish and religious sentiment. The two Beatrices (Chapters 10 and 11) provide a good sense of early asceticism and slower-maturing mysticism in two holy women of the Low Countries in the thirteenth and fourteenth centuries. Chapter 12 on Henry Suso brings us to a person known at first glance for a twenty-year excursion into extremely harsh self-injurious behaviors, but whose rich descriptions of his deep religious grounding and mystical experiences far outshine his ascetic excesses.

Following the saints' lives, Chapter 13 takes up the question asked by medieval and modern persons whether the heroic ascetics and more flamboyant mystics were mentally ill. The dramatic behaviors of a certain number of mystics, and especially ascetics, raised questions about their sanity in the minds of their own contemporaries as well as by modern thinkers. This remains a contentious issue, in which often the conclusions reached appear to reflect one's initial biases or attitudes when first asking the question. We discuss problems with modern Western diagnostic formulations of persons living in other times and cultures in general, and examine in particular the charge that medieval holy persons suffered from hysteria.

We then close with a Conclusion, outlining what we think the book has been about, what it has argued for and against in our understanding of medieval holy persons and the world in which they lived. Finally, we present in an Appendix some of the statistical analyses that we have mentioned in various spots throughout the book, but that would have interrupted the narrative flow had we elaborated on these in any detail.

Part I

PSYCHOLOGY AND BIOLOGY

2

HEROIC ASCETICISM AND SELF-INJURIOUS BEHAVIOR

Why did medieval ascetics practice asceticism? The medieval sources tell us that such behavior was motivated by identification with Christ's passion, service to God, renunciation of the flesh, subordination of the physical to the spiritual, penance for the sins of other individuals or for all of humankind, penance for one's own sins, and combat with the devil. Underlying these reasons were, to varying degrees, the desire to move closer to God and the assumption that carnal thoughts and preoccupations interfered with attainment of this goal.[1]

There is no universally accepted definition of asceticism. Viewed from a cross-cultural perspective, ascetic practices have served as the concrete and tangible expression of various philosophies, found universally, that worldly concerns at every level interfere with transcendental experiences and with an appreciation of the true nature of reality. Mircea Eliade defines asceticism within a religious tradition as "a voluntary, sustained, and at least partially systematic program of self-discipline and self-denial in which immediate, sensual, or profane gratifications are renounced in order to attain a higher spiritual state or a more thorough absorption in the sacred."[2] The centrality of renunciation in Christian ascetic practice is explicated by Noel O'Donoghue, who has noted that integral to the very notion of religious vocation, i.e. literally being called by God, is a sacrificial response that must involve progressively giving up more and more of creature comforts and worldly honors if the response is to be complete and reciprocal to God's invitation.[3]

The role of asceticism in Christian life is both important and controversial. Debate among religious persons arises as to the proper intent underlying asceticism, the proper degree or harshness of asceticism, the proper balance between ascetic discipline as imitation of Christ and charity and love as imitation of Christ, the dangers of pride, competitiveness, and the consequent loss of vision of God, and the risks of debilitating mental and physical illnesses that can occur when the ascetic has no spiritual anchor or guidelines. The basic issues appear to revolve about the centrality of the view that asceticism is a means to an end, not an end in itself; it is a preparation for turning oneself towards God by turning away from sin and the pursuit of temporal values. An integral component of turning away from worldly things is the development of detachment as a prelude toward closeness with God.

Medieval asceticism

An examination of a large number of medieval accounts written by contemporaries and near-contemporaries, which focus on the behavior of those who sought holiness and mystical union with God, makes clear that the majority of religious persons who were considered ascetics pursued a life of moderation of prayer and celibacy, and of abstemiousness in food and drink, often in obedience to one of several available monastic rules. Most of the Western monastic rules were derived from the Rule of Benedict of Nursia, which is a model of common sense and moderation in regard to all forms of asceticism, and is best epitomized by Benedict's own summation in his Prologue:

> Therefore we intend to establish a school for the Lord's service. In drawing up its regulations, we hope to set down nothing harsh, nothing burdensome. The good of all concerned, however, may prompt us to a little strictness in order to amend faults and to safeguard love.[4]

The rationale and motivation for the moderate level of self-discipline recommended by Benedict, in regard to food and wine intake, amount of sleep, clothing proper to the season, and the mental ascesis of obedience and humility, are offered in terms of love and respect for God and man, not in terms of pursuit of union with God. Benedict was concerned with creating an environment in which humans could live peaceably in a small community, a task that he realized was extremely difficult.

There was a smaller group of ascetics, however, for whom a life of cautious poverty and moderate self-discipline was insufficient to satisfy the urgency of their religious vocation. Moderation in asceticism was a form of accommodation that suggested that it was possible to follow Christ and still be part of this world, enjoying even to a limited extent the comforts of this world. But to these heroic ascetics, there could be no reconciliation between the spiritual and corporeal worlds.[5] There was no middle ground between resisting the flesh and yielding to the temptations of the flesh.

These extreme ascetics engaged in a wide variety of physically self-injurious and self-denying behaviors that had profound effects on their health and that were, in many instances, life-threatening.[6] Benedict of Aniane (c.750–821) personifies the heroic ascetic who, "ablaze with heavenly love," cannot rest content with a mild monastic routine. He fasted to the point that his face grew gaunt and his shriveled flesh hung from his bones. He resisted sleep until, when excessively exhausted, he rested on the bare ground only in order to gather some strength so that he could fatigue himself even more by such rest. He would spend other nights in prayer, keeping himself awake by standing barefooted on the icy pavement. He never changed clothes or bathed; "inevitably, a colony of lice grew on his filthy skin, feeding on his limbs emaciated by fasts."[7]

The *vita* proceeds to explain Benedict's drive, despite his abbot's objections, toward heroic asceticism, and his disdain for a monastic rule meant for weaklings:

> Not so much taming a young but ungovernable animal, as mortifying the body, he was compelled by the abbot to exercise rigor against himself more sparingly. But he did not in any way express agreement. Declaring that the Rule of blessed Benedict was for beginners and weak persons, he strove to climb up to the precepts of blessed Basil and the rule of blessed Pachomius. However much the Benedictine Rule might regulate possible things for paltry people, our Benedict explored more impossible things.[8]

It is interesting that Benedict of Aniane, who as a younger man left the court of Charlemagne to form a community that lived according to very harsh ascetic principles, later in life when given the task of reforming the monastic communities in Charlemagne's empire, somewhat modified his own ascetic observances and greatly softened the rigor of ascetic expectations upon members of the community.

The three forms of self-injurious behavior most frequently identified in the medieval hagiographical texts and most often linked together in the mind of the biographer are lacerating, puncturing and burning the flesh, severe fasting, and extreme sleep deprivation. Thus, for example, in the Life of Rusticula (*c*.556–632), a young woman of the Gallo-Roman aristocracy, the text narrates that Rusticula, after election as abbess of the monastery at Arles at the age of 18, strove to make herself worthy of this honor: "began to devote herself to abstinence and vigils taking food only every third day."[9]

The hagiographer provides a scriptural basis for Rusticula's asceticism, thereby legitimizing and making praiseworthy these self-imposed hardships:

> She wore a hairshirt, fulfilling the words of the Apostle saying: "In many labors, in watchings, in fastings." Indeed, in the nocturnal hours, while the other sisters slept, she remained all night long in the church praying with psalms, hymns, and prayers for the flock entrusted to her and for all people with tears to the Lord.[10]

This same triad of ascetic practices is found virtually unchanged six hundred years later in the *vita* of Margaret of Ypres (1216–1237), a young woman from a burgher family in the Low Countries. Thomas de Cantimpre, Margaret's biographer, praises the austerity of her penances: "She very frequently applied the discipline even to the shedding of blood. . . . A child of three could barely have lived on the food she ate while she dwelled in the flesh . . . she scarcely ever slept one entire night."[11] Margaret's heroic asceticism had begun in childhood by piercing her skin with stings and nettles. She died at age 21, after a one-year illness marked not only by bodily pains, extreme weakness, and hemorrhaging, but also by ecstatic visionary experiences.[12]

While lacerating, puncturing and burning the flesh, severe fasting, and extreme sleep deprivation are the most frequently cited and enduring heroic ascetic practices

among medieval holy persons, there are occasional references to other forms of harsh discipline for which individual saints became well known, and which seem to come into and out of vogue in different regions and times during the thousand-year time period under examination. These include prolonged standing in ice water, primarily among the early Celtic saints (Kevin, d.618; Kentigern of Strathclyde, d.612; Neot, d.ninth century; also, at a later time and to a lesser extent, Aelred of Rievaulx, d.1167), wrapping chains about oneself (Nathalan, d.678; Bernard the Penitent, d.1182), pillar sitting, primarily in the Syrian and Near-Eastern saints (Simeon Stylites the elder, d.459; Daniel the Stylite, d.493; Nicetas of Pereaslav, d.1186), and what we would term self-tortures of movement and posture, such as excessive genuflections (Marie d'Oignies, d.1213, who reportedly did 1,100 daily, beating herself with a discipline during the last 300),[13] or of maintaining arms in an extended position for many hours.

While it might be possible to classify harshness of asceticism among the various saints by constructing a quantitative scale of self-imposed pain that is some function of activity times frequency times duration times intensity times individual sensitivity, we prefer to avoid such a calculus and all the mathematical precision that is implied and, rather, to work in a qualitative manner, distinguishing ordinary from extraordinary ascetic practices in a common-sense way. Thus, wearing a hairshirt and scrupulously maintaining a regular liturgical fast and prayer schedule do not qualify in this present study as heroic asceticism, whereas wrapping thorns around one's limbs and torso, binding and pressing them in ever more deeply by the use of a girdle, eating only every third day or restricting food intake to the eucharistic wafer, and voluntarily limiting sleep to a few hours per circadian cycle are considered features of heroic asceticism.

Heroic ascetics were those holy men and women who were well known among their medieval contemporaries and near-contemporaries for the lengths to which they would go in their self-injurious behaviors in order to strive for the ascetic goals of renunciation of the flesh and, in some cases, mystical union with God. The commitment and determination of these individuals are further highlighted by the fact that, in general, they carried out their ascetic practices in the face of rigorous ecclesiastical objections and, for many, considerable public ridicule. The primary question examined here is, Why did bona fide members of the ecclesiastical establishment, i.e. monks, nuns, priests, and those in lesser orders, as well as highly motivated lay persons, engage in such heroic asceticism in clear violation of the norms established by church authorities who prohibited such practices?

Plate 2.1 opposite Colette (1381–1447) was successively a beguine, Benedictine, and a Poor Clare. She became a reformer of the Poor Clares and established convents as part of this reform movement. She was well known for her austerities and mortifications.

Ecclesiastical resistance to heroic asceticism

Giles Constable, in a 1992 article, reviewed the many medieval voices urging moderation in ascetic practices.[14] The list of figures cited by Constable includes Basil and Chrysostom among the Church fathers, Gregory of Tours, Benedict of Nursia, Bruno of La Chartreuse, Bernard of Clairvaux, and Robert of Arbrissel, among others. The advice toward moderation was usually founded upon two principles, the first concerned with the pernicious development of pride and public display in one's feats of heroic asceticism, and the second concerned with the practical effects of starvation and whippings in so weakening the body that the soul too will be weakened in its pursuit of God. Furthermore, excessive self-injurious practices not only endangered the ascetics' health to the point of death, but also threatened their salvation through the commission of sins contrary to religious discipline.[15]

The *Ancrene Wisse*, a thirteenth-century guide written for anchoresses, takes the following unequivocal stand about harsh asceticism, providing evidence of an institutionalized distrust of allowing the zealously ascetic anchoress to determine her own level of ascetic practices without scrutiny by a spiritual director:

> Let no one belt herself with any kind of belt next to the body, except with her confessor's leave, nor wear any iron or hair, or hedgehog-skins; let her not beat herself with them, nor with a leaded scourge, with holly or briars, nor draw blood from herself without her confessor's leave; let her not sting herself with nettles anywhere, nor beat herself in front, nor cut herself, nor impose on herself too many severe disciplines to quench temptations at one time.[16]

What did extreme self-injurious behaviors offer to these devout men and women that was not provided by ordinary patterns of ascetic discipline, much less the traditional penitential practices of the church? Recent scholarly examination of this question has, by and large, been restricted to sociological and psychological explanations.[17] In some instances, explanations of female medieval asceticism have been offered in terms of twentieth-century social values, such as Rudolph Bell's thesis that severe fasting represented, in addition to a method for controlling bodily urges, "a contest for freedom from the patriarchy that attempts to impose itself between the holy anorexic and her God," and Bynum's expansion of this thesis that emphasizes the central role of food and offering of food in the feminine mental landscape.[18] Such theses proceed as if the individual is practically a disembodied soul in a disembodied environment; at best, these writings acknowledge, as a curtsy to human biology, the well-known effects of starvation in suppressing hormonally driven sexual urges. The far-reaching physiological and psychological consequences of extreme asceticism on all levels of human functioning, especially its effects in altering the ascetic's state of consciousness have, by and large, not been explored nor understood.

Publicly performed asceticism

In order fully to answer the question, "Why perform ascetic behaviors?" we must first ask the question, "What are the effects of performing self-injurious ascetic behaviors?" There are many answers to this question, depending upon the level of inquiry upon which one focuses. Publicly displayed ascetic behaviors may serve to define oneself as a holy person, at the same time inviting public responses that begin to delineate a social role, including the risk of being considered either crazy or, worse, a vainglorious seeker of attention. The theme of being considered crazy (or a fool) was doubled-edged since, while it would obviously demean the significance of one's pursuit for God to be considered crazy, the attractiveness of being ridiculed for one's ascetic practices centered precisely around the high value placed on experiencing humiliation and mockery just as Jesus did prior to his crucifixion.

Beatrice of Nazareth (1200–1268), struggling over the insufficiency of her thankfulness for the many graces that God has given to her, searches her mind for ways in which she can suffer disgrace as a further step toward holiness. The text describes how Beatrice,

> Not finding an easier way to follow her heart's desire, she finally gave her whole consent to this plan, that she would feign madness, and so, despised by all who would see her, she would more perfectly cling to Christ's footsteps through this total conformity to abjection and worthlessness.[19]

Beatrice, however, has some misgivings about this plan and decides to postpone implementation of it until she can seek counsel from Henry, a trusted spiritual advisor. Henry, in what can only be viewed as a masterpiece of psychotherapeutic understanding, assures Beatrice that her idea is not of demonic inspiration, as she obsessively feared, but that she should not pursue such a devious course because it would set back her spiritual development. Beatrice agrees and abandons this plan.[20]

Historically and still today, there is often general support and sympathy for publicly performed self-injurious behaviors that ostensibly entail an altruistic, religious, or political motivation or protest, even if the great majority of individuals are themselves not willing to make such sacrifices. Most often, secular forms of publicly sanctioned self-injurious behavior are a protest of the weak against the powerful. In a religious context, self-injurious behaviors have traditionally represented an institutionalized form of sacrifice or propitiation to powerful gods, in order to gain benefits, often communal, and avoid harm. Sacrifices may be made to avoid or cure an illness, to obtain a richer crop, to give thanks for benefits received, and to mourn the dead and ease their travails in the afterworld. Alternatively, if one has behaved improperly or sinfully, a sacrifice through self-denial or self-injury may be made with the hope of avoiding the god's anger and thus forestalling a worse punishment.

Non secus ac cornu tergum si durius esset, *DOMINICVS cõtra stans tartara Loricatus*
Dilaniat sæuis frigida membra flagris . 25 *Sic animam perdit, perditā ut inueniat.*

Plate 2.1   *Dominicus Loricatus* (d.1014) was a monk famous for the severity of his penances. He was born of middle-class parents who bribed a bishop to ordain their son under the canonical age. Dominic was stricken with contrition for this act of simony (see Chapter 12 on Henry Suso for a similar theme), gave up his functions as a secular priest, and became a monk. He wore iron rings and chains around his limbs, scourged himself thousands of times a day, and wore an iron breastplate (*lorica*) at all other times.

There are many examples of religiously sanctioned self-injurious behaviors. Several are present in the Old Testament, including the ritualistic gashing of oneself with swords and lances. One memorable incident is described in 1 Kings 18, in which the prophet Elijah confronts Ahab for his worship of Baal. Elijah proposes a contest between himself, the only remaining prophet, and the 450 priests of Baal. The Baal priests sacrifice a bull and lay it on an altar, calling on Baal to consume the sacrifice with fire. Hours pass by, and nothing happens. Elijah begins to mock them. "'Cry aloud!' he said, 'Surely he is a god; Either he is meditating, or he has wandered away, or he is on a journey, or perhaps he is asleep and must be awakened.' Then they cried aloud and, as was their custom, they cut themselves with swords and lances until the blood gushed out over them."[21]

Publicly performed self-injurious behaviors in the context of religious rituals also occur in the Sun Dance of the Plains Indians,[22] in which warriors hang suspended from a sacred pole by thongs piercing their pectoral muscles, in Hindu festivals in which devotees, while in a trance, pierce their cheeks with rods,[23] and in the organized flagellant processions that broke out intermittently in Europe in the thirteenth through fifteenth centuries.[24] Persons designated or accepted by a society to perform ceremonial self-injurious religious acts usually are not considered mentally ill. Rather, they are given public respect and high status because they have the inner discipline to express deep values of the society in a manner that most other members are unable or unwilling to do.

Secular forms of publicly sanctioned self-injurious behaviors usually involve political protests in which the power differential is vast and the protesting group is disenfranchised. Gandhi's hunger strikes, the Irish Catholic hunger strikers, and the self-immolation more common in Asian cultures, such as the student who set himself on fire in Tiananmen Square to protest the use of army tanks and troops to quash the student protest, are all examples in which honor, rather than the disgrace of a psychiatric diagnosis, accrues to the voluntary sufferer.

In such situations, whether religious or secular, the cultural context renders the self-injurious behaviors meaningful and understandable, and provides a text for decoding the symbolism expressed in these behaviors. The social or religious milieu establishes a framework for making sense out of otherwise highly aberrant behaviors.

Privately performed ascetic behavior

Privately executed ascetic behaviors define oneself differently, in addition to whatever symbolic meaning is associated with being the kind of person who does such things. There is a rich and, perhaps, inexhaustible psychology that can be applied to ascetic individuals. Those who practice their asceticism clandestinely avoid the pitfalls that accompany public admiration and notoriety, but run the alternate risk of solipsistic pursuit of misguided goals. All of these involve retrospective judgments regarding what constitutes misguided goals, a risk that the intensely individualistic seeker after God always takes. As we commented above, there was considerable condemnation for the heroic ascetic who performed self-injurious behaviors without the knowledge and consent of some sort of spiritual advisor or religious superior.

In the twentieth century, persons who privately injure themselves, when it is made public, are generally considered mentally ill, even if they insist that religious reasons inspired such injuries.[25] Our present society in general views self-injurious behaviors as deviant.

For example, a young man who is followed at our psychiatry clinic had the practice of standing motionless for over thirty hours continuously while praying in his apartment, allowing his legs to become grossly edematous until the skin around his toes cracked open. This young man developed a cellulitis and thrombophlebitis (bacterial infection in the tissues and blood vessels of his legs and feet) that would have resulted in amputation or death, had he not been hospitalized several times on an emergency basis and treated (without his consent) with intravenous antibiotics. This young man had delved into Eastern philosophies in college and now, a few years later, was using a combination of Christian and Eastern prayers to bring harmony into the world. Living in a secular age, he is hospitalized, transferred to a psychiatric ward, given a diagnosis of schizophrenia, and treated under court order with antipsychotic medications. Within one week of initiation of this pharmacological treatment, he states that he still believes that he should pray for world peace, but thinks that he is not personally responsible for bringing it about and that it is not necessary to stand immobilized for a day or two while he prays.

The practice of standing motionless for many days while praying is described of the desert father John (late fourth century), who is said to "surpass in virtue all the monks of our own time."[26] The text continues in its description of John's feat:

> He began by standing under a rock for three years in uninterrupted prayer, not sitting at all or lying down to sleep, but simply snatching some sleep while standing. . . . When his feet had swollen and split from his standing motionless for so long, and the discharge had caused putrefaction, an angel appeared . . . and having healed him, made him leave that place.

John was spared the diagnosis of schizophrenia, but presumably someone with authority did come along and order him to abandon his heroic ascetic practice. The miraculous healing power of the angel is noteworthy; our modern young man required intravenous antibiotics. Despite the time spread of fifteen hundred years, the conservative opinion of those who are designated to adjudicate such zealous behaviors is remarkably similar: whatever the self-professed intent, excessive self-injurious behaviors should be interrupted and redirected.

A situation somewhat similar to our young man is described in the psychiatric literature of a young man who gave up his job in order to live in a city park and undergo one-week to six-week long fasts.[27] His parents had him committed after he nearly died of starvation and dehydration while on the longer fast. During most of his psychiatric hospitalizations, the young man appeared calm, intellectually intact, non-delusional, and thoughtful in describing his religious reasons for his ascetic practices. After much controversy, he was finally given a diagnosis of schizophrenia based upon the idiosyncratic nature of his ideas, absence of a social group that endorsed his beliefs and actions, and the life-threatening nature of his ascetic practices. We would point out here that the diagnosis of schizophrenia is based upon somewhat circular evidence and reasoning, namely that extreme fasting based upon idiosyncratic (for the twentieth century) religious ideals constitutes evidence of delusional thinking. Since there is no religious leader available who could order the young man to cease his fast, a diagnosis of schizophrenia by a psychiatrist becomes necessary in order to interfere legally with this young man's freedom to starve himself.

The physiology of asceticism

If, for the moment, we ignore psychological and sociological considerations and restrict our inquiry to the level of the physiological effects of these harsh self-injurious behaviors, we find that there are specific and fairly well-known effects upon various functional systems of the body, such as measurable changes in hormonal levels, basal temperature, and immune mechanisms. In addition to these broad changes in specific bodily functions, however, harsh self-injurious behaviors bring about changes in brain physiology and functioning. Phrased most simply, altered brain physiology is nothing else than an altered brain state which, in turn, is reflected both behaviorally and subjectively as altered states of consciousness.

It was the production or attainment of altered states of consciousness that, at times, allowed the medieval ascetic practitioner to transcend the mundane concerns of daily existence and move to a higher spiritual plane. In fact, in terms of physiological psychology, the self-injurious behavior did not so much "allow" the ascetic person to move to a different state of consciousness as it actually was the mechanism that brought about, or caused, an altered state of consciousness.[28]

The basic physiological effects of mortification of the flesh, sleep deprivation, and severe fasting are essentially identical for all human beings independently of time, place, and culture. To be sure, there are individual differences among human beings based upon genetic variation, age, gender, and, possibly, life experiences. To say that a trait or a function is inherent to human beings is not to say that it is identical in every person. Thus different individuals in all societies will have different sleep requirements, responses to low blood sugar and ketosis, and endorphin (endogenous opiate) responses to tissue damage. Some persons need more sleep and others need less sleep, all other things, such as state of health, being equal.

There is rarely, if ever, sufficient evidence other than circular reasoning to postulate such variation in a given historical individual. In addition, the symbolic meaning of suffering will influence to some extent the perception of and response to the pains and deprivations inflicted upon the sufferer. Tooth pain, for example, may be joyously welcomed by the medieval ascetic and bitterly resented by the modern analgesically oriented person. The first will see pain and pain response as meaningful and necessary to spiritual ascent; the latter as meaningless and avoidable. But while such variations in reception and perception of pain may dampen or increase the amplitude of a given physiological response, nevertheless the range of basic physiological responses, including production of an altered state of consciousness, to the triad of mortification of the flesh, sleep deprivation, and prolonged fasting are firmly fixed and relatively hard-wired by one hundred million years of evolutionary history. It is no coincidence that the instrumental goal of some of the medieval ascetics and the major psychological effects of heroic ascetic practices are the same: to alter one's state of consciousness.[29]

This is not to say that each ascetic consciously said: "Now I will alter my state of consciousness by engaging in self-injurious behaviors." There is not evidence for this, nor is it how self-injurious behavior occurs in clinical situations in the twenty-first century. The sequence in which self-injurious behavior is automatically and regularly followed by an altered state of consciousness establishes operant as well as classical conditioning effects that reinforce this sort of behavior. Since most human behavior is processed and initiated automatically by non-conscious mechanisms, i.e. most decision-making occurs too rapidly and too complexly to depend upon the slow pace of conscious thought, the connection between self-injurious behaviors and altered states of consciousness is established at a non-conscious level.[30]

Neurophysiology of asceticism

Harsh self-injurious behaviors, especially if carried out on a prolonged or habitual basis, literally reshape synaptic pathways in the central nervous system as repeated usage of specific neural connections reinforce these connections and lead to the pruning of less-used neural pathways. These processes provide the underpinning for those predictably repetitive patterns of behaviors that we tend to call habits and addictions. Thus the repeated use of a behavior, such as self-laceration leading to a "desirable" disruption of one's dysphoric mood or an interruption in one's unpleasant or unwanted chain of thoughts, influences the strength of the neural networks underlying this sequence of behaviors in a manner that makes it more likely that a recurrence of similar disturbing thoughts will lead to the same interruptive (self-injurious) patterns of behavior and less likely that the disturbing thoughts will lead to other, perhaps non-destructive, behaviors the next time.[31] The development of such reinforced neural pathways is not a phenomenon isolated to brain physiology experiments in the laboratory, but leads to complementary psychological changes in perception, cognition, anticipation, emotional state, and self-awareness. At a psychological level, deliberate use of thought-deflection techniques denies rehearsal time to memories and images, thus providing success in avoiding prohibited topics and lending further operant reinforcement to the self-injurious behaviors.[32]

It is reciprocally true that cognitive and emotional processes, such as occur in meditation and guided imagery, can bring about brain changes that result in an altered state of consciousness and that alter the perception and interpretation of incoming sensory stimuli as well as internally generated stimuli (thoughts, images, emotions).[33] The well-known ability of hypnosis to bring about anesthesia and analgesia during dental procedures, birthing, and even major surgery are the best examples of mental processes profoundly affecting pain perception.[34]

The essential point here, however, is not whether meditative techniques can bring about altered brain states and thereby altered states of consciousness, which they obviously can, as will be discussed in the next chapter, but that some of those individuals who practiced heroic asceticism in medieval Europe relied on self-injurious behaviors rather than cognitive meditative techniques as their preferred method for altering their states of consciousness.[35] Why they wanted to alter their state of consciousness is a matter of conjecture and a question that we will shortly address, but, for the moment, we merely emphasize that heroic asceticism does indeed powerfully bring about alterations in one's state of consciousness.

An episode in the life of Gherardesca of Pisa (*c*.1200–*c*.1260) captures this interrelationship very clearly. Gherardesca is asked to pray for the return to health of a Franciscan brother, "who was continually suffering prodigious distress of mind." Later that day, while in church, Gherardesca remembers her promise.

> Kneeling on the ground, she began to pray for him most devoutly; and returning to her cell, having removed her clothing, she scourged herself fiercely. While she was lacerating her flesh, she heard clearly from heaven all the reasons for which the aforesaid brother was being afflicted with such great tribulation.[36]

The text does not suggest that Gherardesca mortified herself in order to do penance for the monk, for she appraises the monk on the ways in which he has offended God. Although such a motivation might have been the case anyway, the close juxtaposition of scourging and hearing a voice from heaven makes it likely that Gherardesca used scourging as a form of trance induction. Once in a trance, she then hears the voice of God or an angel speak to her.

Problems raised by ascetic behaviors

We wish to consider three interrelated problems that arise when discussing heroic asceticism in relationship to mysticism. The first is the problem of reductionism, of substituting a biological level of explanation for an essentially psychological or mystical experience. The second problem is that of authenticity of mystical experience when the experience appears dependent upon induction techniques, such as ascetical behaviors or drug ingestion. The third problem raises the question of grace in relationship to mystical experiences. Can ascetical behaviors have any efficacious role in attaining a mystical experience or in obtaining responses from God? Can we pressure God, as sometimes comes up in the saints' *vitae*, by our penances and promises? We will touch upon each of these problems in turn.

The problem of reductionism

Some social historians and theologians may well view our formulation as essentially reductionistic because it explains psychological phenomena in terms of physiological mechanisms rather than as functions of psychological motivations and intentions. However, such an observation would have to rely on a model of a mind–body dichotomy that was not present in medieval theology and is presently untenable in neuroscientific terms. A narrow definition of reductionism would assert that all living phenomena can be understood and explained in terms of the laws of physics and chemistry and, accordingly, mind, and its corollary, consciousness, consist in the physical-chemical operations of the brain.[37]

This is not our position. We are not equating brain and mind.[38] We can fully accept at a pragmatic level the existence of a non-physical "self" as it is immediately given in inner experience while still recognizing that this sense of self, and the phenomena of consciousness and self-consciousness that go with it, are exquisitely sensitive to mood, attention, tooth pain, and sleep deprivation, as well as to alterations in the external environment, such as rhythmic drum-beating or psalmody chanting, and the internal environment, such as variations in blood sugar and blood alcohol.

Wayne Proudfoot, writing about efforts to describe and explain religious experiences, makes a distinction between what he terms "descriptive reduction" (the failure to identify an emotion or experience under the description by which the subject identifies it), which he judges as unacceptable, and "explanatory reduction" (offering an explanation of an experience in terms that are not those of the subject and that might not meet with his/her approval), which he considers as perfectly justifiable and, in fact, normal procedure for the historian.[39] Our point is a fairly straightforward empirical one: whatever the ontological complexities attached to the mind–body problem and whatever the rich metaphorical meanings of asceticism for a given individual in a particular society, fiddling around with one's brain state causes alterations in one's state of consciousness.

These alterations are often predictable after a few rounds of trial and error. Rapid ingestion of several ounces of whiskey usually serves as convincing proof that poisoning the central nervous system has profound and dose-related effects upon one's thinking processes, perception, emotional and behavioral controls, and sense of self. The fact that expectation, setting, intention, and attitude may all influence the intensity and positive or negative emotional direction of the effects of a given dose of alcohol upon an individual does not appreciably alter the basic interactions between alcohol and brain function.

Explanations of ascetic behaviors solely in terms of cultural influences are as incomplete as explanations solely in terms of neurophysiological changes. Intentional behaviors such as self-starvation, sleep deprivation, and damaging the skin with thorns and nails certainly appear to be motivated by personal and religious beliefs and values. There is no argument here. The social, anthropological, and personal psychological explanations for ascetic behaviors, both in medieval Europe and in other societies, have been well formulated for the past hundred years or more and need not be reviewed here.[40] For the moment, we are not examining the psychological motivations underlying heroic ascetic behaviors. Rather, we are interested in tracing out some other causal notions that have not been prominently developed as yet, namely, the effects of extreme ascetic behaviors upon human neurophysiology and, consequently, upon human states of consciousness.

The problem of authenticity of mystical states

A further problem, in addition to the charge of reductionism, that some historians, theologians, and others may have with the thesis that many heroic ascetics relied upon the physiological effects of self-injurious behaviors as a method of inducing a mystical experience is that such an explanation appears to undermine or diminish the authenticity of the mystical experience itself. It is as if a mystical experience is authentic only if it occurs either spontaneously unbidden or in the context of meditative practices alone. Anthropologists, who routinely work with cultures in which transcendental experiences are evoked by drugs and rhythmic activities, rarely get themselves into this quagmire of judging genuine from spurious mystical states, especially when specific and elaborate induction procedures are an integral part of many cultures' religious and healing rituals.

In discussing the noetic quality of mystical states, which can be defined as a sense of authenticity of insights and knowledge obtained during a mystical state, Proudfoot has observed that, although the seeker of a religious experience is aware that induction exercises such as meditation, prolonged fasting, and sleep deprivation will have considerable effect on his physiological and mental state, it is nonetheless

> a *conditio sine qua non* of that experience that he [the seeker] view these manipulations as catalysts, not as sufficient causes. The experience must be perceived by the subject as providing access to some reality beyond himself and his conscious preparations. He must attribute the experience not to the fasting, the exercises, or the chanting alone, but to some power that transcends these natural causes.[41]

In Western Christian mysticism, this transcendent power is conceptualized as grace, a gift from God.

The method of induction into the mystical state has theoretical and practical importance, however, because if the mystical experience of being in the presence of the Ultimate cannot be differentiated from an altered state of consciousness induced by psilocybin ingestion or sleep deprivation, then, according to some, the value of the mystical experience itself, the efficacy of grace, and the knowledge of God, or the Ultimate,[42] that accrues from such an experience, are diminished.

Huston Smith engaged this question forty years ago when there was much serious experimentation in the use of psychedelic drugs (mescalin; psilocybin) to induce "religious" experiences.[43] Smith cites considerable evidence supporting the claim that, phenomenologically, psychedelic drugs can induce religious experiences that are indistinguishable, even from a Western Christian perspective, from experiences that occur spontaneously. This evidence includes a study using either psilocybin or active placebo by 30 Harvard theology students and professors in the setting of a Good Friday service in church. The psilocybin was administered double-blind to 15 participants; the control group of 15 received nicotinic acid, which produces a physiological response (flushing; tingling) but has no psychedelic properties. Neither the researcher nor the subjects knew whether they received placebo or active drug. Some of the faculty and students who received the psilocybin, including Huston Smith, reported the deepest religious experiences of their lives. Smith concludes that, given a proper mental set and setting, experiences of a religious nature induced by drugs cannot be distinguished descriptively from their natural religious counterparts. Smith himself does not further conclude from this, however, that such evidence necessarily casts into doubt the authenticity of religious experiences or the presence of a transcendent reality in the universe.

Much of this controversy was sparked by Aldous Huxley's 1954 book *The Doors of Perception*, in which Huxley reported his drug-induced altered states of consciousness as religious experiences.[44] Huxley introduced Huston Smith to Timothy Leary, the Harvard psychologist, which led to the 1962 Good Friday experiment reported in the paragraph above. Meanwhile, R.C. Zaehner, Professor of Eastern Religions and Ethics at Oxford published an influential book in 1957 (prior to the Good Friday experiment) debating, or rather profoundly disagreeing with, Huxley's conclusions that there are no differences between religiously based mystical experiences and psychedelic drug-induced religious experiences.[45]

According to Zaehner, the underlying issue to much of this controversy is the question of whether, as Huxley and others claim, "'mysticism' is an unvarying phenomenon throughout the entire world and at all ages, and that it may (and does) make its appearance in all and any religious system."[46] Zaehner argues against the claim that mystical experiences are the same everywhere, i.e. that they represent some fundamental getting-in-touch with a greater reality (a state of pure consciousness) that ultimately is not influenced by cultural or religious expectations or intent.

Zaehner's point is that nature mysticism and psychedelic mysticism have superficial points in common with the mystical experience of union with God, including a sense of loss of self and a merging with an entity greater than oneself. But, to Zaehner, these are only the trappings of mystical experiences that are profoundly different from the grace and infusion of God experienced by the Christian mystic. Zaehner himself tried mescalin in his rooms at All Souls College, Oxford, dispensed by the psychiatrist J.R. Smithies and monitored by several witnesses. Zaehner's experiences included perceptual distortions, some bouts of hilarity that were lost upon the witnesses, and a relative trivialization ("Just tripe, like everything else") of works of art and literature that would ordinarily have been of interest and value to him.[47] Zaehner's most interesting insight, which did not seem to lead to any personality or moral changes after the drug effect wore off, was that figures within paintings seemed to be trying to escape from the frames or boundaries of the picture. Zaehner not only did not derive anything religious from the experiment, but actually felt that the altered state of consciousness that he experienced with mescalin was anti-religious. Huston Smith, in his original 1964 article, comments that Zaehner disagrees with Huxley and he (Smith) disagrees with Zaehner, whom he perceives as continuing the age-old conflict between science and religion, between evidence and doctrine.[48]

When the dust settles, a general problem does remain for some: if a "mystical state" is accounted for solely in naturalistic terms, whether drug, mania, or pain induced, then it throws into question the relationship of the transcendent experience to the divine and even the necessity for a divine presence in the causal sequence itself. This problem arises primarily when the mystical state is equated with (or reduced to) the physiological state, but less when the induction techniques are perceived as a preparation for reception of the divine, or, as in the case of drug induction, when the drugs are seen as opening up the person to other levels of reality.

The problem of grace and ascetic attempts to influence God

If God is totally remote and unmovable, there is no purpose in even offering prayers as a way to influence such a divinity. But at the level of daily practice, whatever the theological and philosophical issues raised by human preoccupations with the seeming incompatibility of the divine qualities of justice versus mercy, and omniscience versus omnipotence, humans seek, through prayer and supplication and sacrifice, God's help and intervention. The ideal request of God, it is often said, is for help with changing one's own heart and mind in the direction of loving God and one's fellow humans. The divine response to such a request comes in the form of God's grace. An example of this appears in the mystical writings of Gertrude of Helfta (1261–1301), a Rhineland mystic of the late thirteenth century.

Gertrude the Great of Helfta, in her *Spiritual Exercises*, emphasizes the central role of divine grace in the attainment of a spiritual relationship to God. Gertrude is one of those individuals who embody the slow development in Western mysticism of the utilization and teaching of meditative and contemplative exercises without the use of heroic asceticism to prepare oneself for a relationship of closeness to God. Gertrude writes:

> At this point, invoke the grace of the Holy
> Spirit to make you progress in religion.
> Come, Holy Spirit, come, O God, love; fill my
> heart, which, alas, is empty of all that is good.
> Set me on fire to love you.[49]

While prayer and meditation can be seen as relatively pure forms of requesting either the divine presence or the grace of compassion, the role of heroic asceticism in these requests seems to be more problematic. The problems become deeper when the request of the supplicant is of a more practical nature, even if the motivation is altruistic or generous. The question is whether one can influence, by way of preparedness, the offering of divine presence, as the use of psychedelic drugs, lacerating of the flesh, fasting, and chanting seems to imply, and whether one can influence, by engaging in self-injurious behaviors, the direct intercession of God according to one's wishes. These problems arise in a practical sense in the *vita* of many medieval mystics who, although knowing better in terms of orthodox doctrine, cannot resist demanding special graces and favors from God.

For example, in the *vita* of Lutgard of Aywieres (1182–1246), the narrator describes how Lutgard, fearing, as did Job, God's judgment of her works, demanded reassurances from God:

> Therefore for a long time she implored the Lord daily and wailed that He render her certain at the present moment. She stayed for an even longer time in this desire and one day she heard a voice made most manifest to her: "Be now secure, dearest one, because your life is pleasing to the Lord."[50]

Lutgard, however, is not able to be secure with this single divine reassurance, but, after a brief moment of joy, continues to fret, as the text describes: "Therefore the righteous Lutgard was exultant at the time, but nevertheless she began to tremble with fear again." The Lord offers to repeat his statement in front of a witness, the prioress, but Lutgard demurs out of concern for the prioress's timorousness. She is finally reassured when the divine voice tells her: "In the meantime, dearest, be at rest; soon you will be manifestly and perfectly secure."

Lutgard not only can demand personal reassurances from God, but she bargains for the salvation of souls, using self-injurious behaviors as the medium of exchange. None other than Innocent III appears to her after his death (1216) surrounded by a great flame. He reports that he is to be tortured for three reasons (one reason, although probably not in Lutgard's mind, must have been Innocent's condoning, after the fact, the Fourth Crusade's assault and sack of Constantinople instead of Saracen fortifications in 1204), but that the Mother of Mercy has allowed him to ask Lutgard for her intercessory prayers. Lutgard discusses this with her monastic sisters and they agree that the soul of Innocent should be saved. The text then proceeds: "She herself, having compassion on such a punishment, afflicted herself with wondrous pain for him who appeared to her."[51]

In this little episode, Lutgard and her biographer, under cover of a dream-vision, are able to criticize perhaps the most powerful pope ever, the pope who had Emperor Otto IV deposed, forced King Philip Augustus of France to take back his wife, and laid England under interdict and excommunicated King John for refusing to recognize Stephen Langton as archbishop of Canterbury. This apparently innocent passage in Lutgard's *vita* demonstrates the ways in which political subversion can insinuate its way into the biography of a holy person.

This example also exemplifies, for our purposes, the difficulties that are raised by self-injurious behaviors in the service of one's soul and the mitigation of punishment of another soul. It appears that the original incentive and justification of asceticism, going back to the desert fathers, as a form of discipline to set oneself straight with oneself and with God, has somewhere along the course been diminished and that the penitential aspect of self-injurious behavior has become enhanced.

Asceticism in its broadest sense signifies a personal approach of discipline and self-denial towards the creature comforts of the corporeal world. It often does, but need not, reflect a larger religious commitment. When it does, asceticism will naturally reflect the philosophy, value system, and symbols of that religious community. Further, since religious communities undergo changes that both reflect and influence the surrounding secular society, it is to be expected that the form, purpose, and content of ascetic beliefs and practices will also change as the society changes.

As with many human endeavors, the evolution of a practice need not represent progress (however judged), but may indeed show mixed elements of refined sensibility as well as deterioration of the initial vision and moral purpose. Christian asceticism appears to have struggled with its many threads of meaning. From its initial concept of renunciation of worldly comforts in order to achieve a proper balance between spiritual and secular values and focus, asceticism took on to itself added meanings related to suffering for Christ's sake as well as suffering for its own sake. The notions of sin and penitence through bodily wounds gave final justification for the type of heroic asceticism that infrequently but dramatically punctuated the moderate levels of asceticism ordinarily practiced by those in religious communities and some fervent lay people. As such, heroic asceticism held itself up to the rest of society as the moral, logical, and literal end-point of the eschatological and dualistic element in Christian doctrine. At the very same time, practitioners of heroic asceticism were also viewed by much of society either as inhabiting the lunatic fringe of the Christian community or as truly distorting the salvific and life and love-affirming message of Jesus.

At every level, heroic asceticism raised as many problems as it solved for the ascetic individual and the larger society. Pride and vainglory, publicity-seeking, ambivalent attitudes toward the material universe as representing God's creation, the questionable practice of demanding grace from God, the personal sanity of the heroic ascetic, and the role of the ascetic as either critic of secular values or pathfinder to mystical union with God, are all issues with which Christendom in general and regional and temporal locales had to struggle and define. There was no consensus whether the heroic ascetic represented a holy person or a misguided and distorted individual.

While the psychological, social, and theological facets of asceticism have been much studied and interpreted, the short and long-term physiological effects of heroic asceticism have not attracted as much thought or investigation. The perennial paradox, leaving aside cultural symbolism, is how persons who ostensibly wish to achieve detachment and to minimize the body's influence in their daily lives and their relationship to the divine can accomplish these goals by drawing so much attention to the body. The immediate experience of intense physical pain seems to rivet attention to the body, not away from it. The mental state brought about by sleep deprivation and starvation seems to dull the senses, not make one aware of transcendental universes.

Yet we cannot ignore the persistent presence and, at times, increased appeal and popularity, of harsher and harsher asceticism throughout the Middle Ages in Western Europe. Somehow, there must be something about pain, sleep deprivation, and prolonged fasting that commend themselves to a small number of God-driven individuals. It is our thought that at least part of the appeal of the practice of heroic asceticism is that it brings about altered states of consciousness. Induction of an altered state of consciousness was and is a crucial element in the development of a religious mentality that strives for transcendence.

There are two major components involved here, the first being the struggle to get rid of mental clutter in order to be open to communion with the divine, and the second being the changes in perception, cognition, emotional tone, and sense of reality that are the very stuff of an altered state. Heroic asceticism is not the only method to induce an altered state. Meditation, alcohol and drugs, and chanting and drumming are other methods. But in medieval Europe, asceticism was for much of the time the most effective of the culturally sanctioned methods for interrupting the ordinary stream of mental clutter and for producing an altered state that became, in a Christian practitioner, a state that permitted an increased awareness of the presence of God.

3

MYSTICISM AND ALTERED STATES OF CONSCIOUSNESS

Consciousness, like pain, is something we know directly from experience. Yet, definitions of "consciousness" and "altered state of consciousness" are notoriously elusive and unsatisfactory even in the context of shared cultural assumptions, let alone in an attempt to capture what the experience of an altered state of consciousness was in the context of medieval asceticism and spirituality. It appears that the metaphors we ordinarily employ to describe and understand our daily experiences are based upon our bodily and sensory experiences and therefore are particularly unsuited to the verbal delineation of abstract mental concepts, such as consciousness.[1]

Most modern scientific as well as philosophical literature on this topic begin by acknowledging that no single definition or description of consciousness satisfactorily captures all aspects of the concept.[2] In fact, Ilya Farber and Patricia Churchland suggest that it is premature to expect to be able to define consciousness precisely, given our profound ignorance of the topic. They note that, in the normal course of science, conceptual development goes hand in hand with empirical progress, and only late in the game are explicit definitions more helpful than harmful.[3]

Nevertheless, a basic working definition of ordinary consciousness, however tentative and open to refinement, is necessary.[4] The one that we will use here is taken from psychiatrist Frank Fish: consciousness is a "state of awareness of the self and the environment."[5] Yet there is no consensus regarding the nature of this "awareness" that constitutes consciousness. There has been a tendency, as Hume had observed, to substitute the content of consciousness (what one is conscious of, e.g. particular thoughts or imagery) for the experience of consciousness, but consciousness involves much more than cognitive thoughts and imagery. There are emotional, moral, attentional, arousal, and bodily aspects to consciousness.[6] Consciousness also refers to the sum total of those lived-in and remembered experiences that belong to a person and develop over the course of an individual's lifetime. Dale Purves, in a review of David Dennett's book on consciousness, described consciousness as, first and foremost, "a luminous and immediate sense of the *present*, about which we are quite certain."[7] This Western notion of consciousness resonates with the Eastern notion as explicated by the Dalai Lama, who describes a fundamental state of mind which is unsullied by thought and just in its own state as mere luminosity, the knowing nature of the mind.[8]

Furthermore, one's level of awareness and the sense of luminosity and immediacy are not fixed, but constantly changing. The normal "state" of consciousness is not a unitary state. It involves constant variation in attention and intensity. E. Roy John has offered a technical neuropsychological perspective on this important notion of the flux of consciousness, as follows:

> Consciousness is a process in which information about multiple individual modalities of sensation and perception is combined into a unified, multidimensional representation of the state of the system and its environment and is integrated with information about memories and the needs of the organism, generating emotional reactions and programs of behavior to adjust the organism to the environment. . . . Many levels of consciousness can exist, in which the dimensions are present in variable amounts. The content of consciousness is the momentary constellation of these different types of information.[9]

This description of consciousness may appear to leave out some essential pieces of subjective awareness (self-consciousness) which we usually associate with human consciousness, but it does amply point out the psychological complexity and shifting nature of consciousness. One other very important feature to mention, which is elaborated upon in Chapter 4 (on the asceticism of pain), is that consciousness is a limited-capacity system, such that paying attention to one or two pieces or chunks of information makes it difficult to attend to other pieces of information. This, of course, raises the problem of mental clutter (which shall be discussed shortly), and the use of meditative and ascetic practices as methods for clearing or distracting the mind from its usual cluttered contents in order to allow other thoughts or images to present themselves.

Altered states of consciousness

If consciousness is difficult to define, altered state of consciousness is even more so. Arnold Ludwig has defined an altered state of consciousness as

> any mental state induced by various physiological, psychological, or pharmacological maneuvers or agents which can be recognized subjectively by the individual himself (or by an objective observer of the individual) as representing a sufficient deviation in subjective experience or psychological functioning from certain general norms for that individual during alert, waking consciousness.[10]

The obvious circular elements in this definition make it somewhat unsatisfactory, but it is hard to do much better with a general definition. Charles Tart has offered more elaborate notions of altered states of consciousness, emphasizing that there are system properties to normal consciousness (e.g. logical thinking, selective attention) which must change substantially in order to consider that one is in an altered state of consciousness. It is the different structural properties (altered sense of self, altered sense of reality, altered perceptual processes) of specific altered states of consciousness that describe (or explain) the subjective experience of being in the various altered states.[11] One defining characteristic of those altered states that are considered desirable goals of meditation and prayer is the reduction of mental clutter.

The task in speaking about altered states of consciousness, whether in a medieval or modern context, is to take cognizance of the fact that small and transient shifts of consciousness occur all the time – as when shifting focus from concentrating upon what one is reading to a few moments of reverie or daydreaming (represented in the EEG by a shift from beta to alpha brainwave rhythms) and a subsequent return to deep concentration – without losing sight or trivializing what is meant by major shifts of levels of consciousness. Nor do we mean to imply that the frequent, transient shifts in "attention" are themselves trivial, for considerable creative processing can occur in these brief reveries.

It may be helpful, in considering the nature of what it is that persons said to be undergoing mystical states are experiencing, to examine a sample description of such an experience from a medieval text and then to appraise how well it fits with concepts ordinarily used in the twenty-first century to describe altered states. The passage is from the *vita* of Beatrice of Nazareth (1200–1268), based upon her own (now lost) journal, chronicling the events following her consecration ceremony:

> When the Lord's chosen one, Beatrice, had received this privilege of betrothal, she was immediately so filled with sweet joy and exultation that she took no notice of what was going on around her, since her outer senses were asleep. As often as she had to approach the bishop to receive some of the things pertaining to this rite, she could not present herself to him unless supported by the hands of those around her. When the sacramental rite was over, even though she was closely surrounded by people all day long, she could not notice or attend to anything she happened to see or hear around her. All the noise of outer things was hushed, and she rested sweetly in the arms of her spouse.[12]

We notice in the elements of Beatrice's mystical experience a broad distinction between the normal, wakeful, fairly attentive, logically ordered, reality oriented level of consciousness in which we are simultaneously aware of our inner stream of thoughts and our outer environment, and those altered states in which awareness of the environment is severely narrowed, the stream of inner thoughts is less logically organized and reality directed, the emotional feeling-tone is unusual, the sense of personal identity is altered, and the content and processes of consciousness appear subjectively very different to the person having the experience.

Capacity to experience altered states of consciousness

The capacity to have altered states of consciousness is a fundamental human trait, and if we think about those most common of altered states, namely sleep and dream states, then we can expand this statement to include, at the least, mammals among those species that have such a basic capacity. This capacity is built into the anatomy and physiology of the central nervous system.[13] The shift into certain types of altered states, most notably sleep and dream states, occurs automatically on a relatively fixed schedule and is ordinarily governed by chronobiological mechanisms. In nature, there are many patterns of sleep/wakefulness cycles, the most common one being the usual circadian cycle and the most dramatic one the seasonal hibernation of certain mammals, such as bears, during winter times.

The hierarchical structure of the human brain permits higher cerebral centers subserving cognition, motivation, and emotions to override, to a limited extent, certain basic physiological functions that are ordinarily governed automatically by lower brain centers. It is a basic phylogenetic principle of development that older structures are preserved and newer structures and functions are built upon the older foundation.[14] This hierarchical organization of control, for example, permits us to resist, by conscious effort, going to sleep at inopportune times, despite the pull of a circadian rhythm. Mammals would be in great trouble if the sleep cycle automatically kicked in every sundown or sunrise, despite the apparent necessity of attending to some immediate environmental dangers or even just to social activities.

Once asleep, we do not usually have control of our dream states, although there does seem to be some limited ability to awaken ourselves from upsetting dreams. The recent study and appreciation of the phenomena of "lucid dreams" raises the possibility that individuals may have some control of their dream imagery. Lucid dreams are dreams in which a person becomes aware that he or she is dreaming. Not only is the dreamer able to control or direct some of the dream activities, but there is also a sense of self-reflectiveness that routinely is a concomitant of conscious mental states, but is notably absent in ordinary dream states.[15] While being cautious about jumping onto a facile and trendy explanatory bandwagon, our understanding of this paradoxical dream state has potential implications toward some insight into the experiences of some of the mystics, since there is a coherence and volitional component to the description of the dream-like experiences of many mystics that strongly resemble the experiences described by lucid dreamers.

Trance and hypnotic states

In addition to sleep and dream states, and what appear to be subcategories of dream states, there are a variety of altered states of consciousness within the broader stage of wakefulness that are more or less open to conscious control and manipulation. These are frequently referred to as trance or hypnotic states of various depths. Sometimes we slip into a mild trance state automatically and without wishing to, such as the transient state called "highway hypnosis" which most automobile drivers have experienced. A different type of altered state is that sense of depersonalization and derealization that occurs to people during emergency or danger conditions, such as automobile accidents or combat situations, in which one feels as if outside one's body observing oneself, or as if the event is unreal in some indefinable way, giving the experience a dream-like quality.[16]

In addition to those altered states into which one shifts or slips without conscious effort or volitional intent, humans have learned how to alter intentionally their own states of consciousness through a variety of ingenious mechanisms. Every human culture appears to have developed its own preferred methods and rules by which individuals may alter their states of consciousness. Variations in methods sanctioned and expectations of what the actual experiences of altered states of consciousness will be like are merely cultural shapings of the basic human capacity to move in and out of different states of consciousness. This is analogous to the great variations in eating habits across different cultures, which too represent cultural shapings of an obligatory human activity.

To say that the capacity and desire to alter one's state of consciousness is an inherent human trait, however, is not to say that the capacity is present in all humans to an equal degree, or that training is not useful in improving one's ability to enter, maintain, or exit such a state. On the continuum of skillfulness in altering one's state of consciousness, some individuals are clods and others are masterful. Gherardesca of Pisa (*c*.1200–*c*.1260) appears to have been one such adept. In the previous chapter on asceticism, we provided an anecdote from her *vita* in which a vision follows immediately upon Gherardesca fiercely scourging herself in the privacy of her room. But several lines later, Gherardesca is again asked to pray along with a young woman for the recovery from illness of this woman's brother:

> Then Gherardesca, for she was pious and humble, instantly knelt down and prayed tearfully to the Lord on behalf of the aforesaid sick man. And while she was praying – whether in the body or outside the body, I don't know, God knows – at once she was led into a meadow very beautiful and pleasant. It was full of roses and other kinds of flowers, emitting a most pleasant fragrance.[17]

The *vita* proceeds to describe the approach of three pilgrims across the meadow, one of whom is Jesus himself. Gherardesca sees the wounds in his feet, and her tears fill these wounds. She drinks the water of her tears and is told that her prayers on behalf of the supplicant will be answered. This type of vision, occurring spontaneously and remembered in rich detail, is very different from mystical states without content, and would not even qualify as a mystical state according to the definition of Robert Forman and others, who restrict the definition of mystical states to those restful conscious states without content (often referred to as "states of pure nothingness").[18] Yet Gherardesca's experience exemplifies the strong affective component and attachment to the humanity of Jesus that characterized the dominant form of mysticism of the thirteenth century. It also shows the rapidity and ease with which certain of the mystics could enter an altered state.

In general, the trait or capacity to enter into an altered state should be distributed in the general population along a bell-shaped curve. The capacity to alter one's state of consciousness or, phrased in passive rather than active terms, the capacity to experience an altered state, is a measurable trait that has been studied in recent years under several different psychological constructs. The two most frequently used terms for this trait are hypnotizability and absorption.

Hypnotizability and absorption

Hypnotizability, a notoriously difficult construct to define in other than circular terms as the ability to become hypnotized, is a general measure of the susceptibility of a subject to follow suggestions. Ernest Hilgard defines hypnotizability as the ability to have the experiences characterized by the hypnotized person and to exhibit the kinds of behavior associated with it.[19] Scientifically, it is safest to avoid talking about the subjective components of hypnotizability and to define it operationally in terms of the measurement of a person's compliance or resistance to suggestions when in a hypnotic state. There is ongoing debate whether the compliance or resistance to following suggestions is a voluntary or involuntary function.

Absorption is defined as openness to absorbing and self-altering experiences.[20] It is the capacity to become focused upon a narrowed field of imagery or thought and to block out of awareness most of the mental activity (clutter) which ordinarily preoccupies us. The state of consciousness during an episode of high absorption is characterized by focused, undivided attention to an event, either internal or external, rather than doing a frequent sampling of different types of stimuli. Although the notions of "internal" and "external" are meaningful and usable terms for everyday discourse, descriptions of mystical experiences seem to obliterate such inside–outside distinctions. In terms of their psychological characteristics, mystical states (we are not referring to narrative religious visions) represent states of high absorption.

Hypnotizability and absorption, although different from each other, are highly correlated in most individuals. They tend to predict the presence of a whole range of other psychological traits related to inner-directed mental activities and a broad cluster of characteristics which we shall shortly describe as thin-boundaried. For example, the trait of absorption is associated with measures of phantasy-proneness,[21] and responsivity to meditation and electromyographic (EMG) biofeedback techniques. In general, absorption is seen in persons who also possess increased and more vivid imagery, inward and absorbed attention, and a pattern of positive mood states.[22] It is likely, judging by the facility and rapidity with which many of the medieval mystics experienced ecstatic states, that the constructs of hypnotizability and absorption describe core psychological traits that can be applied in a meaningful and constructive way to the types of persons, medieval and modern, who have mystical experiences.

For example, Margaret of Ypres's (1216–1237) initial mystical experience, which occurred directly upon taking a self-imposed vow of chastity of mind and body, is described in her *Life* as follows: "Absorbed in ecstasy, her head fell upon the psalter which she had in her hands." When Margaret "returned to herself," she reported to her spiritual director that she had had a dream, but that it was a dream unlike any previous ones that she had. Since it was Margaret's first ecstatic experience, she did not recognize it as such immediately, but her director appreciated the mystical nature of this particular dream.[23]

From this modest beginning, Margaret appears to have developed the ability to experience a trance state almost at will. Thus, when her mother complained to her spiritual advisor that Margaret spoke too little to the family, he ordered Margaret to converse with them for as long as it takes to recite seven psalms. Margaret obediently did this, but if the conversation shifted away from God and onto gossip or rumors, "at once she turned away her face and slept." Similarly, if the talk went beyond the appointed time, Margaret "immediately would slump down and lean against the wall and her face and hands would instantly turn livid."[24]

As another example of Margaret's absorption, of her ability to become absorbed in inner thoughts and to block out attention to ordinarily relevant details of the environment, consider the following event: "As the handmaid of Christ was returning from church intoxicated with heavenly delights, she entered the house and found a basket full of raw eggs on a bench. Thinking they were egg shells, she emptied the basket and threw them out of the house."[25]

As is evident with Margaret and other mystics, the mind is absorbed in heavenly delights and does not pay attention to the details of the mundane world, such as the differences between whole eggs and egg shells. Such persons are often called absent-minded, and descriptively this is true, but the critical point is where is the mind when it is "absent"' and the critical question is, how does Margaret manage to shift her state of consciousness so readily, such that she is "absent" to ordinary environmental stimuli?[26]

Altered states of consciousness and altered brain states

An unresolved and stormy debate persists among workers in the various fields that study altered states of consciousness. One part of the debate concerns whether the mental states that persons are in when they are hypnotized or in meditative trance states have distinctive characteristics such that there is reason to think that these types of mental states are different from "ordinary" states of relaxation and drowsiness in which one allows oneself to become suggestible, i.e. hypnotizable. A second part of the debate centers about the word "allows," which implies a voluntary activity under conscious control, as opposed to "susceptibility," which implies a degree of involuntariness in going into a trance state. If hypnotizability is a trait, then highly hypnotizable persons would have less ability or reason to resist going into a trance state, or greater facility in going into a trance state than would those who are not highly hypnotizable. By contrast, in the social–psychological model of hypnosis articulated by Nicholas Spanos, the "hypnotized" subject voluntarily agrees, for reasons such as social agreeableness, to follow the suggestions of the hypnotizer.[27] Spanos argues that hypnotic behavior is a voluntary response strategy rather than a special state in which subjects have lost conscious control over suggestion-induced behavior.

This debate is articulated scientifically in terms of whether there is evidence that the neurophysiology of hypnotic and deep meditative states is different than that of relaxation and drowsiness states.[28] At least part of the debate involves an objection to the assumptions of the modern scientific paradigm that differences in mental states must be demonstrable neurophysiologically or through brain imaging (i.e. as differences in brain states) in order for the very notion of "different state" to be meaningful and discussable. From a scientific viewpoint, a meditative or even a mystical state must have unique neurophysiological characteristics in order for it to be considered as distinguishable from a light trance or ordinary state of relaxation in which the focus of attention is narrowed and the person mentally attends to internally generated stimuli rather than environmentally generated stimuli.

Those who object to such a narrowly scientific approach to the study of transcendental or similar mental states argue that the very act of investigating persons in such states changes or interferes with the practitioner's ability fully to enter such states. Despite these objections, a very large number of studies of varying quality examining associations between meditative and brain states have been pursued and published. What is perhaps most interesting is that, despite several thousand reports in the scientific and lay literature, there remains no consensus or even modest agreement about what the brain is doing when a person is in a meditative or mystical or even "light" hypnotic state.[29]

The extensive review by Michael Murphy and Steven Donovon amply documents this total lack of consensus about whether meditative and hypnotic states differ from ordinary relaxation states.[30] As might be expected, studies that are less scientifically rigorous and those done by researchers who appear to have a personal stake in a particular outcome find greater (or lesser) differences between the efficacy of meditative versus relaxation states in bringing about blood pressure reduction, cardiovascular competence, pain control, and anxiety reduction than do the more controlled and methodologically rigorous studies. Many of the neurophysiological studies which compare meditators to a control sample of non-meditators also seem to fail to take into account the potential sample bias that those who chose to study and practice meditation intensively may represent a very different population from non-meditators. A final problem in this type of research is that there are many forms of meditation induction and meditative states, most strikingly the differences between states of arousal (e.g. ecstatic) and quietude and stillness (e.g. contemplative tranquility) such that neurophysiological findings relevant to one type of meditation may have little crossover to other forms.

One other interesting item is that the number of studies on these topics peaked in the 1970s and early 1980s, when there was intense public interest in meditation and altered states, and that, despite the availability of more sophisticated scientific instruments and the greatly increased philosophical and psychological interest in the subject of consciousness recently, scientific interest in discerning measurable differences in the various altered states seemed to have diminished until very recently. It is likely that the formidable technical and methodological problems of such research into mental states, which make it likely that research outcomes will be tentative and inconclusive, have discouraged large investments of time, money, and effort. However, the combination of technical breakthroughs in brain imagery, the emergence of cognitive neuroscience as a mature discipline, and renewed interest in spiritual matters has seen a growth of more sophisticated studies investigating relationships between brain mechanisms and consciousness.[31]

It might appear to the thoughtful layperson that, surely, if there were important differences between hypnotic or meditative states and states of ordinary drowsiness, then one to two thousand studies would have uncovered such differences. Nevertheless, the intransigence of problems of research methodology, such as finding proper samples of individuals to study, deciding what physiological parameters to measure, and determining what variations constitute significant differences, has not yielded to more sophisticated technology.

Michael West, in 1980, reviewed the scientific literature on findings relating to electroencephalographic (EEG) patterns during meditation.[32] The ordinary state of wakefulness is characterized by two EEG patterns, that of full activation and alertness called beta activity and that of relaxation, closed eyes, and reverie called alpha activity. Most studies reviewed by West demonstrate that both meditation and "ordinary" drowsiness exhibit an EEG alpha rhythm, but that the alpha rhythm is more stable during meditation. This difference can be picked out by experienced EEG readers blind to the state of consciousness of the subject.

A second difference is that the alpha rhythm was not interrupted by external stimuli (e.g. noise) during a deep meditative trance, indicating that the meditator had trained the brain, so to speak, to maintain an internal focus and not attend to external factors, which would be indicated by a shift to a beta (alert) activity pattern. A third difference relates to the notion of coherence in EEG patterns. This refers to how uniform the EEG activity is over the whole cerebral cortex surface. EEG recording of the brain during meditation suggests that there are more periods of EEG coherence during these states than during non-meditative states.[33]

Seemingly contradictory findings were that the usual habituation (decreased EEG response) to repeated stimuli seen normally was not seen in meditating subjects. This means that experienced meditators have trained themselves to maintain uninterrupted awareness of the external environment while not shifting into beta activity, but remaining in a meditative (alpha activity) state. In keeping with this, experienced meditators can maintain an alpha rhythm while meditating with eyes open, whereas in non-meditating subjects, the EEG pattern usually switches over to the more attentive beta rhythm when eyes are open, since the "normal" waking state is to a large extent stimulus-bound or stimulus driven. In modern meditative practice, the meditator follows a technique of mental noting that strengthens mindful awareness. When thoughts, sounds, and sensations arise in consciousness, the meditator remains aware of the environment while practicing letting the sensations pass through without attending to them.[34]

We are such visually driven mammals that it is difficult for us to look at something and not focus on it at least temporarily, which would be reflected in a shift from alpha to beta waves. Finally, meditators appear to spend more time in the slow wave theta patterns than do non-meditators. The theta pattern, most commonly seen in stages of deep sleep, is often associated with altered states of consciousness.

Graffin and colleagues measured the EEG patterns of a group of high and low-hypnotizable subjects.[35] The high-hypnotizable subjects displayed an EEG pattern characterized by greater theta activity in the more frontal areas of the cerebral cortex, although theta activity increased for both groups (high and low-hypnotizable) in the more posterior areas of the cortex during an actual hypnotic induction session. The posterior (occipital) cortical areas are primarily involved with visual processing and interpretation. The authors suggest that anterior/posterior cortical differences are more important than right/left cortical differences for understanding hypnotic processes. This argues against the usually oversimplified assumption that dream and meditative states represent a shift from left brain to right brain dominance.[36]

Aside from the technical findings regarding alpha and theta patterns during hypnosis and meditation, what is most impressive still is the very tentative and modest nature of the research findings. While the conclusion of West[37] in 1980 that "it appears likely that meditation is, psychophysiologically, a finely held hypnagogic state," is supported by later studies such as the one cited above by Graffin *et al.*, it still remains extremely difficult to demonstrate scientifically and in detail the ways in which meditative/hypnotic states differ from states of ordinary drowsiness. Although there is debate about the incorrigibility of the experience of consciousness,[38] nevertheless the cumulative experience of meditators throughout the world is that they experience altered states of consciousness that are very different from states of ordinary consciousness. The differences during meditation are most prominent in its middle stages of mindful awareness of the environment without interruption of the meditative state and in its deeper stages of states of pure nothingness. The task of science is to catch up to experience rather than to deny experiences that, at the moment, are difficult to explain.

The presence of mental clutter

The normal condition of an ordinary state of consciousness consists of an ongoing stream of shifting and fairly fragmented segments of thoughts and images that collectively can best be described as mental clutter. Mental clutter does not constitute the totality of the ordinary stream of consciousness; there is directed, purposeful thinking as well as drifting off into daydreams and free-floating imagery that may have important creative functions. To be human and awake is to be plagued, or blessed, with a constant flow of thoughts and images. Such a normal state of affairs was commented upon by John Locke, in his essay on human understanding: "I grant that the soul in a waking man is never without thought, because it is the condition of being awake."[39] Jerome Singer, the developmental psychologist, has emphasized that "ongoing thought," as he terms it, is much less the product of structured, directed thinking than experimental psychologists have previously assumed. Singer proceeds:

> It seems likely that the baseline or tonic characteristics of normal thought involve a range and variety of intrusions of images and interior monologues of retrospective or prospective scenes played out with greater or less vividness and that all of these are subject to different degrees of attention depending on the external task demands.[40]

Because mental clutter represents the normal operation of ordinary moment-to-moment consciousness that is rooted in everyday petty and profane topics, it thereby becomes the unique characteristic of subjective mental life that most interferes with seeking detachment from the material world and engagement with the spiritual world. A mental state with reduced clutter is a basic characteristic of all altered states considered desirable in the quest for a transcendental or spiritual experience. Therefore the task for all religions that value spirituality and transcendental experiences is to develop techniques and rituals for reducing mental clutter; these are, in essence, techniques for altering one's state of consciousness within certain moral constraints and according to specified rules.

The problem of clutter, moreover, is a general problem of human self-consciousness not restricted to individuals with transcendent aspirations. For some reason, and there is never a shortage of ready explanations, the self-reflective awareness of one's own stream of consciousness, when it itself becomes the object of awareness, is generally experienced as possessing to varying degrees a subjectively unpleasant and even painful quality. This unpleasant emotional tone which accompanies more than just a few moments of self-conscious reflection into one's own thought processes is usually accompanied by a commensurate human propensity to interrupt and escape one's "normal" mental state. The drive to interrupt mental clutter, from a religious and spiritual perspective, reflects a universal tendency to transcend one's base humanity and make contact with a higher reality. It is through our mental clutter that preoccupies us with petty desires, grievances, anxieties, ambitions, and plans that we stay attached to the world. Non-attachment requires solving the problem of clutter.

Much of modern Western secular 'leisure' activities are devoted to filling our lives with distractions from our "normal" (i.e. cluttered) state of consciousness. We ingest legal (alcohol, caffeine, and tobacco) and illegal mood and consciousness-altering substances ("downers" such as barbiturates and opioids, "uppers" such as cocaine and amphetamines); we use car radios, cellular telephones, loud music, and news shows in public places, and as many television sets in a house as can be afforded. It normally takes attention-riveting stimuli to divert a person from attending to the ticker-tape parade of thoughts that flow incessantly, unbidden and often unwanted, in "front" of our minds. Spiritual mantras and intrusive media noise from radios and televisions each perform a similar task in interrupting an unwelcome stream of trivial and disturbing thoughts and images. It is customary for most of us to value the mantra and demean the loud and repetitive beat of rap music, but neurophysiologically, the same process of changing a brain state is occurring.

For some individuals in modern times, such as those suffering from the flash-backs and intrusive imagery of post-traumatic stress syndromes as well as those who experience major discrepancies between what their thoughts happen to drift to and what they think they ought to be thinking about, the stream of consciousness can become an enemy that has to be combated.[41] This conflict between real and ideal has its medieval echoes in those ascetics, usually adolescents and young adults, who appear to have injured themselves in order to interrupt profane thoughts and carnal desires, in contrast to ascetics who appear to have sought primarily a direct experience of the presence of God.[42]

Mental clutter and medieval mysticism

Why was it necessary for Western medieval Christians aspiring toward closeness with God to alter their state of consciousness, usually through a combination of asceticism and prayer? The fundamental premises underlying Western ascetic religious practices are, first, that there are multiple realms of Being arranged in a hierarchy of ascending reality and value; second, that ultimate reality resides in the unseen and non-material worlds rather than the physical world of our senses; third, that attachment to the transient material world, partially in the form of mental clutter, interferes with recognition and participation in the spiritual realms, wherein lie the ultimate values of truth, unity, and permanence; and, fourth, the proper life task for each individual who accepts the three premises outlined above is to strive toward disengagement from the material world and engagement with the spiritual world.

A state of consciousness occupied with mental clutter is incompatible with the state of mind that strives for a close relationship with God. It is the problem of clutter as the enemy of contemplation that Cassian (d. $c.435$), founder of two monasteries in Marseilles, addresses in various ways and that the medieval ascetics sought to solve, at least in part, through ascetical behaviors. Cassian's writings were very influential in Benedict of Nursia's (c.480–547) thinking as he established his rules for monks.[43] The presence of mental clutter in medieval religious, those incessant, intrusive thoughts that swirl unbidden through the minds, constituted a major barrier to the attainment of equanimity and a realization of transcendent values and experiences.

In the first chapter of his *Conferences*, Cassian directly engages this question in the form of a dialogue between Germanus the student and the desert monk Moses, the teacher. Germanus asks how it occurs that despite ourselves, "useless thoughts slide into us, subtly and without our seeing them, so that it is no small thing not simply to drive them away but even to know and to grasp that they are there at all?"

Moses' reply accurately describes the problematic truth about the human stream of consciousness. He answers Germanus,

> It is impossible for the mind to remain undisturbed by thoughts, but anyone serious about the matter can certainly permit them entry or drive them away, and although their origin does not lie entirely under our control we can choose to approve of them or to adopt them.[44]

Moses, the desert ascetic, proceeds to recommend reading of Scriptures and singing of psalms as the best method for giving a spiritual rather than carnal turn to our thoughts. Ridding oneself of mental clutter does not, in itself, provide a gateway to the spiritual world, but it is usually considered a necessary preliminary step.

Cassian returns to the theme of clutter in his long discussion of prayer in Conference Nine. The narrator in this Conference is blessed Isaac, who states that, if the endless unstirring calm of prayer is to be achieved, a succession of obstacles must be overcome. Isaac elaborates on this process:

> First, there must be a complete removal of all concern for bodily things. Then not just the worry but even the memory of any business or worldly affair must be banished from within ourselves. Calumny, empty talk, nattering, low-grade clowning – suchlike must be cut out. Anger and the disturbance caused by gloominess are especially to be eradicated. The poisonous tinder of carnal desire and avarice must be pulled out by the roots. . . . Because of the workings of memory whatever has preoccupied our mind before the time of prayer must of necessity intrude upon our actual prayers.[45]

Historically there have been alternatives to the rather laborious and time-consuming practice of personal discipline recommended by Cassian to rid the mind of clutter. The clearest departures from the usual pattern of intensive and prolonged scriptural study and meditation training are those rare occasions when one is suddenly and unexpectedly "seized" or "rapt" into the presence of Absolute Being or the unity of the universe. Such dramatic experiences highlight the controversy about whether one can prepare in any manner for such transcendent experiences or whether, in Christian terms, they come about purely as the result of God's grace unmediated by any activity, preparation, or merit of the person. The conversion experience of Saul of Tarsus (Acts 9:3–9) on the road to Damascus is the prototypal example of God's grace suddenly and explosively capturing an unsuspecting individual, although it has been argued that Saul's intense animosity toward the new Christian sect was itself a preparation for his conversion.[46]

The sudden conversion of Augustine in the garden, when he picks up the epistles of Paul in response to a child's distant voice saying, "Take it and read," and opens the page to Romans 13: 13, stands as another example of infusion by God's grace upon a somewhat prepared but still resistant sinner. Not accidentally, it is Paul that Augustine turns to at the time of his great spiritual anguish. The conversion experiences of Paul and Augustine served as exemplars throughout the medieval period of one form of sudden mystical illumination.[47]

Despite the theoretical acknowledgment that one cannot force God to bestow his grace, the general theological consensus is that transcendent experiences are more likely to occur to the prepared and God-hungry person, and that preparation usually involves some balance of ascetic and meditative practices. As it is sometimes phrased, in order to let God come into your heart and mind, you must make some room there. Therefore, the question always arises as to what is involved in making room for God. Although the metaphor of making room in one's "heart" strongly implies that there must be a change of emotions in the direction of love and charity, nevertheless, at least part of this change must involve extending the spatial metaphor to making room in one's mind, not just one's heart, for thoughts of God to enter. This conjunction of heart and mind is expressed in the *vita* of Ida of Louvain (d. *c.*1300), a Cistercian nun who finds herself distracted while at mass:

> It once happened at mass time that while the Divine Mysteries were being handled, Ida was for a moment distracted from her goal by him who invented all iniquity, namely, the Devil. Thus was she turning over within herself something frivolous and useless. Forgetful of the Saving Mystery, she was letting her heart and mind apply themselves to some idle outward thoughts.[48]

The description of mental clutter provided here is perfect: frivolous, useless, idle, outward thoughts. To a secular person, such mental meanderings are of no consequence and usually pass unnoticed. But to Ida, such meanderings were not innocuous. They were cause for concern, both because the thoughts led away from God and because of the risk of letting such drifting become habitual. Right after Ida caught herself, she entered into an altered state. Her soul floated from her body and she saw herself and the proceeding of the mass from a vantage point above the altar.

But if clutter is the normal waking state of the mind as well as a description of the contents of the ordinary state of consciousness, and if a mystical state represents a shift toward a wakeful state of consciousness without mental content or sensory images, that is, a state of awareness relatively empty of thoughts and images, as often expressed in both Eastern traditions and the via negativa of Western Christianity,[49] then ridding the mind of clutter becomes a critical first step in the approach toward a mystical state. The very process of clearing or removing mental clutter involves a shift to an altered state of consciousness, since the ordinary state of mind is one filled with clutter. Robert Forman, in a series of articles on "pure consciousness," restricts the definition of mysticism, in true apophatic tradition, to those restful conscious states that are without content and cannot be described in sensory terms. Mental states in which one sees images and hears sounds are considered "visionary" but not mystical states by Forman.[50] Richard Jones, in his philosophical analysis of mysticism, distinguishes between two types of mysticism, that which he designates as a "nature-mystical experience" in which there is imagery and thought content within an unmistakably altered state of consciousness, and "depth-mystical experiences" in which, similar to Forman's description of a state of pure consciousness, the mind is completely stilled.[51] But Jones does not restrict mystical experiences only to the "stilled mind" variety of altered state. Such a restricted definition would remove most medieval mystics from consideration as "true mystics," for much of their mystical experiences involved imagery of physical closeness to Jesus.

The problem of clutter remains central throughout the Middle Ages to all who aspire to a transcendental or mystical pathway. Thus, seven hundred years after Cassian, Lutgard of Aywieres (1182–1246), a mystic from the Low Countries, struggles with unwanted thoughts in language that echo Moses and Isaac, the desert ascetics. Lutgard's biographer recognized the endless nature of the endeavor to rid the mind of its incessant mundane thoughts as he described her attempts to focus her thoughts at prayer exclusively on God:

> she began to apply herself to the task of completely banishing all thoughts from herself when she was saying the Hours, not just evil thoughts but even the good ones as well and to occupy her spiritual consciousness solely on what she was saying – a feat which is impossible in this condition of mortal life.[52]

Simone Weil, in modern times, captured this identical quandary in a single sentence: "The capacity to drive a thought away once and for all is the gateway to eternity."[53]

The saints collectively provided, in various ways, the models for the types of sacrifice and commitment involved in disengagement from the material world. Models were needed for persons in different stations of life, such as Guthlac the warrior (c.673–714) who renounced the world to become a hermit, Francis of Assisi (c.1181–1226) who rejected the mercantile world to recreate an apostolic path, Beatrice of Nazareth (1200–1268), who made her commitment to Christ in childhood, and Gherardesca of Pisa (c.1200–1260) and Angela of Foligno (1248–1309), both of whom served in late medieval lay society as examples of married women who finally follow their souls' desire and give up secular marriage for a heavenly one.

According to her *vita*, Gherardesca, who as a child of 7 ran from home to join a convent, was later persuaded by her mother to return home and eventually marry. Afterwards, however, Gherardesca felt herself distanced from Christ and embarked on a regimen of mortifying her body with prayers and fasting. Several years pass, and Gherardesca realizes that her desire for closeness with God cannot be satisfied while living, even ascetically, as a married woman in the secular world. The text proceeds:

> At length, since the saint unceasingly showed her great desire to leave the world and its enticements and to spend her life in a certain monastery in the service of Jesus Christ, and since she did not believe that it was possible to earn eternity in the world, she started earnestly to admonish her husband. She said that if he would, with her, abandon the transitory things of this world, they could enjoy the fruit of a better life in a monastery and that in the end they would obtain the glory and participation in the heavenly kingdom.[54]

The sentiments expressed in this passage are echoed and lived out in almost every saint's *vita*, since preference for the spiritual and rejection of the values of the secular world are the essence of what defines a holy person. As this passage implies, the multiple realms of reality that compose various theological and cosmological models of the universe can, for purposes of an examination of Western mysticism, be collapsed to two crucial categories. There is the level of reality of the physical world and our participation in it by way of our bodily existence. This contrasts with the level of reality of the transcendent world and our participation in it by way of our spiritual existence.

The goal of life on earth is to appreciate the illusory quality of our present existence and to strive, by proper action and contemplation, to live according to God's will and to seek an ever closer relationship to God. Beatrice of Nazareth (1200–1268) expresses this vocation in her mystical treatise, *The Seven Manners of Loving*, in unequivocal terms:

Plate 3.1 opposite Margaret of Cortona (1247–1297) from a Tuscan peasant family, was the mistress of a young nobleman near Montepulciano. She had one son. After her husband's death, she gave up her life of luxury and became a Franciscan tertiary. When her son reached adulthood, Margaret became more reclusive and devoted her life to prayer and pursuit of God.

LA B. MARGUERITE DE CORTONNE

> The soul desires to lead its whole life so as to work, grow, and ascend to a greater height of love and a closer knowledge of God, until it reaches that perfection for which it is fully made and called by God.[55]

Our bodily existence, manifested by our physical needs and natural desires as well as our psychological and emotional engagement in worldly concerns such as ambition, acquisition, and attachments, is generally assumed to interfere with our awareness of and participation in the transcendent world. As phrased by Walter Nigg in his discussion of the asceticism of St. Anthony, "Spiritual reality can be reached only at the expense of the flesh."[56]

The proper means and procedures by which to diminish (or vanquish) the influence of worldly needs and desires and to increase an awareness of the divine is the problem that medieval ascetics, if not all medieval Christendom, struggled to solve. However, there were also practical problems facing the secular and church leaders and those in religious orders in the early Middle Ages. The immediate concern was the conversion of the emerging barbarian kingdoms to a world view in which social responsibilities and right conduct according to Christian principles were pitted against the reality and power of sin and heresy. At a broad social and political level, conversion of early medieval Europe involved slowly modifying the warrior ethic of the secular nobility and upper clergy drawn from this class to an accommodation with a religion that preached pacifism and other-worldly values. The actual means toward these goals of religious commitment and spiritual development were neither clearly defined nor easy, however, despite occasional guidelines written for the nobility about the proper balance between devotion to the sacred and involvement in the secular world.[57] Given the priority of conversion of heathen and heretical peoples, holiness, other than by adoption of a eremitical and monastic life, was most clearly manifested in the early Middle Ages not by mystical pursuit of God but by high-risk evangelical activities that had the potential to end in martyrdom or near-martyrdom, such as the missions of Gall (died c.640) and Boniface (d.754 or 755) to the barbarian tribes. Boniface, along with 30–50 of his followers, were killed by pagans in Friesland (in present-day the Netherlands).

In general, holiness through martyrdom was no longer available after the conversion of Western Europe to Christianity, although some missionaries did achieve martyrdom proselytizing in Islamic North Africa. With the relative stability and economic expansion of Western Europe by the turn of the millennium, the pursuit of holiness shifted, or returned, from exterior evangelical behavior to interior spiritual behavior.

Mystical states and altered states

Pursuit of inner spiritual growth returns us to a consideration of what it means to shift attention away from the world and to the transcendental realm. Our awareness of multiple levels of reality and our passage through these realms involve changes in our moment-to-moment state of consciousness. Whether the mystic's consciousness of something transcendent "out there" is itself only internally generated stories during or after an altered brain state to explain fragmentary phenomenological data rather than a reflection of a higher reality beyond our material reality is at the heart of the materialistic-theological debate. We do not wish to enter this controversy here, other than to insist that, in either case, there are brain changes that accompany (as cause or effect) changes in consciousness. As every mystical writer has attested, although the specific vocabulary varies, when one feels or knows oneself to be in the presence of the divine, one is in an altered state of consciousness.

The significant variations in our self-reflective state of consciousness constitute the very experience of moving out of the mundane, corporeal level of reality into a "higher," or more spiritual, level of reality. The ecstatic experience of the presence of a higher Reality or a higher Being (usually, in Western culture, God) is, by definition and description, an altered state of consciousness. Bernard McGinn suggests that the expression "presence of" rather than "union" or "identity with" a higher being, is a more useful way of describing the encounter with God. He thinks that if mysticism were defined literally as union with God, there would actually have been very few mystics in the history of Christianity.[58] Nevertheless, one may refer to union with God as the ultimate, even if unattainable, goal of late medieval Christian mystics.

William James, whose work, *The Varieties of Religious Experience*, serves as the gold standard of psychological studies of religious experience, takes for granted that the mystical state is, whatever else, an altered state of consciousness. James writes, "One may say truly, I think, that personal religious experience has its root and center in mystical states of consciousness."[59]

Mysticism and personality traits

Are there psychological traits that predispose a person toward transcendental and mystical experiences? The personality construct of thin and thick boundaries, as developed by Ernest Hartmann, can serve as a model and integrating metaphor for an investigation of this question.[60] Hartmann postulates that thin and thick boundaries constitute a broad dimension of personality and an aspect of the overall organization of the mind.[61] All persons can be placed somewhere along a thin/thick boundary dimension, i.e. as having thinner or thicker boundaries. There is no inherent value attached to being thin or thick-boundaried; the construct is descriptive and heuristic. It is fairly clear that the world needs both types, and that there is benefit and cost to each type.

Although we shall speak of thin and thick as if individuals were purely one or the other, this is in reality not so. We are speaking of a spectrum or continuum from thin to thick-boundaried, along which spectrum each of us can be placed. It is possible that a person's ratio of thin and thick boundariedness may shift as a result of maturation and life experiences, but the notion of a basic dimension of

Plate 3.2 Odile (d.720) was the daughter of a Frankish nobleman. She was reportedly born blind and miraculously recovered her sight at age 12. She refused family pressure to marry and founded a monastery, of which she became the abbess. She is shown in prayer having a vision of the suffering Christ.

personality carries with it some expectation of relative stability. Examples of other postulated stable and basic dimensions of personality and temperament are the traits of risk-taking, novelty seeking, and conservatism. If we think of each of these constructs as embodying a continuum, then all humans can be placed somewhere on separate dimensions of risk-taking, novelty seeking, and conservatism, as well as thin/thick boundaried.[62]

Thin-boundaried individuals are flexible or fluid in their identities. They do not separate themselves from the natural world, but see themselves as continuous with nature, including animals and other humans. They suffer when others, especially children and animals, are hurt, and do not rationalize the pain by intellectual explanations of the natural causes of pain or the inevitable Darwinian chain of events that bring about suffering. They are relatively psychologically undefended, and therefore vulnerable to assault by the world.

Thin-boundaried individuals are more open than thick-boundaried persons to daydreaming activity, which can be defined as task-irrelevant cognitive activity in which internally generated phantasy material intrudes on an individual's primary task of dealing with external events.[63] Although daydreaming, like many other mental activities that are not tightly linked to solving problems in the physical day-to-day world, is often judged pejoratively, meditating and contemplating upon the nature of the Oneness of the universe must fall under this category of internally driven thinking.

Thin-boundaried persons have vague delineations between wakefulness and sleep, and experience many in-between or transitional states of consciousness, such as daydreams, reveries, and phantasies. They may have difficulty distinguishing vivid imagery from "reality," and tend to merge memories with phantasies. They tend to see connections and ambiguities where others do not.

An example of a thin-boundaried person is the narrator in Marcel Proust's *Swann's Way*, who remains in a long transitional period between waking or sleeping states and is unclear not just where he is, but even who he is, when he awakens. He first addresses how it must be for others, and then he describes his own predicament.

> When a man is asleep, he has in a circle round him the chain of the hours, the sequence of the years, the order of the heavenly bodies. Instinctively he consults them when he awakes, and in an instant reads off his own position on the earth's surface and the time that had elapsed during his slumbers; but this ordered procession is apt to grow confused, and break its ranks . . . for me it was enough if, in my own bed, my sleep was so heavy as completely to relax my consciousness; for then I lost all sense of the place in which I had gone to sleep, and when I awoke in the middle of the night, not knowing where I was, I could not even be sure at first who I was.[64]

The personal qualities of many of the medieval mystics appear similar to the qualities of thin-boundaried persons. Every thin-boundaried person is not a mystic, nor do all thin-boundaried traits apply to every mystic. There are several late medieval mystics who also appear to be administrative geniuses, an unlikely but undeniably real combination of seemingly opposite characteristics. Bernard of Clairvaux (1090–1153), Joan of Arc (?1412–1431), and Teresa of Avila (1515–1582) represent an unusual type of mystic each of whom must have possessed enough thick-boundary qualities to negotiate his/her way among powerful secular and religious leaders. But more common are thin-boundaried holy persons who appear to be "not of this world" and are prone to get into difficulties if too much in the world. This is so especially when the world around them is composed of thicker-boundaried individuals who are, stereotypically, intolerant and impatient with the vagueness, fuzziness, and unworldliness of thin-boundaried people.

This is a frequent theme in the *vitae* of many saints, who are ridiculed by their monastic or secular peers for their ascetic ways, their sensitivity to spiritual nuances that others ignore, and the ease with which they fall into trance states. Even as tough an ascetic as Benedict of Aniane is jeered for humbly cleaning and oiling the shoes of other monks at night.[65] Lutgard of Aywieres is teased by her abbess and peers when she refuses to allow the abbot of St. Trond to bestow a kiss on her, as he had done to the other nuns.[66] Giles of Assisi is ridiculed by street children because he goes into a trance when he hears the word "Paradise."[67]

We wish, however, to avoid turning the differences between thin and thick-boundaried persons into grounds for a medieval morality play. Most individuals represent a combination of thin and thick-boundary traits and manage to integrate these opposing tendencies more or less well in their daily lives. There do exist, by contrast, some thin-boundaried individuals who, in the day-to-day operational world, are more vulnerable and need a different type of nurturance and, possibly at times, protection, than thicker-boundaried people.

The traits of hypnotizability and absorption are highly correlated with scores on a Thin/Thick Boundary questionnaire developed by Hartmann,[68] lending construct validity to the thin–thick boundary measure. Absorption and positive-construction daydreaming activity (as opposed to guilty-dysphoric daydreaming) are also highly correlated.[69] Interestingly, women scored slightly, but consistently thinner (in terms of boundaries) than men on Hartmann's questionnaire,[70] and adolescent girls scored higher than adolescent boys in phantasy-proneness in a recent Spanish study.[71] We cannot administer psychological tests to medieval mystics, but the descriptions of the traits of persons scoring high on hypnotizability, absorption, and thin-boundariedness closely approximate the descriptions of the behaviors and personalities of most medieval mystics.

We offer one further bit of speculation about the personality of medieval mystics. Isaiah Berlin has described two contrasting ways by which people arrive at knowledge about the world, which he calls, based on a fragment from the Greek poet Archilochus, hedgehog and fox. "The fox knows many things, but the hedgehog knows one big thing."[72] The fox is an empiricist, a scientist; the edifice of knowledge is painstakingly built piece by piece and is always contingent, ready to be revised as evidence requires. The hedgehog believes knowledge is acquired intuitively, and seeks to discover unifying themes underlying the seemingly disparate and chaotic experiential world. To our knowledge, this construct has not been measured with psychological testing. But, in many ways, hedgehogs fit the description of medieval mystics in their openness to and pursuit of the Absolute, the One, the world beyond the physical. We offer the suggestion that mystics are, in general, thin-boundaried hedgehogs. Foxes are uncomfortable with and, often, inimical to mysticism.

Sad to say, some not-so-thin-boundaried persons yearn to be mystics, but cannot achieve the dissolution of their boundaries with that of the transcendent world.[73] They are earthbound; they cannot soar, although they long to. Some of these persons will show up as a supportive figure in the company of saints and mystics, perhaps as the saint's biographer. In fact, the worldly biographer of an unworldly, and therefore vulnerable, mystic has an important role to play in protecting the mystic from criticism or persecution by skeptics and detractors. Such was the case with Jacques de Vitry, the powerful churchman and future cardinal who, by his endorsement, lent respectability to the beguine and mystic Marie d'Oignies (1157–1228) and, indirectly (in his preface to Marie's *vita*), to Christina the Astonishing (1150–1224).[74]

It is a hardship to want to experience closeness to God, but to be, for whatever reason, unable to do so and also unable to rest content in providing support for those who are mystics. For some of these persons, foxes longing to be hedgehogs, thick-boundaried persons trying without success to enter into transcendental states, heroic asceticism seemed to offer, at some points in medieval Europe, a possible avenue to mystical experiences not otherwise available.

Methods of induction of altered states of consciousness

The factors determining what types of mystical encounters a person shall experience are not exclusively matters of individual temperament. Each culture seems to select, from the totality of available methods and rituals for altering a state of consciousness, those variations that conform to and further shape important values of that culture. In most cultures, certain types of altered states of consciousness appear to be a fundamental component of religious practices. As such, all cultures have specific rules for types of methods that can and cannot be used for induction procedures into altered states of consciousness as well as rules controlling permission and access into such states.

Alcohol and drug use for inducing trance states

Alcohol and drug use (such as LSD, cocaine, and marijuana) are among the most rapid and reliable methods of altering one's state of consciousness. Changes in the state of consciousness occur within minutes of rapid ingestion of as little as several ounces of alcohol. Indeed, the use of mind-and-mood-altering substances forms part of the trance induction procedures in religious ceremony of many cultures.[75] But even here, within a given culture, there is a range of individual responsiveness to the effects of hallucinogens or other drugs that have a primary action upon mental functions. Not all individuals respond alike to a given dose of a drug, even under similar circumstances. Interestingly enough, persons who are more likely to become deeply absorbed in their experiences (as determined by higher scores on the absorption scale) and whose altered states are of a positive affective quality are also those who report a more pleasant mood during marijuana use than persons who score lower on the absorption scale.[76]

Michael Winkelman,[77] in an anthropological study of magico-religious practitioners, has analyzed a stratified subsample of 47 cultures selected randomly from the Standard Cross-Cultural Sample of Murdock and White.[78] As part of this study, Winkelman examined patterns of usage of psychedelic drugs in the induction of altered states of consciousness. The study supports previous anthropological findings that altered states of consciousness have a role in the magico-religious practices in all cultures. Winkelman found clear patterns in the correlation between social organization and the use/non-use of psychedelic drugs in trance induction in magico-religious practices. Psychedelic drug use is found much more commonly in societies with shamanic practitioners and minimal social stratification (class distinctions), such as in villages not belonging to a larger federation. However, not all shamanic practitioners employ psychedelic drugs, since there are a variety of other mechanisms (fasting; auditory driving such as drumming) available for trance induction in religious ceremonies. According to Winkelman's survey and analysis, "the use of psychoactive drugs in ASC [altered states of consciousness] induction procedures declines with increasing political integration of the society."[79]

In Western Christianity, a society with class distinctions and complex political integration, religious specialists traditionally are priests who are not expected to have altered states of consciousness as a component of their religious practices. Consistent with this, psychedelic drugs are, and have been, rejected as a method of induction into a mystical state, although plants with hallucinogenic properties were available in the Middle Ages.[80] Alcohol in the form of wine is used, in great moderation, in the liturgical mass for its symbolic, not pharmacological, properties. In fact, the use of alcohol or psychedelic drugs in a Christian "mystic" to bring about a mystical state would serve to remove such an individual from serious consideration as a holy person.

Meditation for inducing trance states

Meditation, in contrast to psychedelic drug use, is a much slower and more difficult method to bring about an altered state of consciousness. An example of the arduousness involved in reaching, through meditation, the altered state of consciousness that is characterized by Christian mystics as a higher spiritual plane, is the great effort put forth by Cassian ($c.360-435$) and those who followed him to bring the Eastern meditative and mystical teachings of Origen ($c.185-254$), Evagrius ($c.345-399$), and John Chrysostom ($c.347-407$) into the daily life of cenobites in the West.[81]

Nevertheless, the Western distrust in general of altered states of religious consciousness, such as were promulgated in Eastern Orthodoxy and other esoteric (from a Western point of view) religions, resulted in a lack of emphasis in the early medieval West of pursuit of personal closeness to and identification with God. The theological basis of this was articulated by Bishop Irenaeus (130–200) in his opposition to Gnosticism's teachings that man can achieve immediate experience and knowledge of divine reality.[82] The orthodox cautiousness regarding mystical states was reflected later, as Robert Markus points out, in a gradual evolution in Cassian's thinking from an emphasis on ascetic discipline and solitary contemplation toward an acceptance of communal living and scriptural reading as the realistic pathway to a holy life.[83]

Elaine Pagels has examined the far-reaching consequences of Irenaeus' role in resolving the second-century controversy about the distance between God and man.[84] The theology hammered out by Irenaeus and others was central in the development of the orthodox creeds promulgated in the fourth and fifth centuries, which articulated guidelines for believers and strict boundaries for seekers of transcendental experiences. The medieval mystics, as seekers, had to conform to canonical teachings in their understanding and interpretation of what was revealed to them in ecstatic states and not trespass into areas of heresy.

Benedict's *Rule* (*c.*529) represents the codification of this line of development away from the centrality of altered states as the Christian focus, and the triumph for the next five hundred years of an emphasis on community rather than the individual. Those persons who became known for altered states of consciousness, namely the mystics who form the subjects of the present study, were usually and still are, with notable exceptions, on the fringe of the religious hierarchical structure and often under grave suspicion as a result of their mystical experiences.

To the extent that some altered states of consciousness were recognized as legitimate mystical states, meditation, initially as a form of contemplative prayer, has proven to be a more acceptable and respectable method in Western culture than either alcohol or drug use for altering one's state of consciousness toward heightened spiritual awareness.[85]

There is no exclusive type or technique of meditation; all methods are designed to solve the problem of clutter and appear to aim toward an altered mental state that generically can be subsumed under the modern concept of trance. A trance state reached through meditation can be facilitated by ancillary techniques such as rhythmic acoustic stimulation (chanting of a mantra or a scriptural phrase; drum beating), kinetic stimulation (rocking motion), forced hypermotility (whirling dervish), hyperventilation and breathing exercises, visual and sensory deprivation, fixed staring, such as at a crucifix or stained glass window, and seclusion and restricted mobility.[86]

Ascetic practices for inducing trance states

Ascetic practices, a process different than, although at times overlapping with, meditation, are a third method. In Western Christianity, ascetic behaviors of a self-injurious nature have formed a culturally sanctioned, prescribed, and ritualized means of reliably altering one's state of consciousness. An enduring theme throughout the entire development of Christian spirituality is the distinction between the ascetic's goal of interrupting and terminating undesirable mental states (e.g. sexual arousal; anger) in order to achieve the virtues of detachment and renunciation and the goal of moving toward a direct experience of the presence of God. While the latter is obviously the theoretical or ultimate goal for those following a mystical pathway, traditions within Christianity have differed both as to the relative merits of a life dedicated to good works versus strict reclusive contemplation, as exemplified in the prototypal Martha and Mary story in Luke 10:38–42, and as to the practicality and, therefore, the desirability of striving for such ultimate holiness. The dangers of mental unbalance and spiritual floundering are greater when striving for a virtually unattainable goal.[87] In practical terms, medieval hagiographical descriptions of many holy persons, especially during their adolescence, speak very little about union with God as motivation for asceticism, and very much about the goal of combating thoughts of bodily comforts and sexual gratifications.[88]

Metaphors and the ineffable

A few words need to be said about the role of metaphors in describing mental states. There is no language other than the metaphorical for speaking of mental states, especially of a transcendental nature, and more especially those that have characteristics referred to as ecstatic states. Thus we may think of the mind as a container which must be emptied out of certain material, i.e. clutter, excess baggage, etc., in order to have room for other types of goods. But we have no words for describing the "other types of goods" that then come into the mind. Lakoff and Johnson have provided the theoretical understanding why transcendental and mystical experiences are ineffable, namely, that our metaphors, which subserve all our language function, are based upon our bodily experiences, which are precisely the opposite, so to speak, of what we are trying to convey about our transcendental experiences.[89]

Richard of St. Victor (d.1173), one of the most influential figures of twelfth-century mysticism, writes keenly about the problems inherent in trying to convey abstract and transcendent concepts in a language rooted in the material world:

> Everybody knows how difficult or almost impossible it is for the carnal mind still untaught in spiritual studies to raise itself to the understanding of unseen things and fix its eye upon contemplating them. For so far it knows nothing but bodily things; nothing presents itself to its thoughts but what it is accustomed to thinking about, that is visible things. It seeks to see invisible things and nothing meets its eye but the form of visible objects; it desires to consider incorporeal things but dreams of the images of corporeal things only.[90]

The types of problems caused by the embeddedness of our language in our physical experiences is nowhere more manifest than in the long exegetical tradition of transforming the reading of the Song of Songs from an erotic love poem into a mystical text.[91] The literature of the Flemish and Rhineland mystics that speaks of being taken up in the arms of Christ, the heavenly bridegroom, underscores the impossibility of directly conveying ecstatic experiences in any language other than that of metaphors of physical ecstasy. Thus, this passage from Gertrude the Great of Helfta (1256–1301), instructing contemplatives regarding attainment of union with God, merges erotic and spiritual imagery in the genre called Bridal Mysticism (Brautmystik):

> In the evening, entirely melting and growing faint while waiting to enjoy the sempiternal vision of the mellifluous face of God and the Lamb, rush into the embrace of the spouse Jesus, your lover; altogether like a busy bee that clings with a kiss to his amorous heart, plead for a kiss from him.[92]

The alternative to such rich metaphorical language is that embraced by the apophatic tradition, which asserts that the direct experience of God is so beyond human imagery and comprehension that it can only be described by negation, i.e. by saying what the experience is not like.

Feminist critical theorists have observed that, among women mystics of the twelfth to fifteenth centuries, there was a greatly increased emphasis on the description of visceral experiences as correlates for ecstatic emotional states. In the *vitae* of such mystics, the experiences of rapture and mystical ecstasy were expressed in terms of interior processes, primarily cardiac.[93] Attention paid to the heart resonates with Buddhist meditative teaching about the heart as the center of consciousness and, with it, the importance of "training of the heart" as a way of diminishing unwholesome mental states that have already arisen or may arise. It is possible that modern historians have misjudged the medieval mystic's experience of rapture as a physical phenomenon of heart rather than an awareness of the heart as an metaphorical "energy center."[94]

Whatever overall metaphorical terms one employs to designate those self-conscious activities constituting mental "clutter" that interfere with the attainment of spiritual goods, medieval hagiography repeatedly emphasizes the importance of struggling against thoughts and temptations of worldly treasures, food, sex, reputation, competition for holiness, and self-importance, all of which were recognized as sinful desires. Thus, for example, in the Life of Genovefa (*c*.500), St. Germanus gives to the child Genovefa a copper coin to be made into a necklace, and admonishes her to disavow all interests in material possessions "never suffer your neck or fingers to be burdened with any other metal, neither gold nor silver, nor pearl studded ornament. For, if your mind is preoccupied with trivial worldly adornment, you will be shorn of eternal and celestial ornaments."[95]

It is just as likely, however, that the clutter that interferes with the pursuit of spiritual treasures was comprised, not of sexual desires and longing for fame, but of very mundane thoughts anticipating the day's activities, worries about one's aches and pains, petty grievances and gossip against one's neighbor, and the thousand and one ideas and images that pass through our minds all the time and that constitute what we refer to as our stream of consciousness.

To summarize, there are basic differences among individuals in their capacity for entering into altered states, as well as in their interest in pursuing the experiences of different altered states. The efficacy of alcohol and drugs for bringing about certain types of altered states in all who ingest such substances often obscure the fact that some people can enter altered states easily and others with great difficulty and then to a sharply limited degree. While we casually tend to think of these differences as based upon life experience and motivation and, in a religious context, grace or God's call, there is considerable evidence that there are strong biological influences and constraints upon one's propensity for entering into altered or trance states of consciousness. One determining factor relates to the thin–thick boundary distinction that we discussed earlier. A second factor is the characterological trait that Cloninger and co-workers have described under the term "self-transcendence."[96] Self-transcendence "refers generally to identification with everything conceived as essential and consequential parts of a unified whole . . . the person is simply aware of being an integral part of the evolution of the cosmos."[97]

It is very likely that Tellegen's construct of absorption, Hartmann's of thin boundaries and Cloninger's of self-transcendence are attempts at capturing and operationalizing in measurable terms the same or very similar constructs. In all three concepts, the notions include some sort of basic, hereditable, relatively hard-wired trait or disposition that can be modified only slightly by life experiences and personal motivation. There are clear limits to the extent that one can change, or would even want to change, one's basic disposition. Those persons who become mystics would, in general, come to the task with traits of high absorption, openness to transcendental experiences, thin boundaries, and an ability and desire to work at getting rid of mental clutter.

A type of situation in which a person might want to change or mask the expression of these thin-boundaried traits is when one is living in a social environment that greatly values and encourages the opposite pole of the self-transcendence spectrum that one happens to find oneself. Mystically inclined persons living in a materialistic-atheistic environment may meet with skepticism, ridicule and, under totalitarian political systems, even persecution. Alternatively, individuals with little capability for self-transcendence who live in a religiously or spiritually oriented environment may be viewed as pedestrian and, literally, lacking in grace. In each situation, there will be some temptation to conceal one's true nature or to pretend one is more (or less) than one is. We have raised the possibility that this latter description fits some religious communities in the later Middle Ages, in which attainment of altered states was highly valued, both because the experience itself was characterized as the goal of life on earth, and because of the positive light in which it cast the mystic. In such situations, some thick-boundaried individuals might adopt a harshly ascetic life style in an attempt to achieve (or force) an ecstatic state of consciousness that their thin-boundaried peers seem to reach so effortlessly.

Mihaly Csikszentmihalyi has analyzed and discussed factors that contribute to or interfere with achievement of mental states imbued with positive qualities of synchrony of self, task, and universe.[98] Although Csikszentmihalyi does not develop his concept in the vocabulary that we are using, it is clear that what he refers to as the ability to develop the "flow" experience is dependent upon a person's aptitude initially to shift out of the tedious self-conscious stream of consciousness that dominates our usual mental state. Csikszentmihalyi's "flow" experience appears to be similar to the description of states within a religious framework in which the presence of a higher Being is experienced.

In general, the types of positive altered states that are sought usually include altered cognitive processes, use of visual imagery rather than verbal descriptions, distortions in the sense of time, altered sense of bodily perceptions, altered peripheral vision and depth (stereoscopic) perception, blurring of boundaries between ordinary reality and imagination, sense of a reality greater than the ordinary reality, sense of closeness or union with a greater Being, and, finally, difficulty in remembering and describing what this state was like when one is no longer in the state (ineffability). The exact nature of a transcendental state that persons desire and expect to experience, and actually do experience, varies with cultural context, personality, values, and religious orientation.[99] In medieval Europe, these formal characteristics of altered states of consciousness were shaped by a Christian sensibility into the transcendental state that ultimately evolved, in the thirteenth to fifteenth centuries, of a close personal encounter with God.

4
PAIN AND LACERATION OF THE FLESH

Introduction

There are certain paradoxical elements in the use of pain to divert one's stream of consciousness from worldly concerns, for the initial effect of pain is to rivet one's attention to that part of the body that is in pain.[1] Nevertheless, pain is remarkably effective in interrupting the ordinary flow of thoughts, and it is this characteristic that makes the production of pain via laceration of the flesh a useful practice for those ascetics wishing to put a stop to the mental clutter that they are otherwise unable to get under control through customary meditative practices.

Pain, like many primary experiences, is difficult to define, however well acquainted we may personally be with it. Pain can be broadly defined as an unpleasant sensation and emotional state occurring when tissues are damaged.[2] This definition links pain literally to physical damage and the sequence of sensory neural events and subsequent central nervous system processing of these sensory inputs. It also emphasizes that an emotional component is an integral part of the pain experience. We are not speaking here of the metaphorical uses of the concept of pain, such as emotional pain (e.g. heartache), nor does this proposed working definition touch upon more diagnostically problematic types of pain, such as tension headaches, low back pain, and muscle aches that do not seem attributable in a literal sense to tissue damage.

The outstanding psychological feature of physical pain is its unique ability to capture attention, intruding into normal waking consciousness and interrupting and disturbing the ongoing activities and mental preoccupation of the sufferer.[3] Although we are able to elaborate a secondary vocabulary with which to describe subjective features of pain to others, the actual experience of pain is, as Elaine Scarry writes, "language destroying."[4] As the intensity of pain increases, the range of thoughts is progressively constricted, and one's conscious landscape is increasingly occupied with the multiple sensations of the pain and its emotional concomitants, such as anxiety, fearfulness, and anticipation of catastrophic consequences.

One way of understanding this dramatic effect of pain in narrowing the scope of attention utilizes a model of consciousness (defined here as focal attention) as a limited capacity system, i.e. limited in the number of organized chunks of information it can simultaneously keep in the conscious state.[5] Mandler, who proposed this model, suggests that, typically, about five such chunks (or distinct channels) can be accommodated in human consciousness at any given time. The reader can appreciate that one can easily keep three or four chunks or streams of thought going simultaneously.[6] Thus, while one is reading this page, one can also think about lunch, maintain an inconstant awareness of one's back leaning against a chair or one's feet in one's shoes, and have some awareness that the sky is a bright blue. Narrowing of attention refers to focusing (whether intentional or involuntarily) upon one or two chunks while excluding most other environmental and internal stimuli. If one developed a severe toothache while reading this page, it is likely that the pain of the toothache would come to drive out most other less urgent matters from one's mind (conscious awareness).

Essentially, the human nervous system is so constructed that events of high physiological and emotional arousal, such as intense pain, claim and preoccupy so much of the limited capacity "consciousness" system that other, less urgent cognitive functions will be displaced from conscious processing.

Types of pain and summation of pain

Although we may casually speak of somatic pain as a unitary experience, there are, in fact, two very distinct types of pain that have their foundation and explanation in basic neurophysiology. The initial experience of pain, for example, that caused by a laceration of the skin, is carried to the brain (and brought to our awareness) via rapid transmission along thinly myelinated (A-delta) sensory nerve fibers. This immediate experience of pain is of bright quality, precise localization, and sharp sensation, and allows the wounded person to withdraw quickly from the source of pain. As this pain begins to subside, it is followed by pain that is vague, often dull and/or burning, poorly localized, but persistent, and of a disagreeable, nagging quality. The delayed pain is the result of slower transmission of signals along unmyelinated sensory nerve fibers.

More importantly for our considerations of heroic asceticism, this type of delayed pain shows a summation phenomenon, whereby persistent activity in these unmyelinated fibers (subjectively experienced as waves of unrelenting pain) lead to a secondary hyperalgesia. This phenomenon is characterized by enlargement of the painful area beyond the immediate site of the injured tissue, with an increasing sensitivity in this wider area to ordinarily mild (non-painful) natural stimuli superimposed upon the pain from the initial wound, such that even light touch or warmth in the vicinity surrounding the actual injury will be felt as extremely painful.[7] Furthermore, sleep deprivation increases pain sensitivity by decreasing the threshold at which noxious stimuli are perceived as painful.[8]

As a personal example, one of the authors underwent a total hip replacement operation with very little post-operative pain. However, on the day following surgery, the area of skin on the thigh adjacent to the nine-inch sutured incision line was so sensitive that the mere pulling off of a strip of tape two inches away from the incision caused a more intense burning sensation than the pain caused by the rest of the procedure, including the skin incision itself, cutting through the muscle layers, dislocating the hip joint, sawing off the head of the femur, and hammering into place a metal ball-joint prosthesis. This hyperalgesia in the area surrounding the incision remained for about one week before gradually subsiding.

A medieval example

It must be this delayed, chronic, nagging, and persistent pain and hyperalgesia that the medieval ascetic experienced on a continuous basis, as the initial lacerations and puncture wounds by thorns became infected and the entire cutaneous area surrounding the lesions developed an exquisite hypersensitivity to even the light touch of a smooth garment rubbing across the skin, let alone a coarse hairshirt. Nor is it the same as a hairshirt rubbing briefly against intact healthy skin. A brief excerpt from the *Vita* of Beatrice of Nazareth (1200–1265), a Flemish holy woman and Cistercian nun, serves to illustrate specific methods employed to inflict tissue damage and then to keep both types of pain (acute and chronic) constantly in the awareness of this early adolescent ascetic:

> She was accustomed to beat her tender body, from the soles of her feet up to her chest, using sharp twigs and even the prickly branches of the yew tree. She also strewed her bed, from top to bottom, with sharp yew leaves; by them her tender limbs were so hedged in that scarcely any part of her body remained unscratched by the punctures.[9]

The text proceeds to describe the hagiographer's and, presumably, Beatrice's recognition of the intrusive quality of constant pain, as follows:

> She carried the prickly yew leaves in her bosom during the day, and was more harshly pierced by them as her waking senses were forced to be continuously aware of the nagging hurts, and to be constantly harassed with fresh pricks whenever she turned.

As this young ascetic matured into middle adolescence, she became more ingenious in covert self-injurious techniques for keeping pain constantly in the forefront of consciousness, as described in her *Vita*:

> she . . . made a rope with thorns woven into it, and this she used on her flesh as a belt. Its length went twice around her waist, and daily caused her tender body more wounds as its great length and many thorns dug into her. Not content with this torment, she made of the same rope a belt with many knots. . . . To these she added another belt, composed of fifty hard knots, which she wore over her tunic more tightly to compress the other hidden inside, and to pile torment on torment. Yet to all this she

added also a leather strip which she pressed hard on the others inside, so that at times she could not bend one way or the other, or lift or lower her head without fierce pain.

Role of endogenous opiates in modulating pain

The occurrence of tissue damage, both acute and chronic, brings about an interrelated series of physiological and psychological responses for modulating (usually reducing) the perception of pain. Release of endogenous (naturally occurring) opiate peptides, such as endorphins and beta-encephalin, into the bloodstream and into the synapses between nerves, is one of the most obvious and rapid responses. Endogenous opiate peptides are molecules composed of amino acid chains that exert a morphine-like dampening action on the transmission of signals from sensory neurons and other nerve cells involved in the processing of pain information.

The central nervous system pathways concerned with the transmission of pain signals from the periphery to the cerebral cortex are rich in opiate peptide neurotransmitters and receptor sites.[10] Neurotransmitters are chemical messengers that carry the nerve impulse signal from the terminal (axon) of one nerve cell to the receptor sites on the dendrites of the next nerve cells in the network. One needs to think of any single axon as having connections to thousands of dendrites. In addition, activation of the receptor sites of the "next" nerves in the chain may have the effect of stimulating or of inhibiting impulses in the network.

The process of pain modulation is a complex one. The opiate peptides activate neurons in the brain stem that send signals down to the spinal cord that inhibit the rate of impulses sent by neurons that transmit pain messages back to the brain. Since the intensity of felt pain is a function of the rate of firing of the pain fiber, the net effect of the endogenous opiates is to reduce the perception of pain.

Endogenous opiates and reward centers in the brain

At the same time that the endogenous opiates are dampening down the activity of the pain fibers, these molecules appear to exert a separate and direct stimulatory effect on those brain centers and networks that are associated with the mammalian reward function, that is, those centers that appear to subserve motivated behavior, positive mood, and the perception of pleasure. These reward mechanisms are unrelated to the pathways directly subserving pain recognition and response, but "happen" to utilize some of the same chemical neurotransmitters (opiate peptides) that are used in the pain system.

Such a concurrence of a single type of mechanism in widely divergent functional systems is by no means unusual in physiology, and reflects the basic conservatism of evolutionary biological processes. Essentially, as species evolve toward greater complexity and specialization of organ systems, evolutionarily older anatomical structures and mechanisms are not discarded, but provide the foundation upon which modifications and adaptations are superimposed for the development of newer and more specialized organs. This makes for some very interesting anatomical and functional convergence. For example, one of the most obvious of such convergence is the curious adaptation in male higher vertebrates of the urinary (excretory) system for purposes of reproduction, and the further linking of the reproductive system to those brain mechanisms subserving pleasure and drive.

Although we generally accept this delightful (or frightful) conversion of a male anatomical system originally meant for one biological function (excretion of liquid waste products and maintenance of body homeostasis) to a totally different function (delivery of one's genetic material into the reproductive organ of a species-specific mate) as a quirk of blind evolution, in fact, the adaptation of a more archaic system for different purposes is a basic principle of organic evolution.[11]

In a similar way, the complex mammalian (and hominid) brain is the product of continuous evolutionary modifications upon a more primitive reptilian brain.[12] Thus, humans and other mammals have the same basic structures as reptiles in the brain stem for regulation of breathing to insure the proper levels of oxygen and carbon dioxide in the blood. This physiological function of maintaining proper blood chemistry (such as acidity/alkalinity, or pH) within fairly narrow upper and lower limits is too important a life-sustaining metabolic activity to leave to the vicissitudes of conscious judgment about what is best for the organism. Regulation of breathing, therefore, occurs automatically, as the carbon dioxide and pH receptors in the brain stem (outside of conscious control) send feedback signals to the muscles of respiration that constantly adjust the rate and depth of breathing.

In addition, humans, and probably simian species, have higher (cerebral cortex) brain mechanisms for overriding (to a point, for we cannot hold our breath indefinitely) these automatic and homeostatic mechanisms, thus allowing the individual to bring respiration under voluntary control. Examples of this capacity include holding our breath or, its opposite, intentional hyperventilation, or the use of exercises of breath control in meditative practices. The higher cortical brain structures which enable us to splint our rib cage into temporary immobility, or to sigh, or to breathe rapidly until we become light-headed or even pass out, do not replace the older brain stem mechanisms that automatically regulate respiratory rate and depth, but are superimposed (piggybacked) upon them.

In a similar manner, the evolutionary development of complex "reward" centers in the midbrain utilized some of the available networks and opiate neurotransmitters that had been part of the evolutionarily older pain system. Avoidance of pain, and therefore avoidance of tissue damage, is a more basic function for survival than is the pursuit of pleasure (which may be an integral component for reproduction, which is the next evolutionarily important task), and therefore utilizes a more archaic brain system. Thus, the release of opiate peptides (evolutionarily developed for pain modulation) in response to tissue injury has the additional effect of stimulating evolutionarily newer reward centers in the brain that are not inherent components of the pain systems. Stimulation of reward centers in the human brain can have the effect in consciousness of a euphoric state. When this occurs as a result of tissue injury, however, the resultant pain usually overrides appreciation of any pleasurable effects.

The "euphoriant" quality that can be associated with the release of endorphin and other endogenous opiate is thought to be responsible for much of the addictive aspects of pain-inducing behaviors, ranging, in modern times, from self-injuring in individuals with developmental disabilities[13] to self-cutting in adult patients with borderline personality disorders[14] to the violent retching of bulimics[15] and the excesses of some long-distance runners.[16]

Much of these euphoriant effects caused by the release of endogenous opiate peptides into the bloodstream can be blocked by the administration of opiate (morphine) blockers, thereby demonstrating the dual role of endorphins and similar compounds in stimulating the reward centers as well as in down-regulating the activity of the pain system. This provides a concrete example of a mechanism by which inflicting pain upon oneself can have profound effects upon one's thinking processes and mood state far removed from the original conscious intent of the self-injurious behaviors.

Neural pathways modulating pain perception

Equally important as changes in blood levels of circulating substances (hormones, endogenous opiate peptides) which modulate brain states in response to pain, there are extensive neural pathways in place for higher (cerebral cortex) brain centers to influence the perception and emotional valence of pain. These brain structures and pathways provide the neuroanatomical substrate for a variety of voluntary and, to a large extent, learned mechanisms that can powerfully dampen down or enhance the attention paid to and the felt intensity of the pain. Specifically, there are neural pathways directly connecting the frontal cortex, via midbrain centers, to the secondary sensory (pain) neurons in the dorsal horn at all levels of the spinal cord.

The significance of this is that neural activity in the cerebral cortex (i.e. brain networks subserving higher mental activities such as thought, imagination, emotion, and imagery) can exert a direct modulatory influence, either inhibitory or excitatory, on the rate of firing and threshold sensitivity of the assemblies of neurons that signal tissue damage (actual or potential) back to the cerebral cortex. The specific populations of neurons excited, and changes in the rate at which each nerve cell fires (sends an impulse), are the neurophysiological mechanisms that encode the intensity and quality of pain sensation. Thus, any mechanism, such as the effects of endogenous opiates or of morphine-like drugs, that slows down the rate of firing of pain-transmission neurons will diminish the magnitude of felt pain.

Although we have described separately, for the sake of exposition, the brain network (relative hardwiring, so to speak) system and the neurotransmitter-biochemical system as if they were independent units, we are really speaking of a single integrated central nervous system. Impulses are transmitted from one nerve cell to many other nerve cells that comprise neural networks by means of chemical messengers (neurotransmitters). Among the many types of neurotransmitters are the endogenous opiate peptides (such as encephalins and beta-endorphin), which act within the pain system principally by inhibiting the firing of nociceptive (pain) cells.[17]

The perception of pain represents a final vector that is the sum of the incoming pain signals commanding attention and the outgoing modulating signals dampening and distracting attention away from the pain. In essence, the progressive research knowledge of the neurophysiological mechanisms subserving our ability to alter pain perception and response only confirms what we already know from psychological studies of human behavior and from personal introspection of our individual experiences with pain.

Much of this story of pain is well known in basic psychology, but rarely examined by historians or theologians. Thinking about something else will temporarily diminish the intensity of the pain. A state of depression will magnify the perception and negative significance of pain. Intense pain will alter our ordinary modes of thinking. The effectiveness of hypnotic (trance) states in reduction of felt pain is well documented. Subjects in either self-induced or other-induced hypnotic trances are able to undergo major surgical and dental procedures without anesthesia with only a vague awareness of discomfort somewhere in the periphery of their consciousness.

There is ongoing controversy as to whether the hypnotic state is an actual altered state or "only" a normal state of consciousness in which the subject responds to socially learned expectations and high test-demand characteristics.[18] In either case, the hypnotic state is a state of high suggestibility.[19]

Hypnotic alteration of pain perception has been demonstrated not only in clinical situations, but also under controlled laboratory conditions, e.g. tolerance to immersion of one's arm in a bucket of ice water, a procedure that ordinarily causes intense and intolerable pain within a matter of minutes. What is clear is that the human being is able, via mental processes based upon suggestion and imagery, to alter substantially the neurophysiology of pain perception.[20] This means that neural activation begun in our cerebral cortex, which phenomenologically is experienced as conscious thought, can send signals down to lower brain centers or to the synapse centers in the spinal cord which will block or inhibit pain signals from reaching the cortex or, phrased differently, from reaching conscious awareness.

The perception of pain is influenced by social attitudes regarding the moral value and redemptive power of pain, role modeling by others (both in person and in heroic/mythic stories) of how one is expected in a particular culture to respond both publicly and privately to pain and physical damage, and one's physical health, social roles, personal attitudes, psychological makeup, mental and emotional state, and life experiences.[21] At the same time, the biological level of the functional continuum of pain control, such as the release of endogenous opiates and corticosteroids, genetically determined thresholds for noxious stimuli transmission

COMETA ET NICOSA.

Scortator Babylas mimus foedam, edita in arce
Sponte sua inclusus, luxuriem domuit:
Mox quoque scorta Cometa, simulq; Nicosa, pudice
Vt viuant, casulam non procul inde struunt.

Plate 4.1 *Cometa and Nicosa* (d. ?fifth century) were concubines of the mime Babylas in Cilician Tarsus. When he converted upon hearing a sermon, he gave his money to Cometa and Nicosa. However, they gave all the money away and devoted themselves to a religious life, building a small hut near the tower where Babylas lived. One of the two women is seen applying the discipline.

and tolerance, and the neurophysiological changes set directly in motion by tissue damage, provides the effective mechanisms for the progression of an altered state of consciousness that has effects far beyond the dampening of pain.

Pain response and altered states of consciousness

In the context of a study of asceticism, the production of tissue damage and pain is one mechanism employed to alter the seekers' relationship to a transcendent Being. In the history of Christianity, inflicting pain upon oneself has been a common, but by no means constant, method to bring about such alterations in one's state of consciousness. Within the Western Christian spectrum, there has been a radical change from the early to late medieval periods. Specifically, social attitudes toward the role and legitimacy (or desirability) of self-inflicted physical pain as a means of achieving closeness to God has shifted considerably from that of the desert fathers, the original Christian ascetic practitioners, to that of the late medieval heroic ascetics. The desert fathers' lives embodied renunciation of worldly comfort and values; their goal was not suffering in itself, but to achieve a mastery over the physical impulses and needs that normally master the man. Thus the need for sleep, food, and creature comforts was placed under austere discipline.

For example, the major form of ascetic discipline described in the collection *The Lives of the Desert Fathers* was severe restriction of food.[22] Reference to fasting is found in the dialogues with John of Lycopolis, Abba Or, Ammon, Abba Helle, Paphnutius, Pityron, and others. An interesting insight is provided in the dialogue with Apollo, in which the holy man criticizes those who are ostentatious in their asceticism.

> He severely censured those who wore iron chains and let their hair grow long. "For these," he said, "make an exhibition of themselves and chase after human approbation, when instead they should make the body waste away with fasting and do it in secret. Rather than do this, they make themselves conspicuous to all."[23]

There are no examples of self-laceration as a heroic ascetic practice among the desert fathers. In fact, the purposeful inflicting of physical pain was seen as interfering with the goals of asceticism, which was to empty one's consciousness to make room for God.

By the late Middle Ages, the methodical application of self-torture took on a justification of its own among the heroic ascetics despite admonitions against this by more moderate elements in the Church. The verbalized goal was to experience directly the passion of Jesus; the effect was the production of the altered states of consciousness that follow upon the experience of severe and unremitting pain.[24] Our present knowledge of the effects of the many mechanisms of pain modulation, including endogenous opioids, suggests that, whatever their evolutionary survival value (by downregulating pain responses under conditions of stress) in the animal kingdom in general, the processes subserving the modulation of pain has probably taken on more complex and integrated functions in mammals and humans.

Akil and colleagues speculate, in regards specifically to endorphins, but we may generalize to all pain perception mechanisms, that these integrated central nervous system functions include the control of affect and mood, drive and reinforcement, and the process of filtering information and controlling attentional mechanisms.[25] In short, endogenous opiates and other components of the original nociceptive system have been appropriated as components of many other normal activities of the more complex primate brain, including the regulation of mood, motivation, attention, and cognition. When we hurt ourselves (or are hurt), we are doing more than just causing pain, or fulfilling some symbolic function of cultural significance. We are altering our brain state in significant ways.

5

SLEEP DEPRIVATION

They [Beatrice and a teenage companion] had the custom of rising secretly for night vigils when all was quiet. They could not sing them as they were sung in choir, for lack of books, but, doing what they could, they labored to compensate devoutly by the frequent repetition of the Lord's Prayer. . . . They spent the time left over usefully in godly meditations till vigils were almost finished in the nun's choir. When they had finished their devotions properly, they stole away to their beds, hastening their return a little before that of the community so as not to be caught by the others. . . . The monastic custom in force at that monastery did not permit vigils to persons of weak or feeble body.[1]

Human beings, like most other species on earth, have evolved in a world governed by a circadian cycle. This is reflected by the evolutionary development of an internal biological clock that normally synchronizes the daily cycle of sleep and wakefulness to the periodicity of the external environment.[2] The normal sleep cycle appears to be composed of two distinct phases defined as REM-sleep and non-REM sleep. REM is an acronym for rapid eye movement. Most dream activity occurs during this phase of sleep, although dreaming is not limited to REM sleep.

By convention, non-REM sleep (i.e. non-dreaming sleep) is divided into four stages, determined primarily by EEG patterns, which seem to reflect what is commonly considered the depth of sleep. These phases have fairly similar physiological characteristics to each other, and make up what we regularly think of as ordinary sleep. REM-sleep has very different EEG and behavioral characteristics from non-REM sleep. In REM-sleep, there are bursts of rapid eye movements and finger twitching, irregular breathing, loss of muscle tone, and the activation of an altered state of consciousness in the form of a dream state. Sleep itself in healthy adults has a regular sequence and periodicity of phases, with REM-sleep taking place during an intermediate depth of sleep. REM-sleep typically occurs about every 90 minutes through the initial sleep cycles and then more frequently toward the end of the normal sleep time.

Consideration of the effects of sleep deprivation on human behavior, mental functioning, mood, and performance requires that we make several distinctions which reflect the complex nature of the sleep/wakefulness cycle. First, we must examine which phase of the sleep cycle is affected by sleep deprivation, namely, whether there is total sleep, REM-sleep, or non-REM sleep deprivation.[3]

Second, the duration and pattern of sleep deprivation are important factors in determining the various effects under consideration. Following Pilcher and Huffcutt, we distinguish between short-term (less than 45 hours) and long-term (more than 45 hours) continuous sleep deprivation. There is also a separate category referred to as partial sleep deprivation (sleep period of less than 5 hours in a 24-hour period), which has important effects on mental functioning.[4] In addition, there is a category of sleep fragmentation, which refers to the frequent interruption of the sleep phase itself and which has serious effects on daytime alertness, cognition, mood, and performance.[5]

Third, we have to consider that the various types of sleep deprivation may not affect the different physiological and psychological processes underlying mood, perceptual, cognitive, and motor functions in exactly the same way or to the same extent. It may turn out that sleep deprivation affects some mental functions more severely than other functions, and that different types or degrees of sleep deprivation have different effects on different mental functions. Finally, we must consider the influence of age (adolescence, adulthood, old age) and gender upon the various effects of different types of sleep deprivation. Increased attention has been paid in recent years to the disturbances in attention, mood, and behavior seen in school-age children with insufficient sleep[6] and to the performance and judgment problems seen in medical-surgical residents who work under relative sleep-deprived conditions.[7]

REM-sleep deprivation

Although much research and media attention have been directed toward the dramatic behavioral effects of REM-sleep (dream) deprivation in animals under experimental conditions, in point of fact, pure REM-sleep deprivation in humans is almost impossible to achieve.[8] This is because the animal or human deprived of REM-sleep will go into REM-sleep increasingly rapidly in the sleep cycle such that, under ordinary circumstances, the only way to REM-sleep deprive humans is to deprive them totally of sleep.[9] Under laboratory conditions, subjects are deprived specifically of REM-sleep by monitoring their sleep cycle with electroencephalography and electromyography and then rapidly awakening them, with a loud bell or similar intrusive stimuli, as soon as there is evidence that they have begun to dream as indicated by EEG and onset of rapid eye movements. When allowed to return to sleep, the subject will rapidly (within moments) revert to the interrupted REM-sleep phase.

If a human is relatively REM-sleep deprived, the major effect, although one that has relevance to our concerns, will be rebound increased REM-sleep, in which there will be heightened vividness of dreams. There is also good evidence that REM-sleep plays an important role in learning new complex tasks and in memory acquisition. Laboratory studies in animals and humans have shown that increased learning demands are followed by increased REM-sleep activity and that, conversely, interference with REM-sleep and/or total sleep in the 48 hours following introduction of new material or procedural tasks to be learned results in impaired memory and learning.[10]

Total sleep deprivation

Total sleep deprivation for extended periods of time rarely occurs, or at least rarely is documented;[11] it may occur under torture. Military researchers have studied sleep deprivation as part of broader investigations of human performance under extreme conditions.[12] Occasionally a disc jockey or some other publicity seeker will go without sleep for an extended period of time.[13] There is a medical report of a 17-year-old male high school student staying awake 264 hours (11 days) in order to break the record listed in the *Guinness Book of Records*.[14] The young man, after the third day, showed intermittent irritability and had memory lapses and perceptual distortions. By the fifth day, he experienced what were termed "hypnagogic reveries," such as seeing a path running through a quiet forest. The student never showed the gross impairment of reality contact that had been reported in earlier attempts at prolonged sleep deprivation.

The physiological and psychological effects of total sleep deprivation fall into several categories. First, there is deterioration in various motor task performances and in exercise endurance.[15] Second, there are perceptual difficulties including altered stereoscopic vision (depth perception), loss of efficiency in processing peripheral visual information, misrepresentation of visual stimuli, and visual and tactile hallucinations. While the frequency and magnitude of perceptual distortions are related to the duration of sleep deprivation, there also appears to be a strong circadian component to the occurrence of visual distortions. The peak incidence of perceptual distortions during periods of sleep deprivation occurs between midnight and 4 in the morning, with several lesser phases occurring throughout the 24-hour cycle.[16]

Third, there are decrements in cognitive performance such as logical reasoning, mental addition, visual search tasks, and word memory tasks. Finally, there are mood changes, including increased irritability and depression, decreased vigor, occasional feelings of persecution, and, in general, decreased ability to direct and maintain attention. A meta-analysis of nineteen research articles studying the effects of sleep deprivation found that cognitive performance was more affected by sleep deprivation than motor performance, and that mood was much more affected than either cognitive or motor performance.[17]

Physiologically, prolonged sleep deprivation brings about decreased growth hormone release at sleep onset and decreased circulating androgen levels in healthy men.[18] In a separate study, sleep deprivation (REM and non-REM deprivation) resulted in decreased plasma cortisol levels.[19] All of these effects of sleep deprivation are reversible with return to a normal or adequate sleep cycle.

Effects of age and gender

There are no known differences between men and women in the effects of sleep deprivation. Neither gender appears more resilient nor more vulnerable to the various deficits in psychological functioning that result from sleep deprivation.

The case is different, however, when age, especially adolescence, is a consideration. Contrary to much popular belief, sleep need does not decrease with maturational transition from childhood to adolescence.[20] What does decrease, at least in modern times, is the amount of sleep that adolescents actually allow themselves. Given the opportunity, sleep duration will be maintained at a fairly constant level throughout adolescence. It is clear that social and academic pressures rather than biological requirements account for this decrease in sleep duration from early to late adolescence. The average duration of sleep time (seven hours) leaves older adolescents in the United States with a significant sleep debt and measurable daytime sleepiness.

There are two changes in sleep pattern in adolescence, however, that appear to be more related to maturational changes in the biological clock than to social factors. The first is that there appears to be an increase in daytime sleepiness in late adolescents even in the absence of marked changes in total sleep time. Carskadon and colleagues hypothesize that this is related to decreased slow wave sleep time, but the issue is still open.[21] The second change, one that has recently drawn the attention of educators and health counselors, is that there seems to be a shifting in the biological clock to a later time for sleep onset, and a concomitant extension of the sleep period into a little later in the morning, in middle and late adolescence.[22] It is possible that the later sleep onset time of late adolescents reflects a built-in biological rhythm as well as social pressure to stay up late.[23] When this late (midnight–1 a.m.) sleep onset is coupled with a 6:30 a.m. awakening for early high school classes, then the adolescent will go through the week with considerable sleep debt. Most studies have documented poorer academic and driving safety performance under such conditions of relative sleep deprivation.[24]

Toward the other end of the life span, it has been found that older people (age 50–60) show similar psychological and behavioral responses to sleep deprivation as younger adults do, but the changes occur more rapidly, i.e. earlier in the sleep deprivation period.[25]

Partial sleep deprivation

The meta-analysis by Pilcher and Huffcutt reported the fairly surprising finding that partial sleep deprivation (less than 5 hours of sleep per 24 hours) produced greater detrimental psychological effects than short or long-term total sleep deprivation. Specifically, partially sleep-deprived subjects, on average, had larger negative mood changes and performed at a level two standard deviations below that of non-sleep deprived subjects, compared to about a one standard deviation difference for both long-term and short-term deprivation. As with total sleep deprivation, the detrimental effects of partial sleep deprivation upon mood were more pronounced than the effects upon cognitive and motor performance.[26] These negative effects are more pronounced as partial sleep deprivation and sleep fragmentation become chronic.[27]

The pattern of partial sleep deprivation in all likelihood most closely approximates the sleep patterns of medieval religious, especially those heroic ascetics who spent much of the night in prayer. To the effects of partial sleep deprivation must be added the unphysiological sleep schedule of the medieval monastery, which has young adults going to bed by 8 p.m. and awakening around 2 a.m., when their biological tendency is to move their sleep and awakening times several hours later into the night and morning.

Sleep deprivation in medieval asceticism

It is somewhat difficult to estimate with confidence the degree of sleep deprivation that the medieval ascetics underwent. The ordinary daily rounds of monastic life, especially under austere conditions, were such as probably to keep many of the religious in a state of moderate partial sleep deprivation. Any attempt to estimate the amount of sleep that medieval religious obtained on average immediately bumps into the problem that there is no such entity as "on average." Customs varied regionally and by time period, and from one monastery to another even within the same order. There were obvious problems that the monasteries faced in establishing a daily routine in terms of the dramatic differences in time of sunrise and sunset and length of day from winter to summer.

The Rule of St. Benedict takes the seasonal changes somewhat into account in laying down the recommended monastic routine, with the proviso that changes can be instituted within the overall guidelines.[28] Conceptually, Benedict divided the 24-hour day into two periods of equal length, a 12-hour day beginning at 6 a.m. and a 12-hour night beginning at 6 p.m. Dom Paul Delatte, Superior-General of the Benedictines in France, offers his opinion that the monks did not go back to bed after the Night Office. He suggests, citing Cassian, that the "ancient monks feared that this supplementary rest made the soul lose the spiritual vigor that the sacred vigils [Matins and Lauds] had inspired and furnished an occasion for illusions of the devil."[29]

The monastic day was to end with Compline around 6 p.m. in the winter, after which the religious were to go to bed. In summer, this might be extended to 7 or 8 p.m. The day was to begin in winter at 2 a.m. with Matins, followed by Lauds, then private prayer and meditation, and Prime toward 6 a.m. In summer, Matins might begin at 3 a.m., to allow sufficient sleep time in view of the later bedtime. Whether winter or summer, sleep was to be completed by Matins, with no return to sleep between Lauds and Prime. Benedict calculated that the religious should sleep somewhat about half of the night, which technically would be six out of twelve hours, but most likely allowed for an extra hour or so. This assumes that the religious were able to fall asleep rapidly and remain asleep from 6 p.m. until the call to Matins at 2 a.m.

Thomas Merton provides a modern monastic version of the daily life of a Cistercian monk, which appears to follow St. Benedict's Rule closely.[30] The monks arise at 2 a.m. in winter and summer and do not return to bed until 7 p.m. in the winter and 8 p.m. in the summer. At best, a monk would get about seven hours of sleep, which is a little under that recommended by modern sleep researchers as optimal for late adolescents and young adults, but certainly cannot be considered as constituting sleep deprivation. Assuming that there was not an opportunity to catch extra sleep in the time between Lauds and Prime or later on in the day, then a certain number of religious, those who either cannot fall asleep readily at 7 or 8 p.m. or those whose sleep requirements are at the upper end of the normal curve, would function in the daytime with a mild to moderate degree of sleep deprivation. Those whose practices of a more austere form of asceticism included decreasing the amount of time allowed for sleep beyond that regularly allowed by whatever rule they followed would, of course, suffer more severely from the effects of sleep deprivation.

While this overall pattern, both medieval and modern, can innocuously be described as merely being a little short on sleep, it is, in fact, clear that chronic partial sleep deprivation and sleep fragmentation have serious psychological consequences. The most general effect is a loss of a sense of well-being, accompanied by irritability, daytime sleepiness, and a depressed mood. Vitality, interest, and sustained attention to complex tasks and processes all suffer. Perceptual distortions and illusions in which ordinary objects seem to take on altered shapes and unusual characteristics are frequent occurrences.

In addition to the general state of chronic partial sleep deprivation that was most likely the common condition of many of the religious in the more ascetic monasteries, there are two additional factors that must be considered when evaluating the effects of sleep deprivation on mental state and altered states of consciousness. The first is the obvious reminder that sleep deprivation was not occurring in isolation, but was part of a larger ascetic pattern that often included varying degrees of self-injurious behaviors and fasting. Sleep deprivation itself enhances pain sensitivity by reducing the pain threshold (the level at which a noxious stimulus is perceived as painful).[31] Consideration of the interaction of the different forms of ascetic practices will be postponed for a later discussion.

The second factor that requires mention is a basic problem when considering any aspect of human psychology. This is the factor of individual variability. The problem relates to how much of human behavior can be accounted for by general factors common to a group and how much must be attributed to individual variability. Research provides us with group norms upon which we may base our assumptions and historical or scientific explanations. But the norms are usually made up of bell-shaped curves along which a population is distributed. By definition, more persons will fall around the mean of the curve but, also by definition, there will be outliers at one or two or even more standard deviations from the mean. Such considerations hold true for all human traits, including response to administration of pain and response to varying types of sleep deprivation.

Hæc toti ZOERARDE *orbi spectacula præbes?* *Cum pigro tam sæua geris certamina somno?*
Perdius & pernox sic Zoerarde sedes? *Si tu sic dormis, quis vigilare potest?*

Plate 5.1 Zoerard (d. ?eleventh century) was possibly a Polish missionary to Hungary some time after the religious conversion of the Hungarian people by King Stephen; Zoerard was a hermit. It is said that King Ladislaus promoted the sainthood of Zoerard to develop cults that would support his hold on the Hungarian throne. Zoerard here is shown with a clever arrangement designed to prevent sleep.

Thus, while it is likely that most religious in a monastery were able to accommodate to the sleep practices imposed upon them, either by taking catnaps or by suffering with a mild degree of depression and cognitive impairment, it is equally likely that the degree of individual variation in sleep requirements and tolerance to relative sleep deprivation and fragmentation made it more of a trial for some and affected their cognitive, mood, and behavioral performances significantly. In addition, those who practiced heroic asceticism made concerted efforts to limit their sleep even more severely. Even in regard to these conditions, however, we cannot be sure how much catnaps and microsleep such ascetics actually managed to obtain.

Beatrice's biographer provides two example of different methods of preventing sleep; the first, utilizing zealousness in prayer, was cited in the opening passage of this chapter; the second, cited below, incorporates self-injurious behaviors as a technique of avoiding sleep:

She would even bind her shins and legs with the same kind of ropes and cords. Thus she wore her frail body down with whips and piercings. She would sleep not lying down but reclining slightly, and if sometimes sleep took hold of her drooping eyelids, she would be pricked in one place or another by the thorns and would immediately open her eyes and start from her sleep. Yet once or twice a week she used to lay aside these torments caused by the thorny ropes, not to indulge her body or to spare it, but to resume her usual sufferings with more zeal and restored strength, and to add new wounds to old ones, not yet healed over.[32]

It is likely that this moderate degree of partial sleep deprivation brought about subtle, but definite changes in the cognitive or perceptual functioning in the adolescents in question. It is also likely that the effects of sleep deprivation were additive to the other harsh ascetic practices in producing altered states of consciousness, especially under conditions in which there were expectations of a trance state with a religious imagery. If illusions and perceptual distortions were going to occur, these would take their form and content from the religious symbols and spiritual expectations that provided the context of the holy person's life.

6

FASTING AND STARVATION

The major psychological effects of fasting and starvation are difficult to sort out from a person's response to the circumstances under which the fasting occurs. Most of human starvation has occurred involuntarily in the context of famines, warfare, sieges, and, in the twentieth century, concentration camps and other genocidal institutions. Under such situations, it has not been possible to differentiate the effects of threat, torture, intimidation, oppression, and social disruption from those of "pure" starvation on the psychological reactions of the population under consideration. The notion of "pure" starvation is itself an oversimplification, since even inadequate diets have different physical and psychological effects depending upon the quality and nutrient content of whatever foods are available. For example, a diet adequate in calories might be deficient in proteins or essential vitamins, with the subsequent development of various diseases and syndromes of malnutrition, such as rickets, scurvy, and kwashiorkor.

Furthermore, starvation under such broadly adverse conditions bears little resemblance to the enthusiastic voluntary fasting, even in the extreme, carried out by religiously motivated persons in medieval Europe. Interestingly, the classical experimental study of the biological and psychological effects of semi-starvation done by the Minnesota group under Ancel Keys at the end of World War II approximates the conditions and motivations of monastic fasting more closely than do the natural occurrences of large-scale starvation.[1] Keys's study utilized conscientious objectors who volunteered for the research project out of altruistic motivations that the scientific findings would help post-war worldwide efforts at nutritional relief and rehabilitation. The experiment was carried out under regulated conditions at a university laboratory with a 12-week control period, 24 weeks of semi-starvation, and 12 weeks of restricted rehabilitation. The Minnesota study called for two meals a day, with an average daily intake of 1,570 calories that included 50 grams of protein and 30 grams of fat.

There are also important differences beyond the obvious socio-cultural ones between the medieval ascetics and the World War II conscientious objectors who volunteered for the Minnesota study. The Minnesota study employed only males, who were screened for good health prior to entrance into the project. From a nutritional regard, medieval heroic fasting undoubtedly involved protein, vitamin, and mineral as well as caloric deficiencies, while the Minnesota group had a well-balanced diet that was deficient only in calories. Keys and colleagues addressed the question of whether their findings regarding psychological changes under controlled and safe conditions of semi-starvation can be applied to the experiences of starvation under highly adversive and stressful conditions. They concluded that

> differences in attendant conditions must modify the [psychological] responses to the physical deterioration of starvation, but the bond between the physiological status of the organism and the "psyche" is closer than is sometimes realized. The dominance of the "body" becomes prominent under severe physical stress. . . . The magnitude of psychological changes secondary to semi-starvation varies, both in different individuals and in different conditions, but the direction of change is a more fundamental characteristic.[2]

It is important to note that the volunteers steadily lost weight, in the absence of heavy exercise or work requirements, on a 1,570-calorie diet. It is highly likely that the medieval heroic fasters had a much more restricted caloric intake than this. In order to gain a proper perspective, the heroic ascetics' diets must be placed against the "normal" medieval diet, which bordered at the barely subsistence level as often as not. Once again, there is no such thing as a "normal" medieval diet, since availability varied greatly by region, year, climatic conditions, agricultural and pastoral technology, local or widespread famines, and warfare. Nevertheless, there are some maximal values for land productivity that can be calculated for best-case harvest scenarios, and there are minimal values for human nutritional requirements that have not changed since the appearance of hominids on this planet.

In a detailed study of early medieval nutrition, Kathy Pearson has reconstructed the conditions governing upper and lower levels of food production in the temperate lands of Western Europe.[3] Her basic conclusion was that the majority of early-medieval people likely suffered some degree of malnutrition resulting from the irregular availability of foods necessary to a balanced diet. This marginal diet was subject to a variety of risks and hazards with little latitude of safety to compensate for the effects of even partial crop failures. For example, the brief number of days in which to bring in the grain at harvest time before it spoils in the field required heavy effort by all available men, women, and children. A shortage of labor, such as might occur when men were off to war or in the year or two after a pestilence, would very likely result in subsequent food shortages. Pearson calculated a lower range of daily rations of 360 grams of bread, 1 liter of beer, 35 grams of cheese, 77 grams of legumes, and 102 grams of mixed fat and meat, which yields a diet of about 1,986–2,138 calories. She considers this diet inadequate for peasants (or anyone) doing substantial manual labor. As mentioned above, this does not even take into account vitamin and mineral deficiencies, particularly iron and calcium maintenance for menstruating or nursing women.[4]

GVTHLACVM assiduè Plutonia monstra lacessunt,
Cessit at his nunq̃ vis generosa viri.   15   *Cœlite præsenti gaudet, discitq̃ futura:*
Nam gaudent puro pectore Cœlicolæ.

Plate 6.1 Guthlac (d.714) was a warrior who converted to a religious life at age 24. He became a monk, initially living in a monastery, but then retiring to the life of a hermit in the Fens near Ely, England. He is known for his spiritual trials and temptations, especially being assailed by hordes of demons.

While most of the heroic ascetics did not engage in heavy manual labor or child-bearing which would increase their caloric and mineral requirements, their severe dietary restrictions, using the ordinary marginal medieval diet as a taking-off point, were such as to bring them into starvation conditions. For example, Guthlac (674–714), after he became a solitary hermit in the fens of what is now East Anglia, was said to observe the following dietary regimen:

> So great indeed was the abstinence of his daily life that from the time when he began to inhabit the desert he ate no food of any kind except that after sunset he took a scrap of barley bread and a small cup of muddy water. For when the sun reached its western limits, then he thankfully tasted some little provision for the needs of this mortal life.[5]

If we calculate Guthlac's daily diet as one cup of barley bread, this would give him about 700 calories, 19 grams protein, no vitamin A or C, and insufficient B vitamins. It is possible that the cup of muddy water did contain some nutrients and minerals. The effects of such austere diets are additive, even allowing for the possibility of some degree of exaggeration in his asceticism.[6]

The text proceeds to describe how Guthlac was able to resist the temptation, hinted at in many saints' lives, to extend the fast ever more severely. Two devils in human form appear to Guthlac, compliment him on the power of his faith, and offer to instruct him in the lives of the ancient hermits.

> For Moses and Elijah and the Savior of the human race Himself first of all scaled the heights of fasting: moreover those famous monks who inhabited Egypt destroyed the vices of human weakness with the sword of abstinence. And therefore if you wish to wash away your sins committed in the past and to destroy those that threaten, afflict your flesh with the whips of abstinence and crush the arrogance of your mind with the rods of fasting. For in so far as you are broken down in this world, you shall be made whole and firm in eternity.

The two devils suggest that Guthlac should fast for six days and take nourishment on the seventh, but Guthlac rejects this advice. He dispels the demons by praying out loud and immediately began, "even then," to take his daily allowance of barley bread.[7] Elsewhere in the *Vita*, other of Guthlac's intense hallucinatory (or visionary) experiences are described, much of which may be the result of a combination of starvation, isolation, and cultural expectation. It is likely that Guthlac suffered from night blindness and scurvy.

The psychological changes noted in the Minnesota study, which conformed to the general findings of earlier, less systematic studies of natural starvation, included emotional instability, irritability and moodiness, as well as apathy, a tendency toward depression, poor concentration, tiredness, and decreased social initiative. The men became more self-centered, were reluctant to participate in group activities, and spent more time alone. Group cordiality became difficult to sustain, especially compared to the high levels of camaraderie and social involvement seen in the 12-week control period. There was no decline in intellectual capacity on formal testing or to clinical observation, but spontaneous mental effort and achievement declined during starvation and remained at a low level even during the early phase of rehabilitation, only gradually returning to normal. Personality measures on the MMPI showed statistically significant increases on scores of scales measuring hypochondriasis, depression, and hysteria (i.e. scales measuring "neurosis" and low tolerance for stress), with only marginal changes in the "psychotic" side of the test profile.

Sexual interest and expression dropped dramatically until, by the end of the 24-week period, they were virtually extinguished in all but a few subjects. There were decreased sexual phantasies and sexual dreams reported, and decreased masturbation and nocturnal emissions. Starvation is accompanied by profound disturbances in neuroendocrine functioning, especially in decreased thyroid hormone activity and decreased sexual hormones levels. From other studies, it is clear that, in women who achieve a state of semi-starvation, there is regression to a pre-pubertal luteinizing hormone pattern with consequent amenorrhea (absence of menstrual periods).[8]

The modern concept of anorexia nervosa focuses on the anorexic's morbid concern with physical appearance, i.e. the pursuit of thinness and fear of obesity, whereas the medieval sources themselves focus upon fasting as one of several important methods of ascetic discipline and subduing the flesh. The only two psychological criteria for anorexia nervosa listed in the official psychiatric nomenclature, the *Diagnostic and Statistical Manual*, are "intense fear of gaining weight or becoming fat, even though underweight" and "disturbance in the way one's body weight, size, or shape is experienced."[9] This is not the reason that medieval ascetics, or their biographers, offer for the ascetics' refusal to eat. Vandereycken and van Deth provide an informed discussion of the history of self-starvation, and place the medieval fasting saints in the context of an ambivalent social response, both venerating and suspicious of the proclaimed duration and severity of the fasts.[10] Recently, some historians have emphasized the socio-political dimensions of extreme fasting as a protest against male authority, which appears to be an unwarranted extrapolation of a modern concern into a medieval religious framework.[11]

Szmukler and Tantam, in an interesting article reviewing reasons that anorexics offer for their refusal or claims of inability to eat, make the point that anorexics' explanations have varied with the times, perhaps including (during the late twentieth and early twenty-first centuries) what they think their doctors expect to hear. In the nineteenth century, abhorrence of fatness was not offered, as it is today, by the anorexics as an explanation. The authors suggest that behind the varying and confusing accounts of why anorexics do not eat lies a common experience: that they feel "better" if they starve themselves and worse if they eat a substantial amount of food.[12] This basic formulation helps to avoid the ethnocentric assumption that medieval women ascetics must have starved themselves for the same reasons (concern with weight and body shape) that modern anorexics do. Modern diagnostic insistence upon the etiological centrality of concerns about body shape and weight turn anorexia nervosa into a culture-bound phenomenon of late twentieth and early twenty-first-century technological society rather than a relatively rare, but historically and culturally ubiquitous clinical syndrome.[13]

Part II

HISTORY

7
HISTORICAL METHODS
Selecting a database

If we wish to supplement a narrative study of individual medieval holy persons with a quantitative examination of the characteristics of medieval holy persons as a group and of significant correlations between these characteristics, we have to establish some ground rules regarding how membership in the group is defined.[1] Essentially, we need inclusion and exclusion criteria to determine who shall be counted as a holy person and who shall not. In undertaking a quantitative study of the prevalence of various characteristics of a large group of holy persons, it is important not to select or handpick specific saints who happen to have the special characteristics (e.g. heroic asceticism) that we may have already decided are defining markers of holiness. Otherwise we shall discover that almost all holy persons practiced heroic asceticism.

Adoption of a large historical database compiled by other scholars constitutes the only safeguard against not stacking a data set to confirm one's anticipated and favored thesis. Of course, this places reliance on some other scholar's predilections and biases, but if the data set is large enough, has been used in other scholarly studies, and was not collected with our particular purposes in mind, then it protects the choice of a database as much as possible from our own biases.

Once a large database is selected, in this case the saints included in Thurston and Attwater's 1956 revision of *Butler's Lives of the Saints*, then we have to begin narrowing down the sample even further to conform to the time frame and whatever other parameters define our target population. We established as inclusion criteria all entries within the 1956 edition of *Lives of the Saints* whose date of death fell within the years 450–1500. Exclusion criteria consisted of all entries not falling within the designated time frame. This yielded 1,462 holy persons listed and described for this time frame.

Available databases of holy persons

During the past two millennia in Western Europe, thousands of men, women, and even children, have been recognized as holy by their contemporaries as well as by posterity. There have been many attempts to develop and categorize lists of holy persons, with each collection somewhat reflecting the religious, national, regional, and political interests of the group assembling the list. Among the many medieval efforts to develop a compendium of holy persons for various reasons, the collection by Pietro Natali, Bishop of Aquileia, who produced his *Catalogus sanctorum* between 1369 and 1372 with some 3,300 saints, would appear to be the most comprehensive of the lot, despite its early date and the absence of entries over the past half-millennium.[2]

In 1643, publication began of a great compendium, *Acta Sanctorum*, under the direction of the Belgian Jesuit scholars John Bolland and Godefroid Henskens, in which accounts of the lives of a great many of these holy persons have been compiled.[3] As contrasted to medieval compendia, *Acta Sanctorum* stands out as the beginning of modern scholarly efforts to edit and assemble a large collection of "saints' lives." The biographical entries in this compendium include a wide range of historical materials. For example, one can find copies of various types of authentic documents, e.g. charters, wills, saints' lives, that were written during the lifetime of the holy person; these, of course, constitute the "best" evidence to use for historical research. The most comprehensive type of document for hagiographical research purposes are *vitae* or lives written by contemporaries. One may also find in *Acta Sanctorum*, however, *vitae* written much after the holy person died that are of varying scholarly value. In addition, the compendium includes explanatory notes by editors during the past three centuries of its publication, as well as forged documents that still are of historical interest.[4]

Acta Sanctorum by and large serves as the fundamental database for all subsequent compendia of saints' lives. Nevertheless, *Acta Sanctorum* is itself an incomplete and therefore ongoing project. It does not include all persons considered holy by various Christian groups, and its entries in some cases are seriously out of date in terms of modern standards of scholarship and most recent editions of particular *vitae*. Some of the documents placed in the original entries in *Acta Sanctorum* were drawn from the flawed, incomplete, or interpolated manuscript copies that were available at the time when a particular entry was developed. Much new information has been uncovered since the mid-seventeenth century when the saints' biographies were written for the compendium and the documents were collected. In many cases, the full spectrum of material was not available when the Bollandists made their original compilation.

During the Middle Ages, *vitae* and other documents were hand-copied and re-copied in various *scriptoria*, primarily in monasteries and convents. The modern historian has to try to date and compare each manuscript to all other versions, and sort out what appears to be original, what has been added or changed, and what seems to be invented or interpolated at a later date. The modern editor of each *vita* has an obligation to identify and explain alterations in different copies of the saint's life, since the monks who copied manuscripts may have made unintentional copying errors or, alternatively, intentionally added to or deleted material from their version. Without going into great detail, each *vita* was written for the purpose of conveying to an audience a particular view of the subject (holy person). This is as true of later redactions, expansions, abridgments, and interpolations, as it is of the original *vita*.

Each new version, sometimes centuries later, will generally alter the *vita* in terms of the redactors' audience, values, interests, and purposes. One reason frequently encountered is to insert into the *vita* additional signs of holiness, such as miracles or visions, in order to enhance the reputation for true sanctity of the putative holy person. Another reason was to provide greater "evidence" of the healing powers of this saint's shrine, thus attracting more visitors and more benefactors. Additional reasons relate more directly to politics and economics. For example, one finds the insertion of a few lines into a copy of an older manuscript to the effect that a piece of disputed property had been given as a gift to a particular monastery during the lifetime of the holy person. This type of written evidence, supported by association with a holy person, carried a degree of credibility that a secular document, such as a charter, might not convey.

A further reason for finding altered later versions of a *vita* relates to a copyist compiling in a single manuscript abridged versions of several saints' *vitae* (similar to a *Readers' Digest* condensation) usually for a didactic purpose, such as a collection of saints belonging to a particular monastery or monastic order. The abridgment process necessitates selecting which portions of the original version to leave out of the new compilation, but it sometimes is the case that this very abbreviated manuscript was the only one known to an early Bollandist editor. The modern editor has to construct as best as possible an autograph (original) text of a saint's *vita* by studying and comparing all extant copies of the *vita* and cross-checking names and dates and events mentioned in each *vita* against other sources from the same historical period and region. The goal is not to make a composite "*vita*," but to reconstruct a *vita* as close to the original as the various sources permit. This is true as well in regard to all subsequent redactions and editions, each of which illustrates the author's interests.

Application of these scholarly techniques have led to the conclusion that some of the individuals who were thought to be saints in the past, e.g. St. Christopher and St. George, are no longer considered to have been real people much less saints. It should also be noted that modern scholars have "discovered" many medieval persons who were thought to have been holy by their contemporaries or their posterity but who were overlooked or unknown to the early compilers of the relevant volumes of *Acta Sanctorum* when they were completed. In summary, although *Acta Sanctorum* is an extensive database, it can in no sense be considered comprehensive nor can the documents of various types that are printed therein be considered authoritative.

There are many other massive compendia of information, each compiled for different reasons or matrices of reasons that bring together thousands of biographies of holy people in greater or lesser detail. Some of these collections are ostensibly dictionaries, such as that compiled by the Benedictine scholars at Ramsgate, in England, where more than 7,000 "saints" are listed, or Holweck's even more inclusive *Biographical Dictionary*.[5] The *Roman Martyrology*, which is primarily a liturgical compendium, lists some 4,500 individuals as well as a great many more saints identified as anonymous martyrs who died, often in groups, as a direct result of persecution.[6]

Other collections are richer than the above-mentioned compendia (other than *Acta Sanctorum*) in the depth of information that they provide about each saint. Among these, there is general agreement that the *Bibliotheca Sanctorum* is to be regarded as the "most complete."[7] However, Guerin's *Les petites Bollandistes*, which is a summary of *Acta Sanctorum*, really cannot be ignored, even if it is often and rightly claimed to be inaccurate.[8] Baudot's compendium, *Vies des saints*, brings together rather short but very useful biographies of a large number of holy persons and is comparable in its number of entries to *Bibliotheca Sanctorum*.[9] The best known and richest compendia in English, which provide substantial biographical entries, are those by Alban Butler, in its Thurston and Attwater 1956 revision,[10] and Sabine Baring-Gould.[11]

None of the above-mentioned compendia nor any other collection may be considered definitive or inclusive of all holy persons. Indeed, the only "comprehensive" collection is that by Broderick whose limited census includes only 283 men and women. However, his criterion, simply stated, is that he examined only the lives of those who were recognized as saints in a fully canonical manner or, to quote him directly, "whose formal canonization is solidly attested."[12] And even this criterion is open to question.[13]

However, a better idea of the incompleteness of all collections can be seen in the context of J. O'Hanlon's Herculean efforts which resulted in the identification of more than 3,000 Irish "saints," each accompanied by a short biography.[14] On the other hand, David Farmer, who included in his dictionary only English saints dead before 1530 along with a "representative" sample from the rest of the British Isles, records somewhere in the neighborhood of 2,500 holy persons. Interestingly, he ignores the overwhelming majority of Irish saints identified by O'Hanlon.[15]

Concentration on holy persons from a national perspective has been common among compilers of saints' lives, such as O'Hanlon regarding Irish saints. This is, in effect, a medieval phenomenon, as seen in the early collection *Kalendars of Scottish Saints*.[16] By the beginning of the twentieth century, various scholarly groups, interested in some unique populations having features in common other than nationality, also engaged in this sorting process. For example, as early as 1904, Agnes Dunbar produced *A Dictionary of Saintly Women*.[17] As feminist studies have increased during the past two decades, more specialist compendia have been made. Jane Schulenburg has done some very extensive sampling of holy women in the early Middle Ages,[18] Jo Ann McNamara published a compendium on eighteen Merovingian and Carolingian women saints,[19] and Elizabeth Petroff has made a collection of twenty-six medieval women who would appear to have been mystics.[20] It is curious, however, that in a putatively male-dominated field of history no quantitatively structured collections of male saints, e.g. warrior saints or merchant saints, have been made. Medieval royal saints, both men and women, however, have been studied as a group.[21]

In choosing to focus on a particular "national" group, such as the Irish saints, or a particular type of saint, such as late medieval mystic women, any large study must necessarily rely on one or more of the above-mentioned compendia for source material. The process of selection of which saints to include in one's own study requires establishing coherent criteria for inclusion and exclusion. Of modern studies, we can examine that by Michael Goodich as a model of scholarly method.[22] Goodich's work focuses upon the thirteenth century, or more exactly, upon holy men and women "who lived after the Fourth Lateran Council of 1215, and were born prior to 1296." In establishing these limits, Goodich was understandably impressed by the spectrum of papal actions that conditioned the making of saints during this era. Goodich also chose *Acta Sanctorum* as the compendium from which he drew his saints, but limited his selection to those men and women whose "immediate *post mortem* veneration is attested to by at least two independent contemporary or nearly contemporary sources."

From the entire *Acta Sanctorum*, Goodich identified 518 saints who met his inclusion criteria. Use of these criteria, however, results in the curious fact that about half of the saints in his sample are from Italy while the other half are from north of the Alps. In terms of population distribution, it is clear that, even taking into account the fact that Italy, especially the northern region, was, on the whole, the most densely populated region of medieval Western Europe, the distribution of saints on a per capita basis is still heavily skewed toward Italian saints. There are likely many reasons for this, but among these may be Goodich's criteria, namely, the requirement of two immediate or near contemporary written sources. In short, the highly urbanized and densely populated north of Italy was likely better suited to produce such written sources in large numbers than the more rural and less well-populated transalpine regions. Needless to say, Irish "saints" are not represented in Goodich's sample in any way consistent with their number identified by O'Hanlon. However, with the exception of the apparent over-representation of Italian saints, many of the less rigorously defined samples developed by modern scholars on the basis of various compendia are, as will be seen below, very much consistent with Goodich's statistical patterns regarding such matters as social status, gender, and profession.

While Goodich's approach may be considered a scholarly model when applied to the thirteenth century, it is not of equal value throughout the entire medieval period. Thus, Jane Schulenburg, in discussing her selection criteria for female saints of the earlier Middle Ages, comments that she chose not to apply Goodich's criteria of two independent contemporary or near-contemporary sources. Schulenburg explains: "Because of the fragmentary nature of our documentation, as well as the special conditions and problems surrounding the transmission of saints' lives – which seemed to favor male saints – this criterion would be extremely difficult to apply to this early period." Schulenburg points out that applying Goodich's criterion would result in the exclusion of a number of important early medieval women saints for whom contemporary *vitae* or other contemporary sources are not available.[23]

Quantitative studies of saints' lives

In the past 50 years or so, there have been four extensive censuses of saints. The pioneering work was done by the sociologist Pitirim Sorokin, who covered saints throughout the entire history of Christianity.[24] Sorokin based his study on the compendium developed by Butler. A second study was carried out by Pierre Delooz in 1969, which covered the years 1000 to 1967.[25] Delooz relied upon the compendium edited under the direction of Baudot. In 1982, two American scholars, Donald Weinstein and Rudolph Bell, produced a broadly gauged sociological census that covered the period between 1000 and 1700.[26] They too used the Baudot compendium, but with heavy reliance on Delooz's earlier choices. The fourth major census was done by Jane Schulenburg and covers the period 500–1100.[27] It uses the *Bibliotheca Sanctorum* as its data source. One much shorter quantitative study, focused solely on the social status of saints, was produced by Katherine and Charles George,[28] and used the Butler collection.

It must be clear that each extant collection of saints' lives carries various advantages and disadvantages to the scholar, depending upon the design and focus of the study. We decided that our study of medieval asceticism and mysticism would be best served by surveying all saints included in the Thurston and Attwater revision of Butler between the years 450–1500. Our initial choice of this compendium was based upon the fact that the biographies are in English, thus making our source material readily available to an Anglophone audience. Second, even previous studies based upon earlier and less scholarly editions of Butler have proven to provide data that match very closely the data from more demanding research designs. For example, the data on the social class and professional careers of saints culled by Katherine and Charles George from Butler's collection were consistent with that found by Goodich for the thirteenth century, whose database, as noted above, was developed from *Acta Sanctorum* with very rigorous source criteria.[29] It is important to note that, over the years, all the collections and compendia, including the one by Butler, have been the subject of scholarly criticism.

Delooz has written a critique of Sorokin's work, but his criticism does not rest upon Sorokin's choice or utilization of Butler's *Lives of the Saints*, but upon Sorokin's lack of empathy for the Middle Ages and his introduction of modern geographical designations. Problems abound, as Delooz himself concedes, in the selection of any particular compendium for a statistical base, and serve to emphasize that there is not now, and probably never will be, a definitive list of saints. This is because the very notion of what constitutes sainthood changes as society changes. Merovingian saints were more often than not bishops and abbesses drawn from the nobility. Late medieval saints from Italy were often Franciscan monks and laypersons associated with the Franciscans or other religious orders. Patterns of popular veneration of holy persons, social determinants of which Christian traits were valued as saintly, vast geographic and temporal differences (different civilizations, as Delooz puts it, appropriating Toynbee's term), and evolving institutional procedures for canonization, combine, seemingly, to make it almost impossible to study sainthood in general, as opposed to studying particular holy persons in particular locales within graspable segments of time.[30]

Weinstein and Bell are the only scholars to attack the actual number of saints in the Butler collection. However, they call attention not to the modern revised edition, but to the obsolete 1926 edition.[31] Interestingly, the middle (1938) edition of *Butler's Lives of the Saints* edited by Thurston and Attwater was very positively reviewed in 1939 by Hippolyte Delehaye, the president of the Bollandists.[32] Even this highly praised revised 1938 edition of Butler has been further improved by Attwater in 1956. It is worth noting in this context that Butler's original edition had 1,486 separate entries while the Attwater 1956 edition has 2,565 entries.[33]

None of the major or, indeed, minor quantitative works dealing with the sociology of saints exactly parallels our present study. Thus, to reiterate, Sorokin covered all of Christian history and both Delooz and Weinstein and Bell begin in the year 1000, i.e. they do not cover the earlier 550 years that are covered in our work. In addition, Weinstein and Bell carry their study to 1700 while Delooz goes to 1967. Schulenburg limits her study to holy women in the time period 500–1100.

The demographic statistics for the lengthy period covered in these works do not, in general, permit easy comparisons. However, it is possible, as with the example provided from Goodich, to make comparisons for particular centuries with regard to specific geographic areas, social status, or percentage of male and female saints. Indeed, as will be seen, most such comparisons make clear that whether one uses *Acta Sanctorum*, Thurston and Attwater's revision of Butler, Baudot, or *Bibliotheca Sanctorum*, the results in terms of patterns of frequency distributions, such as percentage of male to female saints, are generally in very close agreement. Such comparisons suggest that the group of saints included in the massively revised and augmented 1956 edition of Butler that we use in our study is as representative as the other large collections of saints' lives.

As Schulenburg emphasizes, once a compendium is selected for the statistical base and various criteria are established for inclusion/exclusion, it becomes likely that many saints of interest will be discovered to have been left out of the database. Thus Schulenburg argued for the usefulness of discussing saints who do not appear in her database, but whose biographies are of intrinsic interest to one or another topic under discussion. For example, Schulenburg included only saints from Italy, Germany, France, Belgium, and Britain, thus omitting, among others, Irish and Spanish women saints whose *vitae* corroborate information found in *vitae* of saints included within her statistical net.[34] In this same vein, we found that a number of interesting women who came to be thought of as mystics were not included in the revised Butler compendium. Thus we too have thought it useful to discuss these biographies, although, like Schulenburg, we have not added them to our database.

The list of holy women not included in Butler is a fairly long one, and includes several of the holy women whom we discuss, such as Beatrice of Nazareth (d.1265) and Gherardesca of Pisa (d.1267). A reading of various recent works on medieval women saints turned up many other holy women not found in Butler's compendium. These include, in addition to Beatrice and Gherardesca, Adelheid of Vilich (d.1015), Balthild of Neustria (d.680), Bloemardine of Brussels, Christina of Markyate (d.1160), Christine Ebner (d.1356), Domenica Dal Paradiso, Elizabeth of Reute (d.1420), Elizabeth of Spalbeck, Elsbeth Stagel, Eustadiola of Bourges (d.684), Eve of St. Martin (thirteenth century), Glodesind of Metz (c.600), Hadewyjch of Antwerp (thirteenth century), Ida of Leau, Ida of Nivelles (d.1231), Lutgard of Tongeren, Margarete Ebner (fourteenth century), Margaret of Ypres (d.1237), Marguerite Porete (d.1310), Marguerite d'Oingt (d.1310), and Rusticula of Arles (d.632). The names do not provide a single rationale that explains their omission by Butler. Rusticula, Balthild, Eustadiola, and Glodesind of Metz were Gallo-Roman and Merovingian nobility, most of whom became abbesses. They are included in Jo Ann McNamara's collection of eighteen Dark Age women saints.[35]

Of the collection of twenty-eight women mystics ranging in time from St. Perpetua (d.203) to Magdalena Beutler of Freiburg (d.1458) in Petroff's sampling of medieval women's visionary literature, almost half of the women relevant to our time period are not listed in Butler.[36] Most omissions are of the Belgian and Rhineland late medieval women mystics. A few women (e.g. Marguerite Porete, burned at the stake as a heretic) are not included in Butler for obvious reasons. In this they are in the good company of Meister Eckhart (d.1327, but not at the stake), an acknowledged mystic but not included in most compendia of saints because of his apparently heretical pantheistic beliefs.

Parenthetically, as reference to Meister Eckhart dramatizes, it is not the case that only women and not men were left out of Butler's compendium. Perusal of the last two chapters of Giles Constable's *The Reformation of the Twelfth Century* provides mention of many male religious of the eleventh and twelfth centuries who were considered holy persons by their contemporaries, but who are not listed in Butler.[37] These include Geoffrey of St. Thierry, Gerald of Salles, Gerard of St. Albinus, Guigo of La Chartreuse, Otloh of St. Emmeram, and Richalm of Schonthal. Such lists of names unmentioned in Butler serve to underscore not the inadequacy of Butler as a database, but rather the limitations of all databases for hagiographic research purposes.

As Schulenburg noted, the researcher cannot add names to the data pool, especially since, in the case of the late medieval women mystics, it is precisely the visionary and mystical aspects of these holy women that have earned them recent recognition. Inclusion of these holy women for statistical analysis would obviously shift our results in favor of an even greater percentage of mystics among the religious women of the late medieval period. We return to Delooz's observation: one is limited by any particular list, but there is no simple alternative.

Despite the absence of many holy women and men from Butler's compendia, a comparison of revised Butler with other compendia reveal very close agreement on demographic factors. For the thirteenth century, revised Butler selected 172 lives of holy persons to summarize for his collection. As Michael Goodich has shown, a thorough search of *Acta Sanctorum*, based upon highly stringent criteria, provides a total of 518 *vitae* of holy persons for a similar but not identical time period.[38] To anticipate our next chapter, of revised Butler's 172 thirteenth-century holy people, 26.2 percent are women. Goodich has found 27.9 percent women. Weinstein and Bell, using Baudot, found 22.6 percent women in their sample of thirteenth-century saints. On this gender variable, revised Butler's sample is almost identical with the *Acta Sanctorum* collection for that century, and very close to Baudot's collection as utilized by Weinstein and Bell. Similarly, using a geographical criterion, Goodich found that almost half of the thirteenth-century holy men and women who were canonized were Italian, while in revised Butler's sample for the thirteenth through fifteenth centuries, 58.9 percent were Italian. These two comparisons make clear that, in regard to at least two important measures (gender and geographic region), the Butler data pool is very similar to the larger *Acta Sanctorum* from which it was drawn.

Dividing history into periods

We chose to study all holy persons included in Thurston and Attwater's 1956 revision of *Butler's Lives of the Saints* whose date of death fell within the time period 450–1500. Analysis of the data that we generated from this population of 1,462 holy persons suggested that there were three distinct subperiods, the fifth to tenth centuries, the eleventh to twelfth centuries, and the thirteenth to fifteenth centuries. While our initial decision to use the time period 450–1500 was an external decision based upon the generally accepted time frame of the beginning and end of the Western medieval period, the subdivision into three smaller temporal units was based upon the way the data distributed rather than a judgment externally imposed by any expectations that we necessarily had prior to the study. We wish to spend some time here discussing how one goes about selecting time periods for inclusion in a study.

As suggested above, periodization is roughly of two types. One type is imposed by the materials that survive from the past and the other type is imposed upon the past by scholars and others who synthesize one or more of the schema that are provided by material that has been generated from the past. Each genre of source material has its own intrinsic implicit or explicit periodization scheme. For example, the authors of Annals periodize on a yearly basis, *gesta* (deeds) that deal with the bishops of a diocese periodize according to the reign of the bishops, and dynastic chronicles periodize according to both the dynasty as a whole and the individual leaders of the dynasty. A saint's life written as a "biography" periodizes both in relation to the life of the holy person and afterlife, that is, the miracles worked by God through the saint after the latter's corporeal death.

Historians are often influenced by the internal periodization provided by their sources to create an external periodization. Thus, for example, the era of the Anglo-Norman kings or the Angevin kings betrays a dynastic principle in periodizing English medieval history. In a similar vein, for an economic historian, technological developments and commercial changes might be the more salient criteria that separate one "age" from another. For example, the industrial revolution in early modern times would likely be judged of greater importance than which particular monarch sat on the British throne. The broad categories of medieval, renaissance, and early modern eras are themselves notions externally imposed by historians and others upon the seamless flow of the human past.

Divisions such as medieval and renaissance suggest that scholars often try to blend several streams of social interaction, e.g. religious, political, and military, found in their sources in order to create distinct periods in history. Thus, for example, Constantine's toleration of Christianity, his building of Constantinople, which created two "Roman" capital cities, and the institution of a defense-in-depth concept for the Empire based in part on the development of fortress cities and mobile field armies, have led many historians to see his reign as a critical period in which significant change was inaugurated.

The dating traditions developed in the past also influence the process of periodization in important ways. As recognized by Dionysius Exiguous (sixth century) and popularized by the Venerable Bede (d.735), the divison of the history of the world into the era before Christ (BC) and after Christ (AD) has become the fundamental paradigm according to which subsequent Western generations have dated events. Although we do not ordinarily think of it this way, events during the first five hundred years or so after the birth of Christ were dated according to the year of the reign of the Roman emperor or consul and not according to an *Annus Domini* method of calculation. Thus, although we now read in history books that the sack of Rome by Alaric occurred in AD 410, the sackers and sackees dated the event in the fifteenth year of the reign of Emperor Honorius as sole emperor in the West. For Christians, the birth of Christ marked the beginning of a new world history, but it took five hundred years or so actually to develop calendrical reckoning based upon this broad division of history.

Moreover, even within the fundamental BC–AD paradigm, how one writes the history of the world is still influenced greatly by more specific organizing principles that one may have in mind. For example, if we are interested in early religious institutional history, then events such as Constantine's Edict of Toleration in 313 and the decision of Theodosian II to make Christianity the official religion of the Roman Empire (438) become important landmarks. If we want to look at the central government of the Church, then we might want to start with the designation of Peter as the "rock" upon which the Church was built as recorded in Matthew 16:18. The shift of church authority from Jerusalem to Rome thus is marked by Peter's mission and martyrdom there.

With regard to the history of religious experience in the Christian West, there are a variety of paradigms for periodization, but no scholarly consensus. Each paradigm results from an emphasis on one or another type of behavior, e.g. monastic, papal, episcopal, urban, or spiritual. Thus, if we are interested in a history of monasticism, we might start with the odd individuals separating themselves from society as hermits, and then consider the more or less organized groups who fled to the Egyptian desert, and finally, in the West, the establishment of the Benedictine tradition in connection with the latter's Rule and the Rule of the Master. These few examples in the various axes of interest provide a hint of sorts regarding the complexity of periodizing any area of Christian religious history, much less the history of the Church as a whole.

Textual historiography

We touched earlier on the topic of sources briefly in mentioning the obligations of an editor of a *vita*, but a more extended discussion is needed at this point. Texts in what broadly may be considered the hagiographical genre from which we draw our information, like all other texts regardless of genre, are problematic for this study in many ways. Considerable care must be taken in using *vitae sanctorum*. Much of the information included in the medieval life of a person deemed sufficiently holy to merit a *vita* was dictated by custom. Indeed, it is this very customary choice of data which makes the broad classification of a hagiographical genre rather less controversial than many other putative genres. To put it another way, it is often problematic whether one or another medieval author knew he was writing an "epic" or a "romance," but there is rarely doubt that the author of a randomly selected *vita sancti* knew he was writing within the tradition and expectations of that particular genre.[39]

The very fact that a *vita sancti* usually included a particular, or even obligatory, set of data is both a solace and a problem to the historian. In general, for example, something must be said in each *vita* concerning family background of the holy person. Here two related problems are raised. For many early medieval holy persons, the family background was unknown and thus hagiographers felt little restriction in providing an auspicious and usually noble pedigree. However, even when family background was known to the author, there are instances in which the social status is raised higher than it actually was. Thus we see operative a bias toward giving a holy person an aristocratic lineage.

Asceticism as a sign of holiness

When we turn to the lives of holy persons, some effort is always made in the *vita* to indicate why they merit the distinction they have received. In this context, asceticism, broadly defined, appears with considerable frequency and, in some contexts, great fervor as, for example, in the lives of the Egyptian desert fathers. By comparison, Merovingian bishop saints are often described as being somewhat ascetical, but a lack of emphasis suggests that mention of this is rather pro forma. Within the framework of what has traditionally been considered ascetic behavior in the West, heroic self-injurious behaviors would appear to be a rare phenomenon in general, although on the evidence of the *vitae*, it would appear to be even more rare in some contexts than in others. Only a minority of persons considered holy practiced heroic asceticism. Efforts of varying consistency by the ecclesiastical authorities throughout the Middle Ages to thwart excessive self-injurious behaviors are well documented. The presence of such official policy in regard to heroic asceticism thus may create a bias on the part of the hagiographer to omit accounts of extreme self-injurious behaviors.

One primary question in our research concerns the reliability of reports that one or another holy person practiced excessive self-injurious behaviors (SIB). Since SIB was both rare and of dubious legality in certain of its activities, the author of a *vita*, in reporting such behaviors, took some risk that his intention to press the claim of holiness for his subject would be undermined or even rejected. Many of the *vitae* include a justification of heroic asceticism, an attack on detractors who already have or can be anticipated to criticize the excesses of the holy person, and a warning that such zealous feats are not to be imitated. Jacques de Vitry, in his *Life of Marie d'Oignies* (d.1213), an early role model for Beguine spirituality and an influence on the Franciscan movement,[40] details some of Marie's self-inflicted bodily punishments, and then warns the reader:

> I do not say this to commend the excess but so that I might show her fervor. In these and in many other things wherein the privilege of grace operated, let the discreet reader pay attention that what is a privilege for a few does not make a common law. Let us imitate her virtues, but we cannot imitate the works of her virtues without individual privilege.... Thus what we have read about what those things which certain saints have done through the familiar counsel of the Holy Spirit, let us rather admire than imitate.[41]

Further, in attaching to the SIB a quality of virtue, the hagiographer had to have some sense that the local authorities and the particular audience for this *vita* would be receptive of this officially discouraged behavior. Such a holy protagonist would not be seen as conforming to the norms of legitimate asceticism and thus be vulnerable to post-mortem condemnations of various kinds. Nevertheless, it is clear that there was popular admiration for some holy figures who were known for their heroic asceticism, so there was often considerable tension between popular support and ecclesiastical criticism of such behaviors. It is possible and even likely that more SIB was practiced by the holy person than was reported or recorded by the biographer, but to say more would be little more than guesswork.

On the other hand, recent feminist criticism has suggested that reports of heroic asceticism in late medieval holy women were exaggerated by the male clerical hagiographers of these women saints to reflect, in Amy Hollywood's phrase, "contemporary male expectations and desires" that women's spirituality be centered around ascetical and paramystical (bodily) phenomena.[42] At a broader level, Kari

Børresen has written extensively about a basic fallacy in traditional historical research in which "men's experience and thought are valued as normatively human."[43] Hollywood cautions about the "dangers threatening the historian who accepts the hagiographer's account as if it were a piece of modern historical writing shaped by concerns and conceptions of reality identical to our own."[44]

The danger is in taking the hagiographer's description at face value or as transparent in its signification. We are not aware of any serious historian who takes all that is written in a saint's life at face value. But there is equal danger in determining what can be taken, more or less, at face value and what should be viewed as embellishments, exaggerations, distortions, minimizings, and even outright fabrications according to a preconceived theory of what the hagiographers were "really" up to. Thus, Hollywood asserts,[45] and De Ganck earlier made the same point,[46] that Beatrice of Nazareth most likely did not engage in the severe ascetical practices described in her *vita* because the descriptions were obviously lifted from the *vita* of Arnulf of Villiers, a man notorious for the extremities of his own asceticism who was admired by Beatrice's anonymous biographer.

This is a plausible, but not entirely convincing argument, since the evidence that the biographer openly plagiarized some compelling descriptive passages does not necessarily mean that Beatrice did not engage in similar behaviors. In fact, it is as likely that information on heroic asceticism was as available to the saint to imitate as it was to the hagiographer to copy. Beatrice's asceticism, moreover, occurred only during a few years within her adolescence and is not out of the domain of other medieval descriptions of harsh asceticism or of patterns seen in youthful self-injurious women in recent years.[47] The basic problem in judging what was real and not real in hagiographical accounts is that the modern historian cannot have it both ways. Thus, Hollywood, while rejecting descriptions of Beatrice's heroic asceticism, accepts descriptions of Beguine practices of mendicancy because, given male clerical objections to such activities, the fact that begging is mentioned at all suggests its historical reliability and importance.[48]

In general, the quality of a report of SIB in hagiography must always be viewed cautiously. Information concerning SIB sometimes came to the author of the *vita* from personal observation, sometimes directly from the holy person; on other occasions it came from people who knew the holy person well, and sometimes it seems clear that the source of information is several times removed from the protagonist. Thus, the nature of the source of the information recorded in the *vita* is important to our judgment of the quality of the information. In this context, the motivation and special interests of the author of the *vita* certainly cannot be ignored, and not just in regard to admiring male clerics writing about holy women. There are other grounds for the researcher to suspect that exaggeration has occurred. For example, claims that one or another holy person subsisted and indeed flourished with daily ingestion only of the host must be rejected as exaggerations.[49]

McGinn too tackles the question of historical accuracy in saints' lives, but his focus is more the "visionary explosion" beginning around 1200, as he phrases it, rather than self-injurious behavior. McGinn questions "the extent to which these accounts can be accepted as direct reporting of the experiences of the purported authors themselves or of close associates of the saints whose lives are being presented. In short, how 'real' are they?"[50] McGinn insists that he must continue to point out that we have no direct access to the experiences of thirteenth-century mystics – or any other mystics for that matter. He suggests that these mystical visions be thought of "primarily as 'visualizations' in the sense of powerful imaginative creations based on intense meditation on the imagery of the Bible and the liturgy, as well as artistic representations of Christ, the angels and saints, heaven and hell, and so on."[51] McGinn points out that theological evaluations of these visions have never insisted that they be taken at face value or in a purely literal way.

To summarize, there is no single, authoritative, or complete listing of saints. Various large collections of saints' lives have been put together by different compilers for different purposes, with the results that idiosyncratic inclusion and exclusion criteria make the collections more or less usable for future research, depending on the researchers' focus of interest. In previous research, we have used saints' lives for incidental descriptions of medical and psychiatric conditions which appear fairly accurate, although, or especially because, the purpose of the narrative was unrelated to medical interests as we now define them.[52]

Furthermore, all of the collections are flawed in terms of the scholarly limitations of information at any given time for any given saint. We have chosen to use Butler's *Lives of the Saints* as edited and augmented by Thurston and Attwater for our database. Rationale for this choice, as well as comparison of Butler to other modern compendia are discussed. In general, there is fair agreement across demographic variables in the different compendia that are most often used, suggesting a general validity that the compendia are providing a reasonably representative sample of the population of holy persons. The question of the historical accuracy of any given work of hagiography can only be tentatively approached by close analysis of the *vita* as evaluated in terms of its manuscript history and an understanding of the social and cultural context in which it was written and rewritten.

8
PATHWAYS TO HOLINESS

During the long millennium encompassing the Middle Ages in Europe (AD 450–1500), there were many pathways to holiness.[1] There was a range of pathways to sanctity, from the full sacrifice of martyrdom, heroic asceticism, and voluntary exile at one extreme to the exercise of benevolent, charitable, and administrative power by influential bishops, abbots, and secular princes at the other end. Performance of miracles, usually healing the sick and infirm, but also abatement of storms and fires, and turning back of enemy armies, constituted one important class of evidence for a person's holiness. Other categories of public acts that were perceived as evidence of holiness included notably generous charity (an activity usually limited to those of the very wealthy who chose not to continue to accumulate goods exclusively for themselves and their family), proximity to and support for an even greater saint (often, but not limited to the female relatives of male saints, such as Scholastica (d.543), the sister of Benedict of Nursia), and a life dedicated to celibacy (often but not limited to married persons, since celibacy in a religiously professed person, while admirable, was expected).

Personal qualities of holiness

Along this continuum of holiness, there were also a variety of personal behaviors and intangible features of character and demeanor that, underlying explicit descriptions of service to the church, charity to the poor, heroic ascetic behavior, and evidence of mystical experiences, the local medieval populace and, at times, the church authorities, understood as manifestations of holiness in a person's life and of that person's spiritual connection to God. Such qualities were recognized by those in contact with the holy person, but it is exceptionally difficult for the researcher one thousand years later to reduce such charismatic traits to specific acts. Sometimes the reader, both medieval and modern, is left with the impression that the saint's life is suffused with holiness even beyond that of any specific charitable, ascetic, or miraculous deeds. Such unmistakable but indefinable and intangible impressions are problematic for classificatory purposes, where the identification of specific behaviors provides more reliable evidence.[2]

Plate 8.1 Amelberge (d.690) and her husband Witger are the parents of Gudule, of whom it was prophesied that she would be a holy child. The parents themselves became celibate and retired to respective monasteries. Amelberge is depicted having a vision of the heart and limbs of the suffering Jesus.

This quality of holiness becomes evident in the following description of Cuthbert (d.687), a Northumbrian Englishman, by his anonymous biographer.

> And so for many years he continued to live a solitary life cut off from the sight of men; and also in all conditions he bore himself with unshakable balance, for he kept throughout the same countenance, the same spirit. At all hours he was happy and joyful, neither wearing a sad expression at the remembrance of a sin nor being elated by the loud praises of those

who marveled at his manner of life. His conversation, seasoned with salt, consoled the sad, instructed the ignorant, appeased the angry, for he persuaded them all to put nothing before the love of Christ.[3]

The pathway of martyrdom

The notion of what constituted holiness itself, and the different pathways toward sainthood, however, underwent numerous changes, large and small, as medieval society evolved during the thousand-year period. An obvious example of such metamorphoses was the change in one of the criteria for sanctity, that of martyrdom as the ultimate method of bearing witness for Christ. The understanding of martyrdom as the giving up of one's life for Christ, as he gave up his for mankind, shifted from the literal to the figurative sense as opportunities to die for the faith greatly diminished following the Edict of Milan in 313, which gave toleration to the Christians. Prior to this time, Christians risked execution by the Roman authorities. As expressed by Bouyer regarding the status of Christians in the Roman Empire before the Edict of Milan, "An avowed Christian was *ipso facto* a candidate for martyrdom."[4]

Afterwards, such literal martyrdom could only occur under a unique combination of exceptional circumstances and uncompromising personality, such as the martyrdom of Thomas Becket (d.1170), or of an occasional Dominican inquisitor who applied his commission too zealously, such as Peter of Ruffia (d.1365), who, as inquisitor general for Piedmont and surrounding regions, was murdered by members of a heretical sect. Other individuals exposed to risk of martyrdom included missionaries who were preaching the Word beyond the frontiers of the Christian world. Examples of martyred proselytizers include some of the early Irish and Anglo-Saxon missionaries to the Germanic peoples, such as Boniface (d.754), who was killed with his followers by heathen Frisians (in what is now the northern Netherlands) or, centuries later, Adalbert (d.997), Bishop of Prague, killed by heathen Prussians in Pomerania, or the later Franciscan missionaries to North Africa, such as Daniel (d.1227), the minister provincial of Calabria who, with seven other monks, was beheaded after attempting to preach Christ to the Muslims in Morocco.

As time passed, martyrdom came more and more to be represented by the figurative or metaphorical suffering of the few heroically ascetic hermits and stylites living in their "desert." The concept of "desert" evolved to signify any location to which one voluntarily withdrew from the world in order to pray, live ascetically, and experience physical suffering in imitation of Christ. Thus, for those living in monastic communities or even within the secular community, metaphorical martyrdom came to depend upon self-inflicted heroic ascetic practices.[5] This theme is stated explicitly in several *vitae* of holy persons. For example, the anonymous author of the life of Juliana of Mont Cornillon (d.1258), in describing Juliana's own asceticism as well as her persecution by others, states, "Next we must tell of the trials and persecutions Juliana endured before her blessed departure, out of zeal for justice and love of Christ. She actually took up her cross and followed Christ, if not by death on a cross then by excruciating pain."[6]

Socio-political avenues to holiness

There were also dynastic, monastic, local economic, and even religious doctrinal interests that influenced the perception and promotion of any individual as holy. In general, wealth, power, and status were important factors in the post-mortem campaign to elevate someone to sainthood. In a noble house's rise and maintenance of power, it was considered important to have a saint in the family pedigree. An example of this is the Merovingian dynasty's elevation of their ancestor, Chlodovald (d.560), to the status of a local saint.[7] Chlodovald, whose name in French is Cloud, was the son of Chlodomer and the grandson of Clovis. When his father died in battle in 524, the 4-year-old Chlodovald and his two older brothers were taken into custody by their grandmother, Clovis's widow. However, custody of the three boys was transferred to their two uncles, Childebert and Chlothar, in order to provide them with the proper upbringing for males of the Merovingian royalty. Instead, Chlodovald's two older brothers and their tutors were murdered by their uncles who then divided Chlodomer's kingdom between them. Chlodovald escaped the slaughter with the help of retainers and was taken to safety. As a young adult, he relinquished all claims to the Frankish throne and accepted tonsure as a monk. He was subsequently ordained priest, and lived a quiet life as a hermit in the region of Nogent, instructing the local populace in Christian precepts.

In the years following his death, he was venerated as a saint and a cult was developed with the support of his cousins, the sons of Chlothar, the man who had murdered Cloud's brothers. In promoting the sainthood of their holy relative, the royal descendents of the murderous uncles in one move publicly atoned for their uncles' well-known crimes and gave the local populace a saintly type of Merovingian prince to remember and venerate.

As a later example of attaining recognition as a holy person on the coat-tails of highly influential allies, William of Bourges (d.1209), of the family of the counts of Nevers, was initially a monk at Grandmont and then entered the Cistercian abbey of Pontigny. He became Abbot of Fountainejean (Loiret) and, from 1187, of the royal foundation of Chalis (Oise). In 1200, he was appointed Archbishop of Bourges. William strongly supported papal policy and reforms, which primarily involved protecting ecclesiastical resources (land, labor, and movable wealth) for religious purposes, keeping it out of the hands of would-be despoilers. In canonizing William into sainthood in 1217, Pope Honorius III held William up as the model archbishop who, although belonging to the noble class, placed loyalty to the Church over loyalty to his noble relatives. William's canonization also served the political interests of the Cistercian Order.

Plate 8.2 Bathilde (d.680) was abducted from England, raised in a royal Merovingian household, and married Clovis II. Upon his death, she became Regent for her young son. It is said that she participated in the traditional Merovingian politics of arranging the murders of rival family members. Bathilde was pressured to enter a convent at Chelles.

Pursuit of union with God

From the perspective of a broad spectrum of pathways to sanctity, the intense pursuit of a personal union with God represents just one and, as it turns out, a numerically small one at that, of the many avenues to holiness in medieval Europe. Furthermore, the model by which an interior form of holiness is expressed, namely, pursuit of union with God, appears to have been at least as strongly influenced by changing social and cultural patterns as those externally focused and less problematic pious behaviors, such as charity to the poor or establishment of monastic foundations, that constituted the more common but less dramatic pathways to sainthood. Charity appears to remain a constant throughout the centuries as a behavior that holy and pious persons do, and is a behavior that all witnesses could understand and agree upon, even if the motivation could at times be suspect.

Why the prevalence and intensity of pursuit of union with God should be as dependent upon historical milieu as the more worldly avenues to holiness raises interesting theological, philosophical, and psychological questions. One might take an essentialist position and suggest that there would be a core group of persons in every society who are particularly sensitive to perceiving and answering the call from God. This might be considered a stable and consistent figure independent of a particular culture, although dependent upon that culture for its particular expression.

Nevertheless, our data, as we will show shortly, point toward the opposite conclusion, that intense pursuit of union with God as an expression of religiosity, and a society's expectation and recognition of this, are strongly influenced by social and cultural milieu. For example, our data are in overall agreement with recent research findings of a higher prevalence of mystical and ecstatic experiences in female as compared to male saints. However this is true primarily for saints of the thirteenth to fifteenth centuries time period, and to a lesser extent for saints in the eleventh to twelfth centuries. Vauchez, utilizing canonization proceedings as a database, speaks of a "feminization of sanctity" after 1200.[8] There are no statistically significant gender differences, however, in prevalence of mysticism for saints in the fifth to tenth centuries. In these earlier centuries, religious attitudes and sentiments found other forms of expression than pursuit of an intensely personal relationship to God.

The pathway of mysticism and asceticism

Mystical and visionary experiences refer to descriptions by the holy person (or inferences by witnesses) of altered states of consciousness of an ecstatic, spiritual, and religious quality occasioned by pursuit of the presence or nearness of God. Heroic asceticism refers primarily to the intentional self-injurious behaviors of excessive sleep deprivation, fasting, and laceration of the flesh, as contrasted to ordinary ascetic behaviors, such as a sparse diet or avoidance of meat.

Mysticism and asceticism can each be conceptualized as a continuous or dimensional property. One is not either a mystic or an ascetic or not, but more (or less) of each, and varying across time as one journeys through life. This is especially the case if mysticism is viewed as an aspect of spiritual ascent or progress, such that there can be progressive development (as well as temporary setbacks) and deepening of one's spiritual life, as Nicholas Watson puts it, "from sin to conversion, from tears to joy, from earthly music to heavenly music."[9]

Nevertheless, criteria must be established for converting dimensional properties, such as various ascetic behaviors, into categorical entities, such as, this constitutes heroic ascetic behaviors and is evidence of a holy person. We need to be able to say, for example, whether Peter of Luxembourg (d.1387), who was reported to have been appointed Bishop of Metz at age 15 (an ecclesiastically illegal procedure which greatly troubled Peter himself), and who died at age 18 most likely as a result of his extreme austerities, should be classified as an heroic ascetic in our study.[10] The essential classificatory question is whether the extent of his ascetic behaviors distinguishes him along this dimension from those persons who practiced a moderate and expected level of asceticism for their station in life.

There is no consensus among those who work in history and theology about the definitions or boundaries of what constitutes mystical experiences and heroic ascetic behaviors. We are not speaking here of the problems in using medieval source material, which relate to the nature of information found in our documents. These have been discussed in the previous chapter. Rather we are referring to the problems of establishing a threshold for asceticism in order to differentiate "ordinary" ascetic discipline from heroic asceticism, and to the problems of defining or describing the characteristics of a mystical experience in order to determine who qualifies as a mystic and an ascetic for purposes of inclusion in our database and, ultimately, statistical analysis of the findings.

This involves a degree of circular reasoning, since our modern notions regarding the nature of mysticism have been deeply influenced by late medieval writings. Thus, all discussion of Western mysticism is influenced by the same unresolved controversies discussed in Chapter 3. For example, do visions and affective/ecstatic states constitute "true" mystical experiences, or do only the more apophatic, contentless, contemplative "states of pure consciousness" qualify? There may be less conceptual disagreement as to the thresholds that must be reached to identify heroic ascetic behaviors than regarding the identification of mystical experiences. In either case, it is still necessary to develop a heuristic definition as to what descriptions of spiritual experiences were judged mystical, and what degree of asceticism qualified for heroic asceticism, again taking into account, in this latter case, the historiographical problems that texts cannot be taken at face value and that descriptions of ascetic practices may have been either exaggerated or suppressed for a variety of reasons and that descriptions of the behaviors while in mystical states may have been dramatized to conform to male expectations of female emotionality. For example, as discussed earlier, there is reason to believe that the male biographer of the *vita* of Beatrice of Nazareth was influenced by accounts of excessive asceticism from the *vita* of Arnulf of Villiers (1180–1228), a notorious ascetic, in describing Beatrice's adolescent self-injurious behaviors. Roger De Ganck points out that some of the same words used by Beatrice's biographer to describe her self-castigations can be found in Arnulf's biography. It is possible that Beatrice herself heard or read about Arnulf's heroic asceticism, but there is no direct evidence that she did.[11]

We have discussed many of these knotty issues in the previous chapters. Ultimately, we have to proceed pragmatically with some classificatory decisions. They are as follows. In order to score positively for heroic asceticism, there had to be evidence of extreme self-injurious behaviors (SIB) in any one of the three most common ascetic practices (laceration, sleep deprivation, fasting) that stood out as clearly excessive when compared, as best we can tell, to the accepted ascetic practices within that person's regional and temporal milieu. For example, acts of holding white-hot iron kettles against her flesh in order to burn herself, such as are described in Queen Radegund's *vita*, are not found in any other Merovingian holy woman's life, and therefore constitute acts of heroic asceticism, whereas her practice of cleaning and polishing the sandals of other nuns at night, while it might be construed as indicating sleep deprivation, points to the Queen's virtue of humility, but not necessarily heroic asceticism.[12]

Similarly, in order to be counted as a mystic, there had to be clear descriptions in the texts of reports of ecstatic experiences or of altered states of consciousness of the types that were associated with mystical apprehensions of God. Furthermore, there had to be evidence in the text that the hagiographer and those in proximity to the saint believed that the holy person's pursuit of union with God was of an intensity and dedication that far exceeded the focus of most of the saint's contemporaries, including that of other persons who dedicated their lives to God's work.[13] By contrast, occasional reports of a few dream visions, deathbed visions, or heaven–hell dream voyages did not qualify as evidence of mysticism, a point in which we are in agreement with McGinn.[14]

There is no necessary linkage between self-injurious behavior and spirituality. Certainly in the twenty-first century, those who injure themselves, and those who seek union with God, appear to be on different life trajectories in general.[15] Simone Weil may be a notable modern exception in this regard.[16] There have been historical occasions, however, when self-injurious behaviors and spirituality have been relatively closely associated with each other, at least in popular thinking. The culture of Western Europe during the late Middle Ages is often identified as the milieu in which such linkage between asceticism and spirituality was prevalent.

Overview of data

In Chapter 7, we discussed the process of selection of a database (the group of saints, listed in the Thurston and Attwater 1956 revision of Butler, whose dates of death fell with the years 450–1500) for our study. Once a database is selected, the huge amount of information contained therein has to be further categorized in a manner that permits measurement and correlation of variables with the two major domains of interest in this study, namely, altered states of consciousness and self-injurious behaviors.

Basic questions to be asked of the database begin with who were the saints and what were their demographics? From what century and from what countries or regions do they come? How many men and how many women? What is their age range? What was their social class? Were they from the nobility/aristocracy, or from the non-noble wealthy and middle classes of merchants and successful farmers, or were they from lower echelon artisan and peasant families? Was their adult social role primarily a secular one, or had they entered into a religious vocation, and, if the latter, was it as an early oblate or following an adult decision? How did these demographic features changes over the course of the thousand-year period under study? What is gained and what is lost by lumping individual lives rich in their idiosyncrasies and uniqueness into group categories?

Vauchez expresses misgivings about the use of quantitative methods for studying a "domain as complex and as delicate as the history of spirituality,"[17] but proceeds to do so despite his reservations. Use of statistics calls attention to patterns that cannot be fully appreciated with the use of a few dramatic, but perhaps non-representative examples. We needed to examine quantitatively the many different pathways to holiness that were recognized in medieval Europe, in order to place asceticism and mysticism in broader perspective and to see how the various patterns of attributes of holiness changed both temporally and geographically. Otherwise we may be so impressed with the narratives of a few selected saints' lives that we would conclude that almost all medieval holy persons were mystics who practiced heroic asceticism.

Characteristics of the study sample by gender and time frame

A report describing the statistical characteristics of a large sample of individuals classified according to ten or twenty descriptors (century, gender, social class, geography, religious behaviors, ascetic and mystical behaviors) can rapidly become overwhelming. We shall present an outline of some major patterns relating to gender and time frame that characterize our sample, and place the details and most of the statistical analyses in the Appendix for the interested reader.

There were 1,462 holy persons included in Thurston and Attwater's 1956 revision of *Butler's Lives of the Saints* for the time frame (450–1500) that we have studied. Of these, 1,214 were men and 248 were women. Table 8.1 shows the distribution of male and female saints across the centuries.

We thought that it would be important initially to compare our findings with the results of other large studies of medieval saints, in order to see if there is sufficient correspondence between the studies to lend validity to our procedures and outcome.

If we compare our findings regarding percentage of male and female saints with Weinstein and Bell's figures for the time frame in which our data overlap, we see close agreement in most of the five centuries (eleventh to fifteenth) under consideration (Table 8.2).[18] Second, if we compare the percentage of male and female saints in our sample for the same time period (500–1100) that Schulenburg studied, we come up with 87.8 percent male and 12.2 percent female compared to the 85.4 percent male and 14.6 percent female distribution found by Schulenburg.[19]

Furthermore, except for the dip in percentage of women saints in the ninth century in Schulenburg's study, and the sharper drop in percentage of female saints

Table 8.1 Male and female saints by century

Century	Men	Women	(Women %)	Total
5th (second half)	60	5	7.7	65
6th	188	22	10.5	210
7th	199	32	13.9	231
8th	105	24	18.6	129
9th	76	17	18.3	93
10th	48	10	17.2	58
11th	108	6	5.3	114
12th	131	17	11.5	148
13th	127	45	26.2	172
14th	89	39	30.5	128
15th	83	31	27.2	114
Total	1,214	248	17.0	1,462

Table 8.2 Female saints in three studies (%)

Year	Kroll and Bachrach	Schulenburg	Weinstein and Bell
500–599	10.5	8.5	–
600–699	13.9	16.6	–
700–799	18.6	21.0	–
800–899	18.3	13.6	–
900–999	17.2	18.9	–
1000–1099	5.3	10.4	8.5
1100–1199	11.5	–	11.8
1200–1299	26.2	–	22.6
1300–1399	30.5	–	23.4
1400–1499	27.2	–	27.7

in the eleventh century in our study, our gender rates century by century (i.e. AD 500–900) are similar to those found by Schulenburg, as well as those found by Weinstein and Bell. In each of these other studies, a different compendium of saints' lives was used, the time frames studied differed, and the general focus of interest varied from ours. Yet there is only a 2 percentage point difference between Schulenburg's findings for men and women saints, and only a 0.5 percentage point difference between Weinstein and Bell's study and ours.

It is interesting, in this regard, that both Schulenburg's and our own data set show decreases for the number of women saints in the eleventh century relative to the centuries before and, in our case, since Schulenburg stops at the year 1100, the centuries beyond (thirteenth through fifteenth). Weinstein and Bell also found a low percentage of women mystics in the eleventh century. Weinstein and Bell and our data are in agreement in finding large percentage increases in holy women starting in the thirteenth century.

Michael Goodich reported a statistical study of 518 saints who lived after the Fourth Lateran Council of 1215 but were born prior to 1296.[20] For this time period, Goodich found that 27.9 percent were female. This accords very closely with the rates in our study for female saints of 26.2 percent in the thirteenth century and 30.5 percent in the fourteenth century, and is almost identical to the figure in our study of 28.0 percent female saints averaged for the two centuries. Our figures are somewhat higher than the 22.9 percent of female saints found by Weinstein and Bell for these two centuries, but we have to keep in mind that Goodich's sample set does not include the entire thirteenth and fourteenth centuries.

The distribution of saints by gender and time period in our sample set suggests a division into three time frames. First, there is a slowly rising percentage of women saints from the fifth to tenth centuries, then a downward turn in the eleventh and twelfth centuries. This is followed by a dramatic rise to 28 percent for the thirteenth through fifteenth centuries. Figure 8.1 displays in graphic form the data presented in Table 8.1. These figures suggest that the reformation of the twelfth century was not reflected in an increase in the percentage of women saints until the next century.

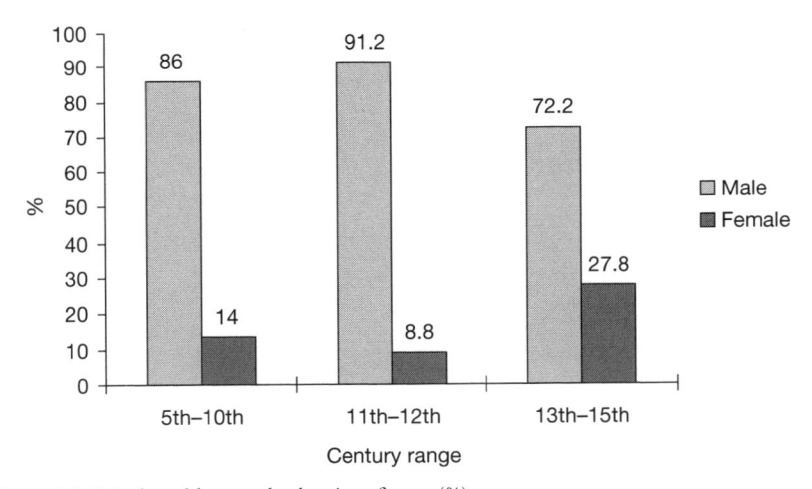

Figure 8.1 Sainthood by gender by time frame (%).

Patterns of heroic asceticism

Overall, 10 percent of our entire sample of 1,462 saints was noted for some form of heroic asceticism. Saints included in this category were scored positively in at least one of the three ascetic subcategories (laceration, fasting, or sleep deprivation). This figure of 10 percent heroic ascetics distributes into 6 percent in the fifth to tenth centuries, 9.5 percent for the eleventh and twelfth, and 18 percent in the thirteenth to fifteenth centuries. These overall figures reveal a steady increase in heroic asceticism across the three periods, with a threefold increase from the early to the late period.

When we examine the data to see whether the rates for self-injurious behaviors are different for men and women saints in different time frames, we see (Figure 8.2) that, in the fifth to tenth centuries, 5.6 percent of the male saints and 10 percent of the female saints practiced heroic asceticism. This figure rises in the eleventh and twelfth centuries to 9.6 percent for male, but drops to 8.7 percent for female saints. The figure for male saints continues to show a modest rise in the thirteenth to fifteenth centuries, increasing from the previous figure of 9.6 percent to 11.7 percent. However, there is a dramatic increase to 33.0 percent in the practice of heroic asceticism among women saints of these latter three centuries. There are no significant differences in heroic asceticism in the ratio of male to female saints for the fifth to tenth and eleventh and twelfth centuries, but the male–female differences in heroic asceticism is highly significant (χ^2 = 26.037, p < 0.001) for the thirteenth to fifteenth centuries. To summarize, there is a gradual and continuous increase (from 5.6 percent to 11.7 percent) from the fifth to the fifteenth centuries in the percentage of male saints who practiced heroic asceticism. By contrast, the percentage of female saints practicing heroic asceticism drops in the eleventh and twelfth centuries, and then sees a very dramatic increase for the thirteenth to fifteenth centuries. In these last three centuries of the Middle Ages, one-third of women saints in our sample, compared to roughly one-eighth of male saints, practiced heroic asceticism.

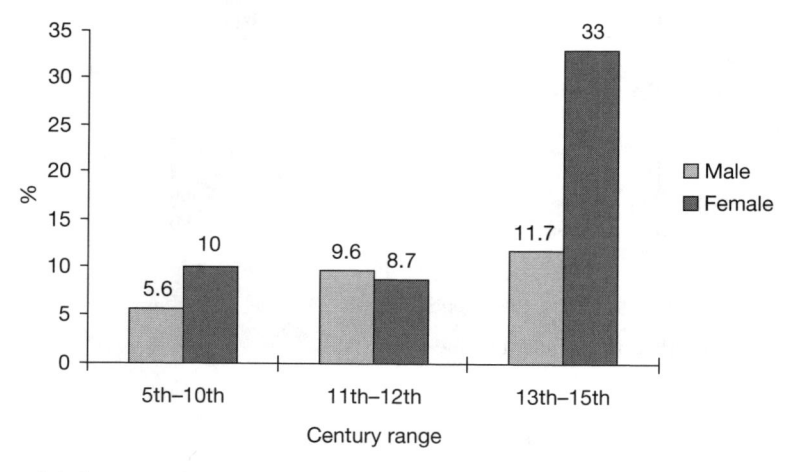

Figure 8.2 Asceticism by gender by time frame (%).

Patterns of mysticism

When we examine patterns of mysticism in our total time period under study (AD 450–1500), we find that 9.4 percent of the 1,462 saints were regarded as mystics in their lifetime. In terms of gender, 6 percent of male saints and 26 percent of female saints were mystics. Furthermore, of the total of 138 mystics, 47 percent were women, although women represented only 17 percent of the complete sample of saints. Looking at the rates of mysticism combined for both genders by time frames, we find a very slight rise from the figure of 3.1 percent in the fifth to tenth centuries to 4.6 percent in the eleventh and twelfth centuries. This is followed by an almost sixfold increase to 24.6 percent in the thirteenth to fifteenth centuries. In this latter time frame, fully one-quarter of the saints in our sample were considered mystics by their contemporaries and/or posterity.

The pattern of change in rates of mysticism is not a constant one, but varies with gender and time frame (Figure 8.3). If we look at the fifth to tenth centuries, we see no significant difference ($\chi^2 = 0.147$, $p = 0.702$) between rates of mysticism in males (3.0 percent) and females (3.6 percent). The percentage of male saints who are mystics remains static at 3.8 percent for the eleventh and twelfth centuries, whereas there is a three-and-a-half fold increase, to 13.0 percent, in mysticism in women saints for these two centuries. Although we are speaking of small numbers here, the difference in percentage of female to male saints for these centuries just reaches statistical significance ($\chi^2 = 4.132$, $p = 0.042$). By the thirteenth to fifteenth centuries, we see almost a quadrupling of the rates of mysticism in male and female saints compared to the eleventh and twelfth-century time frame ($\chi^2 = 57.1$, $p < 0.001$). The rate of mysticism in the women saints in the thirteenth to fifteenth centuries was just above the 50 percent mark.

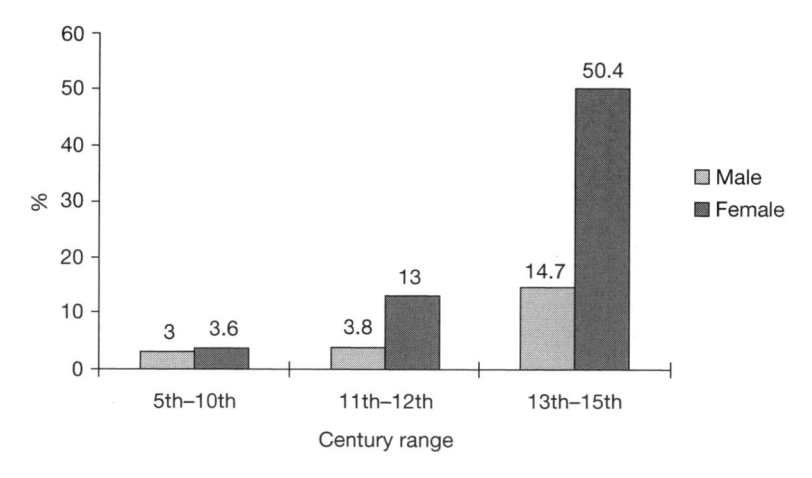

Figure 8.3 Mysticism by gender by time frame (%).

To summarize, in the fifth to tenth centuries, mysticism was a relatively uncommon marker of sainthood for both men and women. In the eleventh and twelfth centuries, mysticism remains rare among male saints, while it begins to claim somewhat greater prominence in the lives of women saints. The thirteenth to fifteenth centuries are marked by an overall increased percentage of saints who are known for their mystical experiences, but even here, the figures remain relatively modest for male saints (14.7 percent), while over half of all women saints in this time period have mystical experiences as one of the major attributes of their holiness.

Our findings of low rates of mysticism in holy persons prior to the thirteenth century are consistent with Peter Dinzelbacher's assertion that there is a lack of historical sources between the seventh and twelfth centuries that contain descriptions or references to the sensations of mystical states (ecstasies, raptures, auditions, sentiments of joy and sweetness) that dominated saints' *vitae* in the late Middle Ages.[21] Dinzelbacher reviews what he terms "premystical phenomena" in twelfth-century English mystical writings, including Christina of Markyate (d. after 1154), Ailred of Rievaulx (d.1167), and Edmund of Eynsham (d. after 1196). From these examples, he concludes that there is no full-grown *Vita Mystica*, understood as a literary genre, in twelfth-century England.[22] Although Dinzelbacher focuses on the expression of mysticism in England, he carries his generalization to the continent too. The characteristics described by Dinzelbacher as evidence of the new mentality of mysticism in late medieval Europe include a turning of the individual to his/her own interior, a loving relationship to Jesus expressed physically, emotional reaction of the mystic at contact with the Divine, the taste of spiritual and bodily sweetness, and ecstatic experiences.

Although our findings support Dinzelbacher's thesis that the flowering of mysticism occurred in the thirteenth rather than the twelfth century, we nevertheless need to comment on some of the problems raised by the particular definition of mysticism that he employs. The problem is that if mysticism is defined strictly in terms of the affective type characteristic of the Rhineland and Low Country mystics of the later Middle Ages, and if that is what we look for in searching the source material for mystics, then most likely we will not find mysticism in earlier centuries. This is because affective mysticism was not the shape that mysticism took in the early Middle Ages.

Parallel problems arise in making cross-cultural diagnoses in psychiatry. The expression of certain mental illnesses may be so different in different cultures that one is no longer sure that the condition is even the same in both cultures. For example, if, as is postulated by many workers, depression is expressed in Western culture by reports of one's subjective emotional state (I feel blue; I am upset) while something akin to depression is expressed in some Asian cultures with physical symptoms (My body feels hot; I have back pain), then it is problematic whether we are describing depression, neurasthenia, or chronic fatigue syndrome, or whether these three conditions are all just cultural variations of a basic depressive-like syndrome.[23]

There is no simple way to solve this sort of classification difficulty, either in cross-cultural psychiatry or in historical studies that range across geographic regions and time spans. In the case of modern researchers who are trying to identify individuals from medieval times who can be classified as mystics, there is conceptual contamination because, as we mentioned earlier, our own modern notions of mysticism are partially shaped by late medieval writings. In reviewing our data source, we were aware of the special characteristics of affective mysticism and strove not to limit our survey of earlier saints to this particular definition. For the earlier centuries, we looked for evidence of a saint's focus on developing or attaining a personal closeness with God, whether or not the notions of affectivity or sweetness were articulated in the text. Even given this broader construct of a mystical focus or experience, mysticism was extremely rare in holy men before the thirteenth century and in holy women before the eleventh century.

Association of heroic asceticism with mysticism

We have examined the data for asceticism and mysticism as each of these dimensions of sainthood vary separately by gender and time frame. We now examine the interaction between mysticism and asceticism to see how likely is the medieval mystic to practice heroic asceticism, and vice versa. It might be helpful first to review overall patterns. Of the 1,462 saints in our sample, 9.4 percent were known for mysticism and 10.1 percent for heroic asceticism. Of the group of mystics, 53 percent were males and 47 percent were females, although, as we mentioned above, females comprised only 17 percent of the total sample of saints. Of the saints known for heroic asceticism, 65.3 percent were males and 34.7 percent were females. The percentage of women who were heroic ascetics is double the percentage of women in the total sample of saints, but is still less than the percentage of women in the group of mystics. To summarize, within the groups of medieval mystics and heroic ascetics, there is a higher percentage of women than one might expect just on the basis of their representation within the total medieval sample of holy persons.

One important question is what is the strength of the association between heroic asceticism and mysticism in our sample of saints.[24] Is the mystic also a practitioner of heroic asceticism, or do mysticism and heroic asceticism occur unrelated to the other? If we analyze the subgroup of male saints noted for their mysticism, only one-sixth of these individuals also practiced heroic asceticism. By comparison, almost half of the female mystics also practiced heroic asceticism.

If we reverse the focus and examine the group of male heroic ascetics, then we find 14 percent were also mystics. Again, by comparison, 59 percent of female ascetics were also mystics. In terms of statistical analysis, there is a very weak (and non-significant) correlation between mysticism and heroic asceticism among male saints, whereas there is a moderately strong correlation between asceticism and mysticism among women saints.[25] Male mystics are not likely to come from the ranks of the heroic ascetics, and vice versa, while there is roughly a 50 percent chance that a woman mystic will practice heroic asceticism, and vice versa.

The importance of this data is that it makes clear that male saints who seek mystical experiences do not seek it primarily through heroic asceticism. This raises the question about whether they had other techniques for entering into the trance-like states of consciousness considered mystical states, such as methods based on the teaching of John Cassian, or whether such altered states can occur spontaneously in a few gifted individuals whatever the specific cultural context. In this latter case, it would appear that, in general, male saints who were not gifted in terms of attainment of mystical states did not utilize heroic asceticism as a stepping stone to mysticism.

If we analyze these figures in terms of time periods (Figure 8.4), we see that in the fifth to tenth centuries, 92 percent of saints were neither mystics nor heroic ascetics. There were 5 percent who were solely heroic ascetics, 2 percent who were solely mystics, and 1 percent who were both mystics and heroic ascetics.[26] The holy person who had mystical experiences and also practiced heroic asceticism represented less than 1 percent of the total number of saints in our fifth to tenth-century sample.

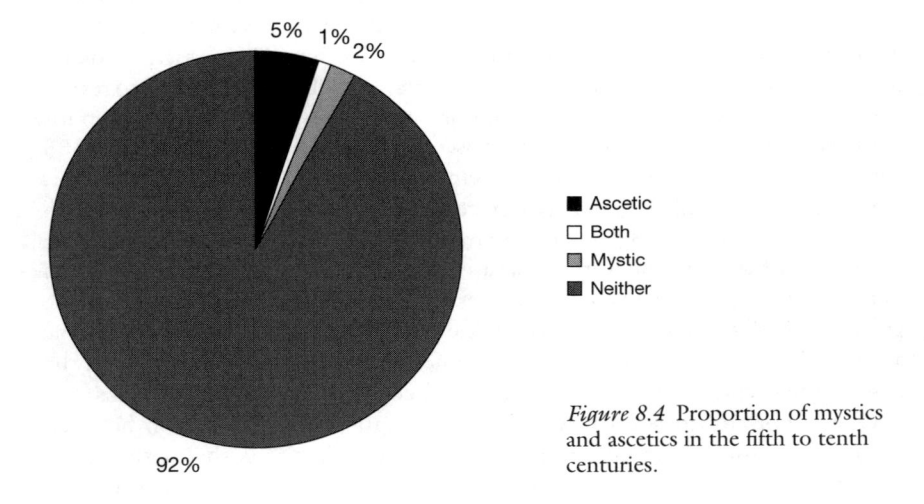

Figure 8.4 Proportion of mystics and ascetics in the fifth to tenth centuries.

In the eleventh and twelfth centuries (Figure 8.5), 88 percent of saints were neither mystics nor ascetics, 8 percent were solely ascetics, representing a slight rise from the earlier time period. There is also a very slight increase to 3 percent of saints who were solely mystics, and essentially there is no change from the previous time period, as shown by the 1 percent figure, of saints who were both mystics and heroic ascetics.[27]

In the thirteenth to fifteenth centuries (Figure 8.6), we see an increase in the number of mystics and heroic ascetics, and in those who were both. But still, 65 percent of saints in this time period were neither mystics nor heroic ascetics. Heroic asceticism without mysticism was seen in 10 percent, and mysticism

Figure 8.5 Proportion of mystics and ascetics in the eleventh and twelfth centuries.

Figure 8.6 Proportion of mystics and ascetics in the thirteenth to fifteenth centuries.

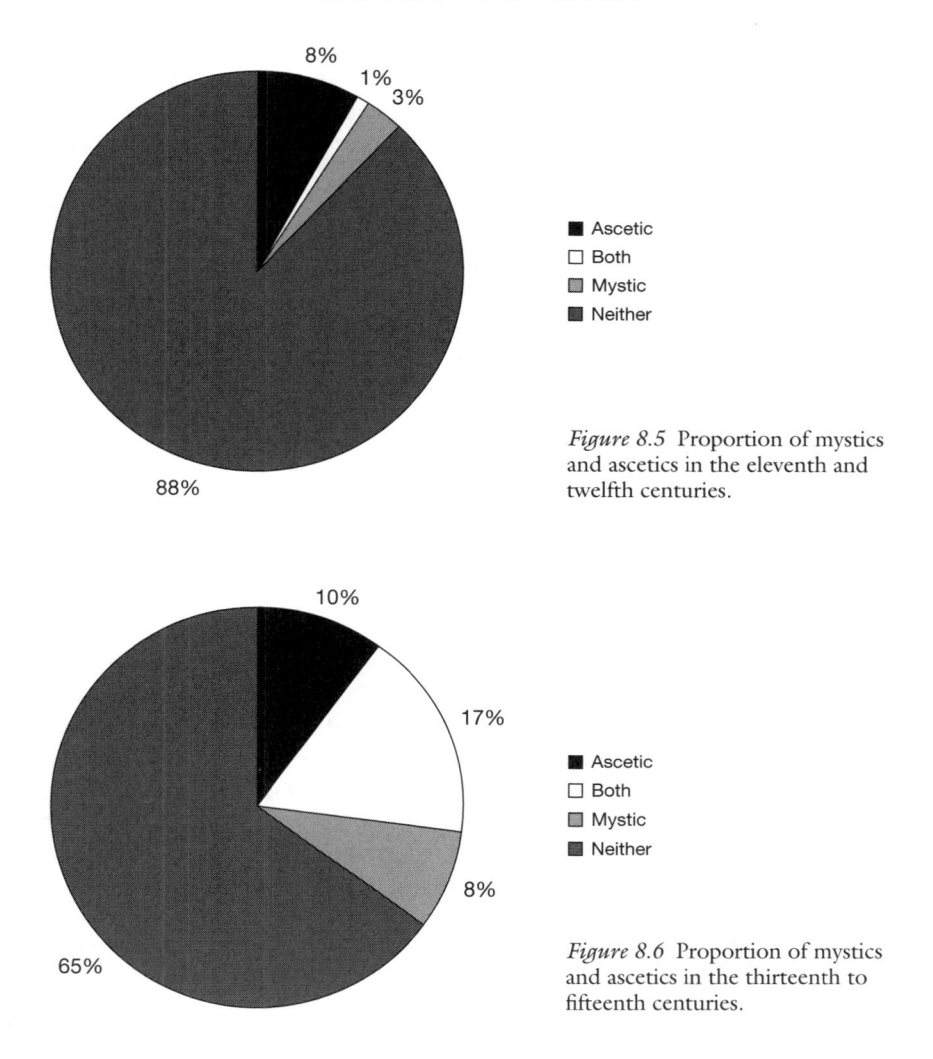

without heroic asceticism was seen in 8 percent of the sample in this time period. The figure for saints who were both mystics and heroic ascetics rises to 17 percent.[28]

Despite a few dramatic examples, such as Francis of Assisi or Henry Suso, in whom one finds a drive toward both heroic ascetic practices and mystical experiences, the combination of heroic asceticism and mysticism is rare in male saints. There is, however, a correlation between these two variables for female saints, such as Beatrice of Nazareth and Angela of Foligno.

The quantity of data generated from a sample size of 1,462 persons analyzed for several demographic, social and ecclesiastical, and religious and spiritual variables can rapidly become overwhelming. We have presented in this chapter just those variables relating to gender, time frame, mysticism, and asceticism. Even here, we have concerns that the amount of detail can obscure some basic patterns that emerged when the data were analyzed. With this possibility in mind, we will pare down the findings to a few salient features.

In line with other large studies of medieval saints, we found that 83 percent of the saints in the time period under study were males and 17 percent were females. We also found, as expected, that the percentage of women saints was not distributed evenly throughout the thousand-year period. We were surprised to see, however, a drop in the percentage of women saints in the middle (eleventh to twelfth centuries) period. This was followed by a dramatic increase of women saints to almost 30 percent of the total sample for the thirteenth to fifteenth centuries.

The patterns for mysticism and heroic asceticism follow, in general, that set by the overall male/female distribution, but again with a few unexpected findings. Mystics, both women and men, were equally and sparsely represented among the group of holy persons of the fifth to tenth centuries. After this time frame, the percentage of women who were mystics rises fourfold in the middle period and tenfold in the thirteenth to fifteenth centuries. In this later time period, fully half of women saints were mystics. By comparison, the increase in percentage of male saints who were mystics rises modestly to 15 percent for the last three centuries.

The pattern for heroic asceticism follows closely that set for mysticism, but with a few exceptions. Male saints again show a modest and steady increase from a low of 6 percent in the early medieval time period to a high of 12 percent in the later time period. Women saints show a more dramatic increase in heroic asceticism from the early to the late period, reaching fully one-third of the group, but there is a downward dip in the middle period which parallels the downward dip in the overall percentage of women saints in the same middle period. This requires an explanation.

We were also interested in the correlations between mysticism and asceticism. It turns out that, for male saints, there are negligible correlations between heroic asceticism and mysticism. Few male mystics practiced heroic asceticism, and few heroic ascetics showed much interest or propensity for mystical pursuits. For the women saints, there are modest correlations between heroic asceticism and mysticism, especially in the thirteenth to fifteenth centuries. In the Appendix we examine in greater detail the relationships between mysticism and the three specific forms of heroic asceticism (laceration, starvation, and sleep deprivation).

Our database covers Western Europe and its environs over the course of the millennium known as the Middle Ages. During this period, there was immense diversity in terms of culture, language, and even in the nature of Christian religious observance. Given this cultural diversity, the data indicating that holy women had more than twice the rate of self-injurious behaviors than holy men raise the question as to whether there are inherent differences between men and women that encourage the latter to fulfill certain of their religious goals or perhaps even affirm their religious identity through self-injurious behaviors. The pattern of higher rates of self-injurious behaviors in women than men is one that has held up in Western cultures since the beginning of the Christian era, both in religious and secular circumstances. The alternative hypothesis to considering fundamental gender differences is that common themes of the Western world view, such as a male-dominant hierarchical structure and social reinforcement of outer-directed aggression in males versus self-directed aggression in females, incline women toward higher rates of self-injurious behaviors. In many non-Western cultures, males have higher rates than females of self-injurious behaviors performed in a religious context.

While general observations and hypotheses regarding fundamental biological differences between men and women with regard to their proclivity to engage in various self-injurious behaviors may help us to understand broadly based behaviors, the role of culture appears to have direct influence on the expression of whatever tendencies may be present. Thus, for example, the data for fasting and laceration of the flesh for the High Middle Ages (eleventh and twelfth centuries) are clearly at odds with the general patterns noted above. One would predict on the basis of statistical analyses that holy women would have around 30–50 percent higher rates of these forms of heroic ascetic behaviors than holy men in this middle time period. Yet the data show that women drop below men in their rates of heroic asceticism in these two centuries.

This very interesting historical pattern cannot be explained away by differences in regard to our data for the eleventh century. Although Schulenburg's and Weinstein and Bell's percentage of female saints are greater than ours for the eleventh century, our data for the twelfth century are consistent with Weinstein and Bell's data set; Schulenburg's research stopped at 1100, so a direct comparison cannot be made. Thus, any recalculations that would have to be done would deal only with half the time frame of this middle period. Moreover, if we look at the raw numbers for the eleventh centuries, they are small in regard to the numbers in the twelfth century. Thus, the discrepancies for the percentage values among the various studies for the eleventh century are less significant than they would be if the problems were with the twelfth century, or with both centuries combined. We are still left to explain the finding that there is a decrease in the percentage of women saints who engaged in fasting and laceration of the flesh in the eleventh and twelfth centuries, especially compared to the percentages in the next three centuries.

Rather than try to explain away the anomaly in the data for the High medieval period as a sampling problem, it seems worthwhile to examine the particular historical circumstances. Broadly speaking, there is general agreement that, during the early Middle Ages, women had many more opportunities to serve God in the church than during the High Middle Ages. Indeed, the expression of religious behavior of women within the church was vigorously curtailed during the very widespread religious reforms of this High medieval period. Let us hypothesize provisionally in this context that the decline in the likelihood of female fasting and laceration of the flesh during the eleventh and twelfth centuries did not merely correlate, but was causally related to church reform. Indeed, we suggest that this pattern of decreased heroic asceticism was the result of the general policy of restriction of the performative and expressive religious behavior of women. In trying to account for this behavioral pattern, it may be noted that both excessive fasting, in the context of common meals, and laceration of the flesh, which caused bleeding, infections, and scarring, were more easily observable than staying awake at night when all others were asleep, even in a monastic dormitory. The observable consequences of sleep deprivation are far less dramatic than those of chronic malnutrition and emaciation, or infection and ulceration.

Furthermore, it is likely not only that heroic asceticism declined during the High Middle Ages, but that, in addition, information concerning female asceticism during this time period was more likely suppressed than during the early Middle Ages. The processes by which holy women provided information regarding their extreme asceticism also very likely had to be more circumspect, and the willingness of the author of a *vita* to record such information may well have been dampened as well.

The crackdown by religious reformers during the eleventh and twelfth centuries on all aspects of female activity within the church may well account for the diminution in excessive fasting and laceration of the flesh during this period. However, what is to account for the massive increases of all types of heroic asceticism in female saints during the later Middle Ages not only as compared to the repressive period preceding it, but also as compared with the early Middle Ages, during which time women putatively had a wide spectrum of ways in which to express their dedication to God?

The position of the church leadership with regard to the role of women in the church was not greatly modified during the later as compared to the High Middle Ages. However, it is clear that, with the emergence of the Avignon papacy in the early fourteenth century, the authority of the pope and the papal office's power to control the church massively declined. One aspect of the diminution of centralized papal power may well have been the inability of the papacy to curtail the latitude of women to express their desire for holiness through heroic asceticism. It may be observed parenthetically that efforts by churchmen to curtail heroic asceticism would appear to have increased during the later Middle Ages but these seem not to have been remarkably successful, despite the success of enclaustration of holy women during this period.

The lack of success at all levels in curtailing the religious expression of women during the later Middle Ages may also be seen as part of the church's periodic difficulties in maintaining various aspects of social control. For example, the later Middle Ages witnessed immense alterations in European life. During the later thirteenth century, the West began to experience what was to become a long-term economic depression. In the mid-fourteenth century, the Black Plague was introduced into Europe with recurring catastrophic effects through the end of the Middle Ages. In addition, Europe suffered periodic famines, which were exacerbated, beginning in the fourteenth century, by a massive climatic cooling trend. These ostensibly natural disasters helped create an atmosphere in which political and social revolts became endemic. These were evident both in bloody urban strife and peasant rebellions. Finally, the Hundred Years War (1339–1453) in the West between England and France, and constant conflict with the Muslims on Europe's eastern frontier, further destabilized medieval society.

A general atmosphere of social, economic, and political upheaval prevailed during the later Middle Ages. The moral authority of the church was particularly emasculated by the reputed degeneracy of the so-called Babylonian captivity of the papacy. Aspiring holy women likely benefited greatly from this very fluid situation in which the traditional sources of authority that had been established during the High Middle Ages broke down. Under these circumstances, it is likely that the inclination of women to seek religious fulfillment, particularly of the affective mysticism variety through heroic asceticism, manifested itself in a dramatic manner. Thus, we see roughly 25 percent of holy women in our sample engaged in excessive fasting and laceration of the flesh, and 17 percent in sleep deprivation, to help them fulfill their religious vocation.

The decline in central church authority and the general sense of crisis in the later Middle Ages can only serve to explain why there may have been greater freedom for women to express their spiritual yearnings, but has little to offer in regard to the specific forms and intensity of these yearnings. Two general directions of explanations arise to account more specifically for the phenomenon of the flourishing of affective mysticism and heroic asceticism in the later Middle Ages.

One explanation frequently put forth is that, in the later Middle Ages, religious women, denied an important institutional role in the Catholic Church and under increasing pressure toward enclosure in cloisters, turned toward asceticism and spirituality as a reaction against male hegemony in religious life. As Elizabeth Petroff states, referring to the women saints, "As children, they were marked by precocious piety, and their rebellion often took the form of asceticism."[29]

The use of explanations based upon analysis of political power is central to late twentieth-century postmodern critical theories. These arguments are built upon a Foucaldian assumption about the centrality of power considerations in determining values and beliefs, thrusting it onto the wholly different culture of middle and late medieval society. Indeed, such a conceptual framework in terms of power runs roughshod over the very essence of spirituality, whether Eastern or Western, ancient, medieval, or modern. An analysis of the religious reforms of the High Middle Ages and the shifts in spirituality toward an interior focus that characterized the later Middle Ages that is offered primarily in terms of power ignores or demeans both the psychological states of mind and the spiritual yearnings of medieval women and, we should remember, of medieval men, since the movement toward mysticism and personal union with God was neither exclusively or predominantly female, however much we may center today on women saints.

The pursuit of God usually took a religious or layperson away from corridors or even alleys of power, although the few outstanding examples of acquisition of influence that come through to us today (Bernard, Francis, Teresa) tend to obscure the fact that they were the very rare exceptions. Religious people on the whole pursued mystical union with God from religious and spiritual motivations, not as political acts.[30] There is no evidence that the obscure self-starvers or ascetics gained more than passing notoriety, often only in death, for their troubles, unless the local populace also sensed some authentic spirituality and intensity of vision to the person who has come down to us as holy. It is misleading at best to impose a twentieth-century political theory on thirteenth and fourteenth-century women who labored diligently for their moment with God.

The second explanation that attempts to account for the increases in women's affective mysticism and heroic asceticism in the later Middle Ages, in contrast to the social protest model, is that there are differences between men and women that predispose women to be more receptive and tuned in to the call from God given the proper cultural conditions. This explanatory model swings in both a positive and negative direction. The positive interpretation of this hypothesis is that women are more open to perceiving a reality beyond a materialistic one and a value system other than a narrowly instrumental or pragmatic one that is so limiting to the male gender.[31] The negative interpretation is that women are more suggestible to emotional and "irrational" trends and that the heightened spirituality of the later Middle Ages provided rich opportunity for their suggestibility to lead to a contagiousness of mystic-like behaviors.

The constructs of "open" and "suggestible" are critical in this discussion. In our society, open-mindedness is usually viewed positively while suggestibility is viewed negatively, carrying a connotation of inauthenticity which, when applied to a mystic, is damning. We have discussed the problems with suggestibility elsewhere, but wish to suggest here merely that the pejorative cast given to suggestibility may itself be a male value asserting itself over a female value, or a Western value in favor of willfulness and "independence" asserting itself over the value of obedience to family and community.[32]

Whether one attaches value or censure to openness and suggestibility, our own hypothesis here is that the attractiveness of affective mysticism and a personal relationship with God which struck such a chord in late medieval women carried with it an increased focus upon heroic asceticism. If we can speculate that the trait of transcendence, as we discussed in Chapter 3, is a stable trait in individuals that is relatively immune to environmental influences, such that the base rate of transcendent-prone individuals in a population is a constant, then cultural pressure to have transcendent experiences, such as ecstatic trance states, will drive some earthbound (low on the trait of transcendence) individuals to turn toward heroic asceticism both as a substitute for the emotional intensity that accompanies affective mystical states, and as a method of induction into such trances when ordinary prayer and meditation fail to work.

To summarize, the data demonstrate a clear increase in the incidence of ascetic behaviors and reported mystical experiences in saints in the thirteenth through fifteenth centuries in comparison to the two earlier time periods. In male saints, however, the increases from the early to later time periods are relatively modest. Furthermore, there is practically no correlation for male saints between heroic asceticism and mysticism in any of the time frames. Male mystics were not necessarily ascetic, and male ascetics were not necessarily known for their mysticism. By contrast, not only is there a dramatic increase in the percentage of female saints known for their mysticism and ascetic behaviors as we move from the two earlier time periods to the thirteenth to fifteenth centuries, but there are moderately strong associations between these two indicators of sainthood.

Correlation does not make a statement about causation. It may be the case that those women who were inclined or motivated toward ascetic behaviors also happen to be the kind of individuals who reported mystical experiences. It may also be the case that those persons (the hagiographers) who wrote saints' lives imposed their belief systems on the *vitae* by looking for, inventing, or embellishing ascetic deeds when mysticism was present, or vice versa. If so, this was done only for female, but not for male saints, and only in the thirteenth to fifteenth centuries. It is more likely that lay and religious persons alike expected holiness in women to manifest itself in mystical experiences in the thirteenth to fifteenth centuries, but not necessarily so in the fifth to tenth and eleventh to twelfth centuries.

It may further be the case that the cultural bias about how feminine spirituality should manifest itself had shifted in the thirteenth to fifteenth centuries in the sense that both the biographers, usually but not always male, and society at large, expected female holy persons to have an affective mysticism that was visibly displayed. This might explain the increase across time of female mysticism, but would not, in itself, explain the accompanying associations with female asceticism. However, it is likely that the saints and their hagiographers, in those cases where the time between saint's life and the writing of the *vita* was relatively close, shared a common cultural environment such that the hagiographer's bias was in synchrony with the mystic's quest and with general cultural expectations.[33]

Our hypothesis, which is consistent with the data and statistical operations reported above, is that, with the intense focus in the late Middle Ages on attaining a personal relationship to the divinity, self-injurious behaviors were employed increasingly by many religious women in an attempt to bring about an altered state of consciousness. Asceticism was a culturally acceptable and symbolically meaningful (because of identification with the human suffering of Jesus) practice that was efficacious in inducing a desired trance state that was interpreted or transformed into a mystical experience of closeness with God.

The question remains, never fully answerable, as to why asceticism was more pronounced in female than in male mystics. One possibility is that men, even holy men, were not as intense in their pursuit of ecstatic mystical states as were women, and were even somewhat distrustful of such states. Thus, there is a need to explain the data in two ways: first, to explain the increased use of asceticism in female holy persons, especially female mystics and, second, to explain the absence of increased use of asceticism in male holy persons, especially male mystics in the later centuries of the Middle Ages. We suggest that there is a base rate in the population, assumedly equally shared by men and women, of relative ease and affinity for entering into altered states of consciousness and that, when a society encourages greater numbers of individuals to participate in activities for which they have modest talents at best, they have to find ways to help nature along. Heroic asceticism is one of those ways.

9

RADEGUND

The life of Radegund (*c*.525–587), a princess of the Thuringian royal house, provides an opportunity to examine in detail an example of heroic asceticism that, as far as can be ascertained, went well beyond the usual practices of asceticism in the Merovingian Frankish kingdoms. We know of Radegund primarily from a brief poem of lamentation[1] and two *vitae*, one written by Venantius Fortunatus[2] (d.609), a poet cleric and later bishop and saint who was Radegund's confessor, supporter, and lifelong friend, and from a separate and later *vita* written by Baudonivia,[3] a nun who lived at the same convent as Radegund in Poitiers shortly after Radegund's death. Baudonivia had direct access to informed persons who had lived with Radegund. Radegund also is mentioned in Gregory of Tours' *History of the Franks*,[4] initially in connection with the events described below, and later as part of his narratives about Merovingian politics.

Radegund was born into the Thuringian royal house *c*.525. According to Gregory of Tours,[5] her father Berthar was killed in battle by his brother Hermanfrid. Radegund, by then an orphan (implying that mother had been killed as well) was then raised in her uncle's household until the age of 5 or 6, at which time Hermanfrid was defeated in battle and killed by two Merovingian Frankish kings, Theuderic I and Clothar I, whom he had offended. This was a decisive victory by the Franks who, according to Gregory, killed so many fleeing Thuringians that their corpses, piled up in the riverbed, served the Franks as a bridge across the river.[6] Subsequently, the Frankish invaders massacred most of the Thuringian ruling house, very likely in the presence of Radegund. Gregory offers an alternative narrative of Hermanfrid's death, reporting that Hermanfrid was killed some time after the battle by being pushed off a wall by Theuderic's men.[7]

Only Radegund and her infant brother survived the massacre. Radegund was taken as war booty by Clothar, who saw to her Christian upbringing and education as his future wife in his royal villa at Athies in Picardy. He married Radegund about a decade later (540), at which time she was about 15 years of age and he was about 40. It is likely that Clothar and Radegund were related, as Clothar's grandmother, Basina, was a Thuringian queen and therefore probably a great-aunt of Radegund.

Shortly after her marriage to Clothar, Radegund is said by her contemporaries to have expressed a very strong desire to devote herself to the church and to abandon both the material advantages and the marital obligations that her royal status carried. She became increasingly ascetic in terms of prayer vigils through the night, prolonged exposure to cold with inadequate clothing, wearing a hairshirt, and adherence to a sparse diet in the midst of plenty. She devoted herself personally to caring for the sick, acting not as a queen but as a maidservant in bathing and washing those with putrescent skin diseases. At night, according to what she later told Fortunatus, she would ask to leave her husband's bedchamber "to relieve nature" and would lie on a cold stone floor near the privy for hours, praying that she might avoid becoming cheap in Christ's eyes.[8]

For about a decade, Radegund followed an established model of the Merovingian queen-saint, dedicating her life to the service of God by way of charitable acts, care for the poor and ill, and intercession for condemned prisoners, while simultaneously residing at the royal court as Clothar's wife. Radegund's remarkable and consistent piety, however, must be appreciated against the full panoply of royal prerogatives exercised by Merovingian queens. Saintliness was not the only model available for a Merovingian queen. Several were reported to have incited their royal husbands into conspiracies, assassinations of kin, and wars of vengence. Fredegund (d.597), queen to Chilperic and the most infamous, plotted against, poisoned, and tortured her enemies.[9] Even Radegund's mother-in-law, the sainted Clotild (d.545), who as queen persuaded her husband Clovis to take baptism in 496, thereby converting the Salian Franks to Christianity, urged her sons to avenge the death of her parents.[10]

Radegund's uneasy balance between devotion to God and devotion to regal duties, not mutually exclusive since part of her Christian obligation was to be a good wife, was broken by Clothar's arranging the murder of her younger and only surviving brother around 550. Such actions were not out of character for Clothar, who years earlier had obtained custody, from Queen Clotild his mother, of his two young nephews (ages 10 and 7), under the pretext of arranging their coronation and subsequently personally murdered them, according to Gregory, by stabbing the oldest under the armpit and the youngest, despite his pleas to his uncle, in the chest.[11]

The murder of Radegund's brother, unlike the earlier murder of the nephews that ostensibly had been committed to eliminate rivals to the throne, must have been completely gratuitous in terms of political necessity, i.e. the brother, even as the presumed heir to a defunct Thuringian throne, could not have represented a real threat to Clothar. Clothar could have spared him as a charitable favor to his wife. The consequence of this murder was that Radegund felt she could no longer remain Clothar's wife in a worldly sense. She fled to the villa at Saix, on the way asking the holy bishop Medard to consecrate her to God. Medard initially demurred; he was fearful of the king's wrath. Radegund, showing great strength of character, told Medard that he ought to fear God more than a king. Faced with this compelling argument, Medard complied and consecrated Radegund as a deaconess.[12] Whatever religious and spiritual conflicts about living as wife to Clothar that Radegund must have stifled and satisfied with her moderate level of

Plate 9.1 Radegund (*c*.525–587) was a Thuringian princess raised in a Merovingian royal household. She was married to Clothar I, but established and retired to a monastery at Poiters after Clothar had her brother murdered. The picture of her exorcising demons must be based upon legends, for these were not mentioned in her *vita*.

asceticism and her admirable charity could no longer be contained following Clothar's murder of her younger brother.

The two *vitae* are diplomatic in saying very little about Clothar's role in the murder of her younger brother, but Radegund's immense grief is expressed in a poem written around 570 either by her personally or by Fortunatus with her collaboration. Radegund retired permanently as a lay religious at the villa at Saix, which had been bestowed upon her as a bridal gift by Clothar.

Clothar initially did not oppose this move, and was even supportive for a time. In 558, however, there was some suggestion that he was planning to fetch back his wife. Radegund reacted violently to this rumor with an increase in her already strenuous level of ascetic practices. The *Vita* by Baudonivia describes Radegund's response as follows:

> Hearing this, the blessed one shook with terror and surrendered herself to the harsher torment of the roughest of hairshirts which she fitted to her tender body. In addition, she imposed torments of fasting upon herself, and spent her nights in vigils pouring out prayers. . . . For she said that if the king truly did want to take her back, she was determined to end her life.[13]

Such a threat of suicide, carrying with it the risk of eternal damnation, is practically unheard of in early medieval *vitae* and reflects the intensity of her fear and fury at Clothar. More effectively, Radegund rallied important persons, such as Bishop Germanus of Paris, to intervene and dissuade Clothar from pursuing his plans for her. This strategy was successful, for Clothar abandoned his spousal claims on Radegund. Once again he became supportive of Radegund's religious vocation and helped her found a convent at Poitiers where she lived out her life. Clothar himself continued to maintain the Merovingian tradition of familicide and executed his son Chramm and family after Chramm's unsuccessful rebellion. Clothar died in 561. Clothar had many children, but apparently none with Radegund.

The severity of Radegund's ascetic practices is remarkable for the Merovingian–Carolingian period. Her initial regimen of physical discipline, self-denial, and ministry to the poor and sick, from the time of her marriage until the moment of her brother's murder, was still in conformity with the range of accepted ascetic practices, although admittedly at the harsh end of such a behavioral continuum, especially for royalty not living within the walls of a monastery.

Two dramatic events, however, appear to have propelled Radegund to change significantly the character of her rigorous ascetic practices from her rather stable baseline to a degree of penitential assaults upon herself almost without precedence in Western hagiography to that point in time. The first event, as mentioned above, was Clothar's murder of her younger brother, which caused Radegund to leave her husband permanently. Following this move to the villa at Saix and the cessation of personal contact with Clothar, Radegund appeared to again achieve some sense of balance in her ascetic behaviors between her inner turmoil against Clothar and her Christian commitment to forgive one's enemy. The second event, however, Clothar's rumored interest, about eight years later, in reclaiming his queen, seems to have so unnerved Radegund that she initially threatened suicide and, then, when the immediacy of the threat receded, began to engage in a truly ferocious assault upon her own body.

It would appear that the dramatic and qualitative shift in the nature of Radegund's ascetic practices, from an established routine of self-denial of tasteful food, adequate sleep, and bodily comforts to a pattern beginning in adulthood of inflicting serious injuries to her body cannot be attributed to a corresponding increase in spiritual fervor alone, although this must be factored in. The depth of Radegund's piety and her exemplary behavior in living out the Christian virtues of charity and gentleness were questioned by no one. Her reputation as a holy woman was well deserved. Nevertheless, considering that vengeance for the death of a kin was a virtual leitmotif among Merovingian royalty, and that Radegund had been exposed to this mentality since age 5, if not from infancy, it would take a saint not to feel considerable anger and even hatred, along with a wish for revenge, under such circumstances, although revenge would not restore the life of her brother. Even saintly Clotild, as we mentioned above, could not resist the opportunity to seek revenge for the death of her parents. Yet none of this is suggested in either *vitae* of Radegund.

If we could hypothesize that Radegund allowed herself to recognize anger toward Clothar, and toward herself for a variety of reasons we can only guess at, such as failure to intervene or to warn or to intuit that her brother was in danger, then, given what we already know of her deep religious commitment to live out a Christian life in all respects, we have to assume that such emotions must have given her enormous trouble. Her psychological conflict could only be expressed and played out in religious terms. The outward sign of her resolution of what must have been a crisis of faith was that she greatly increased the intensity and scope of her ascetic behaviors.

Such a pattern of self-injurious behaviors, seen in adulthood as an immediate response to threatened or actual assaults in individuals who had been seriously traumatized in childhood, closely resembles the picture recognized in our century of adults who have been subjected to traumatic and abusive experiences in childhood.[14] There is great potential for distortion in applying modern psychiatric categories and psychological analyses to the actions of persons who lived 1,500 years ago. Without doubt, analogous behaviors seen in different cultures may have vastly different origins and meanings. Nevertheless, certain patterns of Radegund's life bear such a close resemblance to present-day thinking about childhood trauma and post-traumatic stress responses that the analogies are worth examining. We will proceed with our description and analysis and later discuss the legitimacy and limitations of such psychohistorical endeavors.

By the age of 6, Radegund likely thought of herself as having been twice orphaned and violently so. She may have witnessed at an early age the murder of her parents and siblings by her uncle and his men. She was then raised in this uncle's household until age 6, when she likely witnessed the slaughter of her uncle's family by the Frankish kings Theudebert and Clothar. In addition to having suffered these serious losses of close family, she also lost her elder brother, several cousins, her playmates, and servants. The nature of the culturally prescribed reaction that a young girl born into a royal pagan environment may be expected to have experienced at the time of her loss is beyond recovery. In personal terms, however, it is difficult to accept the notion that, even in the "primitive" warrior society in which she lived as a young child, she had been so completely conditioned or desensitized to violence that she would have no emotional reaction to the many losses described above.

It is safe to hypothesize, from all that we know of the nature of children's responses to personal disaster, that Radegund was, at the very least, terrified and overwhelmed, and perhaps may have experienced, either then or later, a whole range of emotions including depression, demoralization, shame, and what is unsatisfactorily referred to as survivor's guilt.[15] Carl Malmquist, in a study of sixteen children who witnessed their parent's murder, described the psychological consequences of such experiences.[16] All the children had recurrent intrusive thoughts about the episode that came back, sometimes at unpredictable and unwanted moments. They all had nightmares, which were part of a larger fear of going to sleep. They had varying degrees of school difficulties, primarily memory impairments and trouble concentrating. All but one of the children had a significant decline in school performance. The one child who did not went in the opposite direction and became more studious following the parental death. They all had disturbed moods, with anxiety and sadness being the predominant affects.

After Radegund was converted to Christianity and was dwelling in her new although very different "home" at the villa of Athies, we can be certain that her mind was preoccupied, while awake and asleep, with reexperiencing all that had happened to her, both the bloody slaughter which she witnessed and also the happy earlier memories of life as a royal princess. In her new and probably hostile environment, and with the insight that comes with increasing maturity, she came increasingly to appreciate all that she had lost. Indeed, it would be difficult for her not to grasp the fact that King Clothar, her captor and later her husband, was greatly and personally responsible for what had happened.

At least thirty-five years later, in mid-life, and with the help of her friend and confessor, the renowned poet Fortunatus, Radegund expressed to contemporaries and left to posterity a sense of the permanence of her emotional losses in a poem entitled *The Thuringian War*. Through Fortunatus' art, and at a remove of some three decades, Radegund expresses her feelings in terms of a loss of "power" over the course of her life. Fortunatus writes: "her power fell from the heights of glory to the lowest depths." He goes on to detail what this would have meant to a young child. Thus,

> her entourage of servants, standing resplendent,
> her youthful peers
> Were dead in a day.

They were alive at one instant in great courtly brilliance as she was cheered by her playmates. Within the course of a day, all was swept away, and so Fortunatus conveys the suddenness of this sense of loss.[17]

Fortunatus goes on to indicate that "they [the dead from the court] were besmirched with funeral ashes. . . . [and]/Now lie without tomb or funeral service." This, undoubtedly, is an allusion to the burning of the bodies by Clothar's troops in a manner that deprived Radegund's familiars, childhood peers, and powerful officials, alike, of the honor of a religious burial even if it were "only," in this case, a pagan rite. There also would seem to be an effort made on the part of the Merovingian conquerors to carry out a process of *damnatio memoriae* in which burning the bodies and scattering the ashes were intended to efface the Thuringian royal family from human awareness. In this context, Radegund emphasized to Fortunatus that the corpses of the Thuringian dead, in general, lay "shamefully unburied in the field" until they were dumped into a "common grave."[18] For Radegund the adult, moreover, the merger of her now Christian views on the immense importance of a proper burial with her feelings from childhood that something had been wrong when her dead playmates and familiars were desecrated long ago would seem to have enhanced her feelings of helplessness, grief, and, perhaps, guilt.

In addition to the viciousness of the destruction and the poignant sense of loss conveyed in his account of the Thuringian defeat, Fortunatus provides a series of what would appear to be images of Radegund's half-remembered experience of the looting and burning of the court and its immediate aftermath. It seems clear that Radegund lost a much-loved friend, whose "golden hair" was reddened by the flames.[19] There is also recurrent imagery, a flashback, to use a modern term, of a "milk-white woman" who "lies on the ground." Radegund remembers stepping over the body of her slain older brother and seems to recall one of the married women at the court, shoeless, who while being marched off as a captive "walked in her husband's blood." Radegund, the child, undoubtedly was very much impressed by the bloody footprints that were made by "A wife's naked feet." She also retained in sharp focus the image of a little boy torn from his mother's grasp and killed.[20]

Finally, Radegund has Fortunatus express her grief at not being permitted to say goodbye in the appropriate manner. She, "the captive could not place a kiss on the threshold," presumably a pagan ritual of some kind by which one who is departing the house forever says a proper goodbye as a last connection to the household gods. Indeed, the strictness of confinement as a prisoner in Clothar's train would seem to have been so rigorous that she was not even able to "cast one backward glance toward what was lost."[21]

After recounting the imagery of these childhood half-memories to Fortunatus, Radegund, at mid-life, poured out a sense of her feelings of grief. Fortunatus writes in Radegund's voice:

> I, the barbarian woman, do not want to
> recount these tears nor do I want to float
> upon the melancholy created by all of those
> drops.

Indeed, here the inertia of melancholia is adduced to affirm Radegund's choice not to remain the passive victim of this immense tragedy but to be active in seeking her salvation. The allusion to her barbarian, i.e. pagan, background, is juxtaposed so that the reader will focus on the choice between pagan fatalism, i.e. inaction, and the Christian imperative for action to attain salvation. In Fortunatus' words, Radegund tells of her dilemma:

> Each person's tears are unique but I alone cry for all.
> My suffering is both private and public.
> To those whom the enemy [her husband] cut down, Fate was kind.
> I, as the sole survivor, must weep for all of them
> Not only must I mourn for those close to me who died,
> In addition, I grieve for those who are still blessed with life.
> My face is often dampened and my eyes are blurred,
> My words are secret but my suffering endures.[22]

Radegund expresses her responsibility, as a survivor of the massacre, and her grief, each of which adds to the burden of the other. She emphasizes, as well, the hollowness of continued psychological loneliness and isolation born from the deprivation of human love. Indeed, her envy of those who were "cut down by Fate" is a crucial indicator of this form of sorrow. It would appear to be a kind of unexpressed wish for death to alleviate the pain of living with her unrelenting memories. She highlights these feelings of loss and isolation with the lament:

> I search eagerly for some greeting carried on the winds.
> However, nothing comes to me from all my lost relatives in the beyond.

Radegund further writes of her enduring loneliness to Amalfred, her cousin and sole surviving relative, now that her brother was dead. Amalfred was serving as a general in the Byzantine army at Constantinople and, earlier, had survived the Frankish attack because he had been in Constantinople at the time.

This section constitutes the greater portion of the poem and appears to be a *fragmentum* from a letter written by Radegund to Amalfred, which subsequently was rendered into poetry by Fortunatus with the appropriate changes of persons where necessary from the epistolary form to that of a third-person narrative. In this "letter," Radegund emphasizes two themes, first, her love for Amalfred and her emptiness at not having close contact with him and, second, a lament for her dead younger brother. Interspersed throughout the letter turned into a poem are laments for other lost relatives.

Thus, the *fragmentum* of Radegund's letter appears in the poem, beginning at some point after the traditional salutation, and starts:

> [You], whose gentle visage once gave me
> consolation with your love, [are] now torn

> from my embrace by evil Fortuna. Oh,
> Amalfred, do you not remember how things
> were during those early years? How I was
> your own Radegund then. Indeed, how I was
> a young child and you my cherished man. Son
> of my father's brother, kindly kinsman. What
> my dead father could have done, or my dead
> mother, what only a brother or sister could
> be you were to me.

Although it appears that Radegund is idealizing the memory of Amalfred, it is likely, from this description, that Amalfred played a critical nurturing role in Radegund's childhood during the years when, after her parents were murdered by her uncle, she was raised in this uncle's household. Equally important is that, following the massacre of the Thuringian royal house and the abduction of Radegund to what must have been a hostile environment at the villa at Athies, there was no "Amalfred" figure to comfort and protect her, although we postulate later that there must have been some nurturing woman, most likely an educated Gallo-Roman nun who was not caught up in the Merovingian–Thuringian blood feud, who taught Radegund the basics of Christianity.

Radegund continues in her letter to Amalfred in an even more idealized vein: "With the press of a pious hand, with sweet lingering kisses, with your tender speech you soothed the little child." She goes on: "There was scarcely an hour in those days that you did not come to me. Now a great length of time creeps (limps) by without a single word from you." Clearly, she feels deserted by the one person who can give her some connection to her past, a past that, though troubled, is remembered in idyllic imagery and serves in her daydreams as a place to find relief from the painful memories that began with the "Thuringian War." Somehow, grieving child and older warrior cousin had formed a union for a few short years that served both as sustenance and nostalgic focus for the rest of Radegund's life.

Radegund then moves the time frame from past to present and continues:

> Then I was frantic when we did not share a house:
> If you went outdoors, I thought you had gone far away.
> Now the sun rises where you are and sets upon us.[23]

Radegund emphasizes the distance of their separation as a means of giving physicality to the breadth of her suffering. She gives her good wishes for his life, making clear that it is better for him to stay away, especially in light of the assassination of her own brother by Clothar years earlier. Nevertheless, his absence, and especially his silence, is very painful to her. How little it would take for him to relieve her suffering! She appraises her present situation:

> Some have every gift while I lack even tears of solace.
> Oh cruel fate that the more I love, the less I have!

The loss of Amalfred prior to the Frankish massacre of the Thuringian royal family was compounded by the apparent absence of a protector for Radegund immediately upon her arrival at Athies. Although Radegund was raised and educated at the royal villa at Athies in the manner appropriate to a future queen, there must have been some resentment and rough treatment of Radegund by her caretakers, for the text of her *Vita* by Fortunatus reports that she spoke even in her childhood about her wish to be a martyr, and that this wish was partially granted, for "she endured persecution from her own household."[24] It is not clear if this "persecution" entailed some physical mistreatment or was primarily in the nature of criticism and ridicule by her Frankish caretakers for her increasingly religious mannerisms, or perhaps for her, at times, uncontrollable grief over her losses.

Furthermore, we must keep in mind that, from the Frankish perspective, it was Radegund's uncle who precipitated the invasion of Thuringia by breaking a treaty with the Franks and ferociously murdering Frankish women and children. According to Gregory, Radegund's uncle King Hermanfrid had violated a peace treaty with the Franks by murdering Frankish hostages in a particularly brutal manner; the young men were hung up to die in the trees by the muscles of their thighs, and more than 200 young women were put to death, either trampled by horses or staked to the ground and run over repeatedly by heavily laden carts.[25] There must have been considerable animosity toward Radegund as an available and helpless Thuringian scapegoat for the Frankish losses.

On the other hand, it is probable that there could not have been very much physical abuse of Radegund, in view of the likelihood that she would someday be queen, but it is hard to know. Furthermore, in view of Radegund's rapid acquisition of Christian teachings and practices, we would hypothesize, given the educational structure of the early Frankish kingdom, that there were available to care for and nurture Radegund some cultured men and women religious of the Gallo-Roman senatorial and upper class, in the category of the sainted Genovefa (423–502) or Gregory of Tours himself, although clearly not these particular individuals. In all likelihood, as judging by her gentleness, a quality not much in evidence among Frankish royalty, and her strong faith, we make the assumption that she had been placed under the tutelage of a devout and kindly woman.

We again emphasize, however, that the expression in childhood of a desire for martyrdom is not a familiar topos in Merovingian hagiography, and provides evidence of Radegund's profound distress. Fortunatus dresses up this wish to die in the language of precocious religiosity, but it seems to be more a reflection of Radegund's turmoil and grief and, very likely, her own view of herself as already suffering martyrdom. To be sure, there was evidence of Radegund's early religiosity as provided in descriptions of her childhood games and activities: she would bring scraps of food to the gathered children, wash their heads and hands, and, carrying a wooden cross, lead a procession of smaller children singing psalms into the oratory. Descriptions such as these might be employed as hagiographical topoi, although we have no need to doubt, in view of Radegund's lifelong religious devotions, that they accurately depicted her childhood focus. But the wish to die in childhood, even under martyr circumstances, is idiosyncratic to Radegund. This is especially the case in view of the fact that Christian traditions did not have long roots in Frankish culture. As in many barbarian societies, it was the women who led the way toward religious conversion. Even so, we are speaking here only of second generation Christians, dating back to Clovis's formal conversion in 496.

When the 15-year-old Radegund was summoned by Clothar to come to his villa at Vitry, she instead fled to Soissons with a few companions. Soissons was the official capital of Clothar's kingdom and Radegund agreed to marry Clothar there. It is not clear if she had gone to Soissons in order to avoid marriage, or to secure a legal marriage to Clothar in place of becoming another one of his wife-concubines at Vitry. Clothar had several other "wives" both before and after his marriage to Radegund. By insisting on the formal and public nuptial ceremony at Soissons, Radegund saw to it that she was designated "head" queen, so to speak, and received a fitting and substantial dowry and a Christian marriage.

There is no evidence that Radegund resisted the marriage, once Clothar agreed to her terms, or that she resisted fulfilling her marital obligations. Radegund's infertility does raise the issue that she might have avoided sexual relations with her husband as much as she could. It is possible that her dietary restrictions led to amenorrhea or anovulatory cycles, and thus to infertility. This is not too likely, however, since Radegund's fasting at that time consisted of eating a plain diet and avoiding meats and rich foods rather than the very strict caloric limits she placed upon herself later.

Radegund maintained her religious devotions after the marriage, for according to the text, "she was more Christ's partner than her husband's companion."[26] She fed and clothed the poor and established a house at Athies for the care of needy women. It is noteworthy that it is only after her marriage that the text begins to make specific reference to ascetic behaviors. Radegund did not apparently display an early adolescent pattern of bodily mortification practices, such as is described in some of the *vitae* of saintly women of the late Middle Ages. In fact, the pattern of adult-onset heroic ascetic practices in the absence of either an earlier pattern of harsh adolescent asceticism or a dramatic conversion experience in adulthood is decidely unusual in medieval hagiography.

The text explains that Radegund's ascetic behaviors were established to counterbalance the life of riches and comfort that accompany the social role of queen. She feared she would lose status in God's eyes as she advanced in worldly rank.[27] She tried to occupy herself with the business of achieving eternal life. However, the description of her nightly bedchamber activities suggests that there were deeper issues at stake than the generic one of not becoming prideful with worldly rank. The text states that, after she lay with the king, she asked permission to go to the privy, where she would then spend several hours on the cold floor until her whole flesh was prematurely dead (relative to the grave). Her mind was on paradise and was therefore indifferent to her body's torment. She "counted her suffering trivial, if only she might avoid becoming cheap in Christ's eyes."[28]

The implication of the phrase "becoming cheap" is that she who was purportedly married and faithful to Christ was acting the prostitute by sleeping with a carnal man, albeit her husband. But this was no ordinary husband. The husband she was sleeping with, or avoiding sleeping with, was the one who had murdered her uncle and his family in her presence. To complicate her psychological and religious conflicts, the uncle murdered by Clothar was the very one who had killed her own parents and siblings.

What can be the further meaning of the phrase "to avoid becoming cheap in Christ's eyes?" The term implies more than just the general notion that it is preferable, even for a married woman, to abstain from sexual and other physically intimate relationships for the sake of fidelity to Christ. The term has connotations both of prostitution and degradation. Why would a wife, even a very religious one, consider herself a prostitute for sleeping with her husband? Her church and her culture tell her that it is her duty, although the message is obviously ambiguous, since her highest duty is to Christ. We do not know what transpired in Radegund's mind while she lay next to Clothar, but we do know what she did later, not just in terms of lying on the cold stone floor immediately after, but in terms of the general pattern of increasingly harsh ascetic practices.

At the psychological level, the question must be raised as to whether Radegund reexperienced, as Clothar's adolescent wife, some of the terror she must have felt at age 6 when she witnessed this same man murdering her uncle, aunt, relatives, and household retainers. One clue that would suggest this is her threat of suicide and her truly horrific self-inflicted injuries that began when, after having left Clothar following the assassination of her brother, she was faced with the prospect of his reclaiming her. The expression that the nun Baudonivia uses in her *vita* of Radegund is that Clothar had come to Tours, from "whence he might more easily reach Poitiers and possess his queen."[29]

After staying at Saix for a number of years, Radegund endowed a monastery at Poitiers, moved there, and established her kinswoman Agnes as abbess. It was at this monastery, especially after Clothar's expressed interest in recalling Radegund back to the royal court as his wife, that her ascetic practices greatly increased. The text refers to a continuation of Radegund's work in caring for the sick, personally scrubbing away the putrid flesh from those with skin diseases, feeding with a spoon those who were too weak to feed themselves, and kissing the faces of lepers. She maintained her own habits of austerity, wearing a sackcloth and a hairshirt, eating only legumes, green vegetables, and coarse bread except during the forty days of Lent when she had herself enclosed in her room and ate only the roots of herbs or mallow greens and restricted herself to two pints of water for the six-week period. She slept on a bed of ashes, but often stayed up at night either in prayer or in cleaning and oiling the shoes of the nuns. Penitential asceticism of this sort is noteworthy, especially for a queen, but it hardly calls attention to itself as heroic asceticism.

Radegund's behavior at the flourishing convent that she had established at Poitiers would seem to have changed radically following Clothar's expression of interest in reclaiming her as wife. At that time, Radegund not only contemplated suicide, but apparently made her intentions sufficiently well known so that Baudonivia learned about them several decades later from nuns who had known the queen. This is not to say that Radegund abandoned the immensely burdensome and socially humiliating labors within the monastery that she traditionally undertook nor did the queen cease performing the moderate to strong ascetic acts that she had followed for a long time. Indeed, she continued to wear sackcloth and a hairshirt, her diet remained meatless as a combination of vegetables and coarse bread continued to be the mainstay of her sustenance.

Following Clothar's "threat" to bring her back to his bed, there was a dramatic escalation in Radegund's direct ascetic behavior. Thus, for example, Fortunatus reports that on one occasion during Lent: "she bound to herself at the neck and upper arms with three wide but rather small hollow round pieces of iron. She did this by placing chains through these pieces of iron" and then locked the apparatus in place.[30] It should be noted that this kind of an apparatus is not something one likely finds in every convent cell nor even likely in the kitchen. The availability of locks are important here and suggests the help of a smith attached to the convent or the purchase of materials from outside the convent stores. As Fortunatus continues his account of her behavior: "She tied up her entire upper body so tightly that her delicate flesh swelled up and thus formed up over the iron."[31]

However, the extent and consequences of this extreme ascetic practice only become obvious to the reader in Fortunatus' description of Radegund's attempts to unlock the apparatus and remove both the chains and little hollow irons that had been so tightly enmeshed in her skin for the forty days of the Lenten period. Thus, he explains that, after the end of the Lenten fast, "she wanted to remove the chains that had been locked under her skin." However, Fortunatus continues, "she could not do this [without serious injury] because the flesh on her back and breasts, that had grown over the chains, was lacerated when they were removed." Indeed, according to Fortunatus, undoubtedly with a modicum of exaggeration, although it certainly must have appeared so at the time, "The flow of blood [when she withdrew the chains] was so great that her little body was drained to the drop."[32]

While the above-mentioned Lenten "exercise" is both extreme and self-injurious, it seems almost tame in comparison with other of Radegund's self-injurious behaviors that Fortunatus indicates she subsequently undertook. Fortunatus describes in considerable detail an incident that the squeamish reader may have difficulty accepting without some feeling of sympathetic pain. Indeed, Radegund would appear to have told her friend and confessor that "she ordered a brass plate to be made and shaped into the form of a cross." She then made it clear to him that "she heated up this brass cross in her cell and pressed it into her body very deeply in two places so that the flesh was burned through,"[33] that is, producing third-degree burns with destruction of the epidermis layer of skin.

Fortunatus cannot have been pleased by this particular instance of Radegund's ferocious assaults upon herself. Nevertheless, he permitted himself to provide a defense of sort by suggesting that "with her soul aflame she caused her appendages, themselves, to burn."[34] Whether this *apologia* was Fortunatus' report of Radegund's views or rather his own *post hoc* justification in the *vita* as an attempt to deflect criticism of his friend and patron must remain moot. It is clear, however, that the reference to the burning of Radegund's limbs in Fortunatus' explanation cannot refer to the episode of the brass cross. It is likely that Fortunatus confounded at least two discrete instances of Radegund's fiery self-injurious behavior into a single report.

Indeed, there seems to have been no dearth of extreme efforts on the part of Radegund which were known to Fortunatus that either were reported directly to him by the queen or about which he learned from the community. After discussing the flesh-burning brass cross episode, Fortunatus seems to imply that Radegund escalated her efforts of self-injury. Thus, he reports that during one Lenten period, "she thought up a yet more horrible means of suffering with which to torture herself." This would be in addition to the starvation-like hunger and the excruciating thirst that normally she chose to endure during Lent. He goes on to note that "although her skin was suppurating and scraped raw by the hard bristles of her hair shirt, she carried a water basin filled with burning coals." He makes clear, however, that "she steeled herself to the pain" that this caused and "despite the fact that her limbs were quivering [from the pain]" she did even more. Thus, she took the opportunity when "isolated from the rest [of her sister nuns], to press the basin of [white] hot coals to her body."[35]

The theme of burnt flesh, which Radegund inflicted upon herself following Clothar's threat to reclaim her as wife, calls to mind the burning of the Thuringian bodies at the hands of Clothar's Franks that Radegund memorialized in her poem *The Thuringian War*. The peril posed by Clothar's renewed interest in her, after she had resolved to have no marital relations with him, must have stirred up her childhood memories of the massacre juxtaposed to her horror at herself that she had passively consented to be his wife. She planned to respond to the actuality of returning to Clothar with suicide. But after Clothar relented from his plans, after the actual danger was over, Radegund nevertheless proceeded to engage in severe self-injurious behaviors, which by virtue of the symmetry of burnt flesh for burnt flesh must have represented a deeply penitential act.

Radegund would seem to have made her intention very clear to Fortunatus, who reports: "[S]he intended to burn her body and thus she pressed the glowing brass bowl against her body and her burning limbs hissed [as her flesh was consumed by the heat]."[36] This terrible ritual of self-mutilation did not go unmarked. However, when Fortunatus notes that "her skin was burned up and that a furrowed scar remained where the glowing brass had touched her," he seems once again to confound at least two separate episodes of self-injurious behavior. Clearly, there must be a significant difference between the mark left by a red-hot brass bowl and a scar referred to as a "fossa."[37] Nevertheless, as Fortunatus continues his description he seems to merge yet a third episode with the previous two as he characterizes Radegund's wounds as "holes."[38]

Fortunatus, a cultured Italian and an outsider to Frankish society, was Radegund's junior by ten years and dependent upon her patronage. Even though he was Radegund's confidant and confessor, he apparently had no authority other than moral persuasion, which he tried at times, to order Radegund to cease or modify her self-injurious actions, much as they must have troubled him.

At certain junctures in this progression of self-inflicted injuries, Radegund would appear to have attempted to conceal the extent of the damage. Despite the fact that the pain undoubtedly racked her seriously wounded body, Fortunatus reports that she never permitted her suffering to be detected in her voice or in her actions. Indeed, only when the smell of her putrefying flesh became obvious did her wounds, by now undoubtedly infected, attract the attention of her sisters. It would appear that in the context of these discoveries she offered an explanation to either Fortunatus or her community or to both. Indeed, she would appear to have affirmed that she thought that she could "cool her burning soul by burning her body."[39]

Fortunatus would seem to be glossing Radegund's explanations when he writes: "although it was not an age of persecution, she sought to be a martyr."[40] Indeed, Fortunatus seems to have been uneasy about Radegund's extreme asceticism as evidenced both by his contraction of six or more incidents into three and by offering explanations that are at best tendentious in light of contemporary church teachings prohibiting such behaviors. In any case, Fortunatus was loyal to his friend and patron. He makes an unambiguous effort to clarify and soften Radegund's motivations by observing that this woman "was willing to suffer such bitter pain in order to attain Christ's sweetness."[41]

There are a few holy persons who have wrapped chains around themselves that dug into the skin and caused chronic infections; however, the description of Radegund burning herself in this manner is practically unprecedented. We need to point out that the pain and morbidity from burns do not go away overnight or even in a few days. In addition, the secondary infections from burns prolong the duration of pain and pose their own serious threats to life and health.

The question we wish to address is How are we to understand the reasons for Radegund inflicting such serious wounds upon herself? It is our thought that the usual explanations offered in terms of religious motivation or spiritual growth and closeness to God will not do in this situation. This is not to gainsay Radegund's deep devotion. She prayed and meditated almost constantly, and tried to keep the image of Christ always before her. It is likely that the image of Christ reminded her, among other precepts, to "forgive thine enemy."

It is noteworthy that Gregory of Tours makes no mention of Radegund's heroic asceticism (it is possible he did not know the extent of it), and that Baudonivia, who surely must have known of it, if no where else than from the *vita* of Radegund written by Fortunatus, only makes a vague allusion to it. Nor would Fortunatus have invented the details of such extreme asceticism as a demonstration of Radegund's sanctity, although he does try to pose it as such. At no time in church history have the authorities made this sort of self-injurious behavior legitimate or acceptable.

While Radegund's "ordinary" asceticism and service to the sick and poor fall under traditional categories of religious observances, her extremes of self-injurious behaviors suggest that additional psychological reasons were operational. There were no precedents in Merovingian observances of Christian tenets to serve as role models for either the method or severity of this sort of self-inflicted damage, nor did the lives of the desert fathers, who emphasized fasting and other forms of abstinence, describe ascetic practices such as Radegund displayed.

Radegund's behaviors fit more closely a late twentieth and early twenty-first-century model of self-injurious behaviors seen in adults who have been traumatized in childhood and who suffer from what the psychiatrist Judith Herman and others have described as complex post-traumatic stress disorder.[42] The psychiatric literature is very clear that trauma in childhood increases the overall risk for a variety of psychological and emotional troubles in adulthood, including patterns of self-destructive behaviors.[43] While the social conditions of sixth-century Merovingian Gaul and urban or suburban America in the decades of the late twentieth and early twenty-first centuries are so vastly different as to hardly require commentary, it is worthwhile to point out some of the similarities between persons living then and now.

The similarities relate to basic components of what is often described as "human nature." In postulating such a concept, we are adopting an Essentialist position that to a great extent is acontextual. The basic premise is that there are similarities in all human beings in the ways that they process and are affected by overwhelmingly traumatic events, especially events of childhood. This point needs refinement upon refinement, for certainly there are differences from individual to individual even within the same culture, and certainly there are culturally sanctioned, supported, and prohibited ways of incorporating and responding to trauma. For one, the symbolic meaning of trauma and pain is vastly different from society to society, and even from different types of events within the same society. Despite all this, it is in the nature of how we are wired that all traumas that we experience will be played and replayed, with endless variations, in our thoughts and imaginations for a long time afterwards. The only exception to this rule might be some sort of active repression of traumatic memories, but delving into this controversial area would take us too far afield.

Just how long, how intensely, how intrusively, and with what variations and permutations the replaying of traumatic experiences will occur varies greatly according to many factors, but it is certain that the actual events will get replayed in the conscious mind, either during wakeful periods or in the twilight stages of falling asleep or awakening, or, of course, in dreams. It is also a consequence of how we are wired that later events, even years later, that resemble in some way the initial traumatic events will recall and arouse an intensification of the mental and emotional replaying of the events that might have begun to diminish as a function of time and, perhaps, mitigating and ameliorating experiences.

We are postulating that something of this sort happened to Radegund. The philosophy of Christian asceticism and her own personal conviction to experience Christ's sufferings provided the cultural framework and rationale for Radegund legitimately to follow a pathway of service to others and a life of discipline, including a moderate degree of mortification of the flesh. Culture shaped to some extent her ascetic behaviors, but Radegund's drivenness emanated from her unbearable memories, intrusive imagery, and intolerable guilt that never left her, which was greatly rekindled when her husband murdered her only surviving brother, and then again when it was rumored that he had intentions of reclaiming her as his wife. This threat brought back in an immediate way all the horrors and emotions that she witnessed and experienced as a child, as well as the conflicts of the marital bed. She responded with an outpouring of penitential and heroically ascetic behaviors. The continuous physical pain with which Radegund lived must have interrupted and diminished the stream of consciousness of painful memories that plagued Radegund.

Clothar's threat also must have stirred up a deep conflict of faith, for no one with Radegund's intense spirituality could contemplate suicide unless in the presence of an absolute crisis. Clothar died in 561, perhaps giving Radegund some twenty years of relative peace within herself.

10

BEATRICE OF NAZARETH

If the life of Radegund is highly atypical in several important respects for sainthood of Merovingian royal women, the life of Beatrice of Nazareth (1200–1268) is very representative of the flowering of Flemish female mysticism of the thirteenth and fourteenth centuries. Beatrice exemplified the precocious spiritual development, childhood seriousness of purpose, and early dedication to a religious life that embody one of several conventional themes of medieval sanctity.

The externals of Beatrice's life

Beatrice of Nazareth was born in 1200 into a lower middle-class family in the village of Tienen, about thirty kilometers from Leuven (Louvain).[1] Regarding the family's social class, the text refers to "*Parentibus mediocribus sortita.*"[2] It is clear that Bartholomew was not a noble, i.e. upper class. However, within the class of *mediocres*, there was a vast spectrum of wealth. From the data provided in the *Vita*, Beatrice's family was surely not from the class of merchant bankers or manufacturers. By the standards of his time, Bartholomew was likely middle middle class, which, when translated into contemporary understanding, would be lower middle class.

Beatrice was the youngest of six children, with two brothers and three sisters. Her mother, Gertrude, who was literate, early began teaching her daughter the rudiments of learning. However, Gertrude died when Beatrice was not yet 7 years of age, at which time she was sent by her father, Bartholomew, to begin her formal schooling at the nearby town of Zoutleeuw. She boarded at a Beguine house in the town. After a year at school, she was called home and a decision was taken to send her to live with the nuns of the Cistercian monastery of Bloemendaal (Florival) with the intention that she ultimately join the order as a nun. Beatrice's father was the general manager (*dispensator generalis*) for the monastery's temporal goods (*temporalia bona*).

After seven years of study and discipline at Bloemendaal, Beatrice petitioned the abbess and the nuns to be permitted to enter the novitiate and was accepted. This was unusual since she was only 15 years of age and the normal age of admission to the novitiate in a Cistercian house was 18.[3] After a year of "probation" as a novice, Beatrice was permitted to take her vows, i.e. at age 16 and thus three years younger than was the norm. She was recognized as a sister on 16 April 1216.[4]

As a nun, Beatrice was, of course, under the full discipline of the Abbess of Bloemendaal, who apparently saw the young girl's precocious intellectual development as making her suitable to pursue the profession of manuscript copyist. Thus Beatrice was sent at age 16 to the nearby monastery of Rameya (La Ramée), where one of her older sisters had already been professed as a nun, for what would appear to have been a year-long course in learning the skills of a scribe. After successfully completing the course of study marked out for her in the scribal discipline, Beatrice returned to Bloemendaal where she remained, serving as a copyist in the convent's scriptorium for another six years.[5]

During this period, Beatrice's father, two of her sisters, Christine and Sybille, and one of her brothers, Wickbert, came to live at Bloemendaal.[6] It is likely that the second brother, whose name was not thought worthy of noting, remained in charge of the family business.[7] Bartholomew became a lay brother and at this time continued to serve the convent as its *dispensator*. At least one of Beatrice's sisters, Christine, became a nun, and perhaps the other did as well, but this is not clear. Wickbert became a *conversus*, or lay brother.[8]

In 1223, the house at Bloemendaal gained the opportunity to found a daughter house at Maagdendaal which was located in Beatrice's hometown of Tienen. Beatrice was sent to the new house at Maagdendaal to serve as a scribe. At this time, Beatrice's father, who must have been well into his fifties, apparently still carried on as *dispensator* for Bloemendaal and took on as well the task of doing the same job for Maagdendaal.

Beatrice remained at Maagdendaal until 1236 and it was there that she received "consecration as a virgin" along with a group of other *virgines* by the bishops of Liege in 1225. Ten years later, however, the Abbess of Maagdendaal gave permission for the foundation of a new religious community at Nazareth near Lier. At least some of its secular entourage appears to have abandoned Maagdendaal as a result of a decision by the Cistercian order to create a new foundation at Nazareth. Beatrice moved not only with her monastic sisters as well as several of her siblings, but also with her father, who undoubtedly was an old man by this time. Upon the establishment of the new location at Nazareth, Beatrice was elected prioress, i.e. the deputy administrator of the house under the abbess. She held this position until her death in 1268. This election, which required both the preference of the nuns and the approval of the order, clearly marks a major development in Beatrice's monastic career.

Beatrice and her biographer

If this were all that were known of Beatrice's life, her career would make a useful entry in a prosopographical dictionary or handbook. Indeed, she would fit admirably within the contours of what now is well known in terms of family social status, wealth, and education about the group of female religious who flourished during the later twelfth and thirteenth centuries throughout much of northern Europe and especially in the Low Countries.[9] There is no evidence that she ever traveled from her native region of Flanders, that she influenced the local nobility or bishops, or served as a magnet attracting potential mystics and curiosity-seekers, or that in her lifetime she was renowned for spirituality beyond the confines of her immediate locale.

It is clear that Beatrice's reputation, and present-day interest in her, does not rest on the external happenings of her life. Beatrice was unusual not just in her precocity in entering the novitiate and taking her vows early, but, among other things, she also kept a diary. This, of course, was a great rarity among medieval clergy, both male and female.

Beatrice apparently began this diary, written in her vernacular Flemish, at the age of 16. This was when she began her course of study as a copyist at Rameya and thus at a time when she had relatively easy access to expensive and therefore rationed writing materials. Under normal conditions, the inventory of the scriptorium was carefully monitored and the cost of parchment and of other writing materials should not be underestimated. Thus, Beatrice's efforts as a 16-year-old not only to keep a diary but to garner necessary materials to do so provide evidence of her dedication to this matter.

As far as we can tell, Beatrice continued the diary on a regular basis until 1236, i.e. throughout her period of work as a scribe in the scriptorium of her mother house in Bloemendaal until 1223 and then for an additional thirteen years during her stay at Maagdendaal. When Beatrice was elected prioress at Nazareth, she seemed to have ceased keeping her diary in any systematic manner, but apparently continued to add notes to it. Whether this habit of her youth and early adulthood was abandoned due to some changes in spiritual values, or was merely the result of taking on the immense burden inherent in the office of prioress cannot be ascertained. However, as in most normal human decisions of this type, the interaction of many motives and considerations were likely in play.

Unfortunately, Beatrice's diary does not survive in its original form in Flemish, and many of the questions that historians would very much like to ask of this source can only be broached by way of hypothesis. Exactly when this document disappeared is unclear. There is interesting speculation that it may have been destroyed, by the abbess and chaplain/biographer, for protective reasons because it delved into Trinitarian mysteries at a depth that was not considered suitable for women religious.[10] This is possible because the Abbess of Nazareth arranged for a young chaplain (his name has not survived), who was attached to the house, to write a Latin *vita*, based primarily on the diary.[11] It is likely that the chaplain came to serve at Nazareth after Beatrice's death.

Although the possibility that the biographer had met Beatrice in some casual manner at an earlier time cannot be ruled out, he certainly gives us no reason to believe that he knew her in any meaningful personal sense such as would be the case if he were her confessor. The chaplain makes clear, however, that he interviewed at least some of the nuns at Nazareth, presumably those whom he assumed knew their prioress best. He also states that he was provided with information by one of Beatrice's elder sisters, the nun Christine, whose memory, by the early 1270s, may have been transformed by the passage of years as well as by the normal process of reconstruction and embellishment of old memories.

Like the *vitae* of all saints, even those written by contemporaries who had access to a wide spectrum of written and oral sources, the *Life of Beatrice* must be used by modern scholars with great care. It is clear that the diary, along with other of her writing (see below), were given by Beatrice to the abbess sometime in 1267 or perhaps during the previous year, but that prior to that time, they were kept absolutely secret by the author. After her study of these texts, and obviously after Beatrice's death, the abbess decided that a Latin *vita* should be written. Thus, among other things, we must try to ascertain what the abbess may have read and thought that encouraged her to have a formal Latin *vita* written. In short, what was the presumed larger purpose of this new document and how may such a program have affected the final product? In this context, it is important to emphasize that, for the last thirty-two years of her life, Beatrice made no systematic entry to her diary. She did, however, add notes from time to time after 1236, but exactly what, when, and why are not clear. Either as part of these notes or in some other well-structured format, Beatrice wrote a *vita* of her father. The chaplain, who then wrote Beatrice's *vita*, used the life of her father as the introduction to the life of the daughter.[12] Thus, to put it simply, the *Vita Beatricis* as we have it now, in fact, contains two *vitae*, a short or abridged *Vita venerabilis Bartholomi* and a very long *Vita Beatricis*.

In addition to her diary with the added notes and the life of her father, Beatrice also wrote a work of mystical devotion later in life. This is entitled *Seven Manieren van Minne* or *The Seven Ways of Love*.[13] This text has survived in the original Flemish and is the oldest extant devotional work in this vernacular. The work also exists as a partial and substantially reworked translation into Latin by the chaplain-hagiographer that he integrated into his Latin version of *Vita Beatricis*. Since *Minne* was written well after 1236, i.e. after the diary was completed and in the fullness of Beatrice's mysticism, it is generally believed that the effort to integrate parts of this mystical work into the *Vita* represents the efforts of the chaplain.[14]

As part of the general critique of the *Vita*, as composed by the chaplain, we must ask, in addition, how closely did he adhere to Beatrice's text? He claims to have produced what amounts to a translation, not an interpretation. He admits to have added only a small amount of information and to have "changed" very little of what he found in Beatrice's notebooks. However, this is very much open to question on several points of both major and minor importance.[15] Amy Hollywood compares Beatrice's Flemish original with the chaplain's Latin edited abridgment, arguing that the differences between the two texts reflect the male hagiographer's tendency to translate mystical into paramystical phenomenon, and to transform Beatrice's internally apprehended into externally perceptible experiences. Hollywood suggests that the chaplain, in misunderstanding Beatrice's mysticism by accentuating the suffering of the body rather than of the soul, of which the bodily descriptions are merely metaphors, is representative of the limited understanding and systematic misreading of women mystics by their male hagiographers.[16]

It must be assumed, in addition, that the Abbess of Nazareth, who commissioned the *Vita*, did so with a particular purpose or perhaps several interrelated purposes in mind. The abbess most surely made her intentions clear to the young chaplain whom she chose as her amanuensis, otherwise she could not be sure that she would obtain the end product of his labors that she desired. Indeed, the chaplain admits that Beatrice's *Vita* was his first effort in this genre. Even taking into account the topos of inadequacy to the task before him, which the chaplain does not fail to introduce, it must be emphasized that the abbess undoubtedly vetted the final redaction that also had to go to the bishop for his approval.

Further, it should be remembered that Beatrice began the diary at age 16 while at Rameya in 1216. According to the *Vita*, however, she recorded in the diary a considerable amount of very personal recollections regarding her state of mind and behaviors on a variety of matters that took place more than half a dozen years prior to her setting down information on these subjects.[17] Thus, our understanding of the inner life of Beatrice during her childhood and early teenage years must be scrutinized carefully in light of the well-known research on memory as a form of reconstruction.[18] In this context, the possibility of creative elaboration and selection, whether intentional or unintentional, cannot be ignored.[19] Since Beatrice kept the diary secret and certainly had no intention of revealing its contents, or for that matter even its existence, during the period of its construction, it must be assumed that she was not writing for a presumed audience, but only for herself. Exactly what this may mean for our understanding of what she wrote is problematic.

One important way to try to evaluate the information that was supplied by Beatrice regarding her childhood and family background is to compare it with information that likely was provided by her sister Christine. Thus, for example, information that would carry somewhat negative implications from Beatrice's perspective might perhaps have been provided by Christine. Indeed, information on some of Beatrice's interactions with her siblings would seem to have been provided by Christine. In addition, some of the information in the form of anecdotes regarding Beatrice's relations with her father may also have been provided by Christine.

Beatrice's early years

The chaplain introduced a variety of general topoi regarding Beatrice's early years that indicate she was marked out even in her mother's womb for holiness. However, there emerges through the ambiance of these topoi some details, probably provided by Christine, that have a ring of truth. Thus, for example, while trying to demonstrate the specially moral tone of her early childhood, the biographer notes that when Beatrice learned that any of her brothers or the family servants cursed or spoke of indecent things, she told her father and encouraged him to be very severe in punishing the transgressors. Indeed, she was seen to participate with her father in the "correction" of the *delinquentes*.[20]

Beatrice is depicted as the model of restraint and obedience. She had no apparent interest in girlish jokes, she rarely laughed, and rarely went out of the house to play with other children. When she did go outside, she often stayed by herself, having little to do with girls her own age.[21] This behavior might be interpreted as an unwillingness to be sullied by the foolish behavior of her peers, but as the discussion of Radegund in the previous chapter makes clear, the far more likely intent for the future saint was to convert her girlish peers so that they would behave in a more pious manner. At the least, Beatrice appears to have been a shy, restrained, special child who related better to the adult world than to the world of boisterous childhood.

It might be suggested, probably on evidence of Christine reported to the chaplain, that Beatrice's emotional life was somewhat curious. Not only did she reject pretty things, such as fancy dresses, but she did not feel it proper to show too much affection to her own parents.[22] Nevertheless, her mother perceived her daughter to be clever (*ingeniosa*) and began to give her the basics of formal education by the time she was 4 or 5 years of age. By age 5, she is reported to have memorized the entire Psalter and could recite it in the appropriate sequence without an error.[23]

When Beatrice, at 7 years of age following her mother's death, was sent off to attend school and board at a beguinage in Zoutleeuw, the pattern of shy, restrained behavior, and precocious intellectual development continued. Beatrice was considered, most likely based upon information narrated by Christine, "simple and timid" while truthful and prudent, "and, above all, obedient and submissive in all matters."[24] Indeed, at the beguine house, where she was sent to acquire good habits, Beatrice endeared herself to the devout sisters and particularly won over the heart of her personal instructor.

It is likely that young Beatrice, despite the earlier avowal of lack of affection for mother and father, was still grieving and depressed over the loss of her mother and the removal from her father and home environment, for the text mentions that Beatrice feared her tendency toward torpor and cowardice. These particular terms, along with weariness, apathy, and fearfulness, collectively regarded as acedia, are closely connected in medieval thinking as evidence of the sin of sloth, but often appear to be the equivalent of what was considered then to be melancholia, or, in modern terms, severe depression.[25] Further evidence that Beatrice was describing a state of depression after the death of her mother when she made reference to her "torpor and cowardice" is that these particular terms reoccur later in the *Vita*'s account of Beatrice's adolescence and early adulthood in what appear unequivocally to be depressive mood states. The beguines' warm reception of Beatrice must be seen, at least in part, as a response to the sadness that they saw, either expressed or hidden, in the grieving child.

In the town school, which was a coeducational institution and where her teacher was a male, Beatrice tried diligently to avoid any contact with the crowd of students, and paid no attention to what they did or said. This type of reserved and aloof behavior elicited the predictable response from her classmates. Some of them criticized her while others laughed at her. Indeed, she clearly came to be one of those victims whom fellow students harass and belittle, a role of suffering endurance that ultimately would support identification with the humiliated Christ.[26]

Beatrice's immediate response to her self-imposed isolation from the other children was to give her full attention to her classwork, an arena in which she would appear to have excelled. Beatrice explained and defended her actions as the proper response to the worldly and immoral behavior of the other children. What the text does not convey, however, was whether the shy and grieving little girl was as strong in her faith at age 8 and 9 as she wanted to believe of herself a decade later. Furthermore, either Beatrice or her hagiographer used her situation at Zoutleeuw to make several instructive and revealing points concerning the putatively immoral behaviors of adolescent boys and girls. Girls who "do not avoid suspicious conversations with boys" are condemned, as are those who seek the attention of boys. Flirting is characterized as "vomiting out signs" of "lurking lechery" that is within these girls. Indeed, Beatrice's aloofness is held up as a model for young girls, and, in this characterization, one may perhaps see some of the abbess's reasons for having the *vita* written and disseminated.[27]

After a year at Zoutleeuw, Beatrice's father called her home and decided that the next year she should be sent to the Cistercian convent at Bloemendaal where she would, if found suitable, ultimately become a nun. Beatrice apparently emphasized in her diary, with the benefit of hindsight a decade or so later, that the desire and decision to go to Bloemendaal to fulfill her religious calling was, at the age of 8, all her idea and initiative.[28] However, her father undoubtedly had reports both from the Beguines and the school in Zoutleeuw that made it clear to him that Beatrice had gotten on very well in the religious atmosphere of the Beguinage, but had suffered greatly in the coeducational school.

Once at Bloemendaal, the shy little girl with exceptionally well-disciplined learning skills set about becoming a member of the religious community in her own very intense way. She reports that she cried a great deal, but from "fervent devotion and not from bitterness."[29] However, Beatrice's mood seems to have been very excited as she talks about her new habit rather prematurely as a "wedding garment" and notes that she threw herself fully into the "whole discipline of regular observance" and went about investigating each of the "Order's observances." She memorized the rule of the Order, giving special attention to "the mystery of our redemption of the Lord's passion." In addition, she insisted upon repeating everything that she learned to her sister novices. There is a touch of obsessionality here that prefigures Beatrice's entry into harsh asceticism, as she keeps herself awake at night to insure that she has arranged everything (prayers, thoughts, things to be memorized, living area) in an orderly fashion. Her early exposure, following her arrival at Bloemendaal, to the influence of the imagery of the Song of Songs (1:12) found in much Cistercian mysticism, is evident here as Beatrice, identifying with the Beloved, places a sprig of myrrh between her breasts.[30]

It is within this first year at the monastery that the twin themes of asceticism and mysticism, at times in conflict and at times in harmony, become manifested in Beatrice's spiritual life. Despite Beatrice's seemingly uneventful exterior life, her *Vita* documents a fierce and constant interior struggle throughout her adolescence and young adulthood. Beatrice's ascetic practices began in these pre-teen years at Bloemendaal and early took on a ritualistic quality. She began fasting and flagellating herself, whipping herself with sharply pointed thorn branches. She exposed herself to the cold by intentionally wearing insufficiently warm clothing during the harsh Flemish winters. She also secretly recited the psalter of the blessed virgin 150 times a day with genuflections. She frequently wept and sighed. The severity of her assaults upon herself is acknowledged by the biographer who says, perhaps with a modicum of exaggeration, "Nothing known to pertain to the chastising of the flesh or the humiliation of the spirit could escape her experience." He continues, "Many things . . . which were almost unbearable not only to tender girls but also to the strongest ones, she zealously applied to herself, both interiorly and exteriorly."[31]

Clearly, even Beatrice's visible signs of ascetic behaviors such as excessive genuflections and weeping and sighing, let alone the flagellations which Beatrice kept hidden from her superiors, were found unacceptable to the sister who had charge of her. The *Vita* reports that Beatrice was severely reprimanded for these observable actions and obediently curtailed them, while continuing her excessive repetition of prayers in silence. More telling, however, and contrary to the discipline of the house, Beatrice continued to carry on her clandestine lacerations of her flesh.

Having failed to win the approval of her guardian sister and novice mistress as she had earlier endeared herself to her Beguine elder at Zoutleeuw, Beatrice found a companion novice (her name is unrecorded), the only peer friendship noted in Beatrice's childhood and early adolescence, with whom she conspired to continue in the harsh ascetic regimen.[32] Among the particular efforts that the two young girls carried out and which Beatrice thought worth mentioning or, at least, the hagiographer thought worth recording, was rising out of bed at night in order to pray secretly in the chapel. This practice was manifestly against the rule for girls of their age. Indeed, Beatrice admits that she and her companion misled their mistress with trickery, but offers the rationalization that they only did so for the greater good of thwarting the master trickster.[33]

One does not have to imagine what other breaches of monastic discipline the two girls undertook to thwart the devil. Beatrice apparently recorded in her diary that, in order to master her frail body "she frequently used sharp branches from the yew tree to beat herself from the soles of her feet up to her chest." The hagiographer reports that she did this to herself, but it seems likely, given the inaccessible location of the places mentioned, i.e. the soles of her feet, that she and her co-conspirator may have taken turns beating each other.[34] Beatrice filled her bed with sharp yew leaves so that her entire body was cut and scraped. In addition, she filled the bosom of her habit with yew leaves that cut her breasts and gave her pain whenever she moved. To increase her self-mortifications further, Beatrice tied rope with twists or knots around her thighs, while, at the same time, refusing to wear the soft linen undergarments prescribed by the rule, which "she abhorred as superfluous and, indeed, which she considered as something baneful."[35]

As Beatrice moved into her early adolescence, she became more sophisticated in designing self-tormenting devices. She reports that she made a rope with thorns woven into it and with knots spaced every few inches along its length. She wound this belt next to her skin around her waist and, over it, she placed her habit. Over her habit, she tied tightly another belt with fifty knots and, over this belt, a leather girdle was placed as tightly as possible, so that she felt pain whenever she moved any part of her body, even her head. In order to increase the pain, she employed a similar combination of thorns and belts around her shins and legs.[36]

While Beatrice was apparently able to keep much of her self-injurious behaviors secret, she had to risk discovery by taking overt acts affecting her comfort and duration of sleep. She used a stone or a piece of wood instead of a pillow. She would try to get away with sleeping on the hard and cold floor rather than in bed. At times, she slept reclining with her tortuous belts and ropes in place so that, if she dozed, she would awake immediately from the pain. During the winter, she resumed her excessive genuflections in the snow at night when no one was around. According to her diary, as transmitted by the hagiographer, Beatrice maintained these self-injurious practices on a steady basis from the time of her entry into the monastery until she was 15 years of age. Intermittently and briefly she ceased "subduing the body or tormenting the flesh," and then only when her bodily strength had been exceeded. She notes that, once or twice a week, she laid aside her devices so that she could regain her strength and begin again. The biographer notes that all this was done in the days of her childhood, when she had not yet attained adolescence.[37]

Furthermore, Beatrice appears to have suffered physical consequences from her excessive ascetic practices. The narrative states that Beatrice's early adolescence was marked by illnesses that served as scourges to snatch her from eternal torments. The first mention of illness in the *Vita* occurs following the onset of her self-mutilative and other ascetic behaviors; previously, Beatrice appears to have enjoyed good, but delicate health. It is stated that Beatrice had a tertian fever with pustules and open sores from head to foot. The pustules and open ulcers are not surprising in view of Beatrice's lacerations of her skin, and her apparent lack of bodily hygiene. If taken literally, tertian fever could refer to malaria (which was endemic both in Italy and the Low Countries), but a more parsimonious explanation is that the fever was secondary to recurrent skin infections and abscesses. Wound healing might have been impeded by a relative degree of chronic malnutrition, depending upon the severity of her pattern of fasting. Bloemendaal at the time was far from prosperous, and even the baseline diet from which fasting would begin might have been fairly sparse.[38]

Yet despite her pain and chronic skin infections, Beatrice claimed that she frequently "sang with a happy face and a joyful heart."[39] She reports that she rarely missed her classes, even if she could hardly walk. She would crawl to class, if necessary, and often was helped by her fellow novices. Beatrice extended the theme of suffering and deprivation into other areas of her monastic life, such as the clothing she chose to wear. She reports that she wore torn and soiled clothes "like a servant girl who worked for wages." She fooled her father by wearing borrowed clothes when he came to visit, so that he would not know how inadequately she was dressed. Due to her lack of proper clothing, she suffered brutally from the cold, and could barely walk or do what had to be done at the privy.[40]

When one looks beyond the hidden arena of Beatrice's personal struggles with asceticism and examines such behaviors in context as they impacted upon the larger religious community, we see considerable evidence of conflict at two levels. One level relates to how Beatrice perceived the manner in which others in the religious community responded to her. The other level relates to our understanding, reading through the text, of how the community in fact responded to Beatrice. In undertaking this, we recognize that her community was composed of individuals, that there was not unanimity of opinion and judgment about Beatrice, and that a charismatic person such as Beatrice, even at this early age, often served to galvanize others into taking up previously latent positions in support of or opposition to her dramatic religious behaviors. Communities, in the presence of persons such as Beatrice, tend to polarize into supportive and critical camps, into those who will understand Beatrice's struggles and tolerate her excesses until she recognizes and changes them herself, and those who will perceive her solely as a willful youth whose errant path threatens both her and the integrity of the community. The text of Beatrice's *Vita* does not address these issues in twenty-first century vocabulary, but there is considerable evidence of a strained interaction between Beatrice and some members of the community. In addition, it is unlikely that small group dynamics have changed that much in Western culture in the past millennium.

On the one hand, Beatrice presents herself as a joyfully suffering penitent who avoids notice, except for occasional reprimands regarding her excesses. On the other hand, there is a strong sense that comes through in several passages that she felt she was not treated by the others as well as she deserved. She attempts to turn her resentment that she is being neglected when she is too ill to care for herself into an opportunity to learn patience and endurance. She mentions that, when she was in sickbed, her companions forgot to bring her food. Not permitting herself to complain, Beatrice would, with great difficulty, go to the refectory and find a few dry crusts and rough vegetables, foods prepared for the healthy, but unsuitable fare for those with illnesses. The biographer poignantly brings out Beatrice's dilemma about not asking for help, but not understanding why others ignore her needs. "If she could not eat the food at all, or if she could not rise to get it, Christ's poor little one, neglected by the others, would fast all day long."[41]

Since monastic routine ordinarily embraces special care for the sick members of the community, we must ask what possibly could be the reasons for such seeming neglect. We must conclude, first, that the Bloemendaal nuns may have thought that Beatrice was exaggerating her infirmities, and second, and perhaps most importantly, that they were trying to avoid reinforcing those excessive ascetic behaviors of Beatrice that they saw as spiritually and physically unhealthy for her. In a small community such as Bloemendaal, there is more than enough work for everyone. When a member is ill, not only is she unavailable for the workforce, but others are obliged both to do her duties and to care for her. Providing such care is one of the basic charitable acts that members of a community do for one another, but when there is evidence and sentiment that a young member is bringing about her own disability in defiance of monastic discipline, it would take a saint not to feel some annoyance.

Beatrice in transition

As Beatrice approaches her fifteenth year, she is deeply caught up in the full spectrum of defining herself as a spiritual being in the Cistercian tradition, in trying to push to the extreme the ascetic pathway toward identification with the suffering Christ and away from sensual comforts and values.[42] Yet she misreads the still developing Cistercian tradition,[43] as the imperatives of her private struggle with sin and mortification of the flesh bring her into conflict with her own community and move her away from any realization of closeness to God. Although she is beginning to meditate on the humanity of Jesus and the events of his life, these practices appear more in the service of ridding herself of the mental clutter of sinful and trivial thoughts that preoccupied her mind than toward pursuit of positive spiritual goals. As yet, there was little direct evidence of the mysticism that was shortly to develop, although, clearly, self-mortification could represent the early steps in this direction if her focus could expand toward the goal of spiritual perfection. The personal issues of willfulness and entitlement, based upon her sense of specialness and suffering, caused her throughout her adolescence and young adulthood to struggle against the sin of pride as a major impediment to attainment of her spiritual goals and her maturation as a person. The stage was set to move beyond, for her, the limited repertoire of harsh asceticism.[44]

Sometime after her fifteenth birthday, Beatrice began to desire to be accepted to the status of novice, although she knew that, by the Cistercian rule, she was several years too young. With this goal in mind, she very thoughtfully took stock of her situation and not only made a determined effort to alter her behavior, but she also sought counsel. She makes clear that she understood that, if she continued her former course of action, she would have little chance to succeed in convincing the abbess and sisters to make an exception and allow her to become a novice three years prematurely. She apparently relinquished, at least for the year, some of the excesses of self-mortification and self-absorption that had characterized her behavior of the previous years. In short, she reduced the behaviors that had failed to gain the approval of the community and which had seriously, if only intermittently, impaired her health and vitality. She embarked on a program of examining her "exterior action and interior behavior" and substituted orderly prayer and meditation for assaults upon her body. She was rewarded when, with some hesitation and to her own great joy, the abbess and community of nuns made her a novice sometime before her sixteenth birthday.[45]

The year of Beatrice's novitiate would appear to have passed very quickly and smoothly. Beatrice makes it evident that obtaining the habit of the novice gave her the opportunity to apply to herself the stricter discipline appropriate to the role of novice rather than being limited to the rules governing the behavior of children. Being allowed legitimately to follow a moderate program of asceticism rather than none at all, she could, in return, give up the excessively harsh and dangerous self-injurious regimen she had previously secretly practiced. She emphasizes that she now slept well and comfortably on a bed of straw. The example of the bed serves symbolically for the reduction of most of her self-injurious behaviors. Indeed, Beatrice notes that she no longer "suffered the rebuke of her mistress," but was now appreciated. Beatrice understood that the monastery recognized and respected her maturity.[46]

The positive changes in Beatrice during this year, the abandonment of her "private" self-injurious behaviors, her public displays of holiness in the form of dramatic weeping, sighing, and praying, and her frequent illnesses, make clear that these behaviors must have been strongly discouraged by the house. She had been rebuked frequently and had not benefited from special treatment when she became ill as a result of her asceticism. Her behavior was considered a manifestation of childish *levitas* that was to be ignored and curbed. When Beatrice reversed course as she matured into her adolescence, the changes were noted and further encouraged. Making herself accessible to counsel in a serious way was another mark of her evolving maturity and seriousness. The combination of Beatrice's own development and the forbearance of the nuns enabled Beatrice to become a productive member rather than a burden to the community. The author of the *Vita* writes that "the obstacles caused by shyness and reason were removed." He continues that, upon incorporation into the devout community, "it was possible for her to cultivate the entire observance of the Order with great integrity."[47]

Nevertheless, it does not appear that Beatrice was able to progress in her spiritual development much beyond a closed loop of ritualistic scrutiny of her faults and defects that she combated with prayers and penances. Several months after taking her vows, Beatrice was sent for one year to the neighboring monastery of Rameya in order to learn the very demanding skills of a manuscript copyist. It is possible that her abbess and others recognized the excesses of Beatrice's mental and physical scourging and its effects upon her health, and decided that she needed a change of environment. Bloemendaal was undergoing Cistercian reform at the time and may have been emphasizing asceticism. Rameya, on the other hand, had a reputation for interior focus and mysticism.

The year spent at Rameya was to have a profound influence on Beatrice. It removed her from Bloemendaal and perhaps from some destructive role models, possibly including the felt presence of her father, who himself may have been given to excessive asceticism. It gave her a useful occupation that would at least intermittently distract her from her excessive devotional zeal, as well as giving her the opportunity and material to put her deepening thoughts into writing. But most importantly, and perhaps not unbeknown to the Abbess of Bloemendaal, it introduced Beatrice to Ida of Nivelles who, despite her youth (she was one year younger than Beatrice) had already gained considerable local regard for her mystical experiences.[48] Beatrice was stunned by Ida's attainment of a personal relationship with God and begged Ida to intercede so that she too could have such a relationship. Ida became Beatrice's spiritual mother and taught her how to begin to transcend the narrow circle of obsessive scrutiny and physical mortification.

Under Ida's inspired tutelage at Rameya, Beatrice slowly learned that inner development requires more than self-absorption with sins and heroic self-mortification. Ida set her on a spiritually more productive path than the one that she had previously marked out for herself. The impressionable teenager studied Ida, discussed the joys of ecstatic experiences, and begged Ida to intercede with Christ to grant her (Beatrice) a similar grace. Ida agreed to pray for Beatrice and, along with beginning to teach Beatrice the methods of attaining spiritual closeness with God, advised the young nun as follows: "Be prepared on the day of the Lord's holy birth when the good Lord will irresistibly fulfill the desire of your heart, granting you the grace you ask for."[49]

Despite Ida's very positive instruction, Christmas day came and went and Beatrice waited patiently for the long-awaited experience of grace, but nothing unusual happened. The infusion of grace did not occur. Grieved and disappointed, Beatrice was convinced that her own sins were responsible for this failure. She approached Ida for consolation and counsel, who answered and reassured her as follows, "This did not happen because your sins demanded it, as you suspect: but know for certain that what you hope for will happen before the octave day, counting from the first day of the Lord's birth."[50]

A further glimpse of Ida's gentle methods of instruction to Beatrice can be gleaned from Beatrice's account of this incident. Ida explains to Beatrice: "Moreover you should not think that I answered you wrongly even if what I promised for the day of the Lord's birth did not happen."[51] Ida explains that, by the Lord's birthday, she meant the entire eight days as a single event. It was neither Ida's teachings nor the state of Beatrice's soul that was at fault; merely Beatrice's ignorance of the meaning of the symbolism of the religious chronology was at issue. Not discussed in the text, but what also must be at issue here is the question of whether God's grace can be demanded on schedule. Perhaps it was important for Beatrice to learn the answer to this question early in the course of her spiritual life.

Somewhat consoled, Beatrice remained hopeful. Several days later, while in choir at dusk for the singing of Compline, and meditating on the image of David playing the harp, Beatrice is "lifted up and seized in an ecstasy of mind." She sees the "divine and sublime Trinity shining marvelously in the beauty of its splendor" and David with the heavenly singers praising "the majesty of divine power."[52] At the end of Compline, Beatrice remained in a trance state for several hours. A nun had to return from the dormitory to rouse Beatrice. When Beatrice realized that she had been recalled "from heavenly delights to the miseries of the human condition," she sighed and wept, but later that evening, in her bed, she was filled with gratitude and delight at what she had experienced.[53] When Ida and others later approach her, she began, out of gratitude, to break out in loud laughter and felt herself to be floating on air. She recognized that others might view this behavior as immoderate, but could not constrain herself. This abundance of happiness lasted one month; illness and physical weakness left her. The profound changes in Beatrice were apparent to Ida and the other members of the community.

At the end of the month, Beatrice returned from Rameya to Bloemendaal. She was noted to be more mature, but also to be withdrawn in pursuit of constant prayer. Concerned that the admiration of others would cause her to fall into vainglory, however, Beatrice slowly began to curb her practice of public prayers and breast-beating. She even started neglecting some of her devotional observances and exercises. Beatrice, while fleeing a reputation for holiness, was, in the words of the biographer, "succumbing to the wound of squalid sloth through lack of caution."[54]

Over the course of the next few months, Beatrice realized that the joyfulness which she had felt after her ecstatic experience at Rameya was gone; in its place was a sense of spiritual aridity and despair. This desperate state lasted, more or less, for about five years, interrupted by occasional moments of a sense of closeness to God, which seemed to come on at her darkest moments and gave her the strength and will to continue her pursuit of the holy. All in all, however, the five years were a time of intense struggle, of tenaciously practicing various forms of self-scrutiny and ritualistic but joyless observances, the entire time praying for divine revelations or at least signs from God that she could regain his presence.

The *Vita* is ambiguous about the level of Beatrice's ascetic practices while at Rameya and, afterwards, at Bloemendaal. There is a hint, prior to the time at Rameya, that self-mortification continued throughout her adolescence, which, according to medieval reckoning, would have extended to her mid-twenties. There is reference, at Rameya, to physical infirmities, but none specifically to ascetic disciplinary practices. One gets the sense that, while there may have been moderate fasting and sleep-deprivation at Rameya, the harsh self-injurious behaviors of the previous several years, such as wrapping thorns around herself, were much abated, if not entirely abandoned under Ida's spiritual tutelage. However, as her period of spiritual barrenness deepened when back at Florival, Beatrice returned in some form to her earlier ascetic practices. In the wake of several prolonged episodes of struggling with carnal desires and blasphemous thoughts, she purified herself "with daily sighs, tears, and sobs as well as with physical discipline."[55]

The text is not more explicit than this. We hear nothing of thorns, prickly yew leaves, and leather bindings. Beatrice suffers from poor health in general. She is physically weak, has mouth and nose bleeds, and often stays in the infirmary. Descriptively, Beatrice appears to have been quite depressed for much of the five years following her return from Rameya.[56] The despair and physical exhaustion that universally accompanies depression was perceived by Beatrice as part of her penitence, and indeed, the mental suffering that her depression caused may have mitigated somewhat the need for the types of harsh self-injurious behaviors of her early adolescence. However, we think that the matter goes deeper than this.

Beatrice was slowly discovering the lesson that had begun at Rameya, that the road toward spiritual perfection, for her, at least, was not the road of harsh asceticism, but of prayerful contemplation of the generosity of her Creator. In a telling passage, Beatrice, after a month of continuous self-scrutiny for small sins and continuous works of penitence for all these minor infractions, realizes that she had actually lost ground and was showing less honor and reverence to God. She determines to drop this unfruitful and obsessive activity and to shift to a state of finding thanksgiving and praise to God. The *Vita* chronicles that, even after the initial five-year period of struggling against spiritual aridity, Beatrice continued to alternate between times of ecstatic fulfillment of a sense of closeness and even union with God, and more mundane and painful periods where the best that she could do was to hold tightly to ritual observances while waiting for the return of grace. The balance slowly shifted, however, in the direction of *Minne*, the experience of joyful love of God.

While it is likely that fasting and some degree of sleep deprivation in the form of prolonged nighttime prayers continued through Beatrice's life, it does appear that Beatrice's insight that prayer and contemplation rather than extreme asceticism was the proper pathway to union with God grew in strength and practice, and that she never returned to the severe self-injurious behaviors of her youth as a means of combating carnal thoughts, ridding the mind of clutter, or attaining mystical states.

11

BEATRICE OF ORNACIEUX

The life of Beatrice of Ornacieux (d.1303 or 1309) provides an instructive illustration of a fairly typical pattern of an onset of heroic ascetic behaviors in adolescence coinciding with an early blooming of religious fervor, and the subsequent abandonment of harsh asceticism as her meditative practices and spiritual development matured.[1] Little is known of Beatrice's early life, other than that she was born at the castle of Ornacieu in the Dauphine. Since women were expected to bring dowries with them upon entering a Carthusian charterhouse, Beatrice's family must have been of at least comfortable financial status. Beatrice's biographer was Margaret of Oingt (c.1240–1310), a Carthusian nun and a mystic who composed mystical treatises in both Latin and Francoprovencal, her native dialect.

Beatrice entered the nearby Carthusian charterhouse of Parmenie (Isere, France) at age 13. Outstanding in her charity, humility, and compassion, she was equally zealous in the severity of her fasts and abstinences. She is reported to have had many graces bestowed upon her, including the sense that Jesus was always at her side and in her heart. The text reports this experience: "In this manifestation of grace He came to her like a person who kissed her vigorously and lovingly."[2]

Up to this point in the young life of Beatrice, there is no suggestion of heroic asceticism other than that she inflicted severe fasts and abstinences upon herself, an expression which need not convey more than the customary level of asceticism for the strict and austere Carthusian convents. After a year or two, however, the devil began to torment her in all possible ways. Beatrice responded by imposing increasingly severe penances upon herself. Even the biographer Margaret of Oingt acknowledges that Beatrice used practices in her penances "which were sometimes immoderate."[3] When it was Beatrice's turn to cook in the kitchen, she kept her face so close to the heat of the oven that she felt as if her brain was on fire and that her eyes fell out of her head. The text proceeds to provide other details of Beatrice's rapid development of serious self-injurious behaviors:

> She always carried live coals in her naked hands so that her skin burned completely, including the palms. Of all this, she felt nothing. She punished herself so severely that blood was running down her body on all

sides. She evoked the Passion of our Lord so strongly that she pierced her hands with blunt nails until it came out at the back of her hand. . . . When she could not do anything else, she walked through the snow and ice without shoes.[4]

The devil, defeated in his plans for Beatrice's downfall by her great mortifications, began to torment her even more in her sleep with foulness and filth than he had done when she was awake. A critical moment of spiritual insight then occurs. Beatrice realizes that she is losing the battle with the devil and she becomes afraid. What she realizes is that, in the struggle with the devil over control and ownership of her body and its sexual urges, she has tried to fight the fight on the devil's own terms, using her body as the battleground. The more the devil tormented her with bodily urges, the more she mortified her body. Not only was she losing the fight, but she was losing her spirituality too, which is, of course, the terms of the ultimate loss. In what had to be the turning point of her young life, she recognizes the futility of fighting like with like (literally, fire with fire, will with will), since the body and willfulness were the devil's domain, and she turns to prayer. Abandoning her obstinacy, she "implored Our Lady to help and rescue her and in her great pity to protect her from the power and tricks of the devil."[5]

Beatrice has a vision of Our Lady in the form of a beautiful 15-year-old maiden who promises to defend her against the devil. Beatrice immediately felt complete peace. A few nights later, the devil reappeared with the intention of violently tormenting her in another way, but Beatrice, instead of resuming her harsh mortifications, began to recite the Ave Maria and the devil, becoming confused, departed. We hear no more from him.

The lesson of grace through prayer rather than heroic asceticism and illness needed to be taught to Beatrice again. A second moment of enlightenment comes to Beatrice when, after wishing for a long time that she could be dead in order to be united with Christ, she hears a man's sweet voice while she is praying at the altar after vespers.

> While He was speaking to her, He told her clearly not to desire such a thing and not to ask Him for such a thing, "for," He said, "I do not want you to die yet." He told her that so kindly and so lovingly that she was convinced that neither she nor anyone else would ever be able to convey this impression. And the great desire of death that she had left her heart immediately and she was greatly comforted; now she desired to keep on living in the service of our Lord.[6]

As the longing for death left her heart, Beatrice then understood that the illness which had resulted from her weakness interfered with her serving Christ, and she prays to the Lord, because it is his will that she go on living:

to give me health for my soul and my body and especially for the illness of my head so that I may always have your grace and will always be able to persevere in your service with devotion.[7]

The *Vita* leaves unstated just what the "illness of my head" might be. There is no evidence that the illness of her head refers to any of the categories of what we now term major mental illnesses (schizophrenia, mania, melancholic depression), nor does her subsequent spiritual development suggest anything in the way of sustained mental illness. We may assume that she is referring in some manner to the thoughts and emotions that intruded upon her quest for closeness with God. We have referred to these torments as mental clutter, with the terminology of "horrible foulness and filth" as used in the text suggesting some combination of sexual and blasphemous thoughts and images. In desperation, Beatrice utilized self-injurious practices as a means of interfering with her intrusive mental imagery. Furthermore, the reference in the text that she "felt nothing" when carrying live coals strongly suggests either that she was able to put herself in a hypnotic-like trance state in preparation for picking up the coals or that she was already in a trance state mesmerized with sexual and blasphemous imagery. In either case, her self-injurious behaviors interrupted the mental circle of unacceptable sexual associations.

Although adolescence is a stormy period in Western cultures, the medieval religious focus on chastity and continence gave particular salience and urgency to the struggle against the flesh in that society. While asceticism was not for every adolescent, the subculture of the Carthusian monasteries in general and, to a less degree, the general zeitgeist, certainly made it clear to fervent adolescents who were considering a religious vocation that engagement in ascetic practice was one important way committed young individuals were expected to behave. But the ascetic practices of sleep deprivation, fasting, and mortification of the flesh had particular relevance for those God-driven adolescents of the late medieval period that transcended the more personal function of subduing the carnal desires and the important social function of identifying oneself as belonging to an exclusive peer group.

Beatrice's preoccupation with adolescent assaults upon the flesh and the subsequent evolution to a more contemplative pathway toward spirituality represents one typical pattern of the development of holiness. What is so fascinating about Beatrice is that the critical moments of transition are so visibly articulated. There are several complementary factors that drive some adolescents into heroic asceticism. The reasons may differ greatly, but in Western cultures, adolescents manifest their struggles with their pubertal changes by developing various forms of ascetic behaviors. Cultures recognize and institutionalize the apparent necessity for such adolescent practices, shaping and making meaningful the particular way the pubertal struggle will occur. Rites of passage usually mark the entry and exit from this developmental stage. The medieval world provided two common forms by which adolescent women were expected to combat their emerging sexuality:

early marriage or a life devoted to God. If the latter, then a certain measure of healthy asceticism was expected.

Adolescent asceticism in the late medieval framework functioned as the apprenticeship program into the spiritual life. It taught the inspired adolescents both the possibilities and limitations of directly waging war against their bodies. Asceticism is a lesson in applied philosophy of mind, enabling the adolescent to discover, by experimentally varying the type, duration, and intensity of the ascetic exercise, the intricacies of the mind–body relationship. The ascetic regimen, whether orderly or desperate, provides a program for the future holy person in the training and discipline of the body. It teaches the adolescent that doing injurious things to the body does things to the mind, to the thoughts and emotions and spiritual focus.

Adolescent asceticism is early practice in altering one's state of consciousness. Although there are many points of difference between medieval religious adolescents and modern secular youth, much of the relentless training of present-day olympic-class young athletes involves preparation for shifting into altered states at the moment of competition, called flow experiences, that permit truly unbelievable physical performances. The same holds true for the virtuoso performances of gifted musicians, who often transport themselves into some sort of trance state in order to prevent the deleterious intrusion of self-conscious attention into the details of their creative presentation.

Paradoxically, and this point was clearly discovered by Beatrice of Ornacieux, this early asceticism can prepare the way for meditation and deeper spirituality. Since there were few formal procedures and programs in medieval Europe for learning induction techniques into trance states, each adolescent initiate had to learn this more or less for herself/himself, although there were informal peer instruction and the *vitae* of established holy persons.

In general, those adolescents who went on to develop a rich mystical life abandoned heroic asceticism as they realized that the major struggle had to be on a spiritual (intellectual/emotional/contemplative) level rather than a corporeal one. When ones sees either the continuation of harsh self-injurious behaviors into mature adulthood or the onset of heroic asceticism in adulthood rather than in adolescence, as in the case of the Merovingian queen Radegund, than one certainly has to consider the likelihood that we are in the presence of neurotically driven rather than, or alongside of, spiritually driven motivations. In Radegund's case, there is the strong sense that her extremely harsh self-injurious behaviors beginning in mid-adulthood are at least as much in the service of attempts at resolution of painful childhood and adolescent memories of the massacre of her family and its aftermath as they are related to direct pursuit of closeness with God. This is an idiosyncratic pattern of heroic asceticism that is in contrast to the more usual pattern that peaks in adolescence or young adulthood exemplified by the two Beatrices.

12

HENRY SUSO

When William James, in his 1901 Gifford Lectures on Natural Religion at the University of Edinburgh, later published as the classic *The Varieties of Religious Experience*, was casting about, in his extended discussion of asceticism, for a figure to exemplify a psychopathic individual, he could come up with none better than Henry Suso (1295–1366).[1] Suso's almost ceaseless dedication to designing instruments and garments with which to inflict wounds upon his flesh has no model for modern comprehension and empathy other than as an expression of mental illness. We could understand and even excuse or forgive a mentally ill person for these harsh self-injurious behaviors; otherwise, James seems to imply, it suggests a masochism that could only be viewed as sick.

Yet in many ways, Suso represents the culmination (apotheosis) of several strands of medieval religious and spiritual development prominent in those holy persons dedicated to the individual pursuit of God.[2] If we condemn or dismiss Suso as mentally ill, must we not also do so, even if to a lesser extent, to those other holy persons who led the way on Suso's ascetic path to holiness, even if less ferociously? Suso pushed the limits of self-mortification of the flesh, not in terms of near-lethality of his heroic ascetic practices, but with an unrelenting intensity that drove him to greater and greater assaults upon his body. Yet there is never the sense, despite James's judgment, that Suso elevated this practice into a virtuous end in itself, for he states repeatedly that suffering was necessary as identification with the suffering Christ, as subduing bodily desires, as combating his tendency to settle for a comfortable level of mediocre religious sentiment, and as submitting his will and willfulness to the will of God. Suffering, both physical and moral, was the first and prolonged step on the pathway to God, leading to the attainment of detachment, which itself was essential as the intermediate step toward mystical union with God. In the *Little Book of Truth*, the disciple asks Eternal Wisdom how the person who is truly detached acts. The reply is:

> He withdraws from himself and all things withdraw along with this self.
> ... He exists in an ever-present now, free of selfish intentions and perceives his perfection in the smallest thing as the greatest.[3]

Even during his most intense periods of self-injurious behaviors, Suso did not remain mired in his mortification practices, for these paralleled, and possibly helped create an avid pursuit, at both an intellectual and ecstatic level, of an increasingly close relationship with God that had as its goal mystical unification with the Godhead. Since union with God can only be a temporary state which one moves into and out of while living with a bodily existence in this world, the achievement of detachment, the diminution of the importance of self, represents the relatively permanent change of character that signifies the coming of holiness.

Henry Suso was born Heinrich von Berg near Constance in 1295 to a family of the minor nobility. Little is known of his childhood because Suso's writings, including his "autobiography," record his spiritual development with a minimum of commentary on his life in the world except as it pertains to his persecutions and spiritual struggles. Suso's life story, such as it is, is contained in *The Life of the Servant*, a third-person narrative in which it is understood that Suso is the servant. However, the authorship of *The Life of the Servant* is unclear. Suso gave spiritual direction to Elsbeth Stagel (?–1360), a nun of the Dominican convent at Toss, whom Suso considered his spiritual daughter. During their meetings, Elsbeth asked Suso to provide personal examples and experiences from his life that would help her understand the pathway to God. Unbeknownst to Suso, Elsbeth, who was herself of the nobility and well educated, kept his letters to her and also wrote down all that Suso told her, not only his theology, but also his extreme penitential practices and his personal struggles in yoking himself to the will of God. When Suso learned about this, he demanded that Elsbeth turn over the writings, which he then began to burn. However, a celestial voice commanded him to save the second installment of manuscripts because they might be helpful in the edification of other religious persons. Probably toward the end of his life, and after Elsbeth's death (sometime between 1360 and 1365), Suso reworked the texts left by Elsbeth and, so that posterity would not disseminate partial and corrupted texts of his works, collected the biographical portions as *The Life of the Servant*, added several other religious treatises, and two of his sermons, all under the title of *The Exemplar*.

In view of this background, it is open to conjecture as to what parts of *The Life of the Servant* is Elsbeth's writing and what is Suso's. The answer to this question, unanswerable with the information available to date, will determine whether *The Life of the Servant* is to be considered autobiographical, biographical, or autohagiographical. Suso himself writes that his work is not always to be taken literally, but rather in the spirit of what he was trying to convey about the role of suffering and detachment and the pathway to God. Frank Tobin, in his introduction to *The Exemplar*, discusses the literary and historical controversies that have ensued regarding the authorship of *The Life of the Servant*.[4] To the extent that a significant portion of *The Life of the Servant* was written by Elsbeth Stagel, this would represent a reversal of the usual hagiographical pattern in which a male cleric writes the *vita* of a holy woman who has been his spiritual guide.

We have reason to believe that Suso was considered a frail and sickly child. Once, while in an internal dispute with a youthful angel who informs him that God will make his burdens even heavier, Suso complains:

> Dear Lord in heaven, what do you want from me? Am I the only sinner around and is everybody else just, that you use the rod only on poor me but spare it with regard to so many others? You have been treating me like this since I was a child when you tormented my tender nature with long, hard periods of sickness. I thought by now it was enough![5]

We have few specifics about Suso's parents, other than that mother was devout and "full of God" and would have liked "to live in a religious manner." Father, by contrast, was "full of the world and opposed this [mother's religious aspirations] with unrelenting severity."[6] Suso refrains from further direct criticism of father but his antipathy toward father is evident indirectly. In *The Life of the Servant*, a vision is described in which Suso's father appears to him after his death, shows Suso the "sorry sight of his suffering in purgatory," and asks for Suso's help in release from purgatory, which Suso gives. Father returns in a later vision to thank his son for his intercessions.[7] Suso's mother also appeared to him in a vision and, by contrast, showed him "the great reward she had received from God."[8]

Further evidence of Suso's regard and love for his mother and his unhappiness with father is that Suso dropped the family name of von Berg and took on his mother's family name (Sus) as his own.[9] Adoption of mother's family name involves rejection of the von Berg patronymic and, presumably, much of the worldly values that it signified. One could imagine that father's unrelentingly severe rejection of mother's pleas for a religious marriage, presumably referring at the least to her request for celibacy between the couple, was equally matched by his scorn for his sickly and whiny child who embodied none of the paternal lineage's virtues of virility and stoicism. After reading passage after passage of Suso's complaints about pain and suffering, we could see that William James's aversion to this behavior must be mild compared to father's contemptuous responses.

It is too much of a modern topos to refer to Suso as a "mother's boy" but such was surely the case. The relevance of this for our purposes is that Suso identified himself with mother's virtues, especially her long-suffering patience as a victim of father and, ultimately, her spiritual aspirations, while rejecting not just father's class values, but also, more importantly, those particularly objectionable characteristics of father that he also found in himself. If we can assume that Suso has in mind his own sexual lusts when the text refers to his blood having been "cooled and his nature crushed,"[10] then he must have been aware that this was one of father's conspicuous vices. The autobiography makes mention that Suso's mother confided in him how much she suffered from the "vexing dissimilarity between her and her husband," and his unrelenting opposition to permitting her to live in a religious manner.¹¹ He must have been aware that part of what father would not surrender was his spousal privileges. This passage also establishes that young Henry became his mother's confidant, a problematic role for a young boy.

The problem of what to do with Henry was happily solved by placing him in a Dominican monastery in Constance at the age of 13. This was a good fit, although young Suso probably suffered from the separation from his mother (and vice versa). A new problem for Suso arose, however, for Dominican rule did not allow entrance into religious life of youth under the age of 15 years. Presumably, a family donation to the monastery secured his early acceptance there. In later life, Suso was much tormented by thoughts that nothing he did was of spiritual value because his entrance into the Dominican order had been secured through simony, the purchase of religious appointment through a material gift.¹²

Suso received the customary theological education at the monastery, which included study of the Bible, the Divine Office, rules and regulations of the Order of Preachers, and lives of the saints, including the Desert Fathers who were known for their asceticism. Many aphorisms of the desert fathers are included, as advice to Elsbeth Stagel and other beginning religious, in Part II of *The Life of the Servant*.¹³ Suso would also have studied philosophy later, especially Aristotle and Aquinas.

Suso, by his own description, was an unexceptional and undistinguished novice and friar. That his entrance into the monastery at age 13 must not have been the result of precocious religious sentiment is made evident by his own comments in the opening paragraphs of *The Life of the Servant*:

> The first beginnings of his life as the servant occurred when he was eighteen years old. Although by that time he had already worn the habit of his order for five years, his spirit was full of distraction. If God would keep him from those many failings, which might compromise his reputation, then, it seemed to him, things would in general not be so bad.¹⁴

Here the theme is struck early of concern with his reputation, which becomes prominent in Suso's later struggles with pride, vanity, and the opinions of others. The other note expressed here, one that resonates with Suso's ongoing ambivalence about strict discipline, is the temptation just to get by with minimal to moderate exertion. Suso seems to be saying that, if only he can slide by without doing anything egregious that would reflect badly on him (and perhaps his mother), this sort of comfortable life would be acceptable. Suso does, however, allude, with intimations of Augustine prior to his conversion in the garden, to "his noticing an emptiness within himself whenever he gave his attention to things he desired. It seemed to him that there must be somehow something else that would calm his undisciplined heart, and his restlessness caused him torment."¹⁵ This uneasiness about the direction his life was taking, his desuetude about his spiritual indifference served as the preparation for a relatively sudden conversion experience. Suso makes clear that this change, which surprised everybody, came about by God touching and calling him.

This sudden calling from God was only the beginning of years of struggle between his intense spiritual quest and his habitual aversion to discomfort, effort, and discipline. He would argue back and forth to himself, and to God, about the reasonableness and wisdom of taking the easy road, of living a religious life, but with restraint. Such a struggle, although not often articulated as clearly as Suso does, is a prominent theme in the spiritual life of many ascetics, who cannot rest content with a life of comfortable and moderate commitment to God. The struggle is much too monumental, and yielding to the temptation of moderation, of not overdoing one's asceticism, of not offending others with one's zealousness, is perceived as complete capitulation to the devil.

Shortly after Suso's conversion around 18 years of age, he embarked on a path of heroic asceticism that proceeded almost relentlessly until a vision at age 40 told him that self-injurious behavior was no longer a necessary or desirable course for him. Sometime after his youthful conversion, he had had his first ecstatic experience while in the choir after the community had eaten their midday meal. His soul was swept up and he lost all sense of time and bodily desire and sensation except for an awareness of bright light and "a bursting forth of the delight of eternal life, present to his awareness, motionless, calm."[16] The text remarks that what Suso saw and heard cannot be expressed. The experience, judged to last about a half-hour to an hour, left Suso filled with the sweet taste of heaven and with the feeling as if he were floating on air, although he realizes that, to the outside observer, he appears unchanged.

This mystical experience had a profound effect on Suso, leaving him with a sense of what union with the divine was like and an intense longing to return to God's loving embrace. However, Suso was early into his mystical pathway. While the mystical experience fortified him against the many barriers he would encounter, these difficulties mounted in the form initially of an inner struggle between his desire for union with God and God's demands that renunciation of all earthly comfort and attachment to all worldly pleasures and relationships are necessary to win God's love. The path to Christ entailed experiencing the suffering that Christ experienced in his passion, the scorn, derision, the flagellation, the bitterness, and all accepted joyfully. But suffering did not come easily to Suso; he was a complaining, not a joyful sufferer. Once when he was supposed to contemplate the suffering of Jesus and to devote himself to imitation of such suffering, he found it hard and bitter. The text proceeds:

> Because of this he was then severely scolded by God, And he heard it being said inside him: "Don't you know that I am the gate through which all true friends of God must force their way if they are to achieve true blessedness? You must fight your way through by means of my suffering humanity if you are really to come to my true Godhead."[17]

Or again, Suso, in his ongoing back-and-forth debates about the linkage between the necessity for renunciation and harsh self-inflicted pain and the pursuit of God, counters his own pleas for moderation with the following divinely infused thought: "No one can be a suitor unless he is a sufferer, nor can anyone be a lover unless he is a martyr."[18] Suso embarks upon a course of harsh asceticism, described in bloody and anguished detail, that goes on for twenty-two years. Interspersed with these self-imposed tortures of the flesh are descriptions of ordinary-type visions of conversations with angels and saints, and moments of extraordinary raptures and mystical closeness with God. But it was these unrelenting assaults upon his own body that brought William James, ignoring Suso's mystical side, to the judgment of Suso as the example par excellence of an abnormal personality utilizing religious principles in the service of one's sickness.

What is it that James is referring to? The first mention of Suso's self-injurious behavior is rather tame and innocent compared to that which progressively evolved, and has symbolic significance as opposed to the later fierce attacks on his body. Soon after his initial mystical experience in the choir of the church, Suso takes his stylus and began to make a series of stab-like strokes forming the name IHS into the flesh above his heart. Blood poured profusely from his flesh and ran down his chest, but because of his burning love he hardly noticed the pain. "The letters were about as thick as a flattened piece of grass and as long as a section of the little finger."[19] Suso carried the name in secret over his heart until his death. During times of adversity, looking at the name engraved on his skin made his trials easier to bear.

The text alludes to the, at times, close connection between self-injurious behaviors and the altered states of consciousness in which visions and ecstasies occur: "And once in the morning after a period of suffering it happened that he was surrounded by the heavenly hosts in a vision."[20] Following the passage, and within a section of the text that describes many other visions to help him endure his sufferings, Suso, on the eve of the feast of the Angels (September 29) puts on a new penitential chain. This occurs nine months after his initial ecstasy in the choir, which took place on the feast of St. Agnes (January 21).

Prior to the descriptions of the full intensity of Suso's self-inflicted scourging, the text also describes Suso's attempts at, and conflicts about, imposing the discipline of denial in the areas of food, warmth, and human companionship. He finds himself in a dream craving a piece of fruit, and claims in that dream that his preference is only for dear Wisdom (Jesus) and not for the fruit. However, he immediately realizes with admirable self-honesty that this bravado claim is not true, that he really does desire the apple (symbolic significance of the apple is not noted in the text). When he awakens, he is ashamed of the strength of his yearning and vows to deprive himself of fruit, a resolve that he maintains for two years.[21] He does not allow himself to enjoy the pleasures of food, wine, and warmth as did his brethren in the monastery. As Lent draws near, he vows not to partake of the "fleeting harmful pleasures of the earthly carnival" and mentally prepares to have his own spiritual carnival. But the sacrifice does not come easily.

During carnival time he had entered a warm room before compline to warm up because he was cold and hungry. However, nothing was as bad as the thirst he suffered. He saw people eating meat and drinking good wine. Because he was hungry and thirsty, this disturbed him inwardly. He then went outside and began to feel sorry for himself, sighing deeply from the bottom of his heart.[22]

Suso's asceticism remained at this moderate level of denial of comfort and pleasures, and the text informs us that "God spoiled him for a long time with divine consolations [visions] which he craved passionately." But Suso was lukewarm in contemplating and imitating the sufferings of Jesus, which he found hard and bitter. Finally he was scolded by God as to the centrality of suffering in the achievement of true blessedness. Frightened, Suso, every night after matins, went to the chapter room and began to focus his attention on the Stations of the Cross. His imagination was so vivid that he felt as if he were walking by Jesus' side. He surrendered his will to God. When he reached the cross, Suso took his discipline (a whip made of knotted cords) and "with heartfelt agony nailed himself on the cross with his Lord, begging him that neither life nor death, joy nor sorrow be able to separate his servant from him."[23] By far the major portion of these nightly observances were devoted to imagining that he literally walked and suffered along with Christ each of the harrowing events that ensued after the Last Supper; it was only as he imagined Christ being nailed to the cross that he physically participated by whipping himself.

Shortly thereafter, Suso begins his extremely harsh self-injurious behaviors in earnest. The text makes it very clear that pain and deprivation were alien to Suso's nature; he complained to God frequently about the hardship of his yoke, but God's replies were always that Suso's efforts at asceticism had to be increased. The middle section of *The Life of the Servant*, from Chapters 15 to 22, describe in detail the lengths to which Suso was driven to inflict upon himself sufficient chastisement in order to reach his goal. Troubled by his lively nature, the meaning of which is never fully spelled out, but which we take to mean bodily desires of many types, including sexual ones, Suso practiced rigorous penances to make the flesh subject to the spirit, some of which he describes as follows:

> For a long time he wore a hairshirt and an iron chain until he bled like a fountain and had to give it up. For his lower body he had an undergarment made secretly with thongs worked in to which a hundred and fifty pointed nails had been attached. They were of brass and had been filed sharp. The points of these nails were always turned toward his body. He would tighten the garment around him, binding it together in the front so that it would fit more tightly against his body and the pointed nails would press into his flesh. The garment was made long enough to reach up to the navel. He would sleep in it at night. In summer, when it was hot and he was weak, or when he had gone for bloodletting and was

lying a captive of his misery and tortured by vermin, he would sometimes lie there, groaning to himself and gnashing his teeth, and he would turn this way and that, as a worm does when it is being pricked with a sharp needle.[24]

But even these sufferings were not enough to chasten Suso sufficiently. He draped a leather belt around his neck and fashioned two slings that held his arms and hands tightly against his neck all night long. Then he hit upon the idea of placing brass tacks within a pair of leather gloves with the sharp points sticking outward, so that, if he tried to remove his hairshirt or even scratch at the vermin eating his body, the tacks would scratch him and leave big, ugly gashes. The skin of his arms and chest would begin to fester, thus increasing the pain caused by each new wound.[25] If he stopped for a few days to permit recovery, he would begin again all the more and cause fresh wounds. Suso had the thought that his body should bear some direct sign of his sympathy for the sufferings of the crucified Jesus. He made for himself a wooden cross about a long as the span of a man's outstretched hand and hammered thirty iron nails into the cross. He fastened the cross to his bare back and carried it against his flesh day and night for eight years. In the last year, he hammered seven more needles into the wood, but left them sticking out even further.

The text proceeds to mention that when Suso first fastened the cross to his back, he did not think he would be able to endure it. He took the cross off and bent the nails a bit on a stone. But "soon he regretted his unmanly cowardice, and so he sharpened them all again with a file and put it back upon himself. It rubbed his back open where the bones were, making him bloody and torn."[26] Again, not content with these tortures, Suso experimented with variations on these themes, whipping himself with the discipline that carried a hook that would get under and rip his skin. He rubbed salt and vinegar into the wounds to increase his suffering.

Suso included heroic fasting, tortures of posture, and sleep deprivation within his ascetic practices. He never bathed nor, presumably, cleansed his festering wounds. In winter, he slept, wrapped just in a heavy cloak that did not cover his feet, on a doorframe. If he stretched his legs out, they froze; if he pulled his legs under him, he felt the pain of the sharp needles.

> His feet became diseased, his legs swelled up as though he were getting dropsy. His knees were bloody and open, his hips full of scratches from the undergarment of hair, his back covered with wounds from the cross. His body was wasted because of immoderate fasting, his mouth parched from not drinking, and his hands shook from weakness. In such torment he spent day and night.[27]

When Suso's twenty-two years of self-inflicted bodily torments were coming to a conclusion, "his whole physical being had been so devastated that the only choice open to him was to die or give up such exercises."[28] God ordered him to cease his self-injurious behaviors. As far as we can tell from reconstructing the inexact time frames of when Suso met Elsbeth Stagel and when his heroic asceticism ceased, it appears that they both occurred when Suso was around 40 years of age. We can conjecture that the special relationship to Elsbeth influenced a softening in Suso's drives toward self-injurious behaviors. At the least, Suso's gradual physical deterioration would have made it increasingly difficult for him to travel to the monastery at Toss and other monasteries where he provided spiritual guidance to Dominican nuns. But equally important might have been his concern that Elsbeth would take up heroic asceticism herself, based upon her admiration for her spiritual teacher. She did begin to increase her disciplinary practices and Suso told her to stop, that his form of heroic asceticism was not for everyone.

When Suso was told by God to cease his own self-injurious behaviors, he was initially elated; he wept for joy. He thought that he had earned the right to live out his life in relative comfort, sleeping on a straw mattress and eating and drinking when hungry and thirsty. But he came to understand that he now had to work on the inner man. God informed Suso that these exterior penitential practices were nothing more than a good beginning and a breaking of the undisciplined man within him. It was time for Suso to make further progress, but in a different manner, if he were to reach his goal. With startling self-assessment, Suso realized that his "self" was still there, that he had not learned detachment, but was still dependent upon the opinion and praise of others. He told himself:

> You blanch at the sight of your adversary. When you should stand firm, you run away. When you should boldly show yourself, you hide. When someone praises you, you are all smiles. When someone finds fault with you, you are depressed. It can well be that you are in need of this advanced schooling.[29]

There followed ten years or more of Suso's spiritual journey in which he was vilified both by important persons and those he considered friends in his Dominican order and by the public. He is accused of writing heretical treatises, of being a poisoner, of fathering a child, of sacrilegiously stealing waxen figures from a local shrine at night, and of faking the bleeding of stigmata on a stone figure of Christ at which he prayed. He is scandalized when his sister runs away from her convent and takes up with bad company. He feels totally shunned by the members of his own religious community. At great discomfort to himself, he tracks her down to a hut in winter, but not before he falls into a stream at night and lies there freezing and almost lifeless for a time. When he finally reaches the hut, he faints into her arms. After he revives, he berates her at length for all the humiliation she has brought upon him. "Alas, my child, my sister, what I have had to go through because of you!"[30]

His sister, in a long and heartfelt speech, points out that she now fully realizes that she has brought misery upon him as well as herself by her sins, and apologizes for this. She tells Suso that he can best show his devotion to God by forgiving her, as he would show to others who were not his close kin. The text is ambiguous as to whether Suso perceives that, at the moment of forgiveness, his reflexive self-centered response, his focus on how much misery she has caused him, is replaced by a deeper understanding that his suffering is slight compared to what his sister has suffered, and that the charity of forgiveness changes both the judger and the sinner. For love of God, Suso forgives her and she returns to a richer religious life, literally and spiritually.

But scandal, malicious gossip, and rejection by townspeople and Dominicans alike continued to plague Suso. His despair is metaphorically described in Chapter 38 of *The Life of the Servant*:

> This suffering man was treated like a skinned carcass that has been torn to shreds by wild animals and still exudes a stench. Finally the hungry insects fall upon it and completely strip the bones that the animals have gnawed on, and they fly away with what they have sucked in. Thus was he carried away piece by piece into distant lands by these seemingly good people.[31]

Finally, Job-like, Suso retreats into privacy and groans again and again from the depths of his being. He says to himself, "Oh God, what do you have in store for me?" Suso hears God's answer within himself, "Is this your detachment? Is this the steadfastness in joy and sorrow that you have so often brought others to appreciate – that one should leave oneself for God in patience and have no other support?" Suso, as before, continues to protest that detachment in such circumstances is not possible, but then, as before, a half-day later, he becomes calm and surrenders himself to God's will, saying, "If it cannot be otherwise, you will be done."[32] Sometime afterward, "when it seemed time to God, the sufferer was compensated for all the suffering that he had endured by interior peace of heart, calm repose, and radiant grace."[33]

During all these years of hardship, Suso's spiritual development toward mystical union with God does proceed, almost despite himself. God gives him consolations in the form of conversations, visions, and ecstasies. Once, during a period of harsh physical asceticism, he laments his surfeit of suffering, crying, "Why was I ever born into this world that I have to suffer such want in the midst of abundance?" He hears a voice in his soul telling him to cheer up, that God will soon console him and make him joyful.[34] When he goes to bed thirsty, he has a dream of a woman from heaven assuring him that she will bring him not a drink for the body, but a spiritual drink of great purity. At another time, Suso, deep in contemplation about his misery, importunes God to "let some sweet fruit of good teaching spring forth so that we poor struggling men might bear our suffering with more patience and can better offer up our afflictions for the praise of God." Suso is transported into himself and beyond himself, and in a state of withdrawal from his senses feels his soul dissolved in his body and the arms of his soul stretched forth to the far ends of the world in heaven and on earth. Suso thanks and praises God and asks that he might offer himself up as a sacrifice to bear the suffering of others who have ever suffered.[35] There is a progression in *The Life of the Servant* from conversations with God and angelic young men about the rationale for suffering to metaphoric visions of heaven to the types of raptures and ecstasies in which Suso's soul is caught up in union with God.

If the measure of Suso were limited just to his extreme austerities and years of self-inflicted tortures, it would be difficult to disagree with William James's assessment. There are many aspects of Suso's behavior and personality that are downright disagreeable and embarrassingly transparent in their self-pity and self-centeredness, at least to the modern reader. The episode narrated previously about his sister's fall into sin exemplifies how Suso places his own discomfort and inconvenience at the center of events that most directly affect others more than himself. Much of the spiritual teaching in *The Life of the Servant* involves the process whereby one achieves detachment from worldly concerns. Had Suso reached any degree of detachment at the time of this episode, his embarrassment at his sister's disgrace would not have been the primary issue. For Suso, detachment comes slowly and only at the cost of repeated painful lessons.

Even God becomes impatient with Suso's incessant whining and weeping. In passages that employ the knighthood metaphor, Suso almost gives up on God because of the serious suffering that God visited upon him. He forgets all about the promises he made to God in his resolve about spiritual knighthood. He becomes sad and irritable with God. But the next morning, calm enters his soul and with his senses withdrawn something speaks within him:

> "How is it now with your outstanding knightly endeavors? What good is a knight of straw and a man made out of cloth? Great daring in good times and then giving up in bad times – no one has ever won the ring you long for that way.[36]

Suso does not back down immediately, even to God. He continues the inner dialogue by noting that the tournaments one has to endure for God are much too long and difficult. The response is that the rewards for knightly fidelity and service are constant and last forever. Suso is struck by this and acknowledges that he had missed the point, but then cannot resist one last bid humbly to complain: "Lord, I was wrong, but allow me to weep in my misery, for my heart is so full." But the reply is swift. "You miserable creature! Are you going to weep like a woman? You are disgracing yourself at the court of heaven. Wipe your eyes and act cheerful so that neither God nor man notice that you have wept because of your suffering."[37]

But Suso has many saving graces that more than balance his lachrymose martyrdom. He does have a sense of humor and can even make fun of himself when he is not too caught up in his own complaining. When he loses sight of his ultimate goal, it is only briefly, with a full return to his spiritual commitment. What we can appreciate most about Suso, once we recover from and look past the horrendous details of his self-injurious behaviors followed by his complaining about how he has to suffer, is that, perhaps more than any other ascetic/mystic, he articulates and integrates a theology and personal psychology of the centrality of suffering within his life. With or without self-injurious behaviors, for he acknowledges that heroic asceticism is not for everybody nor is it the only form of suffering, Suso describes the steps on the road to closeness with God. Suffering, even heroic asceticism, are not goals in themselves, but means to detachment and the surrender of one's will to God.

In the *Little Book of Eternal Wisdom*, eternal Wisdom describes the suffering that she as the human Jesus endured at the crucifixion, and explains to Suso:

> No one can reach the heights of the divinity or unusual sweetness without first being drawn through the bitterness I experienced as man. The higher one climbs without sharing the path of my humanity, the deeper one falls. My humanity is the path one takes; my suffering is the gate through which one must pass who will come to what you are seeking. . . . Stir yourself to boldness, because your heart must often die before you overcome your nature and must in fear pour out bloody sweat because of much painful suffering in which I shall make you ready for me. . . . After this you shall be let out with me along the desolate way of the cross, as you withdraw from your own willing, give up yourself and all creatures, and become as truly free of all creatures in things that can interfere with your eternal salvation as a dying person when he is about to leave and has nothing more to do with the world.[38]

This passage, and many other similar ones, convey the multileveled role of suffering initially as controlling and overcoming one's nature and one's will, as perceiving the transience and emptiness of worldly goods and accomplishments, as developing Jesus' compassion for mankind by way of experiencing Jesus' suffering, and as the way to detachment which, ultimately, is the pathway to mystical union with God. Suso also takes up the question, which we all must ask, of why his suffering has to be so severe and so prolonged. The answer, again given in various forms in various passages of his writing, could only be twofold, that this is the amount of suffering necessary, because of his particular nature, to undergo the changes that encompass purification of the soul, and that this is the amount of suffering that he can endure, even when he does not think that he can. Why does Suso need so much suffering? It is in the nature of his willfulness, self-centeredness, pride, and his inordinate attachment to comfort that necessitates such a long and arduous ascetical pathway. For Suso, the pathway to detachment is through suffering.

God says to Suso:

> Your childlike reckoning you have presented me with arises from your not being always aware of the words and conduct of Christ in his suffering. You should know that God is not satisfied with the kind heart that you possess. He wants more from you. He expects this from you also: When you are mistreated by someone's words or conduct, you must not suffer it patiently. You must forget yourself so utterly that you do not go to bed until you have approached those who mistreat you and, as far as you are able, calm their raging hearts with your sweet and humble words and actions. By means of such meekness and humility you take the swords and knives out of their hands and render them powerless in their malice. Look, this is the old way of perfection that Christ taught his disciples when he said, "Behold, I send you as sheep among wolves."[39]

Suso emerges from the altered state of consciousness in which he received this communication and finds his new task very onerous. It is difficult to think about, and even more difficult to carry out. Nevertheless, he listens to God and begins to learn denial of self and charity to others. These exercises lead ultimately to detachment, which is described in various passages as "withdrawing from oneself and all things – such people's hearts and minds are so completely lost in God that they somehow have no consciousness of self."[40] In the *Little Book of Truth*, Suso asks Truth about the attributes of the detached person. He is told that the detached person, in respect to time, "exists in an ever present now, free of selfish intentions"; in respect to others, the detached person "enjoys the companionship of people, but without their making a deep impression on him. He loves them without attachment, and he shows them sympathy without anxious concern." The detached person is not freed from exterior exercises, i.e. some degree of ascetical practices, but continues to practice the usual exercises, performing them more or less frequently as strength and the occasion permit.[41]

Detachment, unlike asceticism, is an intermediate goal in itself, because it is the foundation for proper relations to humankind and God. One must have detachment for the worldly level of existence in order to have attachment or closeness and, ultimately, union with God. Furthermore, Suso learned that he must also give up attachment not just to worldly goods but to the consolations and visions that God gave him to carry him through difficult periods, for these consolations too, which he craved so passionately, can distract the seeker from moving beyond the joys of visions and heavenly music to the absence of self and self-consciousness that is union with God. In essence, the risk is that the holy person will pursue and settle for vision-experiences as the final goal, because they offer such comfort as well as worldly approbation, failing to understand that even this represents one more attachment that interferes ultimately with closeness to God.

Union with God goes beyond the consolations of conversations with holy persons or angelic figures or even with Christ as eternal wisdom or truth. In union with God, which is in essence indescribable and ineffable to human comprehension, "a person's created spirit is drawn up to where it could not come by its own power. This rapture takes from him images, forms, and multiplicity [all is one]; he loses all awareness of himself and all things."[42] When his spiritual daughter (Elsbeth) asks him about where and how one experiences the Godhead, Suso, in Chapter 52 of *The Life of the Servant* replies:

> Now where is the "where" of the pure divinity of the Son? It is in the brilliant light of divine unity, and this is according to his nameless name a nothingness; according to one in rapture a stillness in being; according to one returned to himself the single nature of the Trinity; according to his own individuality a light of himself, as he is the uncreated source; the is-ness giving being to all things. And in the darkness beyond distinct manners of existing, all multiplicity disappears and the spirit loses what is its own. It disappears with regard to its own activity. This is the highest goal and the "where" beyond boundaries. In this the spirituality of all spirits ends. Here to lose oneself forever is eternal happiness.[43]

As best he can, Suso is describing, in Ursula King's phrase, his experience of "ultimate reality as eternal, uncreated truth in which all things have their source and being."[44] This is the "state of pure consciousness" as represented by the apophatic tradition in which all attributes and positive descriptions of God are negated.[45]

A few words appear necessary at this point to tackle the question of Suso's mental stability. The best way to do this is to argue the various points back and forth, just as Suso does with himself in regard to the values of comfort versus suffering. The problem with modern diagnostic and psychodynamic reasoning in such situations is that, under conditions of uncertainty and scanty information, arguments can become reduced to a formula, either diagnostic (anyone who hears voices is schizophrenic or anyone who ruminates about sin is obsessional) or psychodynamic (anyone who repeatedly hurts himself has sexual fixations). In light of these difficulties, the alternative risk to informed speculation is intellectual cautiousness to the point of paralysis.

Did Suso have a diagnosable mental illness? Given Suso's own descriptions of twenty-two years of horrendous self-injurious behavior, it is impossible not to agree with William James in part, that Suso did indeed exceed the boundaries or the limits of what can be considered normal behavior, even for the time and community in which he lived. In Karl Jaspers's sense of abnormal personality, that is, having certain personality features well in excess of those about him,[46] Suso had an abnormal personality. However, Jaspers emphasized that an abnormal personality is a disposition that represents an extreme variation of human nature and is not an illness. The features exemplified by Suso centered about his drivenness as to what was sufficient to live his life according to the suffering demanded of him by God. His heroic asceticism is a manifestation (or, medically, a symptom) of this drivenness to God and does not in itself constitute or secure an illness diagnosis.

For the notion of an abnormal personality is a descriptive and statistical construct, not a diagnosis of mental illness. Furthermore, at least to the non-psychoanalyst diagnostician, hypotheses about Suso's psychodynamics purporting to explain his behavior and reasoning do not secure a psychiatric diagnosis. As the psychiatric classification system exists at the present time, Suso does not fit into any diagnosable pattern, either of a mental illness or a specific personality disorder. This may reflect the inadequacy of a diagnostic system[47] that is limited, out of the vast richness of personality traits, to ten categories of personality disorder (paranoid, schizoid, schizotypal, histrionic, narcissistic, borderline, antisocial, dependent, obsessive-compulsive, avoidant) and a limited number of illness categories (schizophrenia, manic depressive and depressive, anxiety disorders and circularly defined impulse disorders such as gambling, credit card abuse, and sexual peculiarities). Suso is none of the above. Suso himself tells us that most of his conversations with God and his other auditory and visual perceptions occur in his thoughts and imagination and are not to be taken literally. These are not the types of hallucinations found in schizophrenia or mania. Nor is there evidence of mood disturbances in Suso's life that would argue for a diagnosis of manic-depressive illness.

One further problem regarding diagnosis that just cannot be circumvented is the controversy as to whether religious phenomena, unlike all other considerations, represent a special case that in many situations defy diagnostic categorization. Recognizing that this represents a case of special pleading, we nevertheless succumb and plead, precisely because Western culture postulates and widely accepts a transcendent universe in which religious experiences, behaviors, and ways of life can causally interact with our material universe. Experiences that would otherwise be considered pathological in our culture (hearing voices, speaking in tongues, belief in non-physicalistic interventions such as miracles) are widely held as evidence of a divine presence and reflect positively upon persons having or mediating such experiences. These experiences when occurring in religious context do not form a basis for justifying a psychiatric diagnosis. We are not speaking here of those individuals who committed suicide in response to the apocalyptic aliens hiding behind the Hale-Bopp comet, but are aware even in saying this that there is no hard-and-fast line that allows us easily to separate mental illness from eccentricity from God-driven and martyr-type behaviors. Special pleading represents special dangers, the wedge in the door of cultural relativism in which no judgments can be made by one culture about another.

Jackson and Fulford discuss the question of whether descriptive psychopathology and diagnostics can distinguish between certain classes of religio-spiritual and psychotic experiences.[48] They conclude, after examining a number of contemporary psychiatric cases, that descriptive psychiatry cannot find differences in the form (characteristics) or content (subject matter) between apparently healthy visionary experiences and the delusional/hallucinatory experience of schizophrenic and manic-depressive individuals. They suggest that one look to outcome, to the integrity and wholesomeness of the person's life before and after the religious experience, in order to form a judgment about health and pathology. But it is our opinion that this sort of judgment, while seemingly making good sense, is so much the victim (or ally) of one's own biases and values as to render suspect judgments about any but the most obviously extreme cases of mental illness. If one were to judge by the success of the immediate outcome, then Jesus, Peter, and Paul would be judged harshly. In the case of contemporary situations, where the judgment is to release or confine in hospital the excessively or eccentrically religious person, one does not have the benefit of decades or centuries to reach a decision. In addition, there is the element of moral luck, as expounded by Bernard Williams in his essay of the same name.[49] If the "future" prophet or holy person were to meet with an untimely death in an automobile accident or at the hands of an assassin before the full development of mature spirituality, then how are we ever to know if this person was a saint in the making or merely one more fervent but misguided soul?

In his environment, Suso's asceticism was excessive, but was understandable and supported in principle by the values and traditions of his society. He just lived these principles out a little more literally than most other persons, including most others in religious life. If he were to do these self-injurious behaviors today, he would most likely be committed in most jurisdictions, although interesting questions of freedom of religious practice might be raised.

If formal diagnostic activities are of little help, do psychodynamic considerations provide some insight? Whereas diagnoses are based upon what a person has in common with other persons of similar conditions, psychodynamics is based, or ideally ought to be based, on what is unique, on what makes this person the person he/she is.

Suso presents himself as requiring such heroic ascetic practices in order to subdue, initially, his attachment to desires for comfort and pleasures. If one measure of the strength of a person's drives and desires are the psychological and behavioral defenses established to bring these drives and desires under control, then we would have to assume that Suso thought that his willfulness and love of comfort and gratification of desires required excessive asceticism as a curb.

We have postulated that Suso, in his heroic asceticism, might have been attacking those sensual and selfish characteristics of his father that he saw within himself. His great efforts to prevent touching himself in any pleasurable way by use of gloves with protruding brass tacks suggests a great conflict with sexual self-stimulation, itself a common problem in adolescence and young adulthood. But the ordinary stricture of sleeping with his hands outside the blanket would not do for Suso. Suso's body was the battleground for those aspects of mother's piety and father's worldliness that he took inside himself. His tendency toward excessive complaining and seeing himself as victim may have represented identification with his mother, for he comments that mother complained to him about father. Of course, much of Suso's positive religious and spiritual sentiments also derived from the influence of his mother.

Suso and the two Beatrices display several points in common in regard to the place of asceticism in the development of their turn towards spirituality and mysticism. Their ascetic practices began in adolescence and rapidly intensified beyond the ordinary ascetic practices expected in monastic life. In the *vita* of each of these three holy individuals, mortification of the body was employed to help resolve several typical adolescent issues, most notably burgeoning sexual impulses, but also more generic problems as to who is the master of the house. Willfulness, pride in one's ascetic feats, and self-centeredness remain important issues of the adolescent that extend into mature adulthood even after sexual impulses may abate. Identification with the suffering Christ was a prominent theme in Suso's life and, to a lesser extent, in the lives of the two Beatrices too.

Earlier for the two Beatrices, and somewhat later for Suso, who in this regard appears to have had a prolonged adolescence, heroic asceticism falls away as a mature mysticism develops with its focus on closeness and eventual union with God. The excessive asceticism that was used to bring about, at times, an altered state of consciousness that is experienced as closeness to God and as consolations in the form of visions is no longer necessary or helpful in this endeavor. It finally comes about that extreme asceticism interferes with the state of mind that can best appreciate the ecstatic nature of union with God.

13

MENTAL ILLNESS, HYSTERIA, AND MYSTICISM

Even casual perusal of the descriptions of ferocious self-injurious behaviors and ecstatic states of altered consciousness found in some of the saints' *vitae* cannot help but raise questions to the modern reader of the mental stability and perhaps sanity of these medieval holy persons. How culturally relativistic do we have to be to say that a Henry Suso or a Christina Mirabilis is not pathological in his or her basic personality structure, or to say that what appear as manifestly gross excesses to observers in our culture make sense and are not abnormal given the context of another culture, such as Western Europe in late medieval times?

The modern scientific sensibility has had great difficulty in understanding and assimilating the religious "excesses" of other cultures, a problem made manifest by the absence of clear boundaries between the secular and the religious elements in most of non-Western societies. Our modern notion of separation of "church and state" is in fact a distinctly unusual social and political model in a world where the interpenetration of the divine and the mundane has always been a fact of life. Psychiatry and psychology have in general been the spokespersons for this scientific viewpoint, offering psychodynamic explanations and descriptive diagnoses for what are, to our minds, some very aberrant and almost incomprehensible experiences and behaviors.

This chapter shall examine several issues relating to psychiatry and religious experiences. The first takes up the question of whether religiosity and spirituality are factors that bring about or reflect mental instability and illness or, conversely, are factors that point to a healthy personality and moreover offer some protection against such troubles. The second topic is the question of whether diagnostic formulations developed in one culture, such as our own, have relevance to individuals of another culture, such as medieval Europe. The third topic uses the cross-cultural debate as a point of departure and looks specifically at the contentious issue of hysteria, especially but not exclusively when applied to female mystics and heroic ascetics.

Religiosity and mental illness

Psychological inquiry traditionally has taken the unsympathetic viewpoint that mysticism and extreme asceticism are manifestations of some sort of mental illness. The precise nature of the putative mental illness seems not to have been particularly important, since the labels applied to "excessive religious enthusiasm" undergo changes according to the latest explanatory models and, less elegantly, diagnostic fads and fashions. One hundred years ago, intensely religious individuals who incorporated religious excesses into their daily lives were diagnosed with hysteria, fifty years ago with paranoid schizophrenia, epilepsy, and, again, hysteria, and more recently with manic-depressive illness, anorexia nervosa, obsessionality, and borderline personality disorder.

There has been a parallel line of thought, one clearly in the minority within medical circles, that perceived these exceptional medieval individuals as God-driven persons for whom moderate asceticism proved unsatisfactory to fulfill their passion to subdue the demands of the flesh and their discomfort with embodied existence in general, and for whom the desire for an intense personal encounter with God could not be contained within ordinary bounds of pious expression. According to this more sympathetic psychological approach, the passion for God inspired and drove some individuals to do things that others would not do, but this, in itself, is not necessarily evidence of mental illness. Thus, O'Donoghue cites Peter of Alcantara (1499–1562) and John Vianney (1786–1859) as examples of an excessive asceticism, but ones that "cannot be understood except as expressions of an all-absorbing love."[1]

The debate about the mental balance and well-being versus the neurotic and/or psychotic qualities of heroic ascetics and mystics is only one aspect of a broader debate about whether religious beliefs and practices of almost any type are evidence of mental stability or vulnerability.[2] There are actually two questions: (1) Does religion primarily appeal to persons already mentally ill and vulnerable, versus to those who are relatively mature and stable? (2) Does religion contribute to health and stability or to maladjustment and mental illness in its practitioners and followers?

It must be clear that all of the terms employed in these debates are extraordinarily difficult to define and operationalize, and that a researcher or public attitude pollster can skew the findings by various choices of wording and implicit attitudes and by selecting the population to investigate and the questionnaires to be used for research.[3] Any correlation between mental health and religiosity presupposes that we know how to define and then measure all the terms in such an equation. But if we acknowledge that there is no value-free construct of mental health, then each definition of health will reflect the particular attitudes about normal personality development and functioning that a research group has come to hold within a given culture. Furthermore, it is difficult to avoid circularity in examining the relationship between mental health and religiosity, since our religious beliefs and attitudes themselves have influenced our ideas about healthy personality traits and codes of behavior. Thus, if religious precepts advocate non-violence, then personality traits that embody some degree of aggressiveness will be evaluated as undesirable and unhealthy. If independence and autonomy are valued as indicators of health, the interdependence and attachment to family or community will be viewed as evidence of pathological dependency.

The problems of setting forth standards of mental health and definitions of mental illness are more than matched in difficulty by the problems, first, of defining religiosity and spirituality, and then determining which forms of religiosity and spiritually are healthy and which are pathological. Basic problems, such as how to measure religiosity – shall we use church attendance, or hours of private prayer and reading of scriptures, or intuitive sense of spirituality – resist consensus.[4] If this were not problem enough, it is harder still to define spirituality.

As an example of such difficulties, we can examine one reasonable and thoughtful attempt to develop a research instrument to measure spirituality that is not exclusively linked to Christian beliefs and ideology, although the items of the scale do reflect a Western notion of spirituality in which faith is conceptualized as personal relatedness to an ultimate being.[5] Although the scale, named the Spiritual Experience Index, was designed with the assumption that mature spirituality would be measured along a single dimension such that a person has more of or less of whatever it is to be spiritual, field testing in fact showed that the scale consisted of two distinct dimensions. One dimension, named Spiritual Support, is about reliance on faith for sustenance and support (e.g. I gain spiritual strength by trusting in a higher power). The second dimension, named Spiritual Openness, refers to a receptive attitude toward new spiritual possibilities (e.g. I feel a strong spiritual bond with all of humankind). Vicky Genia, the researcher who designed the spiritual scale, postulates that a faith that focuses exclusively on Spiritual Support ("I gain spiritual strength by trusting in a higher power") tends to be rigid and exclusivistic, whereas a spirituality that is predominantly directed toward Spiritual Openness without a commitment to a self-chosen faith ("I feel a strong spiritual bond with all of humankind") tends to be undifferentiated and incomplete. Spiritual maturity in Genia's paradigm is defined as a balance of the two dimensions.

This example serves to illustrate the formidable difficulties in attempting to develop definitions and measures of very important but abstract constructs of human behavior and beliefs. Particularly interesting is the discrepancy between the theoretical expectation that spirituality consists of a single dimension and the empirical finding that spirituality is more complex, showing up in this study as two distinct dimensions. It also appears that Genia's definition of mature spirituality as a balance of the two dimensions of spiritual support and spiritual openness is predicated on Western enlightenment values and might not find agreement among religious groups that believe that they hold canonical Truth.

The broad distinction developed by Gordon Allport between intrinsic and extrinsic religiosity plays heavily in our culture in determining whether religious individuals are seen as healthier or less healthy than their non-religious counterparts, but this may be because many academic researchers tend to be more liberal than conservative and therefore weight the research instruments in favor of intrinsic, self-directed religious attitudes and behaviors.[6]

Intrinsic religiosity refers to the centrality of God and faith within one's daily life and thoughts. Items on an intrinsic religiosity scale include such statements as: "Nothing is as important to me as serving God as best I know how," and "My religious beliefs are what really lie behind my whole approach to life." Extrinsic religiosity refers to the use of one's religion for purposes of personal support in times of adversity and for social membership in one's community. Items on an extrinsic religiosity scale include such statements as: "Although I am a religious person, I refuse to let religious considerations influence my everyday affairs" and "It doesn't matter so much what I believe as long as I lead a moral life." The literature on the relationships between intrinsic/extrinsic religious orientation and a host of variables, such as mental health, is voluminous; the conclusions of studies, as might be anticipated, are ambiguous.

The distinctions between intrinsic and extrinsic religiosity are themselves controversial.[7] Initially each concept was defined primarily in terms of behavioral focus (e.g. church attendance; time spent in private prayer), but field studies indicated that motivation and intent were more significant in defining differences between the two types than behavioral measures, since, for example, a frequent church attendee might do so for intrinsic devotional reasons rather than for social support reasons. Our own study of 420 college students indicates that the division of religiosity into intrinsic and extrinsic no longer holds. Principal components analysis of a 29-item religiosity scale in our study yielded a single large component that accounted for most of the variance. This component contained a mixture of traditionally intrinsic and extrinsic items, suggesting that church attendance and deriving social support from belonging to a church are no longer incompatible with a personal quest for God.[8]

In general, there is no evidence that religious individuals exhibit greater emotional maladjustment or prevalence of mental illness than non-religious individuals.[9] Alternatively, many attempts to demonstrate that religious beliefs and practices are associated with better mental health have also failed, despite some reports of higher rates of recovery from medical illnesses among religiously oriented as opposed to non-religiously oriented individuals.

Thus, to cite just a few studies, Harold Koenig and colleagues examined the time to recovery from depression in 111 geriatric patients hospitalized on a medical ward who were incidentally found on admission to have diagnosable depression.[10] Two major dimensions of religiosity were measured: intrinsic religiosity and several questions relating to church attendance and participation. Koenig and colleagues found that intrinsic religiosity, but not church attendance or private religious activities (prayer and bible reading), were positively correlated with earlier remission from depression, as determined by four follow-up interviews each 12 weeks apart. In this study, intrinsic religiosity seems to be associated with a more rapid recovery from a clinical depression. The study does not inquire into what the mechanism might be that leads to a better outcome, or even whether the type of person that scores higher on intrinsic religiosity scales is also the type of person who recovers more readily from depression.

Kenneth Kendler and colleagues, utilizing a large sample (N = 1,902) of female twin pairs from their ongoing research into genetics and epidemiology, examined correlations between religiosity and various psychiatric symptoms as well as current and lifetime substance use and dependence.[11] Religious measures included church affiliation and attendance and two self-report scales of personal devotion and conservatism. The results of the study showed no strong association between any religious dimension and lifetime mental illness and current psychiatric symptoms, although low levels of depressive symptoms were related to high levels of personal devotion. Other than this interesting but relatively minor finding, measures of religiosity and mental health or illness were not related to each other. By contrast, personal devotion and personal and institutional conservatism appeared significantly to protect against current and lifetime risks for alcoholism and nicotine dependence.

In a related study of 2,616 male and female twins designed to examine the dimensions of religiosity in greater depth, as well as relationships between religiosity and psychiatric illnesses, Kendler and his group, using a 78-item religiosity scale, identified seven religiosity factors: general religiosity, social religiosity, involved God (on a day-to-day basis), forgiveness, God as judge, unvengefulness, and thankfulness.[12] Similar to our recent findings, religiosity and spirituality did not separate out into different domains in the study sample. Spirituality experience and religious practices items loaded equally into the general spirituality domain. In terms of associations between religiosity domains and mental illnesses, there was, as before, protection by religiosity factors against alcohol and drug use problems, and a complex but in general modestly positive relationship between several religiosity factors and lower risk for depression and anxiety, but not for panic disorder.

In a study more relevant to our present interest in mysticism and psychological abnormality, Leslie Francis and T. Hugh Thomas sampled 222 male clergy in the Church of Wales to examine whether charismatic religious attitudes and experiences were correlated with neuroticism and instability, as measured by the Eysenck Personality Questionnaire.[13] The Eysenck neuroticism scales measure emotional lability and tendency to worry. They found, contrary to many popular prejudices that expect charismatic individuals to be unstable and histrionic in character, that charismatic experience was correlated negatively with neuroticism, positively with extraversion, and unrelated to psychoticism (aloofness and antisocial attitudes).

Since emotional lability and over-reactivity are among the traits commonly attributed to medieval mystics, particularly mystics of the affective type, it is interesting to find these features absent in a sample of male Anglican clergy whose religiosity, unlike traditional conservative Anglicanism, emphasizes the gifts of the Spirit, including physical healing, baptism in the Spirit, and speaking in tongues. While we would not push the similarity between charismatic Anglican male clergy in the late twentieth century and medieval religious of either gender with affective mystical inclinations, each group represents a movement within their respective churches toward the central importance of a personal experience of God. In this sense, it is instructive regarding blanket assumptions about hysterical qualities in medieval mystics and ascetics to examine the psychological profile of a group of modern Anglican charismatics. In general, the psychiatric literature often points to dramatic cases of heroic asceticism and ecstatic mysticism, past and present, as proof that there is something inherently unhealthy about being too religious, or too emotional about religion. Yet such assumptions are not borne out by the study on Anglican charismatics.

Psychiatry diagnoses and religion

The controversy regarding the applicability of psychiatric diagnoses to medieval ascetics and mystics raises basic questions that are at the core of much anthropological-psychiatric debate about the legitimacy of imposing Western cultural categories of health and disease upon other cultures or subcultures. At the broadest level, there is debate whether all mental illnesses are so culturally constructed and shaped that there is practically no equivalence between illnesses in very different cultures or, conversely, whether some mental illnesses are diseases in the biological sense of the term, similar to infectious diseases and heart attacks, and therefore appear in all cultures with essentially very similar symptoms and signs.[14] It is our opinion that this question has been reasonably resolved. All cultures examined to date have psychotic forms of behaviors recognized by the indigenous population as illnesses. These illnesses share formal characteristics with our own notions of schizophrenia and manic-depressive psychoses.[15]

Nevertheless, acceptance of evidence that the group of conditions that we call schizophrenia appears to have underlying brain abnormalities and are found in all cultures need not justify extending the categorical designation of "disease" to an assortment of eccentricities that appear to be variations or exaggerations of normal behavioral and personality patterns. For example, in recent times, many socially disruptive behaviors, such as sexual assault and other forms of violence,[16] "bizarre" sexual preferences, and intemperate gambling, are "medicalized" by inclusion of these behaviors in diagnostic tables and by increasing attempts to "treat" these behaviors with medications. While this approach can be seen as a purely scientific question in the sense that we are coming to specify in what ways the neurotransmitters and brain circuitry underlying deviant behavior differ from that of conventional behavior, it still remains a question of cultural values of how to conceptualize these differences along a health–illness continuum.[17]

Furthermore, it is impossible not to be cognizant of economic and guild interests that influence psychiatric classification strategies. Thus, the convergence of the psychiatric profession and the pharmaceutical industry acts as a powerful force to expand the range of behaviors that can be considered evidence of psychiatric disease and therefore in need of pharmacological treatment.[18] If characteristic human emotions such as sadness and if socially deviant behaviors cannot readily be classified as psychiatric diseases within one's own culture, it is easy to see the problems that can arise when applying value-laden standards of normal and abnormal behavior to an alien culture.

These considerations are relevant to the question of the legitimacy of applying early twenty-first-century secular standards and diagnostic criteria even to what admittedly constituted deviant behavior, as judged by their contemporaries, in sixth or twelfth-century devoutly religious persons. The alternative, however, is to abandon all external standards and judgments about what constituted normal and abnormal forms of human behavior in other cultures.

One common observation is that often it is those individuals with mental illnesses, severe neuroses, and personality disorders who are attracted to and participate in fringe social and religious movements, or complementarily, once in these groups, it is the unstable individuals who will carry the espoused group principle to an extreme. Examples of this just within the past few decades in our society are so commonplace as to scarcely need commentary. The Jonestown mass suicides, Branch Davidian cult disaster in Waco Texas, assassination of Prime Minister Rabin by a religious zealot, and the murder of an "abortion" doctor in Florida by a religious fanatic acting in the name of God, all provide unequivocal evidence that evangelical and messianic religious movements do attract a certain number of certifiable lunatics and a larger group of impressionable and unstable followers.

Nevertheless, a problem remains by virtue of the broad recognition that, in many cases, such extremist individuals and groups embody the literal application of a dominant value espoused by some segment of the society at large. Anti-abortionists speak, at a theoretical level, to the sanctity of human life and the Jonestown participants sold their personal property in order fully to live an apostolic, communal life. In its less extreme forms, many modern religious and secular communes embody Judeo-Christian ideals of proper conduct in this temporary, earthly dwelling place.

Medieval ascetics who lived in voluntary poverty and practiced extreme fasting were living out an accepted religious ideal that the pathway to God was through mortification of the flesh and subjugation of the will. In a parallel fashion, modern anorexics who starve themselves, and bulimics who binge and purge ostensibly to become thinner or at the least to avoid gaining weight, are living out our society's secular preoccupation with dieting slimness, and what constitutes desirable body contours. In both cases, of course, conventional society ambivalently condemns the literalness of these zealous individuals, while upholding the ideals of abstinence, or thinness and fitness, as the case may be. In both cases, furthermore, social attitudes and pressures seem to have very little impact in changing the convictions and excessive behaviors of such individuals.

What is the nature of the vulnerability or special qualities of these persons such that only a few members, and not the majority, of the total population exposed to the same social environment and values become notorious by carrying their behavior to an extreme? Modern psychiatric explanations tend to be framed in terms of prevailing theories and models of the moment. Recent overlapping explanatory models include the role of genetic influences as manifested in altered brain physiology and temperament, errors in brain software programming, childhood experiences, Freudian psychodynamics, family pathology, personality constellation, and underlying psychiatric or medical illnesses.[19] The details are not important here; the basic position is that disturbed individuals will utilize available social patterns, including religious attitudes and beliefs, to express their psychopathology, and medical diagnosticians will utilize available disease models to define and explain psychopathology. A problem clearly arises for the diagnostician when the "disturbed" behavior pattern closely resembles a strongly and widely held belief system such that the boundaries between normal and excessive (or fanatic) endorsement are blurred, as in the cases of zealots within a religious society.[20]

While a psychiatric model undoubtedly explains, or accounts for, a certain number of deviant individuals, there is something circularly unsatisfactory and ethically objectionable about defining all behaviorally deviant persons (i.e. deviating from statistical norms) as having a mental illness. There are persons who perform outstanding feats both intellectually and creatively (usually considered geniuses) and physically (mountain climbers, four-minute milers, prima ballerinas) whom we would not want to call abnormal. Yet we recognize that these persons possess a degree of drivenness of purpose and resolve, as well as talent that, by definition, very few others even approach. It does not matter, but it is interesting commentary on our society, that most of our modern examples of outstanding performance tend to be secular. If a present-day religious person literally spent as many hours and as much intensity training for spirituality as a long-distance runner spends training for the Boston marathon, we would seriously question that person's mental balance. We admire the outstanding athlete or performer for accomplishing what we might aspire to, but can never achieve, just as medieval heroic ascetics were admired for the excesses of their self-injurious practices by others who had no intention of literally emulating them.

But, in fact, many of the medieval ascetics were viewed as deranged by those who knew them. The issue is not simply that we are retrospectively judging some medieval ascetics as being psychologically disturbed. This was the judgment of many of their contemporaries. For example, the life of the beguine Christina of St. Trond (1150–1224), nicknamed Christina the Astonishing, describes how, following either an illness and near-death experience or a prolonged ecstatic state accompanied by a heaven–hell vision, Christina's flight to deserted forests where she lives in trees is interpreted by the townspeople as madness, not holiness.[21] She is captured and bound with iron chains, a procedure of last resort to keep deranged persons from further harming themselves. Christina escapes and flees, and enters into a pattern of extreme self-injurious behavior, including a report that she jumped into a cauldron of boiling water. At other times, she stood in the icy waters of the Meuse for days on end. Reportedly, also during the winter, she held onto a waterwheel throughout its entire cycle so that the water ran over her head and limbs. The townspeople consider Christina mad and demon-possessed despite the fact that she had explained to them, after recovery from her initial unconscious state or near-death experience, that God approved of her plan to offer her own sufferings as penance for those poor souls already suffering in purgatory.

Christina has proven an irresistible if problematic subject for scholars of medieval mysticism. Her life is like a litmus test for one's tolerance and understanding of the excesses of Low Country and Rhineland spirituality while resisting the urge to declare the *vita* as totally untrustworthy and the saint as lunatic. Fanning withholds judgment and presents a straight forward description.[22] McGinn comments on "the difficulty modern readers have with such extreme expressions of impossible ascetic feats and often bizarre mystical phenomena."[23] McGinn suggests that Christina's story is best viewed as something close to modern science fiction that some readers find valuable because it resonates with their own hopes and fear. Amy Hollywood presents a feminist perspective of Christina's life in which Christina suffers not in order to torture her flesh, but to atone for the sins and thus reduce the extent of suffering of those in purgatory.[24] Amy Hollywood, in discussing Carol Gilligan's theory of gender differences in moral development and moral values in modern contexts,[25] refrains from pointing out that Christina's altruistic behavior exemplifies the feminine virtue of "caring" as opposed to the male virtue of "justice" as expounded by Lawrence Kohlberg.[26] In a footnote, Hollywood comments on the problems of the ahistorical use of gender theories of moral development and therefore might be reluctant to make such cross-cultural transformations.[27]

One of the problems in modern hagiographic studies is that many scholars and students comment on the excesses of the saints' behaviors, but, unlike McGinn, seem to shrink from drawing obvious conclusions.[28] It is as if to acknowledge that some of the putative holy persons were really very strange and that a percentage of these strange ones most likely had a psychiatric illness would be to vitiate the entire hagiographic enterprise. But the refusal to acknowledge mental disorder of some sort when it is obviously present and the failure to discriminate between holiness and eccentricity calls into question judgments about the more bona fide holy persons in the community of saints.

Mysticism, heroic asceticism, and hysteria

New movements, which gain notice by those elements of novelty (whether profound or trivial) that distinguish them from the routine and traditional, attract a certain number of abnormal characters who are drawn to the novelty and excesses of the movement. We use the concept "abnormal character" as defined by the German philosopher and psychiatrist Karl Jaspers, as personality "dispositions which deviate from average and appear as extreme variations of human nature."[29] This definition is applicable whether we are speaking about radical or reactionary politics, clothing and hair styles, or religious movements.

The abnormal characters actively participating in religious movements can usually be classified into one of two major stereotypes: fanatics and hysterics. The fanatics often bear some resemblance to paranoids. They have discovered a Truth, protect this Truth by a distorted form of logic, and divide the world into friends and foes. They sometimes become charismatic leaders themselves and attract a band of followers for whom a conspiracy theory defining a common danger forms a central rallying point. Religious fanatics are rarely considered as saints, since their paranoid features of distrust and anger are inimical to the Christian saintly virtues of charity and humility.

Hysterics are much less likely to attract many adherents to themselves, although their flamboyance will be imitated with copy-cat behaviors by others. Hysterics are likely to be personally irksome because of their dramatic qualities, but are usually much less socially persuasive or dangerous because, in general, they do not have leadership qualities, do not develop conspiracy theories, and are less likely to be taken seriously on a large scale. While the hallmark of the fanatic is paranoia, the hallmark of the hysteric is suggestibility and, along with this, an ease for shifting in and out of altered states of consciousness.

If there is a heart of the matter in regard to the question of whether the medieval mystics and heroic ascetics were mentally ill, it must reside somewhere in the domain of hysteria, especially with its pejorative historical linkage to female anatomy and feminine style. But what does "hysteria" stand for, and what is expressed in referring to an individual as having "an hysterical character?"[30]

The term hysteria one hundred years ago merged gynecological with neurological constructs, as the concept shifted from hysterical symptom to hysterical (female) character. In Janet Beizer's phrase, the image of the hysteric caught on in the popular imagination in the late nineteenth century.[31] Historically, the medical diagnosis of hysteria encompassed symptoms of suffocation, vomiting, palpitations, convulsions, fainting, paresthesias (altered sensation), and speech disturbances. The hallmark of hysteria was, and still is, the mimicking of physical symptoms in the absence of physical disease. However, the social definition of hysteria in nineteenth-century Europe expanded it from physical symptoms to character traits, such as a mobile and impressionable nature, insufficiency of willpower manifested primarily as suggestibility, primacy of passions over rationality, excessive emotionality, tendency toward frequent and unmotivated fits of crying, capriciousness and fickleness, egotism, proneness to exaggeration, flights of excessive imagination, and deceitfulness and insincerity. This is not exactly a list of admirable character traits, and one can see how easily it can be applied to medieval mystics and heroic ascetics by nineteenth or twentieth-century scientists or historians prejudiced against the "Dark Ages."

Freud took this *mélange* of protean medical symptoms and constructed a psychodynamic model of symptom formation that involved repression of unconscious sexual conflicts. According to the psychodynamic model, repression of unconscious impulses resulted in symptomatic behavior that symbolically represented a compromise between forbidden desire and superego inhibition. Furthermore, this model of hysteria that postulated the "conversion" of sexual energy into physical symptoms was placed within Freud's theory of psychosexual developmental stages at the Oedipal stage, thus linking the physical symptoms of hysteria to the type of personality that theoretically emerged from unresolved Oedipal problems, namely the hysterical personality. These personality characteristics took on the exaggerated features which males traditionally believed were well-established feminine weaknesses, such as dramatization, exaggeration, and abnormal displays of emotionality, either excessive or absent, as in "la belle indifférence." Although it was technically acknowledged that hysteria in any of its forms could occur in males, the prototypic hysteric and hysterical behavior were caricatures of femininity at its least rational. To refer, one hundred years ago, to a woman medieval mystic as hysterical was a claim that the mystical behaviors, most likely trance-like and ecstatic, were derived from repressed sexual desires and conflicts.[32]

The sexual repression model for the etiology of hysteria and hysterical personality has had a mixed fate. In some quarters, it shows astonishing persistence and continues to be tossed in as an almost reflexive assumption whenever medieval mystics, especially women mystics, are discussed. For example, Herbert Moller attributes the periodic rise and fall of affective mysticism to periodic decreases in the numbers of males available for marriage. While not necessary to his thesis, which is after all an empirical one that can be tested by population demographics as well as historical sources permit, Moller then adds the assumption that the psychodynamic link between a shortage of males and affective mysticism in females is the transformation of sexual frustration into mystical longings.[33] The cure for such hysteria, of course, was sexual intercourse.

Since there rarely is sufficient information about the developmental histories of medieval saints upon which to build a psychodynamic formulation, the reasoning behind the designation of hysterical as relating to sexual frustrations has to be primarily *post hoc* and circular, namely, that specific adult behaviors presumably point back to specific childhood experiences/problems and sexual conflicts.[34] Because late medieval mysticism had a strong component of erotic imagery and language, nineteenth and twentieth-century secular and anti-religious writers, having no understanding or sympathy for the historical context of this mysticism, automatically assumed that the sexual repression dynamics putatively at play in Victorian Europe were present in late medieval Europe.

Christina Mazzoni, in examining the assumptions of Charcot and other late nineteenth-century neurologists, offers the following trenchant question:

> For is the mystic's body language, then, a symptom, uttering and muttering a repressed trauma, like the hysteric's, or is it a miracle, the result of a porousness between the supernatural and the natural?[35]

If the metaphors and imagery of union with God were conceptualized in terms of bridal and erotic language because, being human, how else could one find language to describe such intense and loving experiences, then there is no basis to apply a sexual repression theory invented six hundred years later in a vastly different society. It is also worth noting that it was a male cleric, Bernard of

Clairvaux (d.1153) who was the most influential promoter of the erotic imagery of bridal mysticism.

In most psychiatric circles, despite occasional claims such as those made by Moller cited above, the sexual repression theory of hysteria has by and large been discarded. What remains, then, of "hysteria?" Hysteria by now has come to refer primarily to a personality style characterized by exaggeration, dramatization, suggestibility, self-centeredness in reference to other persons' actions and intentions, inauthenticity, and emotional incontinence. It is to these character traits that we now have to turn our attention.

Karl Jaspers described the "hysterical" type of personality as follows (a description that, by the way, takes it completely out of the realm of sexist bias):

> To characterize the type more precisely, we have to fall back on one basic trait: Far from accepting their given dispositions and life opportunities, hysterical personalities crave to appear, both to themselves and others, as more than they are and to experience more than they are ever capable of. The place of genuine experience and natural expression is usurped by a contrived stage-act, a forced kind of experience. This is not contrived "consciously" but reflects the ability of the true hysteric to live wholly in his own drama, be caught entirely for the moment and succeed in seeming genuine.[36]

The essence of the hysterical personality, then, can be encompassed along two primary traits, the first of suggestibility and imitation, the second of exaggeration and inauthenticity. These are the very traits to which critics of mysticism are referring when they claim that mystics are hysterics. There are certainly enough examples in medieval source material to provide suspicion that suggestibility and imitation play a powerful role in shaping some components of popular pious behavior. For example, there must have been at least a few individuals among the flagellant confraternities in Italy and elsewhere whose participation was motivated by suggestibility and presentation management.

The suspicion of hysterical or exaggerated behavior posing as religious fervor is not unique to the late twentieth and early twenty-first centuries. In an earlier chapter, we cited the desert father Apollo, who censured those who wore chains and let their hair grow long as wanting to make an exhibition of themselves and of wanting approbation.[37] Likewise, the anonymous author of *The Cloud of Unknowing*, writing in the latter half of the fourteenth century, had little good to say about those who ostentatiously display their spirituality. He speaks of those young disciples and "would-be contemplatives" who, misunderstanding the meaning of the spiritual senses, "strain as if to see spiritually with their physical eyes, and to hear within with their outward ears, and to smell and taste and feel and so on."[38] The text of the *Cloud* continues in its description of this "counterfeit contemplation" as follows:

> Whoever cares to look at them as they sit at such a time, will see them staring (if their eyes are open) as though they were mad, and sniggering as if they saw the devil. . . . Some squint as though they were silly sheep that have been banged on the head, and were going soon to die. Some hang their heads on one side as if they had got a worm in their ear. Some squeak when they should speak. . . . Some cry and whine.[39]

The *Cloud* author speaks as a purist of speculative mysticism, and it is clear that not all will agree with his austere stance against outward displays of emotionality in pursuing one's spiritual path. It is, nevertheless, easy to recognize Jaspers's description of the hysterical type, of pretending to be what one is not and simultaneously believing it, in the *Cloud's* blistering depiction of those individuals who publicly strive so hard for holiness. The *Cloud* author's caricatures do convey a sense of an exhibitionistic quality to much that passed as spiritual fervor in his times. He would be, no doubt, critical of some of our favorite Flemish mystics, although he was speaking predominantly of men, not women, in his writings.

But the author of *The Cloud of Unknowing*, and other critics of exaggerated pious behavior, were able, without using the term or construct "hysterical" and without linking it to gender-based stereotypes, to convey their disapproval of behaviors that they viewed as exaggerated. It is a nineteenth and twentieth-century practice to label mystics as hysterics. What is the basis for this? It may be instructive to examine some descriptions of the behavior of a woman mystic, Angela of Foligno (1248–1309), who is sometimes considered a hysteric.

Angela of Foligno grew up in upper middle-class society near the town of Assisi, under the influence of the Franciscan movement (Francis: 1181–1226). She herself was conventionally hedonistic and materialistic. After her religious conversion, she listed her sins as washing, combing and perfuming her hair in order to be admired by others, dressing in luxurious clothes, indulging in fancy foods, coveting possessions, hearing empty and harmful conversations and maligning others, letting loose with fits of anger and pride, and engaging in illicit caresses and seductive behavior. She may have been unfaithful to her husband.

Around 1285, at age 37 or so, she experienced a religious conversion, the details of which are unknown. This type of conversion conformed to the stereotype for male saints, namely a somewhat licentious and worldly life followed by a relatively abrupt conversion and a dramatic rejection of former values and pursuits. The more prototypal female saint was known for piety since childhood, with her spiritual development occurring as a slow and uninterrupted process.

Local opinion had grave doubts about Angela's mental stability as she became preoccupied with meditating on the suffering of Christ and the enormity of her own sins. She just was not the old Angela whom they knew so well. She took off her clothes in the chapel of a church and placed them on the altar, and then progressively gave away, after the death of her husband and sons, all her wealth to the poor. This included selling her jewels and landed property.

Two pieces of Angela's behavior are often pointed to as "hysterical" for those who view religiosity in such constructs. The first relates to seemingly uncontrollable screaming, sobbing, and falling to the ground. On a trip to Assisi early into her spiritual conversion, Angela was deeply engaged, day and night, in her meditations. In the church in Assisi, she had a vision inspired by looking at a stained glass window of Jesus embracing Francis. She later described it as follows: "I saw something full of such immense majesty that I do not know how to describe it, but it seemed to me that it was the All Good."

She heard Christ telling her:

> Thus I will hold you closely to me and much more closely than can be observed with the eyes of the body. And now the time has come, sweet daughter, my temple, my delight, to fulfill my promise to you. I am about to leave you in the form of this consolation, but I will never leave you if you love me.[40]

After God had withdrawn. Angela began to shout and cry out without any shame, "Love still unknown, why do you leave me?" However, as she describes it, "These screams were so choked up in my throat that the words were unintelligible."[41] Her cousin, a Franciscan monk at the church, is so scandalized and embarrassed by this outrageous behavior that he chastises her and tells her never to visit that church in Assisi again. Afterwards, there were times when Angela was so caught up in the fire of the love of God that if she heard anyone speak about God she would scream. Again, in her own words:

> Even if someone stood over me with an axe ready to kill me, this would not have stopped my screaming.... Moreover, when people said I was possessed by the devil because I had no control over my inordinate behavior – for which I was greatly ashamed – I would concur with their judgment and likewise think of myself as very sick and possessed. I could not answer those who spoke ill of me.[42]

At other times, Angela would fall to the ground and lose her power of speech when, in meditation, she would feel the sweetness of God's presence.

The second class of religious observances exemplified by Angela that is often attributed to mental illness of the hysterical type involves severe penances in the form of self-injurious behavior. Angela never provides details about her daily practices in this regard, but she does mention two particular episodes that can serve as indications of her heroic asceticism. One occurred when personal vices, which she thought to be dead in her, were reawakened from the outside by demons, and along with those, some vices that had never been there before. She states:

> My body (which nonetheless suffers less than my soul) experiences such burning in three places – the shameful parts – that I used to apply material

fire to quench the other fire, until you [her confessor] forbade me to do so.⁴³

A second episode involves washing the hands and feet of lepers, especially one leper whose wounds were festering and in an advanced stage of decomposition.

> Then we drank the very water with which we had washed him. And the drink was so sweet that, all the way home, we tasted its sweetness and it was as if we had received Holy Communion. As a small scale of the leper's sores was stuck in my throat, I tried to swallow it. My conscience would not let me spit it out, just as if I had received Holy Communion. I really did not want to spit it out but simply to detach it from my throat.⁴⁴

It is interesting to note that brother Giles of Assisi (d.1262), whose life and locale overlapped with Angela's, was also given to altered states in response to special words. Giles was referred to as mad but, being a male, has been spared the modern label of hysteric. The passage from the *Life of Giles* is as follows:

> For if any man conversed with him concerning the glory of the Lord and His sweetness or concerning Paradise, immediately he fell into an ecstasy and moved not from the spot.⁴⁵

It would appear that Angela's behavior was very much in keeping with patterns of affective mysticism of thirteenth-century northern Italy. Drinking the water used to wash lepers' sores is a not uncommon topos in medieval saints' lives. There is certainly nothing in Angela's *vita* to suggest inauthenticity, that she was not fully committed to the pursuit of a life of charity on earth and of spiritual union with God, or that she was behaving in dramatic style in order to attract attention.

The convergence of hysteria, hysterical personality, and mysticism has been enormously exaggerated and exploited to the detriment of sincere religious commitment, serving minimal purpose other than disparaging a group (both men and women) whose vision of what is valuable in life and worth struggling for differed radically from a materialistic, scientific viewpoint. We are still left to puzzle out the resemblance of some mystics whose public displays of weeping and suffering closely resemble the public dramatic behaviors of those labeled hysterics in present times, or in late nineteenth-century France and Germany. It would appear that not every mystic was a perfectly saintly character. In what sense can some of the medieval mystics be considered as displaying hysterical features?

We discussed earlier the traits of absorption and suggestibility. Neither of these are pathological traits. In fact, they are correlated with psychological openness and certain forms of creativity. The suspicion of hysteria must arise when there is high suggestibility in the absence of those qualities and traits that predispose toward

Plate 13.1 Gudule (d.712) was the daughter of Count Witger and Amelberge, a married couple who became celibate and are considered saints themselves. Gudule is known for her religious devotions and good works. The Devil was always trying to blow out her candle.

having transcendental experiences. Under such a constellation, there is a risk that a person may substitute the appearance of piety and ecstatic experiences for the authentic experience. It is inconceivable that in the Middle Ages, and today, there are not some individuals who long to be mystics, but do not have the necessary ability to experience transcendent altered states, or who lack grace, and make a great pretence or show of convincing themselves and their neighbors that they are the real thing. It is likely that such aspirations in a "wanna-be," or a copy-cat or look-alike, leads to the exaggerated behaviors that seem to irk some people and lead to the label of hysteria.

But why the term "hysteria"? It is here that we come back full circle to male-dictated stereotypes of femininity. If we mean by "hysteria" merely exaggeration, attention-seeking, and inauthenticity, why not just say so? If we mean by this that any expression of affective mysticism, rather than speculative mysticism or apophatic mysticism characterized by the negation of all sensory and perceptual experiences or by the experience of pure consciousness without thought or imagery content, is inauthentic, then we are narrowly confining mystical experiences to one particular conservative model that accords with a masculine intellectualized version of how to behave in the presence of God, and at all other times too.[46] Affective mysticism can only be felt through the body, and will be experienced in part as a physical ecstasy. The question is whether we can accept the possibility that there are states of physical ecstasy that are not sexual, and not the same as the experience of sexual orgasm?

One problem of religious phenomena is that the religious person lives and acts under the assumption of the real existence of a transcendental realm that is non-physical and non-material and that can and does interact with the physical and material realm upon which our ordinary notions of causality and experience are based. If we make judgments about the mentality and behavior of the former applying scientific criteria based upon the latter, then most religious persons will be defined to have some psychopathology.

In Chapter 3, we tried to soften this judgmental stance. Hysterics are suggestible and often are thin-boundaried, in the sense of having less delineation between their own sense of self and the traits and attitudes that belong to others. Mystics are thin-boundaried too, with an ability to shift more comfortably between different levels of reality, to soar with the angels, than can those whose sense of material reality and commitment to scientific methodology as the basis of all knowledge is unshakable. Furthermore, mystics are suggestible too, although not necessarily in terms of being impressionable to the influence of others, but in being able to take their imaginative musings and let these lead them along various creative paths.[47] In a person who is high in the trait of transcendence, defined as having an awareness of being an integral part of a unitive principle, the creative pathway leads to a mystical apprehension of the divine.[48]

The problem in all this is that if a mystic and a hysteric spend much time together, the hysteric will begin, as much as possible, to think like a mystic and take on the behaviors of the mystic, although often in exaggeration. Such must have been the condition in many monasteries and other religious establishments in the late Middle Ages. Watching someone go into a trance state is a great help in getting oneself into a trance state, or a reasonable facsimile thereof. After a while, it is nearly impossible for an observer to know who is communing with God and who is just having an ordinary altered state of consciousness.[49] It is not as if we have special methods or expertise for evaluating the quality of the experience of someone in an altered state. We can try to discern who is which, if we think it is important enough, but the enterprise does a disservice to human complexity. At the least, judgment about mental health is often based upon the ways in which mystical experiences appear to bring about change in a person for the better. Although there is no "gold" standard, and judgments will differ, it does not appear to be that difficult to recognize when one is in the presence of a holy person. The psychiatrist, usually severely limited by professional biases and cultural assumptions, is primarily trained to comment on symptoms and to think in terms of illness as opposed to recognizing virtue and health.

The problem for the psychiatrist/psychologist and also, we suggest, for the historian of religion, is to begin to delineate in what ways, if any, some of these charismatic personalities were abnormal or problematic and then, more importantly, to examine what is the relationship between their character abnormality and their spirituality. We do not necessarily detract from a person's saintliness by attributing some character problems to them. It very well may be that part of the challenge or task toward spiritual perfection was precisely the necessity to combat and surmount one's own disagreeable personality traits, such as vanity, self-centeredness, and willfulness. In previous chapters, the issue of willfulness in the case of Henry Suso and depressive mood swings in Beatrice of Nazareth have been presented as obstacles to overcome rather than as pathological evidence that should detract from their pursuit of holiness. If the saint has no struggle toward holiness, how can a saint's life serve as an exemplar to the rest of us?

The question is whether a psychiatric approach has something additional to offer the established historical explanations of why heroic ascetic practices of fasting and sleep deprivation seemed to wax at the time of the desert fathers,[50] wane throughout the first two centuries of the second millennium in Western Europe, and increase again, with an additional emphasis on laceration of the flesh, coincident with the renewed commitment to a more personal and mystical relationship to God that arose in the twelfth century. Bernard McGinn has suggested that a new surge of piety beginning about 1200 stressed the "possibility of attaining mystical perfection in all walks of life", thus encouraging the seeking of a personal relationship to God in present time rather than waiting for the hereafter.[51]

Our hypothesis is that there was increased emphasis on self-injurious behavior in the thirteenth century because it accommodated two separate but related themes central to the religious reforms of the preceding two centuries. First, it gave tangible expression to the emerging focus on identification with the human aspects of the suffering Jesus, as this imagery captured the religious imagination.[52] Second, for those individuals who did not have sufficient access to or were not able to utilize a relatively overlooked tradition of meditative teaching and practice to assist them in their intensely religious motivation to achieve transcendental or mystical states, harsh asceticism seemed to promise attainment of such altered states.

Prior to the religious reforms of the eleventh and twelfth centuries, the goal of most founders of monastic movements was eternal salvation after death, not union with God in life. The combined practical effect of the writings of Augustine,

Cassian (despite his initial emphasis on solitary meditation), and Benedict had been toward the development of communal worship with a concomitant reduction of the central importance of both an intensely personal relationship to God and the use of either heroic ascetic or disciplined contemplative methods to achieve it. Benedict's notion was that it was so difficult for individuals just to live in peace in a closed community that the spiritual emphasis had to be toward obedience and civility rather than toward a mystical relationship with God.[53]

Toward the end of the Middle Ages, with the waning of a literal identification with the passion of Christ as a dominant form of religious expression, and as Western Christianity rediscovered, initially through the Rhineland mystics and then with the writings of such mystics as John of the Cross and Ignatius of Loyola, its own theory and practice of meditation as a method of achieving a closer personal relationship with God, the prevalence and intensity of heroic ascetic practices declined. Extreme self-injurious behavior, always formally discouraged by the ecclesiastical authorities, could be dispensed with because more acceptable methods of altering one's state of consciousness by meditation became available. Moderate levels of ascetic practice remained because its goals were discipline and sacrifice, not altered states of consciousness.

Despite the rediscovery and further evolution of the meditative tradition within Western Christianity, the recent proliferation of interest in studying the meditative techniques of the Buddhist and Hindu mystical traditions highlights the relative underdevelopment and cautiousness of Western meditative theory and practice, right up to the present time, to satisfy the longings of Western culture for transcendental experiences. The very popularity of recently published books and weekend workshops on Zen and Hindu philosophy and practice attest to the Western interest in Eastern meditation.[54] The relative weakness and even historical suspicion of a Western meditative tradition has been addressed from within the Catholic Church. For example, Raymond Gawronski, writing in the *New Oxford Review*, comments on the ambivalence of the contemporary Catholic Church in regards to assimilating Far Eastern spirituality. Gawronski asserts that the contemplative tradition of the Western church has languished for decades. He further notes that Eastern religions offer the West three possibilities: first, a traditional wisdom, near the heart of which is a traditional discipline; second, experience, especially silence; third, a technique, one which is nonpersonal. Of the third, he writes: "Although some teachers would no doubt hold that technique, in its highest reaches, might be discarded, it is very much at the heart of the practice of meditation. As such, it would seem to be perfectly adapted to modern, technical consciousness."[55]

This theme of the relative insufficiency or mistrust of a meditative tradition within Western Christianity and the unsuitability of the "old religious training" for the contemporary person is closely echoed by William Johnston, a Jesuit author, in an essay on asceticism and Zen Buddhism.[56] Johnston, after citing the achievements of Ignatius of Loyola in systematizing spiritual exercises and ascetical practices as a preparation for mysticism, which he describes as the direct action of

God on the soul, proceeds to speak of recent discontent with Ignatian exercises. Johnston writes:

> First of all, there was dissatisfaction with the traditional ways of praying. Here the Jesuits came under fire for teaching a dull, methodological, discursive prayer which they imposed on the whole Church. No less a person than Aldous Huxley accused the Jesuits of destroying Western mysticism with their plodding emphasis on reasoning and thinking. Where was the vibrant mysticism of medieval Europe? What had happened to Julian of Norwich and Meister Eckhart? Where was *The Cloud of Unknowing*?[57]

A major part of the problem that early twenty-first-century Western culture has in adopting fourteenth-century medieval mystical practices is that there are no comfortable modern models for understanding and accepting a healthy and constructive asceticism, which was so prominent a piece of medieval spirituality. Modern society abhors discipline and sacrifice. The dominant model, both secular and religious, that we presently have for asceticism is a medical model that perceives self-injurious behaviors as pointing toward mental illness. Pain is something to avoid, not pursue. Furthermore, early twenty-first-century Western mysticism, such as it is, is predominantly a joyous and, for the most part, a nature or pantheistic mysticism, whereas fourteenth-century mysticism is now perceived as a darker, apophatic mysticism. In fact, there was a joyous component to medieval mysticism, as exemplified by some of the Flemish mystics such as Gertrude of Helfta, but here too, their joyous and uninhibited ecstatic behaviors ring too much like hysteria to Western conservative thinking to be available as a model for modern mysticism.

Whereas medieval mysticism saw the impediment to closeness with God as stemming from our propensity to sin, early twenty-first century mysticism perceives the analogous impediment to closeness with God as the narcissism of self-absorption that defines our culture. In a similar fashion, the remedy for sin for the medieval mystic was introspective contemplation, penance and redemption and, in some cases, community service. The modern remedy to the problem of self-absorption is, paradoxically, further self-absorption through meditation and contemplation, but of the Eastern variety which, if done successfully, will diminish the focus on self. Henry Suso, in fact, speaks extensively of the importance of detachment in the pursuit of God, but most readers have difficulty seeing past his excessive asceticism to benefit from his mystical insights. In general, the model of medieval affective mysticism has been, until lately, suspect to the modern spiritual seeker.

The few examples of medieval mystics that are accepted as models today are either of the very controlled and accomplished type, such as Julian of Norwich, with no trace of conflict or neurosis, or the more feisty and dynamic ones, such as Teresa of Avila or Margery Kempe, who are used by feminist groups not as models of mysticism, but as political examples of feminine assertiveness. In either case, the true richness of medieval mysticism, which included a moderate component of asceticism, is unavailable to early twenty-first-century persons interested in developing a closer relationship to God because of our failure to discern the authentic spirituality of that era, including the spirituality of those who were excessive, by almost all criteria, in their heroic asceticism.

14

CONCLUSION[1]

Of the 1,462 persons who lived between the years AD 450 and 1500 listed as saints in Thurston and Attwater's 1956 revision of *Butler's Lives of the Saints*, only approximately 10 percent were recognized by their contemporaries as mystics and approximately 10 percent as heroic ascetics. There is overlap between mysticism and heroic asceticism in the same person, but less than is commonly assumed and varying according to time frame. There was little overlap (1 percent) in the early and middle periods of the Middle Ages. It is only in the religious revival of the late Middle Ages (thirteenth to fifteenth centuries), in which the possibility and aspiration developed of achieving closeness to God in this lifetime rather than in the hereafter, that the confluence between mysticism and heroic asceticism (17 percent) reaches notable proportions. It was also in these later centuries that mysticism, especially in women, far outdistanced asceticism as the dominant form of the expression of holiness.

The traditional pathways to holiness more often involved good works rather than intense and often introspective pursuit of closeness to God. Again, it was only in the latter Middle Ages that religiosity and holiness were expressed to any significant degree in avenues other than good deeds of varying sorts, such as service to the poor, service to the church, and evidence of character traits of exemplary Christian virtues, such as humility and unmistakable goodness, that indicated one was touched by God. Yet it is the mystics and heroic ascetics who fascinate, who unsurprisingly rivet our attention to their very excesses that cause admiration in some, repulsion in others, and bewilderment in most modern persons who pause to take an interest in such oddities. These holy individuals were seen to exist at the interface of humanity and divinity in a literal sense that has little equivalence in recent times.

The modern person is in general ill-equipped to come to the topics of medieval mysticism and heroic asceticism with a sympathetic approach. Our scientific and medically informed world view has no lens to view excessive self-injurious behaviors except through the microscope of mental illness. It is a given in our culture that pain is to be avoided and individuals who voluntarily inflict pain and other forms of suffering upon themselves are generally assumed to be disturbed.

Mysticism suffers from somewhat different cultural distortions, a bit more subtle but no less damaging, to an understanding and appreciation of the particular forms of mysticism that flowered in the late Middle Ages. First of all, it is a basic assumption of mysticism that the mystical experience cannot be exhaustively accounted for in naturalistic (scientific) terms, which runs counter to a materialistic world view that can only account for human behavior and psychological states in scientific terms. According to this perception, mystical experiences represent altered states of consciousness ultimately explainable by biological processes, thereby undercutting an essential component of what a mystical experience entails. Accordingly, the late nineteenth–early twentieth-century approach to medieval mysticism in its ecstatic representation, which continues to shape our thinking, was that it was a form of hysteria and, as such, an expression of womanly weaknesses, suggestibility, and tendencies toward dramatic exaggeration.

Even among those interested in and sympathetic to mysticism in general, an appreciation of medieval ecstatic mysticism has suffered because the late twentieth and early twenty-first century model for "proper" mysticism has been an Eastern model (as described by religious philosophers such as Forman, Stace, Staal, and Zaehner among others) that holds up contemplative pathways and the experience of silence and nothingness as the highest form of pursuit or union with the Absolute, no longer necessarily the Christian God or Godhead. Since medieval mystics in general pursued union with a loving Jesus (or Godhead) expressed in corporeal and erotic terms that echoed the Song of Songs and St. Bernard's (1090–1153) commentaries upon them, these ecstatic and joyful experiences are often judged as lesser forms of mystical experiences, or even as hysterical or at best as intermediate steps along the mystical pathway, in comparison to the states of pure consciousness and emptiness sought by Eastern mystics (Buddhists and Hindus) and Western followers of Eastern meditative techniques.

One further obstacle to a sympathetic reading of medieval saints is our tendency to assume naively that a holy person must have a saintly personality and disposition and conform to a higher standard, and that any evidence of neurotic or irritable behavior or self-centered motivations or other human failings negates the possibility that we have a holy person here. But it is only in sketchily drawn saints' lives that conform more to an outline of stereotypic goody-goody behavior and bleach out the imperfections of human character that we come across saints without faults.

In the longer and richer narratives comprising some of the biographies of holy persons, we get to see the conflicts, peculiarities, and even the unattractiveness of the personalities of the saints. For example, Suso includes in his biography an incident in which he is deep in meditation and communion with God and "his heart was full of the holy joy of jubilation." The porter of the chapter house comes to Suso and tells him that a woman is at the door of the cloister wanting to make her confession only to him. Suso speaks harshly to the porter and is unreceptive to the requests of this suffering woman whose heart is burdened with sin. He does not want to interrupt his interior delight. When he attempts to resume his joyous state of mind, he finds that he is unable to, that God is suddenly unavailable. He then hears a voice tell him that just as he was unavailable to the woman in crisis, so God will be unavailable to him.² Suso is not a novice at this time, but a seasoned mystic although an imperfect person. It takes this extreme a response of God's withdrawal from him for Suso to appreciate that to be Christ-like is not just to contemplate the Godhead, but to be charitable and loving to others even when it is inconvenient. While this little episode is intended to serve as a homily with a moral to others, it nevertheless also shows us that Suso is willing, as part of his life journey, to acknowledge and expose his faults. He may not place his attachment to a special relationship to God above his duty to a suffering human being. Critics of Suso may see even his tendency to display his faults as one more example of narcissistic exhibitionism, but no piece of behavior is invulnerable to such an uncharitable charge.

An incident is described in the *vita* of Beatrice of Nazareth in which she considers feigning insanity in order to heap public humiliation upon herself, in imitation of Christ's humiliation. Her spiritual director advises against this dissimulation and the matter is dropped.³ Again, the incident is presented with a moral, but it also casually acknowledges that even saints have, like the rest of us, less than saintly motivations and methods. Other sections of Beatrice's *vita* present what we have considered her struggles with recurrent depressions. Although this is a modern reading of Beatrice's elations in the presence and agonies in the absence of God with which others may not agree, we see an important aspect of Beatrice's holiness precisely in her having to come to terms with the instability of mood swings without losing sight of her relationship to God and without yielding to a despair that crushes her beyond hope.

In our own clinic, we have treated an elderly nun whom we considered holy in her service to others. She had depressions, headaches, joint pains, insomnia, and fatigue. She was a social activist who lamented that she no longer had the energy to travel to anti-war protest demonstrations and get herself thrown into jail. She started and operated on a shoestring a soup kitchen and drop-in center in the most run-down neighborhood of the city. She could be irritable and crotchety and at times insufferable about her pains, but her charity never ended. When I asked her about her relationship to God, hoping to engage her in a "deeper" discussion of her theology, she looked at me and said "Huh?" I took this to mean that her pathway to holiness was works, not contemplation, that in serving those who had nothing, she was serving God, and that she would forgive me my impertinent question. Here was a woman to be valued for her deeds, not for the perfections of her personality or her pursuit of mystical experiences.

Given the many cultural, philosophical, and psychological impediments in our modern approach to medieval mysticism and heroic asceticism, this book has assumed a viewpoint that both takes the medieval mystics and heroic ascetics at their word in regard to what they were trying to do, and also utilizes modern understanding of the physiological and psychological effects of sleep deprivation, chronic starvation, and self-laceration upon states of consciousness in the quest for closeness with God. The Christian world view of a transcendental universe and an infinitely distant but paradoxically approachable and loving God forms the cultural context within which mystics and ascetics are to be approached and studied.

The modern medical or physiological approach to the effects of self-injurious behaviors on states of consciousness is complemented by our twenty-first century philosophical understanding of the role of language and subjectivity as limitations upon our ability to comprehend someone else's descriptions of mystical experiences. It is not just mystical experiences that are ineffable and indescribable; all aspects of the experience of consciousness, including or especially altered states of consciousness, are relatively ineffable. This is an ordinary observation about the human condition, not particularly profound. It acknowledges that we are bound or limited by two very problematic processes, subjectivity and language. The problem of subjectivity is the perennial problem, tackled without closure by most great philosophers, of how we know about other minds. Although there is philosophical debate about whether consciousness provides privileged information to the mind that owns it, there is little debate that no one knows what is in or on my mind, nor is what is in my mind singular or orderly.

It is not just the subjectivity and privacy of my consciousness that interferes with others' empathy and understanding. Language itself limits our ability to convey and receive a rich sense of what we experience and how we interpret it, although perhaps it is even misleading to speak of experience, interpretation, and language, which cannot be so easily separated and juxtaposed, as if they were three discrete processes. Nor can language ever do more than approximate what we are trying to say.

Compared to problems in approaching mysticism in general and medieval mysticism in particular, the issue with examining asceticism in the Middle Ages appears more straightforward, because here we are looking at an observable and confirmatory behavior. Problems with asceticism relate initially to the quality or reliability of information, to questions of accuracy or exaggeration of reports of fasting or sleep deprivation and unseen self-inflicted injuries. But questions about motivation, subjective experiences, and effects of ascetic behaviors bring us back to the same problems with subjectivity and language. Here the question of whether the ascetic's explanation of why he/she engages in these behaviors may not be privileged in the sense that the ascetic may not be in the best location to understand his/her own motivation. The basic point of psychodynamic theory is that individuals are not privy to what drives them to do what they do.

The questions we asked in our introduction were: Who were the mystics and heroic ascetics? What did they experience and do that distinguished them from their religious but less intense peers? Are there patterns and interactions to mystical and ascetical practices that are overlooked by studying just a few famous or outstanding holy persons? How can we explain the relationships between mysticism and asceticism?

In the course of addressing the question of who were the saints, prime importance was given to considerations of historical methodology. Along with some recent historians (Goodich, Schulenburg, Weinstein and Bell), we are strongly of the opinion that a statistical examination of sainthood provides a necessary balance to the enticing tendency of supporting historical generalizations by presentation of a few carefully selected cases. When this is done, we realize that the vast majority of medieval saints received contemporary recognition of holiness not for mystical and ascetic experiences, but, for the most part, by leading exemplary Christian lives of charity, humility, and service. It is also clear that some individuals benefited from family and institutional connections in the pursuit of recognition of holiness.

Other methodological problems relate both to the technical problems of figuring out who wrote each saint's life, the question of when the *vita* was written relative to when the saint lived, the many questions about what kinds of sources the biographer had at his/her disposal, the various intents of the biography in writing about this particular holy person, and the many transformations and distortions that the biography in front of us may have undergone during the many centuries from medieval times to now. Recent feminist investigations have examined the effects of the androcentric premises that inform and mold how women were perceived in the religious consciousness of the Middle Ages and in modern interpretations of medieval life. We have commented on these important issues throughout the course of this book.

When all is said and done, however, we are still left with the biographies of these extraordinary men and women. Although not representing the majority of those individuals who were considered as holy, the mystics and ascetics served as examples and constant reminders of the transcendental foundations upon which quotidian life rested. Charity, love, humility, detachment, rejection of physical comforts and pleasures, and pursuit of closeness with God were the values that underlay the Christian consciousness in the Middle Ages. These values were always in conflict with the demands and attachments to the physical and social worlds of medieval Europe, and we can see them played out in dramatic form in the lives and struggles of mystics and ascetics.

Our own notions about the interaction of self-injurious behaviors and mystical pursuits are tempered by an examination of the data of the 1,462 saints in our sample. It is only in the later time frame (thirteenth to fifteenth centuries) that these two forms of intense religiosity are found to any significant extent in the same individuals. Without wishing to overstate our case, we have focused on the effects of excessive self-injurious behaviors upon altered states of consciousness, a connection that we think has been overshadowed by thinking about asceticism from a purely social or religious historical perspective. Starvation, laceration of the flesh, and sleep deprivation have profound psychological effects and we postulate that some God-driven individuals who were not able to achieve the altered states of consciousness that are experienced as closeness with God utilized techniques of heroic asceticism in an attempt to reach this closeness. In some holy persons, such as Beatrice of Nazareth and Henry Suso, the ferocious excesses of relatively youthful asceticism fall away as they reach a more mature spirituality and mystical apprehension of the Godhead.

Finally, we find that modern attempts to diagnose medieval mystics and ascetics out of context to their environment and disregarding a commitment to God that constituted the urgent and central feature of their lives is an exercise in cultural insensitivity and conceit. The medieval mystics and ascetics did not have the major forms of mental illness such as schizophrenia and manic-depressive disorders and their drive to God cannot be explained by recourse to such formulations. The question of whether they displayed abnormal personality traits is itself almost a rhetorical question, for most persons who distinguish themselves in the intensity and even ferociousness of the pursuit of some form of excellence or exceptional experiences are by definition different from the crowd of persons with normal desires and drives. The mystics carried the ideals of their society beyond what most others would consider, and in doing so defined their specialness.

APPENDIX
Statistical analyses

In the Introduction, we discussed the importance of gaining an overall sense of the types and characteristics of persons who came to be regarded as holy during the Middle Ages. What were their demographics and backgrounds, and what was special about them that the reputation or designation of a holy person was bestowed upon them? While the main focus in the preceding chapters has been on the changes in patterns of mysticism and heroic asceticism in relationship to gender and time frames, this chapter initially examines two demographic sets, namely social class and formal role with regard to the institutional church (job description or lay status). This perspective should help us to understand the composition of the community of holy persons in the Middle Ages and provide a quantitative underpinning to some of the generalizations made throughout the book as a whole. In the second half of this chapter, we will pick up on some of the more detailed analysis from Chapter 8 regarding the relationship between mysticism and the three categories of heroic asceticism (laceration of the flesh, sleep deprivation, extreme fasting) as these vary by gender and time frame.

As shown in Table A.1, it was far more likely for individuals under priestly vows, both those who served secular society and those who lived under a rule for monks, to be recognized for their holiness than it was for laymen or for women, whether lay or religious. Popes, archbishops, bishops, abbots, and abbesses along with monks and nuns and a small number of ordinary secular priests, account for more than 80 percent of individuals recognized as holy during the unfolding medieval millennium under consideration. The relatively small number of women, in both absolute (248 of 1,462) and percentage terms (17 percent) who were recognized as holy can be attributed in part to the fact that there were very few convents in Europe as compared to monasteries for men. Women, of course, were not permitted to enter the priesthood, then as now. Some laywomen, however, provide an exception to the general pattern favoring male sainthood in so far as these women attained holy reputations in the course of their lives through actions such as extensive charitable acts, 'saintly' character virtues of humility and generosity of spirit, and either noteworthy ascetic behavior or widely recognized pursuit of mystical connection with God. Some of these women maintained themselves as lifelong virgins or as married women who, upon being separated from their

APPENDIX: STATISTICAL ANALYSES

Table A.1 Distribution of saints by ecclesiastical status

Church position	Number	(%)
Abbott/abbess	315	21.5
Nun/monk	293	20.0
Minor orders	51	3.5
Beguine	3	0.2
Lay hermit	31	2.1
Pope	40	2.7
Bishop/archbishop	472	32.3
Priest	48	3.3
Layperson: widow	28	1.9
Layperson: virgin	45	3.1
Layperson: other	136	9.3

respective spouses, either by choice while he was alive or through widowhood, gave up sexual relations and a materialistic life style. Both of these types of "virginity" were highly praised in laywomen and considered a sign of holiness while, of course, taken for granted among professed nuns.

As a corollary to the high proportion of religious of all types comprising those recognized as holy, persons of royal status, nobility, and the wealthier classes too were more likely to have their sanctity recognized than were those of inferior status (see Table A.2). Men and women from the upper echelons of society comprise 45 percent of all holy persons in our sample. Taking into account the invariable difficulty historically in defining and locating the "middle class," our study permits the identification of almost 14 percent from this group as attaining holy status. Finally, only 4.5 percent of all holy persons for the entire medieval millennium can be identified with certainty as having belonged to the urban poor and peasant classes. Joan of Arc (c.1412–1431) is one outstanding example of a saint arising from the peasantry. This low figure of 9 percent, however, is likely misleading. The social status of 36.7 percent of our sample cannot be identified with certainty and it is likely that most of these persons came from the lower or, at best, lower middle classes.

This peculiarity, i.e. that members of the lower classes were likely to have their background or origins go unrecognized or unmentioned, is due to the fact that during the Middle Ages elevated social background was thought to be virtuous while lower status was not. As a result, the family background of important persons was more likely to be remembered and remarked upon than the background of non-entities. In this context, men and women of high status bruited about the fame and distinction of their own ancestors, and those people in their entourage did so as well in order to bask in the reflected prominence of their patrons. It was important to have saints as well as distinguished warriors in one's pedigree, as we discussed in Chapter 8 in regard to St. Cloud (520–560), whose saintliness was used by his family to offset their own predilection for violence and familicide.

APPENDIX: STATISTICAL ANALYSES

Table A.2 Distribution of saints by social status

Social class	Number	(%)
Royalty	111	7.6
Nobility	401	27.4
Wealthy	148	10.1
Middle class	200	13.7
Peasant	48	3.3
Urban poor	17	1.2
Unknown	537	36.7

This set of aristocratic-oriented values may well be understood today by those who work out their family genealogies in search of auspicious progenitors, but will be less appreciated by populists who value more highly the rags-to-riches model of a Horatio Alger type. In medieval society, snobbism was far more important than individual merit, especially when merit was evident in one from the lower classes.

During the Middle Ages, the vast majority of men and women selected to high positions in the church, such as bishops and abbots and abbesses, were drawn from the noble and wealthier classes in society. As a result, there is a convergence of upper social class with ecclesiastical positions. In addition, since a considerable dowry was often required to enter monastic life, both monasteries and convents always drew the greater number of their monks and nuns from the higher classes of society even if, in absolute terms, larger numbers of poorer people had access to the cloistered life, especially as lay brothers and sisters during the later Middle Ages. The monastic orders, as they became numerically and politically powerful, also had a vested interest similar to the nobility in promoting the more distinguished of their membership to the status of sainthood.

The broad generalizations about social class and church position evident from the data in Tables A.1 and A.2 are appreciably refined by examining the findings from our sample of 1,462 saints in relation to the time frames of early, middle, and later Middle Ages. In essence, lumping the data across a one-thousand year period of time serves to highlight some features, such as the high percentage of saints drawn from the upper social classes and to obscure other features, such as changing patterns of composition of social class, ecclesiastical rank, and gender in those individuals regarded as holy. Most importantly, episcopal and abbatial figures, who were charged with the responsibility for administering the church and representing its interests to the lay authorities, are seen to play a decreasing role, as the Middle Ages evolved, among those who are recognized as holy. As Table A.3 shows, this decline across the time frames in the identification of holiness among bishops ($\chi^2 = 111.5$, $p < 0.001$)[1] and abbots and abbesses ($\chi^2 = 43.3$, $p < 0.001$) is dramatic and correlates with a rise in the recognition of holiness of the regular clergy ($\chi^2 = 37.1$, $p < 0.001$) and the monastic orders ($\chi^2 = 131.5$,

APPENDIX: STATISTICAL ANALYSES

Table A.3 Distribution of saints by time frame by church position

Curch position	Centuries					
	5th–10th Number	(%)	11th–12th Number	(%)	13th–15th Number	(%)
Abbott/abbess	199	25.3	73	27.9	43	10.4
Nun/monk	77	9.8	41	15.6	175	42.3
Minor orders	1	0.1	2	0.8	48	11.6
Beguine	–	–	–	–	3	0.7
Lay hermit	19	2.4	3	1.1	9	2.2
Pope	30	3.8	5	1.9	5	1.2
Bishop/archbishop	332	42.2	91	34.7	49	11.8
Priest	21	2.7	6	2.3	21	5.1
Layperson: widow	15	1.9	2	0.8	11	2.7
Layperson: virgin	29	3.7	2	0.8	14	3.4
Layperson: other	63	8.0	37	14.1	36	8.7
Total	786		262		414	

$p < 0.001$). The reversal of the earlier pattern also reflects changing criteria of what constitutes holiness from evangelical and public service to the church and the populace in general in the earlier time periods to the private pursuit of an intense relationship to God in the later times.

As seen in Table A.4, the proportions of holy persons emerging from the middle class ($\chi^2 = 72.7$, $p < 0.001$), and even from the peasantry ($\chi^2 = 11.6$, $p < 0.003$) and urban poor ($\chi^2 = 21.4$, $p < 0.001$) increase over time while the percentage of royalty ($\chi^2 = 7.1$, $p = 0.029$) decline and the nobility remains about the same. Reciprocal with this increase in the percentage of holy persons drawn from the lower classes is a decrease in the percentage in our sample of persons whose social status cannot be ascertained.

This decrease across time in the number of saints whose *vita* do not provide information about social class is consistent with the realities of a growing interest in the identity of lower class persons in a society that was becoming increasingly urbanized and bureaucratized. It was necessary for people from the lower classes to be listed in regard to their wealth and family background on tax roles, corvey (military conscription) lists, and numerous other types of documents that made social anonymity increasingly difficult. This of course does not mean that the snobbism inherent in an aristocratic society lessened.

In the second part of this Appendix, we shall examine separately the correlations between gender and time frame and the three subcategories of self-injurious behaviors (laceration, fasting, sleep deprivation) to see if there are different patterns attached to different forms of asceticism, such as has been suggested, for example, by Rudolph Bell,[2] Caroline Bynum,[3] and others in regard to the connection between fasting and holy women. At appropriate locations, we shall compare our findings to those of other large surveys.

Table A.4 Distribution of saints by time frame by social class

Social class	Centuries					
	5th–10th		11th–12th		13th–15th	
	Number	(%)	Number	(%)	Number	(%)
Royal	73	9.3	16	6.1	22	5.3
Nobility	212	27.0	87	33.2	102	24.6
Wealthy	77	9.8	16	6.1	55	13.3
Middle class	54	6.9	46	17.6	100	24.2
Peasant	15	1.9	10	3.8	23	5.6
Urban poor	1	0.1	3	1.1	13	3.1
Unknown	354	45.0	84	32.0	99	23.9
Total	786		262		414	

To recapitulate briefly from Chapter 8, from our database of 1,462 saints who flourished during the Middle Ages, 10 percent practiced some form of heroic asceticism. When we examine the overall distribution of heroic asceticism by gender, it is clear that there is a substantial disparity in the excessive self-injurious behaviors practiced by women as compared to men. Only about 8 percent of male saints during the entire Middle Ages were likely to engage in heroic ascetic behaviors, while slightly over 20 percent of female saints were engaged in excessive fasting, laceration of the flesh, or sleep deprivation. This difference is statistically significant ($\chi^2 = 36.477$, $p < 0.001$). However, when we turn to the details of the gender distribution of these specific types (laceration, sleep deprivation, starvation) of ascetic behaviors in the three time frames of the Middle Ages, the patterns take on certain nuances that are lost when averaged across the long millennium (see Table A.5). We will examine our data to test whether the correlations between mysticism and fasting, as well as mysticism and the other two forms of heroic asceticism (sleep deprivation and laceration of the flesh) are as strong and constant as has been commonly assumed by recent scholarly writings.

Table A.5 Types of heroic asceticism by time frame (%)

Centuries	Male			Female		
	Laceration	Sleep deprivation	Fasting	Laceration	Sleep deprivation	Fasting
5th–10th	2.7	1.6	4.1	6.4	3.6	6.4
11th–12th	5.4	2.9	7.1	4.3	4.3	4.3
13th–15th	8.4	5.0	4.7	22.6	17.4	23.5
Total	4.6	2.7	4.9	13.7	10.1	14.1

APPENDIX: STATISTICAL ANALYSES

Extraordinary fasting

From our database of 1,462 holy people, 6.4 percent were recognized in their lifetimes for their extraordinary level of fasting. If we examine these data with regard to gender for the entire medieval period, 5 percent of male saints compared to 14 percent of female saints ($\chi^2 = 29.306$, $p < 0.001$) engaged in this form of heroic asceticism. Thus, the probability that a holy woman would seek God through excessive fasting was almost three times greater than the likelihood for a holy man.

The above data are in line with our expectations about differential patterns of male and female fasting among medieval saints. But these overall figures only tell part of the story. First of all, if we look at the overall figures for the three time periods, we see a steady rise in fasting saints, from 4.5 percent in the fifth to tenth centuries to almost 7 percent in the eleventh and twelfth centuries, and then to 10 percent in the thirteenth to fifteenth centuries. Again, this meets our general expectations given what we know of the religious revival of the twelfth century and beyond.

Furthermore, if we look at the details of patterns of male and female fasting across time periods, we see that both genders have fairly low rates for the first two time periods, with no significant differences in heroic fasting between men and women saints. Thus, in the fifth to tenth centuries, 6.4 percent of holy women and 4.1 percent of holy men ($\chi^2 = 1.097$, $p = 0.295$) practiced excessive fasting, a minor difference that is of no statistical significance. Interestingly, in the eleventh and twelfth centuries, proportionately less women (4.3 percent) than men (7.1 percent) were excessive fasters, but again, these differences do not reach statistical significance ($\chi^2 = 0.251$, $p = 0.617$). Although the numbers are small, percentage-wise there were more men than women heroic fasters in the eleventh and twelfth centuries. This is a finding that runs counter to conventional assumptions about fasting as the almost unique domain and preferred pattern of ascetic behavior of holy women.

As we move into the thirteenth and fifteenth centuries, we return to the expected pattern. The rate for male fasting saints of almost 5 percent returns closely to its early medieval levels. By contrast, the percentage of fasting female saints increases by more than fivefold from 4 percent in the previous two centuries to 23 percent in the late Middle Ages. This difference is statistically highly significant ($\chi^2 = 32.886$, $p < 0.001$). It appears that the much discussed linkage between religious women and fasting, and the broad theoretical implications of this as a form of feminine spirituality and protest, is, at best, meaningful only for the late Middle Ages. Prior to the thirteenth to fifteenth centuries time period, there are no distinguishing features to female as compared to male fasting patterns.

Sleep deprivation

Of our cohort of 1,462 saints, 4 percent were recognized in their lifetimes or by posterity for their extraordinary degree of voluntary sleep deprivation. From the perspective of gender, 3 percent of holy men compared to 10 percent of holy women engaged in this form of heroic asceticism (χ^2 = 29.299, p < 0.001). Thus, holy women were more than three times as likely as holy men to practice excessive sleep deprivation.

Similarly to heroic fasting, the pattern of heroic sleep deprivation showed a steady increase across the three time periods. During the fifth to tenth centuries, only 2 percent of saints were likely to engage in excessive sleep deprivation. In the eleventh and twelfth centuries, the percentage increases to 3 percent. There is then almost a threefold increase in heroic sleep deprivation to 8.5 percent in the thirteenth to fifteenth centuries (χ^2 = 31.196, p < 0.001).

Gender differences for sleep deprivation are noteworthy, as they were for heroic fasting, but the patterns are different. For the fifth to tenth centuries, women saints show a higher rate (4 percent) than men saints (2 percent) in this form of heroic asceticism. As can be seen, however, the percentages are quite low and the difference between males and females do not reach statistical significance (χ^2 = 2.040, p = 0.153).

When we turn to the eleventh and twelfth centuries, we see virtually no change in the percentage of female sleep deprivers and a minimal increase in male sleep deprivers to 3 percent, but, obviously, this single percentage point difference between male and female rates is not statistically significant (χ^2 = 0.143, p = 0.706). What is noteworthy in these numbers is that there was not a decrease in the percentage of female sleep deprivers from the early to middle medieval periods, in contrast to the decrease in the percentage of female heroic fasters. Again, these findings raise questions about the exaggerated importance given in recent years to fasting in women saints.

When we come to the thirteenth to fifteenth centuries, gender differences in regard to heroic sleep deprivation finally emerge. During this time period, 5.0 percent of male saints engaged in this form of asceticism, representing a modestly progressive increase over the three time periods that reaches statistical significance (χ^2 = 9.056, p = 0.011). The proportion of women saints engaging in heroic sleep deprivation increased from 3.6 percent in the early medieval period to 4.3 percent in the middle period and then dramatically to 17.4 percent in the late medieval period, a change that is highly significant (χ^2 = 12.654, p < 0.002).

It is the difference in regard to heroic sleep deprivation between male (5.0 percent) and female (17.4 percent) saints in the thirteenth to fifteenth centuries that is most dramatic (χ^2 = 16.433, p < 0.001). We see that the 800-year-old pattern of relatively equal rates of heroic asceticism between male and female saints is shattered, with women saints showing a 400–500 percent greater likelihood compared to male saints to engage in heroic sleep deprivation and fasting in the last three centuries of the Middle Ages.

APPENDIX: STATISTICAL ANALYSES

Laceration of the flesh

From our database of 1,462 holy persons, 6 percent were recognized in their lifetimes for the extraordinary fervor of laceration of their flesh. For the entire time period, 14 percent of women saints exhibited this type of direct self-injurious behavior as compared to only 5 percent of men saints ($\chi^2 = 29.499$, $p < 0.001$). Thus, women saints were almost three times more likely to lacerate their flesh than men saints. This compares closely to the gender differences for heroic sleep deprivation and fasting.

The distribution of these patterns over a millennium provides additional insights. During the early Middle Ages (fifth to tenth centuries), 2.7 percent of holy men engaged in laceration of the flesh. This figure tracks well with 1.6 percent for sleep deprivation and 4.1 percent for excessive fasting. Thus, excessive fasting was roughly twice as common as the other two forms of heroic asceticism in male saints in the early medieval period. This relative emphasis on fasting among male heroic ascetics may have reflected the residual influence of the Egyptian desert fathers on preferences between various forms of asceticism.[4]

The incidence of laceration of the flesh among male saints doubled to 5 percent during the middle medieval period (eleventh and twelfth centuries), and rose to 8 percent during the final three centuries of the Middle Ages. The increases of this form of heroic asceticism in male saints across the three time periods is statistically significant ($\chi^2 = 15.761$, $p < 0.001$). When we compare the three different categories of heroic asceticism for the late medieval period, we see that laceration of the flesh is one and one-half to almost twice as frequently employed as sleep deprivation and excessive fasting.

The distribution patterns over the millennium provide even greater insights when we look at the data for holy women. Thus, during the fifth to tenth centuries, 6 percent of women saints engaged in heroic laceration of the flesh, compared to a drop to 4 percent in the eleventh and twelfth centuries, and, again, a dramatic increase to 23 percent in the thirteenth to fifteenth centuries. When we compare the three forms of heroic asceticism for holy women within this latter time frame, we see that the practices of laceration of the flesh and excessive fasting are roughly the same in the 22–24 percent range, and are more common than the 17 percent figure for sleep deprivation.

Correlations between ascetic subcategories and mysticism by gender and time frame

We will now consider whether any of the subcategories of heroic asceticism are correlated with mysticism. In this analysis, we used a Phi coefficient to test for association between categorical variables. In analyses of data using a Phi coefficient, scores range from −1.0, representing perfect negative correlation to +1.0, which represents perfect correlation between the variables. Thus, for example, a correlation of 1.0 in regard to mysticism and fasting for women saints in the thirteenth to fifteenth centuries would signify that every female mystic fasted and that every female faster was a mystic.

When we look at the population of saints in toto for the entire time period (fifth to fifteenth centuries), we see only modest correlations between mysticism and the three ascetic variables. The Phi coefficients range from r = 0.170 for laceration to r = 0.192 for fasting. While these associations all reach statistical significant ($p < 0.001$), they are actually of very modest strength in terms of predicting how each ascetic category will co-vary with mysticism. The three ascetic subcategories themselves (laceration, sleep deprivation, and fasting) are, as we would expect, highly correlated with each other, i.e. if one engages in laceration, it is highly likely, although not invariably, that one also engages in fasting and sleep deprivation. It is only when we analyze the sample by gender and time frame that we begin to see a pattern to the correlations between mysticism and specific types of heroic self-injurious behaviors.

Correlations for male saints: entire time period

The correlations between mysticism and the three categories of heroic asceticism in male saints for the entire period under study (AD 450–1500) are extremely weak, and do not even reach statistical significance except for the correlation between mysticism and fasting (Phi = 0.088, p = 0.002). This indicates that, for male saints, mysticism and heroic ascetic behaviors, except for the weak interaction between mysticism and fasting, are not related to each other. Few of the ascetic male saints were engaged in mystical pursuits, and few of the male mystics practiced heroic asceticism.

Correlations for female saints: entire time period

In contrast to our finding for male saints, there are respectable correlations between mysticism and heroic asceticism for female saints across the entire millennium. These correlations are all of similar magnitude (laceration: Phi = 0.322; sleep deprivation: Phi = 0.288; fasting: Phi = 0.285; all at $p < 0.001$). The correlation between laceration of the flesh and mysticism is stronger than between the other two ascetic categories and mysticism, although all three are quite close to each other in strength. Correlations of 0.3 and above represent substantial association between a pair of items, such as, in this case, mysticism and laceration of the flesh.

Correlations for male saints: three time frames

There is no significant association between subcategories of asceticism and mysticism in male saints in any of the time periods. In fact, laceration of the flesh and mysticism are negatively correlated (although not reaching statistical significance) in the first two time periods; sleep deprivation is negatively correlated with mysticism for the middle time period, and fasting is very weakly negatively correlated with mysticism for the last time period. In essence, there are no meaningful associations between mysticism and any of the three subcategories of asceticism taken separately. If anything, there is a very weak and non-significant trend suggesting that mysticism and the subcategories of asceticism may be inversely related. Thus, male saints who are mystics tend to be less likely to engage in heroic ascetic behaviors than the male saints in our sample who are not mystics. But statistically, all that one could say is that these variables are unrelated to each other.

Correlations for female saints: three time frames

The three types of ascetic behaviors begin to separate from each other in terms of correlations with mysticism for female saints in the three time periods. In the first time period, there is a modest correlation between sleep deprivation and mysticism, and very weak and non-significant correlations between fasting and laceration and mysticism. The same is true for fasting and mysticism in the middle time period. In fact, there is even a very weak and non-significant negative relationship (Phi = -0.083, p = 0.692) between fasting and mysticism in the eleventh and twelfth centuries, whereas laceration and mysticism in this middle time period are strongly correlated (Phi = 0.550, p = 0.008). The absence of an association between fasting and mysticism in the early and middle time frames, as we mentioned earlier, certainly should make us reconsider the current thinking about the role and dynamics of fasting in female saints, especially if generalizations are made about the importance of fasting in women saints that include women of the fifth to twelfth centuries. It should also invite us to think more about the characteristics of women saints who did and did not fast.

In the eleventh and twelfth centuries, of the three subcategories of asceticism, only laceration of the flesh is correlated with mysticism. All in all, heroic ascetic practices and mysticism have not much to do with each other in holy persons, both men and women, in Western Europe prior to the thirteenth century.

Unlike the male saints in the thirteenth to fifteenth centuries, there are definite although modest correlations between mysticism and all three ascetic subcategories in women saints. The correlations are all of the same magnitude: between sleep deprivation and mysticism: Phi = 0.225, p = 0.016; between mysticism and laceration: Phi = 0.245, p = 0.009; and between mysticism and fasting: Phi = 0.221, p = 0.018. The association between mysticism and each category of asceticism is considerably stronger in thirteenth to fifteenth century women saints compared to women saints of the earlier centuries. It is again interesting to note that heroic fasting occupies no special place among the subcategories of ascetic behaviors in these later centuries. It is indistinguishable from laceration of the flesh and sleep deprivation in its relationship to mysticism. All told, mysticism and each subcategory of ascetic behaviors are modestly correlated in female saints of the thirteenth to fifteenth centuries.

NOTES

1 INTRODUCTION

1 This chapter is intended as an outline or road map of what is to come. As such, almost each sentence containing a factual claim or explanatory hypothesis needs to be expanded and supported by examples and notes. In order to present our basic position in this introductory chapter clearly and to avoid repetition, however, we have purposely refrained from elaborate definitions, justifications, clarifications, and supportive notes. Each of the points presented in this introduction will be picked up and developed in the texts and notes of the relevant chapters.

2 HEROIC ASCETICISM AND SELF-INJURIOUS BEHAVIOR

1 See Henry Chadwick, "The Ascetic Ideal in the History of the Church," *Studies in Church History*, 1985, 22: 1–23. See also Johannes Lindworsky, *The Psychology of Asceticism*, trans. Emil Heiring, London, H.W. Edwards, 1936.
2 See Mircia Eliade (ed.) *Encyclopedia of Religion*, New York, Macmillan, 1987, Vol. 1, pp. 441–2. For a discussion of the principles of Christian asceticism, see Paul K. Meagher, Thomas C. O'Brien, and Consuelo M. Aherne (eds.) *Encyclopedic Dictionary of Religion*, Washington, DC, Sisters of St. Joseph of Philadelphia, 1979, pp. 280–2. See also Owen Chadwick, *Western Asceticism*, Philadelphia, Westminster, 1958.
3 Noel Dermot O'Donoghue, "Vocation," in Noel D. O'Donoghue, *Heaven in Ordinaire: Some Radical Considerations*, Springfield, IL, Templegate, 1979, pp. 24–6.
4 *The Rule of St. Benedict*, Collegeville, MN, Liturgical Press, 1982, Prologue, lines 45–47. See also, Dom Paul Delatte, *The Rule of St. Benedict: A Commentary*, London, Burns, Oates & Washbourne, 1921. For a thoughtful essay on the relevance of Benedict's Rule to modern life, see Esther de Waal, *A Life-Giving Way: A Commentary on the Rule of St. Benedict*, Collegeville, MN, Liturgical Press, 1995.
5 See L. Bouyer, "Asceticism in the Patristic Period," in Walter Mitchell, ed. and trans., *Christian Asceticism and Modern Man*, London, Blackfriars, 1955, pp. 15–29, for a discussion of the guiding principles of patristic asceticism. See also, Peter Brown, *The Body and Society*, New York, Columbia University Press, 1988.
6 The vast amount of data collected by Donald Weinstein and Rudolph Bell, *Saints and Society*, Chicago, University of Chicago Press, 1982, provides many examples.
7 *The Emperor's Monk: Contemporary Life of Benedict of Aniane* by Ardo, trans. Allen Cabaniss, Ilfracombe, Devon, Arthur Stockwell, 1979, p. 51, Ch. 2.3–2.4. See also Bede Lackner, *The Eleventh Century Background of Citeaux*, Washington, DC, Cistercian Publications, 1972 for a discussion of the influence of Eastern asceticism upon Benedict, and Benedict's subsequent influence on Western monasticism.

NOTES

8   *The Emperor's Monk*, p. 52, Ch. 2.5.
9   "The Life of Rusticula, or Marcia, Abbess of Arles," in Jo Ann McNamara and John Halborg (eds. and trans.) *Sainted Women of the Dark Ages*, Durham, Duke University Press, 1992, Chapter 7, p. 126.
10 Ibid.
11 *The Life of Margaret of Ypres*, by Thomas de Cantimpre, trans. Margot King, Toronto, Peregrina Press, 1990, pp. 48–50, Ch. 16, 17.
12 Ibid., pp. 76–80, Ch. 41–5.
13 *The Life of Marie d'Oignies*, by Jacques de Vitry, trans. Margot King, Saskatoon, Peregrina Press, 1986, p. 28, Ch. 29.
14 See Giles Constable, "Moderation and Restraint in Ascetic Practices," in Haijo Jan Westra (ed.) *From Athens to Chartres: Neoplatonism and Medieval Thought*, Leiden, E.J. Brill, 1992, pp. 315–27.
15 See Brenda Bolton, "Via Ascetica: A Papal Quandary," *Studies in Church History*, 1985, 22: 161–91, for Innocent III's role, by way of the Fourth Lateran Council and other actions, in stressing the values of a moderate form of asceticism and the dangers of extreme self-mortification. See also C.H. Lawrence, *Medieval Monasticism*, second edition, London, Longman, 1989.
16 Anne Savage and Nicholas Watson (trans. and eds.) *Anchoritic Spirituality: Ancrene Wisse and Associated Works*, New York, Paulist Press, 1991, p. 202.
17 See, for general discussions about medieval asceticism and spirituality, Bernard McGinn, *The Foundations of Mysticism*, New York, Crossroad, 1991; Steven Fanning, *Mystics of the Christian Tradition*, London, Routledge, 2001; Lackner, *The Eleventh Century Background of Citeaux*; Peter Brown, *The Body and Society*, pp. 213–40, 421–2; Richard Kieckhefer, *Unquiet Souls*, Chicago, University of Chicago Press, 1984.
18 Rudolph Bell, *Holy Anorexia*, Chicago, University of Chicago Press, 1985, p. 116. Bell briefly discusses (pp. 13–16) the medical and psychiatric consequences of starvation, but makes no reference to changes in states of consciousness. See also, Caroline Walker Bynum, *Holy Feast and Holy Fast*, Berkeley, University of California Press, 1987.
19 *The Life of Beatrice of Nazareth, 1200–1268*, trans. and ed. Roger De Ganck, Kalamazoo, MI, Cistercian Publications, 1991, Bk. III, Ch. 6, sec. 209 (pp. 241–3).
20 Beatrice, *Life*, Bk. III, Ch. 6, sec. 212 (p. 245).
21 1 Kings 18:28, in *The New Oxford Annotated Bible*, eds. Bruce Metzger and Roland Murphy, New York, Oxford, 1991, p. 454. Other citations to self-injurious behaviors are: Deuteronomy 14:1; Leviticus 19:28; Jeremiah 16:6, 41:5, 47:5.
22 Joseph E. Brown, *The Gift of the Sacred Pipe*, Norman, University of Oklahoma Press, 1971; William K. Powers, *Oglala Religion*, Lincoln, University of Nebraska Press, 1975, pp. 95–100.
23 J. Bowker, *Problems of Suffering in Religions of the World*, Cambridge, Cambridge University Press, 1970.
24 See Norman Cohn, *The Pursuit of the Millennium*, New York, Oxford University Press, 1970, pp. 127–47.
25 See Jerome Kroll and Bernard Bachrach, "Visions and Psychopathology in the Middle Ages," *Journal of Nervous and Mental Disease*, 1982, 170: 41–9; also, by the same authors, "Medieval Visions and Contemporary Hallucinations," *Psychological Medicine*, 1982, 12: 709–21.
26 *The Lives of the Desert Fathers*, trans. Norman Russell, Kalamazoo, MI, Cistercian Publications, 1981, Ch. 13, sec. 3–8.
27 Brian Falloon and Ewald Horwath, "Asceticism: Creative Spiritual Practice or Pathological Pursuit," *Psychiatry*, 1993, 56: 310–20 (with commentary by William Meissner).
28 See E. Roy John, "A Model of Consciousness," in Gary E. Schwartz and David Shapiro (eds.) *Consciousness and Self-Regulation*, New York, Plenum, 1976, pp. 1–50; Karl H.

Pribram, "Some Observations on the Organization of Studies of Mind, Brain, and Behavior," in Norman Zinberg (ed.) *Alternate States of Consciousness*, New York, Free Press, 1977, pp. 220–9. See also the chapter on hypnagogic states and transcendent experience, in Benjamin Kissin, *Conscious and Unconscious Programs in the Brain*, New York, Plenum, 1986, pp. 321–35.

29 See, in general, Donald Price, *Psychological and Neural Mechanisms of Pain*, New York, Raven Press, 1988; J.D. Parkes, *Sleep and its Disorders*, Philadelphia, Saunders, 1985; H. Remschmidt and M.H. Schmidt (eds.) *Anorexia Nervosa*, Toronto, Hogrefe & Huber, 1990.

30 See Daniel M. Wegner and Thalia Wheatley, "Apparent Mental Causation: Sources of the Experience of Will," *American Psychologist*, 1999, 54: 480–92; and, John A. Bargh and Tanya Chartrand, "The Unbearable Automaticity of Being," *American Psychologist*, 1999, 54: 462–79, for a rich discussion of these issues.

31 See Paul Smolensky, "On the Proper Treatment of Connectionism," *Behavioral and Brain Sciences*, 1988, 11: 1–74; see also, William Ramsey, Stephen Stich, and Joseph Garon, "Connectionism, Eliminativism, and the Future of Folk Psychology," in Scott Christensen and Dale Turner (eds.) *Folk Psychology and the Philosophy of Mind*, Hillsdale, NJ, Lawrence Erlbaum, 1993, pp. 315–39.

32 See Gordon Bower, "Awareness, the Unconscious and Repression: An Experimental Psychologist's Perspective," in Jerome L. Singer (ed.) *Repression and Dissociation*, Chicago, University of Chicago Press, 1990, pp. 209–31, for a discussion of these principles in relation to memory.

33 See, for example, B.K. Anand, G.S. Chhina, and B. Singh, "Some Aspects of Electroencephalographic Studies in Yogis," *Electroencephalography and Clinical Neurophysiology*, 1961, 13: 452–6; D. Spiegel, P. Bierre, and J. Rootenberg, "Hypnotic Alteration of Somatosensory Perception," *American Journal of Psychiatry*, 1989, 146: 749–54; J. Kamiya, "Operant Control of the EEG Alpha Rhythm and Some of its Reported Effects on Consciousness," in Charles T. Tart (ed.) *Altered States of Consciousness*, Garden City, NY, Doubleday, 1972, pp. 519–29. See also, F.W. Putnam, T.P. Zahn, and R.M. Post, "Differential Autonomic Nervous System Activity in Multiple Personality Disorder," *Psychiatry Research*, 1990, 31: 251–60. Ignoring for the moment the controversial designation of some patients as having multiple personalities, the normal controls in this study were able to alter their skin conductance and heart rate with hypnotic suggestion. For an exhaustive, if at times uncritical, review of the many studies examining the effects of meditative practices, see Michael Murphy and Steven Donovon, *The Physical and Psychological Effects of Meditation: A Review of Contemporary Research with a Comprehensive Bibliography 1931–1996*, second edition, Sausalito, CA, Institute of Noetic Sciences, 1997.

34 For a summary of the EEG changes related to hypnotic induction and hypnotic states, see Nancy Graffin, William Ray, and Richard Lundy, "EEG Concomitants of Hypnosis and Hypnotic Susceptibility," *Journal of Abnormal Psychology*, 1995, 104: 123–31. See also W.G. Brose and David Spiegel, "Neuropsychiatric Aspects of Pain Management," in Stuart Yudofsky and Robert Hales (eds.) *Textbook of Neuropsychiatry*, Washington, American Psychiatric Press, 1992, pp. 245–75.

35 See Maureen Flynn, "The Spiritual Uses of Pain in Spanish Mysticism," *Journal of the American Academy of Religion*, 1996, 54: 257–78, for a discussion of utilizing pain to bring about an altered state of consciousness in St. John of the Cross, Teresa of Avila, and others.

36 "The Life of the Blessed Gherardesca of Pisa," trans. Elizabeth Petroff, *Vox Benedictina*, 1992, 9: 227–85.

37 See W.F. Bynum, E.J. Browne, and Roy Porter, *Dictionary of the History of Science*, Princeton, Princeton University Press, 1985, pp. 248 and 265–6. See Thomas Nagel, *The View from Nowhere*, New York, Oxford University Press, 1986, pp. 13–19 for a

critique of the weaknesses of physical reductionism, and pp. 28–37 for the problems encountered by dualism as a solution to the mind–body problem. See also Richard Rorty, *Philosophy and the Mirror of Nature*, Princeton, Princeton University Press, 1979, pp. 17–32 for a discussion of mental states.
38 See Mary Midgley, "One World, But a Big One," *Journal of Consciousness Studies*, 1996, 3: 500–14, for a thoughtful review of the issues relating to different levels of analysis of reality.
39 Wayne Proudfoot, *Religious Experience*, Berkeley, University of California Press, 1985, pp. 196–209.
40 For a cross-cultural review of the anthropological and psychological literature on self-injurious behavior, see Armando Favazza, *Bodies Under Siege*, second edition, Baltimore, Johns Hopkins University Press, 1995.
41 See Proudfoot, *Religious Experience*, pp. 136–7.
42 For a discussion of the problems involved in finding a vocabulary for the Ultimate, see Richard H. Jones, *Mysticism Examined: Philosophical Inquiries into Mysticism*, Albany, State University of New York Press, 1993, especially Chapter 5: "A philosophical analysis of mystical utterances" (pp. 101–23).
43 Huston Smith, "Do Drugs Have Religious Import?" *Journal of Philosophy*, 1964, 61: 517–30. This article is reprinted in a more recent volume of old and new essays by Smith, bringing his thoughts on the topic up to date. See Huston Smith, *Cleansing the Doors of Perception: The Religious Significance of Entheogenic Plants and Chemicals*, Boulder, CO, Sentient Publications, 2000. The neologism entheogens refers to "mind-changing substances when they are taken sacramentally" (p. xvi). See also Dmitri Tymoczko, "The Nitrous Oxide Philosopher," *Atlantic Monthly*, May 1996, pp. 93–101, which describes William James's experiments with nitrous oxide as a method of inducing transcendental mental states. The article then proceeds to examine the question of whether drugs can play a role in authentic religious experience.
44 Aldous Huxley, *The Doors of Perception*, London, Chatto & Windus, 1954.
45 R.C. Zaehner, *Mysticism Sacred and Profane*, Oxford, Clarendon Press, 1957.
46 Zaehner, *Mysticism*, p. 198.
47 Zaehner, *Mysticism*, p. 222.
48 Smith, "Do Drugs have Religious Import?" 1964, pp. 23–4.
49 Gertrude the Great of Helfta, *Spiritual Exercises*, trans. Gertrude Jaron Lewis and Jack Lewis, Kalamazoo, MI, Cistercian Publications, 1989, p. 37 (Ch. 2, lines 31–5).
50 *The Life of Lutgard of Aywieres*, by Thomas de Cantimpre, trans. Margot King, Saskatoon, Peregrina, 1987, pp. 32–3 (Ch. 5).
51 Ibid., p. 35. Margot King, the translator, suggests in a footnote that one of Innocent's three crimes was likely the prohibition of new monastic orders, legislated at the Fourth Lateran Council the year before Innocent's death.

3 MYSTICISM AND ALTERED STATES OF CONSCIOUSNESS

1 See Lakoff, George (1987) *Women, Fire, and Dangerous Things*, Chicago: University of Chicago Press, pp. 349–52.
2 See, in general, Dennett, D.C. (1991) *Consciousness Explained*, Boston: Little, Brown; Coan, R.W. (1987) *Human Consciousness and Its Evolution: A Multidimensional View*, Weston, CT: Greenwood; Klein, D.B. (1986) *The Concept of Consciousness*, Lincoln: University of Nebraska Press; Armstrong, D.M and Malcolm, N. (1984) *Consciousness and Causality: A Debate on the Nature of Mind*, Oxford: Basil Blackwell. See also, John F. Kihlstrom (1987) "What This Discipline Needs is a Good Ten-Cent Taxonomy of Consciousness," *Canadian Psychology*, 28: 116–18.
3 See Farber, I.B. and Churchland, Patricia S. (1995) "Consciousness and the

Neurosciences: Philosophical and Theoretical Issues," in Gazzaniga, Michael (ed.) *The Cognitive Neurosciences*, Cambridge, MA: MIT Press.

4 Anthropologists have pointed out that there is no such state as an "ordinary mental state," since what is ordinary in Western culture may not be so in other cultures. In the present context, we refer to the "ordinary mental state" as the relatively attentive, relatively alert, waking mental state that accompanies alpha and beta brain wave patterns as defined by EEG (personal communication, Annual Meeting of the Society for the Anthropology of Consciousness, Berkeley, CA, March 3–4, 1995).

5 See *Fish's Clinical Psychopathology* (1974) ed. Hamilton, M., Bristol: John Wright, p. 82. See also, Natsoulas, T. (1978) "Consciousness," *American Psychologist*, 33: 906–14, which analyzes the seven definitions offered by the 1933 *Oxford English Dictionary*.

6 See, for a discussion of the components of consciousness, Kissin, B. (1986) *Conscious and Unconscious Programs in the Brain*, New York: Plenum, pp. 81–4.

7 See Dale Purves (1992) Book Review of David Dennett, "Consciousness Explained," in *Science*, 257: 1,291–2.

8 Dalai Lama (2002) *How to Practice: The Way to a Meaningful Life*, New York: Pocket Books, p. 221.

9 John, E.R. (1976) "A Model of Consciousness," in Schwartz, G.E. and Shapiro, D. (eds.) *Consciousness and Self-Regulation*, New York: Plenum, p. 4.

10 Ludwig, Arnold M. (1966) "Altered States of Consciousness," *Archives of General Psychiatry*, 15: 225–34.

11 Tart, Charles T. (1977) "Putting the Pieces Together: A Conceptual Framework for Understanding Discrete States of Consciousness," in Zinberg, N. (ed.) *Alternate States of Consciousness*, New York: Free Press, pp. 158–219.

12 *The Life of Beatrice of Nazareth* (1991) trans. and ed. De Ganck, Roger, Kalamazoo, MI: Cistercian Publications, Bk. I, Ch. 77 (p. 101).

13 For an extended discussion, see Laughlin, C.D., McManus, J., and d'Aquili, E. (1990) *Brain, Symbol and Experience: Toward a Neurophenomenology of Human Consciousness*, Boston: Shambhala, pp. 281–4. See also, Winkelman, M. (2000) *Shamanism: The Neural Ecology of Consciousness and Healing*, Westport, CT: Greenwood.

14 For a particularly clear exposition of the application of this principle of conservation to the evolution of the mammalian brain, see MacLean, P. (1990) *The Triune Brain in Evolution*, New York: Plenum. See also Jerison, H. (1991) *Brain Size and the Evolution of Mind*, New York: American Museum of Natural History.

15 See Green, C. and McCreery, C. (1994) *Lucid Dreaming: The Paradox of Consciousness during Sleep*, London: Routledge. See also LaBerge, S. (1992) "Physiological Studies of Lucid Dreaming," in Antrobus, J.S. and Bertini, M. (eds.) *The Neuropsychology of Sleep and Dreaming*, Hillsdale, NJ: Lawrence Erlbaum, pp. 289–303. See also, note 11 above for a reference to lucid dreaming and personality.

16 See Simeon, D., Gross, S., Guralnik, O., Stein, D., Schmeidler, J., and Hollander, E. (1997) "Feeling Unreal: 30 Cases of DSM-III-R Depersonalization Disorder," *American Journal of Psychiatry*, 154: 1,107–13, for a presentation of depersonalization as symptom of mental illness. See also Simeon, Daphne and Abugel, Jeffrey (2004) *Feeling Unreal: Depersonalization Disorder and the Loss of Self*, New York, Oxford University Press. The point should be made explicit, however, that altered states such as depersonalization are also normal phenomena.

17 "The Life of the Blessed Gherardesca of Pisa" (1992) trans. Petroff, Elizabeth, *Vox Benedictina*, Ch. 3, Sec. 25, pp. 247–8.

18 See the series of essays, *The Problem of Pure Consciousness* (1990) ed. Forman, R.K.C., New York: Oxford University Press.

19 See Hilgard, E. (1965) *Hypnotic Susceptibility*, New York, Harcourt, Brace and World, where he defines hypnotizability as the ability to become hypnotized, p. 67.

20 See Tellegen, A. and Atkinson, G. (1974) "Openness to Absorbing and Self-altering Experiences ('Absorption'), A Trait Related to Hypnotic Susceptibility," *Journal of Abnormal Psychology*, 83: 268–77.
21 Rhue, J. and Lynn, S.J. (1989) "Fantasy Proneness, Hypnotizability, and Absorption – A Re-examination," *International Journal of Clinical and Experimental Hypnosis*, 37: 100–6.
22 Pekula, R., Wegner, C., and Levine, R. (1985) "Individual Differences in Phenomenological Experience: States of Consciousness as a Function of Absorption," *Journal of Personality and Social Psychology*, 48: 125–32.
23 *The Life of Margaret of Ypres* (1990) by Thomas de Cantimpre, trans. Margot King, Toronto: Peregrina Press, p. 35, Ch. 8.
24 Ibid., pp. 42–3, Ch. 13.
25 Ibid., p. 47, Ch. 15.
26 There is a construct called the "hidden observer," which refers to the observation that a certain percentage of hypnotized subjects, even under suggestion of amnesia, seem to retain "somewhere" in their psyche for later recall an awareness and memory of that which they ostensibly were not aware of. See Hilgard, E. (1985) *Divided Consciousness*, New York: Wiley, Ch. 9, pp. 185–202.
27 See Spanos, N.P. (1986) "Hypnotic Behavior: A Social–Psychological Interpretation of Amnesia, Analgesia, and 'Trance Logic'," *Behavioral and Brain Sciences*, 9: 449–566. Spanos's article is followed by several commentaries discussing his thesis.
28 d'Aquili, E. and Newberg, A.B. (1999) *The Mystical Mind: Probing the Biology of Mystical Experience*, Minneapolis: Fortress Press.
29 See Hilgard, E. and Hilgard, J. (1975) *Hypnosis in the Relief of Pain*, San Francisco: William Kaufman, pp. 20–3, for a description of depth of hypnotic states; see also Kroger, W. (1977) *Clinical and Experimental Hypnosis*, second edition, Philadelphia: Lippincott, Ch. 8, pp. 50–2.
30 Murphy, M. and Donovon, S. (1997) *The Physical and Psychological Effects of Meditation*, second edition, Sausalito, CA: Institute of Noetic Sciences.
31 Lloyd, D. (2002) "Functional MRI and the Study of Human Consciousness," *Journal of Cognitive Neuroscience*, 14: 818–31; Dehaene, S. and Naccache, L. (2001) "Towards a Cognitive Neuroscience of Consciousness: Basic Evidence and a Workspace Framework," *Cognition* 79: 1–37.
32 West, M.A. (1980) "Meditation and the EEG," *Psychological Medicine*, 10: 369–75. See also the discussion of EEG patterns in meditation, in Austin, J.H. (1998) *Zen and the Brain*, Cambridge, MA: MIT Press, pp. 88–91.
33 Ibid., p. 89.
34 Goldstein, J. (1994) *Insight Meditation*, Boston: Shambhala.
35 Graffin, N.F., Ray, W.J., and Lundy, R. (1995) "EEG Concomitants of Hypnosis and Hypnotic Susceptibility," *Journal of Abnormal Psychology*, 104: 123–31.
36 See, for support of this, L. McCormick, T. Nielsen, M. Ptito, F. Hassainia, A. Ptito, J.-G. Villemure, C. Vera, and J. Montplaisir (1997) "REM Sleep Dream Mentation in Right Hemispherectomized Patients," *Neuropsychologia*, 35: 695–791.
37 West, *Meditation and the EEG*, p. 372.
38 Dennett, D.C. (2002) "How Could I Be Wrong? How Wrong Could I Be?" *Journal of Consciousness Studies*, 9: 13–16.
39 John Locke, in "An Essay Concerning Human Understanding," in E.A. Burtt (ed.) *The English Philosophers from Bacon to Mill*, New York: Random House, 1939, p. 252.
40 See Singer, J.L. (1977) "Ongoing Thought: The Normative Baseline for Alternate States of Consciousness," in N. Zinberg (ed.) *Alternate States of Consciousness*, New York: Free Press, pp. 89–120 (p. 95).
41 See Horowitz, M.J. (1987) *States of Mind: Configurational Analysis of Individual Psychology*, New York: Plenum, for a rich discussion of this topic; see also, Kroll, J.

(1993) *PTSD/Borderlines in Therapy*, New York: W.W. Norton, pp. 79–109; Halligan, S.L., Michael, T., and Clark, D.M. (2003) "Posttraumatic Stress Disorder Following Assault: The Role of Cognitive Processing, Trauma Memory, and Appraisals," *Journal of Consulting and Clinical Psychology*, 71: 419–31.

42 While one can say that, in all humans, both motivations will necessarily be present, nevertheless, the medieval sources provide many examples in which little if any mention is made of anything other than combating carnal thoughts. See P. Brown (1988) *The Body in Society*, New York: Columbia University Press pp. 213–24, who emphasizes the early desert ascetics' struggle primarily with hunger rather than sexuality. But, see also, Columba Stewart (1998) *Cassian the Monk*, New York: Oxford University Press, who considers that the struggle for chastity was omnipresent and pressing, and was closely related to the desert monks' concerns about discipline regarding gluttony.

43 See McGinn, B. (1994) *The Growth of Mysticism*, New York: Crossroad, pp. 26–30.

44 John Cassian (1985) *Conferences*, New York: Paulist Press, Conference One, Sec. 17 (pp. 51–2).

45 Ibid., Conference Nine, pp. 101–2. See, Stewart, *Cassian the Monk*, especially Chapter 7, in which Cassian's views on prayer are discussed.

46 One of the more contentious ongoing debates between medical and religious models has been the attribution of Saul's mystical experience to temporal lobe epilepsy. See Fenwick, P. (1996) "The Neurophysiology of Religious Experience," in Dinesh Bhugra (ed.) *Psychiatry and Religion: Context, Consensus, and Controversies*, London: Routledge, pp. 167–77.

47 Saint Augustine (1961) *Confessions*, New York: Penguin, Bk. 8, Ch. 12 (pp. 177–9). For discussion of the question of Augustine's mysticism, see Bernard McGinn (1991) *The Foundations of Mysticism*, New York: Crossroad, Ch. 7, esp. pp. 228–32. See also Steven Fanning (2001) *Mystics of the Christian Tradition*, London: Routledge, pp. 76–8.

48 *The Life of Ida of Louvain*, trans. Martinus Cawley, Lafayette, OR: Guadalupe Translations, 1990, Bk. 2, Ch. 6, Sec. 10 (pp. 40–1). Acta Sancorum, ed. Johannes Bollandus *et al.*, 64 vols. Paris, 1863–present. (AASS, April, v.II, pp. 155–89).

49 See Ramamurthi, B. (1995) "The Fourth State of Consciousness: The Thuriya Avastha," *Psychiatry and Clinical Neurosciences*, 49: 107–10, for a discussion of the neurophysiological basis of meditative states.

50 See Forman, *The Problem of Pure Consciousness*, pp. 6–8, and, by the same author (1998), "What Does Mysticism Have to Teach Us about Consciousness?" *Journal of Consciousness Studies*, 5: 188–201.

51 Jones, R.H. (1993) *Mysticism Examined: Philosophical Inquiries into Mysticism*, Albany: State University of New York Press, pp. 2–4.

52 *The Life of Lutgard of Aywieres* (1987) by Thomas Cantimpre, trans. Margot King, Saskatoon: Peregrina, p. 45, Ch. 2, Sec. 17.

53 Weil, S. (1987 [1963]) *Gravity and Grace*, London: Routledge, p. 107.

54 "Life of the Blessed Gherardesca of Pisa," 9: 227–85 (pp. 233–4).

55 *Life of Beatrice of Nazareth*, Bk. III, Sec. 247.

56 Walter Nigg (1972) *Warriors of God*, New York: Knopf, p. 22.

57 As an example of how the organized Western Church went about the christenization of barbarian Europe, Rosamunde McKitterick has documented, from the ninth century on, the prevalence of Florilegia, those handbooks of compilations of moral teachings for the purpose of guiding the social and personal behavior of noble laypersons. See McKitterick, R. (1977) *The Frankish Church and the Carolingian Reforms, 789–895*, London: Royal Historical Society, Chapter 5: "The Florilegia," pp. 155–83.

58 McGinn, *The Foundations of Mysticism*, p. xvii.

59 James, W. (1952 [1902]) *The Varieties of Religious Experience*, New York: New American Library, p. 380.

NOTES

60 See Hartmann, E. (1991) *Boundaries in the Mind*, New York: Basic Books.
61 Hartmann, *Boundaries*, p. 49.
62 Cloninger, R.C., Svrakic, D., and Przybeck, T. (1993) "A Psychobiological Model of Temperament and Character," *Archives of General Psychiatry*, 50: 975–90.
63 Hoyt, I., Nadon, R., Register, P., Chorny, J., Fleeson, W., Grigorian, E., Otto, L., and Kihlstrom, J. (1989) "Daydreaming, Absorption, and Hypnotizability," *International Journal of Clinical and Experimental Hypnosis*, 37: 332–42 (p. 333). This study describes daydreaming; it does not speak of thin and thick boundaries. See, however, a study by Michael Schredl and Daniel Erlacher (2004) "Lucid Dreaming Frequency and Personality," *Personality and Individual Differences*, 37: 1,463–73, in which lucid dreaming was associated with thin boundaries, absorption, and imagination (collectively considered as the personality factor: openness of experience).
64 Proust, M. (1992) *Swann's Way*. Volume I of *In Search of Lost Time*, trans. C.K. Scott Moncrieff and Terence Kilmartin, New York: Modern Library, p. 4.
65 Ardo (1979) *The Emperor's Monk: Contemporary Life of Benedict of Aniane*, trans. Allen Cabaniss, Ilfracombe, Devon: Stockwell, Ch. 2, Sec. 4 (p. 51).
66 *Life of Lutgard*, Ch. 21 (p. 23).
67 *Giles of Assisi* (1918) trans. Walter Seton, Manchester: Manchester University Press, p. 22.
68 Hartmann, *Boundaries*, p. 105.
69 Hoyt *et al.* "Daydreaming, Absorption, and Hypnotizability."
70 Hartmann, *Boundaries*, p. 66.
71 Sanchez-Bernardos, M.L. and Avia, M.D. (2004) "Personality Correlates of Phantasy Proneness among Adolescents," *Personality and Individual Differences*, 37: 1,069–79.
72 Berlin, I. (1993) *The Hedgehog and Fox*, Chicago: Ivan Dee, pp. 1–2.
73 A recent study of 15 male subjects in Sweden has suggested that the serotonin system in the brain is associated with the trait of self-transcendence and with openness to spiritual experiences. Again, to spell out that this is not an argument for reductionism, it does speak toward the beginning delineation of a biological underpinning for the types of persons who are more likely (or less likely) to have and accept as valid a variety of transcendental experiences. See, Borg, J., Andree, B., Soderstrom, H., and Farde, L. (2003) "The Serotonin System and Spiritual Experiences," *American Journal of Psychiatry*, 160: 1,965–9.
74 *The Life of Marie d'Oignies* (1986) by Jacques de Vitry, trans. Margot King, Saskatoon: Peregrina. See also, Fanning, *Mystics of the Christian Tradition*, pp. 94–8.
75 See, for example, Clark, W.H. (1970) "The Psychodelics and Religion," in B. Aaronson and H. Osmond (eds.) *Psychedelics: The Uses and Implications of Hallucinogenic Drugs*, New York: Doubleday, pp. 182–95. See also De Rios, M.B. (1989) "Power and Hallucingenic States of Consciousness among the Moche," in Colleen A. Ward (ed.) *Altered States of Consciousness and Mental Health: A Cross-Cultural Perspective*, Newbury Park, CA: Sage Publications, pp. 285–99.
76 Fabian, W. Jr. and Fishkin, S. (1991) "Psychological Absorption: Affect Investment in Marijuana Intoxication," *Journal of Nervous and Mental Disease*, 179: 39–43.
77 For an anthropological survey of the use of psychedelic drugs in trance induction for religious and healing ceremonies, see Winkelman, M. (1992) *Shamans, Priests and Witches: A Cross-Cultural Study of Magico-Religious Practitioners*, Tempe: Arizona State University Anthropological Research Papers, No. 44, pp. 117–21, 149–68; see also Winkelman, *Shamanism*.
78 Murdock, G. and White, D. (1969) "Standard Cross-Cultural Sample," *Ethnology*, 8: 329–69.
79 Winkelman, *Shamans, Priests and Witches*, pp. 108–9.
80 For a discussion of knowledge and availability of potent mind-altering drugs in medieval Europe, see Rothman, T. (1972) "De Laguna's Commentaries on Hallucinogenic

Drugs and Witchcraft in Dioscorides' Materia Medica," *Journal of the History of Medicine*, 46: 562–7.
81 See Cassian, *Conferences*, particularly Conferences Nine and Ten on prayer. See, Stewart, *Cassian the Monk*; see also Rousseau, P. (1978) *Ascetics, Authority, and the Church in the Age of Jerome and Cassian*, Oxford: Oxford University Press, pp. 169–234. See also Bede Lackner (1972) *The Eleventh Century Background of Citeaux*, Washington, DC: Cistercian Publications, pp. 58–61.
82 Irenaeus of Lyons (1992) *Against the Heresies*, New York: Paulist Press. Elaine Pagels discusses the early controversy regarding Gnosticism in *The Gnostic Gospels*, New York: Random House, 1979. See also McGinn, *The Foundations of Mysticism*, pp. 89–101.
83 Markus, R. (1990) *The End of Ancient Christianity*, Cambridge: Cambridge University Press, pp. 181–97.
84 Pagels, E. (2003) *Beyond Belief: The Secret Gospel of Thomas*, New York: Random House, pp. 163–64.
85 Baumeister, R.F. (1991) *Escaping the Self*, New York: Basic Books, pp. 177–200, develops a similar thesis.
86 See, for example, Jilek, W.G. (1989) "Therapeutic Use of Altered States of Consciousness in Contemporary North American Indian Dance Ceremonials," in Ward, *Altered States*, pp. 167–85, for a fuller discussion of the induction rituals into a trance state in several North American tribes.
87 See Markus, *The End*, pp. 199–211, for a discussion of this conflict.
88 Kroll, J. and De Ganck, R. (1986) "The Adolescence of a Thirteenth Century Visionary Nun," *Psychological Medicine*, 16: 745–56.
89 Lakoff, G. and Johnson, M. (1986) *Metaphors We Live By*, Chicago: University of Chicago Press, pp. 29–30. See also, the essay by Richard Jones, "A Philosopical Analysis of Mystical Utterances," in Jones, *Mysticism Examined*, pp. 101–23, which attempts to untangle the dilemma of trying to say something about or to describe the indescribable. Wolfgang Riehle, in *The Middle English Mystics* (London: Routledge & Kegan Paul, 1981), discusses at length the different metaphors used for the different phases of mysticism: preparation for mystical union, for speaking about God, and for mystical union and ecstasy itself, in relation to the English mystics.
90 Richard of St. Victor (1983) *The Twelve Patriarchs* (also called *Benjamin Minor*), Ch. 14, trans. Patrick Grant, *Literature of Mysticism in Western Tradition*, New York: St. Martin's Press. See the extended discussion of Richard of St. Victor in McGinn, *The Growth of Mysticism*, pp. 398–418.
91 See McGinn, *The Growth of Mysticism*, particularly Chapter 5 on Bernard of Clairvaux and Chapter 6 on William of St. Thierry.
92 Gertrude the Great of Helfta (1989) *Spiritual Exercises*, trans. Gertrude Jaron Lewis and Jack Lewis, Kalamazoo, MI: Cistercian Publications, p. 79 (Ch. 5, lines 67–72).
93 See Biddick, K. (1993) "Genders, Bodies, Borders," *Speculum*, 68: 389–418 (p. 414). See also Beckwith, S. (1986) "A Very Material Mysticism: The Medieval Mysticism of Margery Kempe," in David Aers (ed.) *Medieval Literature: Criticism, Ideology and History*, New York: St. Martin's Press, pp. 34–57. See also, Lochrie, K. (1991) *Margery Kempe and Translations of the Flesh*, Philadelphia: University of Pennsylvania Press.
94 See Goldstein, *Insight Meditation*, especially pp. 32–3. We are not suggesting a familiarity of medieval mystics with Eastern teachings, but rather a congruence of experience in a state of rapture.
95 "Life of Genovefa" (Chap. I. 4), in J. McNamara and J. Halborg (eds.) (1992) *Sainted Women of the Dark Ages*, Durham, NC: Duke University Press.
96 Cloninger *et al.* "A Psychobiological Model of Temperament and Character," 50: 975–90.
97 Ibid., p. 981.

98 Csikszentmihalyi, M. (1990) *Flow: The Psychology of Optimal Experience*, New York: Harper & Row.
99 There is, at present, a dispute among philosophers of religion as to whether all "mystical experience" is fundamentally and ultimately the same or is shaped in important ways by one's culture and language. There does not seem to be much controversy, even in the absence of a generally accepted definition of "mystical state," that this state, whatever it is, represents an altered state of consciousness. For the universal form of mystical experience, see Stace, W.T. (1960) *Mysticism and Philosophy*, London: Macmillan. For the opposite viewpoint, see Prigge, N. and Kessler, G. (1990) "Is Mystical Experience Everywhere the Same?" in Robert K. C. Forman (ed.) *The Problem of Pure Consciousness*, pp. 269–87; see also Robert Gimello (1983) "Mysticism in Its Context," in Steven T. Katz (ed.) *Mysticism and Religious Traditions*, Oxford: Oxford University Press, pp. 61–88; and Katz, S.T. (1978) "Language, Epistemology, and Mysticism," in Steven T. Katz (ed.) *Mysticism and Philosophical Analysis*, New York: Oxford University Press, pp. 22–74.

4 PAIN AND LACERATION OF THE FLESH

1 For a working model and review of the research literature on this topic, see Eccleston, C. and Crombez, G. (1999) "Pain Demands Attention: A Cognitive-Affective Model of the Interruptive Function of Pain," *Psychological Bulletin*, 125: 356–66.
2 Chapman, C.R. (1980) "Pain and Perception: Comparison of Sensory Decision Theory and Evoked Potential Methods," in John J. Bonica (ed.) *Pain*, New York: Raven Press, p. 111. See also Fernandez, E. and Turk, D.C. (1992) "Sensory and Affective Components of Pain: Separation and Synthesis," *Psychological Bulletin*, 112: 205–17. Mark Sullivan (1996) "Key Concepts: Pain," *Philosophy, Psychiatry, Psychology*, 2: 278–80, provides a philosophical analysis of the problems involved in definitions and concepts of pain.
3 See Melzack, R. (1986) "Neurophysiological Foundations of Pain," in R.A. Sternbach (ed.) *The Psychology of Pain*, second edition, New York: Raven Press.
4 Scarry, E. (1985) *The Body in Pain*, New York: Oxford University Press, p. 21.
5 Mandler, G. (1979) "Thought Processes, Consciousness, and Stress," in Vernon Hamilton and David M. Warburton (eds.) *Human Stress and Cognition*, Chichester: John Wiley, pp. 179–201.
6 See Miller, G.A. (1956) "The Magical Number Seven, Plus or Minus Two: Some Limits on Our Capacity for Processing Information," *Psychological Review*, 63: 81–97. Miller cites many different laboratory experiments in cognitive psychology and information theory, such as the ability to discriminate auditory pitch (tones) and the ability to remember items scattered on a flat surface, in which human performance diminishes rapidly after seven (more or less) bits of information.
7 See Chapman, C.R. (1986) "Pain, Perception, and Illusion," in Sternbach (ed.) *Psychology of Pain*, pp. 156–8.
8 Onen, S.H., Alloui, A., Gross, A., and Eschallier, A. (2001) "The Effects of Total Sleep Deprivation, Selective Sleep Interruption and Sleep Recovery on Pain Tolerance Thresholds in Healthy Subjects," *Journal of Sleep Research*, 10: 35–42.
9 *The Life of Beatrice of Nazareth* (1991), trans. Roger De Ganck, Kalamazoo, MI: Cistercian Publications, Bk. I, Chap. 5. The critical edition is Leonce Reypens (1964) *Vita Beatricis. De Autobiografie van de Z. Beatrijs van Tienen O. Cist., 1200–1268*, Studien en tekstuitgaven van Ons Geestelijk Erf 15, Antwerp: Uitgave Van Het Ruusbroec-Genootschap.
10 See Iversen, S.D. (1983) "Brain Endorphins and Reward Function: Some Thoughts and Speculations," in James E. Smith and John D. Lane (eds.) *The Neurobiology of Opiate Reward Processes*, Amsterdam: Elsevier, pp. 439–68.

NOTES

11 One argument in support of the evolutionary superiority of the female sex is the observation that the female mammal has a separate organ system specialized for the function of reproduction, whereas the evolutionarily backwards male still has his excretory system do double-duty as a reproductive system, which gets him into all types of troubles, e.g. enlarged prostates.
12 Paul MacLean (1990) *The Triune Brain in Evolution*, New York: Plenum.
13 Sandman, S. (1991) "The Opiate Hypothesis in Autism and Self-Injury," *Journal of Child and Adolescence Psychopharmacology*, 1: 237–48.
14 Kroll, J. (1988) *The Challenge of the Borderline Patient*. New York: Norton; Russ, M., Roth, S., Kakuma, T., Harrison, K., and Hull, J. (1994) "Pain Perception in Self-Injurious Borderline Patients: Naloxone Effects," *Biological Psychiatry*, 35: 207–9; Roth, A., Ostroff, R., and Hoffman, R. (1996) "Naltrexone as a Treatment for Repetitive Self-Injurious Behavior: An Open-Label Trial," *Journal of Clinical Psychiatry*, 57: 233–7.
15 Mitchell, J., Laine, D., Morley, J., and Levine, A. (1986) "Naloxone but Not CCK-8 May Attenuate Binge-eating in Patients with Bulimia," *Biological Psychiatry*, 21: 1,399–406; de Zwaan, M. and Mitchell, J. (1992) "Opioid Antagonists and Feeding in Humans: A Review of the Literature," *Journal of Clinical Pharmacology*, 32: 1,060–72.
16 See Yates, A., Leehey, K., and Shisslak, C.M. (1983) "Running: An Analogue of Anorexia?" *New England Journal of Medicine*, 308: 251–5. See also, Colt, E.W.D., Wardlaw, S.L., and Frantz, A.G. (1981) "The Effect of Running on ß-endorphins," *Life Sciences*, 28: 1,632–40.
17 For a full discussion of the physiological mechanisms involved in modulating incoming pain information and central nervous system pain perception, see Frank, H., Cannon, J.T. Lewis, J.W., and Liebeskind, J.C. (1986) "Neural and Neurochemical Mechanisms of Pain Inhibition," in Sternbach (ed.) *Psychology of Pain*, pp. 25–39. See also, Wise, R.A. (1983) "Brain Neuronal Systems Mediating Reward Processes," in Smith and Lane (eds.) *Neurobiology of Opiate Reward Processes*, pp. 405–37; Akil, H., Watson, S., Young, E., Lewis, M., Khachaturian, H., and Walker, J.M. (1984) "Endogenous Opioids: Biology and Function," *Annual Review of Neuroscience*, 7: 223–55; and Fields, H., Heinricher, M., and Mason, P. (1991) "Neurotransmitters in Nociceptive Modulatory Circuits," *Annual Review of Neuroscience*, 14: 219–45.
18 For a strong proponent of hypnosis as a "voluntary response strategy," see Spanos, N.P. (1986) "Hypnotic Behavior: A Social-Psychological Interpretation of Amnesia, Analgesia, and 'Trance Logic'," *Behavioral and Brain Sciences*, 9: 449–502. For the opposing position, that hypnosis is a special (dissociative) state, see Hilgard, E. (1986) *Divided Consciousness*, New York: Wiley.
19 See Hilgard, E. (1991) "Suggestibility and Suggestions as Related to Hypnosis," in John F. Schumaker (ed.) *Human Suggestibility: Advances in Theory, Research, and Application*, New York: Routledge, pp. 37–58.
20 Johnson, M.H., Breakwell, G., Douglas, W., and Humphries, S. (1998) "The Effects of Imagery and Sensory Detection Distractors on Different Measures of Pain: How Does Distraction Work?" *British Journal of Clinical Psychology*, 37: 141–54.
21 Harris, S., Morley, S., and Barton, S.B. (2003) "Role Loss and Emotional Adjustment in Chronic Pain," *Pain*, 105: 363–70.
22 *The Lives of the Desert Fathers* (1981) trans. Norman Russell, Kalamazoo, MI: Cistercian Publications.
23 On Apollo, in *The Lives of the Desert Fathers*, pp. 78–9 (ch. 59).
24 See Bouyer, L. (1955) "Asceticism in the Patristic Period," in Walter Mitchell (ed.) *Christian Asceticism and Modern Man*, London: Blackfriars, pp. 15–29.
25 Akil *et al.*(1984) "Endogenous Opioids," p. 235.

5 SLEEP DEPRIVATION

1 *The Life of Beatrice of Nazareth, 1200–1268*, trans. and ed. Roger De Ganck, Kalamazoo, MI: Cistercian Publications, 1991, Bk. I, Ch. 5.
2 Charles Czeisler, Martin Moore-Ede, and Richard Coleman, "Resetting Circadian Clocks: Applications to Sleep Disorders Medicine and Occupational Health," in *Sleep/Wake Disorders: Natural History, Epidemiology, and Long-Term Evolution*, Christian Guilleminault and Elio Lugaresi (eds.), New York, Raven Press, 1983, pp. 243–60.
3 See James Horne, *Why We Sleep*, Oxford, Oxford University Press, 1988; see also J.A. Hobson, *The Dreaming Brain*, New York, Basic Books, 1988.
4 June J. Pilcher and Allen I. Huffcutt, "Effects of Sleep Deprivation on Performance: A Meta-Analysis," *Sleep*, 1996, 19: 318–26.
5 M.H. Bonnet and D.L. Arand, "Clinical Effects of Sleep Fragmentation Versus Sleep Deprivation," *Sleep Medicine Reviews*, 2003, 7: 297–310.
6 E.T. Aronen, E.J. Paavonen, M. Fjallberg, M. Soininen and J. Torronen, "Sleep and Psychiatric Symptoms in School-age Children," *Journal of the American Academy of Child and Adolescent Psychiatry*, 2000, 39: 502–8.
7 E.E. Whang, A. Perez, H. Ito, M.M. Mello, S.W. Ashley, and M.J. Zinner, "Work Hours Reform: Perceptions and Desires of Contemporary Surgical Residents," *Journal of the American College of Surgeons*, 2003, 197: 624–30.
8 The classical study of REM-sleep deprivation is by William Dement, "The Effect of Dream Deprivation," *Science*, 1960, 131: 1,705–7. For a historical review of the discovery of REM-sleep, see David Foulkes, "Dream Research: 1953–1993," *Sleep*, 1996, 19: 609–24.
9 See G.W. Vogel, "A Review of REM Sleep Deprivation," *Archives of General Psychiatry*, 1975, 32: 749–61; also D.B. Cohen, "The Cognitive Activity of Sleep," *Progress in Brain Research*, 1980, 53: 307–24.
10 See Carlyle Smith, "Sleep States and Memory Processes," *Behavioral Brain Research*, 1995, 69: 137–45; also Carlyle Smith, "REM Sleep and Learning: Some Recent Findings," in *The Functions of Dreaming*, Alan Moffit, Milton Kramer, and Robert Hoffman (eds.), Albany, State University of New York Press, 1993; also E. Hennevin and B. Hars, "Post-learning Paradoxical Sleep: A Critical Period when New Memory is Activated?" in *Brain Plasticity, Learning and Memory: Advances in Behavioral Biology*, B.E. Will, P. Schmitt, and J.C. Dalrymple-Alford (eds.), New York, Plenum, 1985, pp. 193–203; also, Avi Karni, David Tanne, Barton Rubenstein, Jean Askenasy, and Dov Sagi, "Dependence on REM Sleep of Overnight Improvement of a Perceptual Skill," *Science*, 1994, 265: 679–82.
11 For reviews of the effects of total sleep deprivation, see R.T. Wilkinson, "Sleep Deprivation," in *Physiology of Survival*, O.G. Edholm and A.L. Bacharach (eds.), London, Academic Press, 1965, pp. 399–430. See also J.A. Horne, "A Review of the Biological Effects of Total Sleep Deprivation in Man," *Biological Psychiatry*, 1978, 7: 55–102.
12 G.L. Belenky, "Unusual Visual Experiences Reported by Subjects in the British Army Study of Sustained Operations," *Military Medicine*, 1979, 144: 695–6.
13 L.J. West, H.H. Jantzen, B.K. Lester, and F.S. Corneilson, "The Psychosis of Sleep Deprivation," *Annals of the New York Academy of Sciences*, 1962, 96: 66–70.
14 John J. Ross, "Neurological Findings After Prolonged Sleep Deprivation," *Archives of Neurology*, 1965, 12: 399–403.
15 M. Koslowsky and H. Babkoff, "Meta-analysis of the Relationship between Total Sleep Deprivation and Performance," *Chronobiology International*, 1992, 9: 132–6.
16 Harvey Babkoff, Helen Sing, David Thorne, Sander Genser, and Frederick Hegge, "Perceptual Distortions and Hallucinations Reported During the Course of Sleep

NOTES

Deprivation," *Perceptual and Motor Skills*, 1989, 68: 787–98; D.J. Mullaney, D.F. Kripke, P.A. Fleck, and L.C. Johnson, "Sleep and Nap Effects on Continuous Sustained Performance," *Psychophysiology*, 1983, 20: 643–51; Harold Williams, Gary Morris, and Ardie Lubin, "Illusions, Hallucinations and Sleep Loss," in *Hallucinations*, Louis J. West (ed.), New York, Grune & Stratton, 1958, pp. 158–65.
17 Pilcher and Huffcutt, "Effects of Sleep Deprivation," p. 323.
18 V. Cortes-Gallegos, G. Catenada, R. Alonso, I. Sojo, A. Carranco, C. Cervantes, and A. Parra, "Sleep Deprivation Reduces Circulatory Andogens in Healthy Man," *Archives of Andrology*, 1983, 10: 33–7.
19 J. Born and H.L. Fehm, "Interactions between the Hypothalamus–Pituitary–Adrenal System and Sleep in Humans," in *Sleep and Health Risk*, J.H. Peter, T. Penzel, T. Podszus, and P. von Wichert (eds.), Berlin, Springer, 1991, pp. 503–11.
20 Mary A. Carskadon, E. John Orav, and William Dement, "Evolution of Sleep and Daytime Sleepiness in Adolescents," in *Sleep/Wake Disorders: Natural History, Epidemiology, and Long-Term Evolution*, Christian Guilleminault and Elio Lugaresi (eds.), New York, Raven Press, 1983, pp. 201–16.
21 Mary Carskadon and William Dement, "Sleepiness in the Normal Adolescent," in *Sleep and its Disorders in Children*, Christian Guilleminault (ed.), New York, Raven Press, 1987, pp. 53–66.
22 Amy Wolfson and Mary Carskadon, "Early School Start Times Affect Sleep and Daytime Functioning in Adolescents," *Sleep Research*, 1996, 25: 117.
23 Mary Carskadon, C. Vieira, and C. Acerbo, "Association between Puberty and Delayed Sleep Preference," *Sleep*, 1993, 16: 258–62.
24 W. David Brown, Paul Finn, Charyn Desautel, and William Mezzanotte, "Adolescence, Sleepiness, and Driving," *Sleep Research*, 1996, 25: 459.
25 W.B. Webb, "A Further Analysis of Age and Sleep Deprivation Effects," *Psychophysiology*, 1985, 22: 156–61.
26 Pilcher and Huffcutt, "Effects of Sleep Deprivation", p. 324.
27 Dinges, D.F., Pack, F., Williams, K., Gillen, K.A., Powell, J.W., Ott, G.E., Aptowicz, C., and Pack, A.I., "Cumulative Sleepiness, Mood Disturbance, and Psychomotor Vigilance Performance Decrements During a Week of Sleep Restricted to 4–5 Hours per Night," *Sleep*, 1997, 20: 267–77.
28 *The Rule of St. Benedict*, Collegeville, MN, Liturgical Press, 1982, see especially Chapters 8–18. Chapter 22 sets out the sleeping arrangements for the monks.
29 See Dom Paul Delatte, *The Rule of St. Benedict: A Commentary*, London, Burns, Oates & Washbourne, 1921, pp. 140–1.
30 Thomas Merton, *The Waters of Siloe*, New York, Harcourt Brace Jovanovich, 1949, pp. x–xi.
31 Onen, S.H., Alloui, A., Gross, A., and Eschallier, A., "The Effects of Total Sleep Deprivation, Selective Sleep Interruption and Sleep Recovery on Pain Tolerance Thresholds in Healthy Subjects," *Journal of Sleep Research*, 2001, 10: 35–42.
32 *Life of Beatrice*, BK. I, Ch. 5.

6 FASTING AND STARVATION

1 Ancel Keys, Joseph Brozek, Austin Henschel, Olaf Mickelsen, and Henry Taylor, *The Biology of Human Starvation*, 2 vols., Minneapolis, University of Minnesota Press, 1950.
2 Keys *et al.*, *Biology of Human Starvation*, Vol. II, pp. 767–8.
3 Kathy L. Pearson, "Nutrition and the Early-Medieval Diet," *Speculum*, 1997, 72: 1–32.
4 Pearson, "Nutrition and the Early-Medieval Diet," p. 22.
5 Felix's *Life of Saint Guthlac*, trans. Bertram Colgrave, Cambridge, Cambridge University Press, 1956, Chapter 28, pp. 94–5.

NOTES

6 See our discussion on the influences of Guthlac's daily diet on his visionary experiences, in Jerome Kroll and Bernard Bachrach, "Visions and Psychopathology in the Middle Ages," *Journal of Nervous and Mental Disease*, 1982, 170: 41–9.
7 *Life of Guthlac*, Ch. 30, pp. 98–101.
8 See Manfred M. Fichter and Karl-Martin Pirke, "Psychobiology of Human Starvation," in *Anorexia Nervosa*, eds. Helmut Remschmidt and Martin H. Schmidt, Toronto, Hogrefe & Huber, 1990, pp. 13–29; see also Claire Pomeroy and James E. Mitchell, "Medical Complications and Management of Eating Disorders," *Psychiatric Annals*, 1989, 19: 488–93; also Manfred M. Fichter and Karl-Martin Pirke, "Disturbances of Reproductive Function in Eating Disorders," in, *The Menstrual Cycle and its Disorders*, eds. K.M. Pirke, W. Wuttke, and U. Schweiger, Berlin, Springer, 1989, pp. 179–88.
9 American Psychiatric Association, *Diagnostic and Statistical Manual*, fourth edition, revised, Washington, DC, American Psychiatric Press, 1994.
10 See Walter Vandereycken and Ron van Deth, *From Fasting Saints to Anorexic Girls*, New York, New York University Press, 1994, pp. 14–32.
11 This thesis is most developed, although differently by each, in Caroline Walker Bynum, *Holy Feast and Holy Fast*, Berkeley, University of California Press, 1987, and Rudolph Bell, *Holy Anorexia*, Chicago, University of Chicago Press, 1985; see also a review of Bell's book by Jerome Kroll in *Mystics Quarterly*, 1989, 15, 43–6.
12 George I. Szmukler and Digby Tantam, "Anorexia Nervosa: Starvation Dependence," *British Journal of Medical Psychology*, 1984, 57: 303–10.
13 For nineteenth-century descriptions and theories of anorexia nervosa, see Ron van Deth and Walter Vandereycken, "Was Nervous Consumption a Precursor of Anorexia Nervosa?" *Journal of the History of Medicine*, 1991, 46: 3–19; also, Walter Vandereycken and Eugene L. Lowenkopf, "Anorexia Nervosa in 19th Century America," *Journal of Nervous and Mental Disease*, 1990, 178: 531–5.

7 HISTORICAL METHODS: SELECTING A DATABASE

1 Historians have not been quick to accept the incursion of statistical methods (cliometrics) into the traditional narrative manner of writing history. This ambivalence is acknowledged in Andre Vauchez's (*The Laity in the Middle Ages*, Notre Dame, University of Notre Dame Press, 1993, p. 171) semi-apology for employing statistics in his study of female sanctity: "At the risk of offending my readers, I will begin this essay with a few statistics – not in order to conform to the current fashion for quantification, which is not a great help in a domain as complex and as delicate as the history of spirituality, but to call attention to some especially striking evidence." But, we may ask, why would a reader be offended at the use of statistics to place the narrow focus of interest into broader perspective?
2 Petrus de Natalibus, *Catalogus sanctorum et gestarum eorum ex diversis volumnibus collectus*, ed. Antonio Verlo (Strasbourg, 1513). For discussion of Petrus and other medieval collections, see Michael Goodich, *Vita Perfecta: The Ideal of Sainthood in the Thirteenth Century* (Stuttgart, Anton Hiersemann, 1982), pp. 11–12.
3 Sixty-three volumes to date of the third edition (Antwerp–Brussels–Paris, 1863–1940) have appeared. David Knowles, *Great Historical Enterprises* (London, Nelson, 1963), pp. 3–22, provides an excellent introduction to the work of this Jesuit group which has come to be called "The Bollandists."
4 For useful guides to dealing with *Acta Sanctorum*, see R.C. van Caenegem and F.L. Ganshof, *Kurze Quellenkunde des Westeuropäischen Mittelalters* (Gottingen, Vandenhoeck & Ruprecht, 1962), pp. 202–3; and Jacques Berlioz, *L'Atelier du Medieviste*, (Turnhout, Brepols, 1994), pp. 195–6, and, more recently, Sofia Boesch Gajano, *Agiografia altomedioevale* (Bologna, Mulino, 1976).

5 St. Augustine's Abbey at Ramsgate, *The Book of Saints*, fourth edition (New York: Macmillan, 1947). It would seem that Frederick G. Holweck, *A Biographical Dictionary of Saints* (St. Louis, Herder, 1924) provides reference to even more holy persons than those found in the Ramsgate collection. For a brief overview on these compendia, see John F. Broderick, "A Census of the Saints (993–1955)," *American Ecclesiastical Review*, 1956, 135: 87–115. For a more recent overview of various compendia, see Jane Schulenburg, *Forgetful of Their Sex: Female Sanctity and Society, ca. 500–1100* (Chicago, University of Chicago Press, 1998), pp. 9–11.
6 *Martyrologium Romanum* (Torino, 1949).
7 *Bibliotheca Sanctorum*, 12 vols., Pontificia Universita Lateranse, Instituto Giovanni XXIII (Rome, Città Nuova, 1960–1970).
8 Paul Guerin, *Les petites Bollandistes*, 17 vols., third revised edition (Paris, 1882–1888). Regarding problems with the above, see Goodich, *Vita Perfecta*, p. 1, n. 1.
9 *Vies des saints et des bienheureux selon l'ordre du calendrier*, eds. Jules Baudot and Leon Chausesin, 13 vols. (Paris, 1935–1959).
10 *Butler's Lives of the Saints*, edited, revised, and supplemented by Herbert Thurston and Donald Attwater, 4 vols. (London, Burns & Oates, 1956).
11 Sabine Baring-Gould, *The Lives of the Saints*, 16 vols. (London, 1916).
12 Broderick, "A Census of the Saints," pp. 87–115.
13 See Eric W. Kemp, *Canonization and Authority in the Western Church* (London, Oxford University Press, 1948).
14 J. O'Hanlon, *Lives of the Irish Saints*, 10 vols. (Dublin, 1875–1913).
15 David Hugh Farmer, *The Oxford Dictionary of Saints*, second edition (Oxford, Oxford University Press, 1987).
16 *Kalendars of Scottish Saints*, ed. A.P. Forbes (Edinburgh, 1872).
17 Agnes Dunbar, *A Dictionary of Saintly Women*, 2 vols. (London, G. Bell & Sons, 1904–1905).
18 Schulenburg, *Forgetful of their Sex*.
19 Jo Ann McNamara and John Halborg (eds.), *Sainted Women of the Dark Ages* (Durham, NC, Duke University Press, 1992).
20 Elizabeth Petroff, *Medieval Women's Visionary Literature* (New York, Oxford University Press, 1986).
21 Robert Folz, *Les saints rois du Moyen Age en Occident* (Brussels, 1894).
22 Goodich, *Vita Perfecta*, pp. 3 and 15 for the quotations, respectively.
23 See Schulenburg, *Forgetful of Their Sex*, p. 11.
24 Pitirim A. Sorokin, *Altruistic Love: A Study of American "Good Neighbors" and Christian Saints* (Boston, Beacon, 1950).
25 Pierre Delooz, Sociologie et canonisations. Collection scientifique de la Faculté de Droit de l'Université de Liège, no. 30. (Liège, 1969).
26 Donald Weinstein and Rudolph Bell, *Saints and Society: Christendom, 1000–1700* (Chicago, University of Chicago Press, 1982).
27 Schulenburg, *Forgetful of Their Sex*.
28 Katherine and Charles George, "Roman Catholic Sainthood and Social Status: A Statistical and Analytical Study," *Journal of Religion*, 1955, 35: 85–98.
29 Goodich, *Vita Perfecta*, p. 18.
30 Pierre Delooz, "Towards a sociological study of canonized sainthood in the Catholic Church," in *Saints and their Cults: Studies in Religious Sociology, Folklore, and History*, ed. Stephen Wilson (Cambridge, Cambridge University Press, 1983), pp. 189–216.
31 Weinstein and Bell, *Saints and Society*, p. 7.
32 Hippolyte Delehaye, *Analecta Bollandiana* 1939, p. 57.
33 See *Butler's Lives of the Saints*, eds. Thurston and Attwater, preface, p. v.
34 See Schulenburg, *Forgetful of Their Sex*, p. 12.

35 McNamara and Halborg, *Sainted Women*.
36 Petroff, *Medieval Women's Visionary Literature*.
37 Giles Constable, *The Reformation of the Twelfth Century* (Cambridge, Cambridge University Press, 1966), pp. 257–328.
38 Goodich, *Vita Perfecta*. Goodich studied the 1215–1334 time frame, but we shall refer to this in our text for the sake of brevity as the thirteenth century.
39 See Hippolyte Delehaye, *The Legends of the Saints*, trans. Donald Attwater (New York, Fordham, 1962).
40 B. McGinn, *The Flowering of Mysticism* (New York, Crossroad, 1998), p. 37, considers Marie's " extravagant ascetical practice and ecstatic rapture" as pointing to the way of "the new mysticism."
41 *The Life of Marie d'Oignies*, by Jacques de Vitry, trans. Margot King (Saskatoon, Peregrina Press, 1986), Bk. I, Ch. 2 (p. 14).
42 Amy Hollywood, *The Soul as Virgin Wife*, Notre Dame, University of Notre Dame Press, 1995, p. 49.
43 Kari Elisabeth Børresen, "Women's Studies of the Christian Tradition: New Perspectives," in Ursula King (ed.) *Religion and Gender* (Oxford, Blackwell, 1995), pp. 245–55.
44 Hollywood, *Soul as Virgin Wife*, p. 29.
45 Ibid., p. 30.
46 *Life of Beatrice of Nazareth*, ed. De Ganck, (Kalamazoo, MI, Cistercian Publications, 1991), p. x.
47 Jerome Kroll, *PTSD/Borderlines in Therapy* (New York, W.W. Norton, 1993).
48 Hollywood, *Soul as Virgin Wife*, p. 42.
49 See Jerome Kroll and Bernard Bachrach, "Visions and Psychopathology in the Middle Ages," *Journal of Nervous and Mental Disease*, 1982, 170: 41–9 (p. 44), in which a nutritional analysis is provided of Guthlac's daily diet of half a cup of barley bread; and see Chapter 6 this volume.
50 McGinn, *The Flowering of Mysticism*, p. 27.
51 Ibid., p. 30. Ernest Gombrich, *The Story of Art* (New York, Phaidon, 1972, p. 157) has commented on the increasingly popular use of smaller statues of precious metal or ivory in private chapels in the fourteenth century and that were intended not "to proclaim a truth in solemn aloofness, like the statues of the great cathedrals, but to excite love and tenderness."
52 See Jerome Kroll and Bernard Bachrach, "Sin and the Etiology of Disease in Pre-Crusade Europe," *Journal of the History of Medicine*, 1986, 41: 395–414. We discuss in another article the uses of other medieval source material, such as chronicles and contemporary histories, for medical diagnoses. See, by the same authors, "Justin's Madness: Weak-mindedness or Organic Psychosis?" *Journal of the History of Medicine*, 1993, 48: 40–67.

8 PATHWAYS TO HOLINESS

1 See S. Fanning, *Mystics of the Christian Tradition* (London, Routledge, 2001), pp. 216–20 for a related discussion.
2 The problem of reliability versus validity is almost identical in psychiatric and, in this case, medieval holiness classification. To look just at overt behaviors is to increase reliability (likelihood of agreement between two observers), but runs the risk of ignoring essential elements of what makes a person the type of person that he or she is. Criminal actions may make for more reliable identification of some sociopaths, but the traits of immorality or lack of empathy may go to the core of sociopathy, although harder to identify, just as the trait of compassion may define the core of holiness but be harder to measure than the behaviors of charitable generosity.

NOTES

3 Anonymous, "Life of St. Cuthbert," in Bertram Colgrave, trans. and ed., *Two Lives of St. Cuthbert* (New York, Greenwood, 1969), Bk. III, Ch. 7 (pp. 105–7).
4 L. Bouyer, "Asceticism in the Patristic Period," in Walker Mitchell, trans. and ed., *Christian Asceticism and Modern Man* (London, Blackfriars, 1955), p. 20.
5 See Richard Kieckhefer, *Unquiet Souls* (Chicago, University of Chicago Press, 1984, pp. 64–6) for a discussion of the fascination and fantasies of martyrdom manifested by many of the saints of the fourteenth century, and the replacement of actual martyrdom with self-inflicted injuries and joyful suffering through painful illnesses.
6 *The Life of Juliana of Mont Cornillon*, trans. Barbara Newman (Toronto, Peregrina, no year), Bk. II, Prologue (p. 72).
7 The story of Cloud and his brothers was narrated in bloody detail by Gregory of Tours (d.594), a contemporary of these events. See Gregory of Tours, *The History of the Franks*, trans. and ed. Lewis Thorpe (Harmondsworth, Penguin, 1974), Bk. III, Ch. 18 (pp. 180–2). The only extant *vita* of Cloud was written, about one hundred years after his death, during the reign of Charlemagne. This *vita* was apparently based upon an earlier one, now lost. See also Bernard Bachrach, *Anatomy of a Small War* (Berkeley, University of California Press, 1995).
8 Andre Vauchez, *The Laity in the Middle Ages: Religious Beliefs and Devotional Practices* (Notre Dame, University of Notre Dame Press, 1993), p. 172.
9 Nicholas Watson, "The Methods and Objectives of Thirteenth Century Anchoritic Devotion," in *The Medieval Mystical Tradition in England: Exeter Symposium IV*, ed. Marion Glasscoe (Woodbridge, Suffolk, Boydell & Brewer, 1987), p. 135.
10 See Kieckhefer, *Unquiet Souls*, pp. 33–44, for an extended discussion of Peter of Luxembourg's ascetic behaviors and early death.
11 See *The Life of Beatrice of Nazareth*, trans. and ed. Roger De Ganck (Kalamazoo, Cistercian Publications, 1991), p. x, for discussion. See also Amy Hollywood, *The Soul as Virgin Wife* (Notre Dame, University of Notre Dame Press, 1995), pp. 29–32, and Chapter 10 of the present volume.
12 See Jo Ann McNamara and John Halborg, eds., *Sainted Women of the Dark Ages* (Durham, NC, Duke University Press, 1992), for a compendium of Dark Age women saints.
13 Kieckhefer (*Unquiet Souls*, p. 70) defines fourteenth-century mystics as persons who "cultivated an intense consciousness of God's presence and of personal union with God, a consciousness which sometimes blossomed in ecstatic mystical experiences."
14 B. McGinn, *The Flowering of Mysticism* (New York, Crossroad, 1998), pp. 25–6.
15 Nancy N. Potter, "Commodity/Body/Sign: Borderline Personality Disorder and the Signification of Self-Injurious Behavior," *Philosophy, Psychiatry, Psychology*, 2003, 10: 1–16.
16 S. Weil, *Gravity and Grace*, trans. Gustave Thibon (London, Routledge, 1963).
17 Vauchez, *Laity in the Middle Ages*, p. 171.
18 D. Weinstein and R. Bell, *Saints and Society* (Chicago, University of Chicago Press, 1982), pp. 220–2.
19 J.T. Schulenburg, *Forgetful of their Sex* (Chicago, University of Chicago Press, 1978), p. 63; see also, Jane T. Schulenburg, "Sexism and the Celestial Gynaeceum, from 500 to 1200," *Journal of Medieval History*, 1978, 4: 117–33.
20 M. Goodich, *Vita Perfecta: The Ideal of Sainthood in the Thirteenth Century* (Stuttgart: Anton Hiersemann, 1982), p. 20.
21 Peter Dinzelbacher, "The Beginnings of Mysticism Experienced in Twelfth Century England," in *The Medieval Mystical Tradition in England: Exeter Symposium IV*, ed. Marion Glasscoe (Woodbridge, Suffolk: Boydell & Brewer, 1987), pp. 111–31.
22 Ibid., p. 119.
23 See, Arthur Kleinman, "Neurasthenia and Depression: A Study of Somatization and Culture in China," *Culture, Medicine, and Psychiatry*, 1982, 6: 117–90; Simon Wessley,

"Neurasthenia and Chronic Fatigue: Theory and Practice in Britain and America," *Transcultural Psychiatric Research Review*, 1994, 31: 173–209; Jerome Kroll, Marjorie Habenicht, Thomas Mackenzie, Mee Yang, Sokha Chan, Tong Vang, Tam Nguyen, Mayjoua Ly, Banlang Phommasouvanh, Hung Nguyen, Yer Vang, Langsanh Souvannasoth, and Robert Cabugao, "Depression and Posttraumatic Stress Disorder in Southeast Asian Refugees," *American Journal of Psychiatry*, 1989, 146: 1,592–7.

24 We used a Phi coefficient as a measure of association. The Phi coefficient is expressed as a decimal between −1, which indicates perfect negative association (no mystic is an ascetic; no ascetic is a mystic), and +1, which indicates perfect association (every mystic is an ascetic; every ascetic is a mystic). Phi coefficients of less than 0.2 are considered indicative of a weak association; coefficients between 0.2 and 0.4 are considered indicative of modest to moderate associations; coefficients above 0.4 are considered indicative of strong associations. Generally, in social science research, correlations above Phi = 0.3 between variables are considered as representing meaningful associations between the variables in question. The Phi coefficient for the association between mysticism and heroic asceticism for the entire population (N = 1,462) is 0.227, p > 0.001. This modest correlation between mysticism and asceticism for the entire sample reaches statistical significance because of the large size of the sample, and reflects the finding that most holy persons fell into the "not mystic–not heroic ascetic" category.

25 For male saints, Phi = 0.093, p = 0.001; for female saints, Phi = 0.377, p < 0.001. Here again, although the association between asceticism and mysticism is statistically significant in both male and female saints, the association in the sample of women saints is much stronger. Expressed in terms of explanation of variance, a Phi of 0.377 explains 14 percent of the variance, whereas a Phi of 0.093 explains only 0.8 percent of the variance. Accounting for 14 percent of variance is a respectable figure in the social sciences.

26 For males, Phi = 0.147, p < 0.001; for females, Phi = 0.259, p = 0.007.

27 For males, Phi = 0.085, p = 0.191 (not significant); for females, Phi = 0.339, p = 0.104 (not significant). In the eleventh and twelfth centuries, the association between mysticism and asceticism is very weak for males, and appears moderately correlated for females, but the correlation fails to reach statistical significance because the number of female saints in this time frame is too small.

28 For males, Phi = 0.025, p = 0.666; for females, Phi = 0.290, p = 0.002. There is no association between asceticism and mysticism for male saints in the thirteenth to fifteenth centuries, compared to a moderate association for female saints in the same time period.

29 Elizabeth Petroff, *Body and Soul* (New York, Oxford University Press, 1994), p. 20.

30 See G. Constable, *The Reformation of the Twelfth Century* (Cambridge, Cambridge University Press, 1966), pp. 226ff., and pp. 317ff., for trenchant critiques of viewing the religious reforms primarily as reactions against earlier values.

31 The possibility of gender differences in values has its echoes in the modern controversy between psychologists Kohlberg and Gilligan as to whether justice (an instrumental value) or caring (a social value) represents the higher or "more moral" value and whether these traits are differentially distributed by sex.

32 Although not formulated in gender terms, Iris Murdoch's discussion of two basic forms of the modern novel ("The existentialist novel shows us freedom and virtue as the assertion of will. The mystical novel shows us freedom and virtue as understanding, or obedience to the Good") parallels this distinction between individual and community values. See Iris Murdoch *Existentialists and Mystics* (Harmondsworth, Penguin Books 1999), p. 223.

33 See Hollywood, *Soul as Virgin Wife*.

9 RADEGUND

1 Bruno Krush, ed. Monumenta Germaniae Historica, Auctores Antiquissimi, Berlin, Hanover and Leipzig, 1826–present. MGH, AA I: 271–5, Fortunatus, "De excidio Thoringae." Translations used here are by Bernard Bachrach. For English translations, see *Sainted Women of the Dark Ages*, eds. and trans. Jo Ann McNamara and John Halborg, Durham, NC, Duke University Press, 1992, pp. 60–105.
2 Bruno Krush, ed. MGH, Scriptores Rerum Merowingicanum, 2: 358–405, Fortunatus, "*Vita Radegundae*."
3 Baudonivia, *Vita Rad*, Krush (ed.) MGH, SRM 2: 358–405.
4 Gregory of Tours, *Historia Francorum*, Bk. III, Ch. 7. For English translation, see Gregory of Tours, *The History of the Franks*, ed. and trans. Lewis Thorpe, Harmondsworth, Penguin, 1974.
5 Greg., *Hist.*, III, Ch. 4.
6 Ibid., Ch. 7.
7 Ibid., Ch. 8.
8 Fort., *V. Rad.*, Ch. 5.
9 Gregory of Tours spends much ink describing the misdeeds of Fredegund. For example, Fredegund plotted the assassination of King Sigibert (Greg., *Hist.*, IV, 51). She sent her stepson to a town where there was an epidemic in hopes that he would die. When he did not catch the disease, she maligned the young man to his father, King Chilperic, who had him imprisoned. Fredegund then arranged for his assassination (Greg. *Hist.*, V, 39).
10 Greg., *Hist.*, III, Ch. 6.
11 Ibid., III, Ch. 18.
12 Fort., *V. Rad.*, Ch. 12.
13 Baud., *V. Rad.*, Ch. 4.
15 There is an immense literature, often controversial, regarding this complex topic. See, Judith Herman, *Trauma and Recovery*, New York, Basic Books, 1991; see also, Jerome Kroll, *PTSD/Borderlines in Therapy*, New York, W.W. Norton, 1993.
15 See Jerome Kroll, "Posttraumatic Symptoms and the Complexity of Responses to Trauma," *Journal of the American Medical Association*, 2003, 290: 667–70.
16 See, Carl Malmquist, "Children Who Witness Parental Murder: Posttraumatic Aspects," *Journal of the American Academy of Child Psychiatry*, 1986, 25: 320–5. This particular issue of the journal (May 1986) has an entire section devoted to children's reactions to severe stress. See also, Judith Cohen, Lucy Berliner, and Anthony Mannarino, "Psychosocial and Pharmacological Interventions for Child Crime Victims," *Journal of Traumatic Stress*, 2003, 16: 175–86, and Nathaniel Laor, Leo Wolmer, Meltem Kora, *et al.*, "Posttraumatic, Dissociative, and Grief Symptoms in Turkish Children Exposed to the 1999 Earthquakes," *Journal of Nervous and Mental Disease*, 2002, 190: 824–32. For a discussion of the effects of childhood trauma on subsequent neuro-biological development, see Christine Heim, Gunther Meinlschmidt, and Charles Nemeroff, "Neurobiology of Early-Life Stress," *Psychiatric Annals*, 2003, 33: 18–26.
17 Fort., *De excidio Thoringae*, 11.
18 Ibid.
19 There is much discussion regarding the text, which reads *amati*; several commentators have suggested amiti, i.e. aunt.
20 Fort., *De excidio Thoringae*, 11. There is considerable recent literature arguing that claims which suggest the general unreliability of retrospective reports of childhood experiences have been exaggerated; see Chris Brewin, Bernice Andrews, and Ian Gotlib, "Psychopathology and Early Experience: A Reappraisal of Retrospective Reports," *Psychological Bulletin*, 1993, 113: 82–98. Similarly, studies of children who have to testify at forensic situations provide evidence of age-related suggestibility effects, but

conclude "that even very young children are capable of recalling much that is forensically relevant." See, Stephen Ceci and Maggie Bruck, "Suggestibility of the Child Witness: A Historical Review and Synthesis," *Psychological Bulletin*, 1993, 113: 403–39.
21 There may be some confusion here regarding exactly who said goodbye. It seems that this refers both to the married woman who was carried off as a captor who could not say farewell to the household gods, and Radegund who could not "press a kiss to the threshold." It is not fully clear what is autobiographically descriptive and what refers to the experiences of others.
22 Fort., *De excidio Thoringae*, 11.
23 Ibid., 11.
24 Fort., *V. Rad.*, Ch. 2.
25 Greg., *Hist.*, III, Ch. 7.
26 Fort., *V. Rad.*, Ch. 3.
27 Ibid.
28 Ibid., Ch. 5.
29 Baud., *V. Rad.*, Ch. 6.
30 Fort., *V. Rad.*, Ch. 25.
31 Ibid.
32 Ibid., Ch. 25. Jo Ann McNamara, in a footnote to her translation of this *Vita*, suggests that Fortunatus was overly anxious to promote Radegund as a martyr and therefore exaggerated the extent of her mortification of the flesh. See McNamara and Halborg, *Sainted Women*, p. 81, fn. 71.
33 Fort., *V. Rad.*, Ch. 26. As with the making of the apparatus of chains, little hollow circles of iron, and locks, it is clear that a smith or some other artisan provided the devices that Radegund required. It is unlikely that Radegund revealed her intentions to the smith.
34 Fort. *V. Rad.*, Ch. 26.
35 Ibid.
36 Ibid.
37 Ibid.
38 Ibid. The word "foramina" is used to describe the injuries.
39 Fort. *V. Rad.*, Ch. 26.
40 Ibid.
41 Ibid.
42 Herman, *Trauma and Recovery*; see also, Kroll, *PTSD/Borderlines in Therapy*.
43 Lenore Terr, "Childhood Traumas: An Outline and Overview," *American Journal of Psychiatry*, 1991, 148: 10–20; Bessel van der Kolk, J. Christopher Perry, and Judith Herman, "Childhood Origins of Self-Destructive Behavior," *American Journal of Psychiatry*, 1991, 148: 1,665–71; Erik de Wilde, Ineke Kienhorst, Rene Diekstra, and Willem Wolters, "The Relationship between Adolescent Suicidal Behavior and Life Events in Childhood and Adolescence," *American Journal of Psychiatry*, 1992, 149: 45–51; Robin Malinowsky-Rummell and David Hansen, "Long-Term Consequences of Childhood Physical Abuse," *Psychological Bulletin*, 1993, 114: 68–79; Paul Mullen, Judy Martin, Jessie Anderson, Sarah Romans, and G. Peter Herbison, "Childhood Sexual Abuse and Mental Health in Adult Life," *British Journal of Psychiatry*, 1993, 163: 721–32.

10 BEATRICE OF NAZARETH

1 For the critical edition, see Leonce Reypens (ed.) (1964) *Vita Beatricis: De Autobiografie van de Z. Beatrijs van Tienen O. Cist.*, 1200–1268, Antwerp, Uitgave Van Het Ruusbroec-Genootschap. There are four extant Latin manuscripts, three in libraries in Belgium and the fourth in Vienna. See also the three-volume edition encompassing

NOTES

the *Vita* itself in Latin–English translation with two volumes on the historical context of Flemish mysticism by Roger De Ganck: Vol. I, *The Life of Beatrice of Nazareth*; Vol. II, *Beatrice of Nazareth in her Context*; Vol. III, *Towards Unification with God*, Kalamazoo, MI, Cistercian Publications, 1991.
2 De Ganck, *Life of Beatrice*, Bk. I, Ch. 8.
3 See John H. Lynch, "The Cistercians and Underage Novices," *Citeaux*, 1973, 24: 283–97.
4 See De Ganck, *Life of Beatrice*, p. xvi.
5 There do not seem to be any surviving manuscripts from Bloemendaal that can be identified as Beatrice's work.
6 De Ganck, *Life of Beatrice*, p. xvii.
7 The failure to identify the older brother is basically consistent with the fact that he remained in secular life.
8 It is clear (De Ganck, *Life of Beatrice*, p. xvii) that Sybille, Christine, and Wickbert, like Bartholomew, were all under the discipline of the Abbess of Bloemendaal.
9 See Ernest McDonnell, *The Beguines and Beghards in Medieval Culture, with Special Emphasis on the Belgian Scene*, New Brunswick, NJ, Rutgers University Press, 1954, for the general background to the beguines and mystics of the Low Countries.
10 See De Ganck, *Life of Beatrice*, pp. xxix–xxxii, for a discussion of the activity of the papal inquisition in the Brabant and Cambrai regions in the last half of the thirteenth century.
11 For the likely identification of the chaplain, see De Ganck, *Life of Beatrice*, pp. xxii–xxvii. See also Roger De Ganck, "The Biographer of Beatrice of Nazareth," *Cistercian Studies*, 1988, 22: 319–29.
12 *V. Beatricis*, I, 1 (8–15) is in essence the *Vita venerabilis Bartholomi*, which the chaplain indicates that he has abbreviated "brevitatis causa compendiose digestis."
13 For the critical edition, see Leonce Reypens and J. Van Mierlo, *Beatrijs van Nazareth: Seven Manieren van Minne*, Leuven, 1926. See also H. Vekeman, "Vita Beatricis en Seuen manniern van Minne: Een Vergelijk Studie," *Ons Geestelijk Erf*, 1972, 46: 3–54. There are several English translations of this short treatise. See S.M. Carton, "Beatrice of Nazareth: The Seven Steps of Love," *Cistercian Studies*, 1984, 19: 31–42; also Beatrijs of Nazareth: "There are Seven Manners of Loving," trans. Eric Colledge, in Elizabeth A. Petroff (ed.) *Medieval Women's Visionary Literature*, New York, Oxford University Press, pp. 200–6.
14 The fact that the Flemish original of *Minne* survives in four *manuscripts* makes it clear that the edited abridgment was not intended to replace the original treatise as some sort of "sanitized" official version of Beatrice's views and experiences in these matters, unlike the possibility regarding the disappearance of the original Flemish diary. See De Ganck, *Life of Beatrice*, pp. xxv–xxvii for a discussion of the biographer's method of integration of texts.
15 De Ganck, *Life of Beatrice*, p. xxv.
16 A. Hollywood, *The Soul as Virgin Wife*, Notre Dame, University of Notre Dame Press, 1995, pp. 30–5.
17 Of course, 1216 is the earliest date at which she could have put this information into her diary. It is possible that she placed it there at an even later date.
18 See C.R. Barclay, "Schematization of autobiographical memory", in D.C. Rubin (ed.) *Autobiographical Memory*, New York, Cambridge University Press, 1986, pp. 82–99. See also M. Ross and M. Conway, "Remembering One's Own Past: The Construction of Personal Histories," in R.M. Sorrentino and E.T. Higgins (eds.) *Handbook of Motivation and Cognition: Foundations of Social Behavior*, New York, Wiley, 1996, pp. 122–44.
19 De Ganck, for example, has considerable doubt that Beatrice's asceticism was as severe as is reported in the *Vita*. However, he postulates that the biographer, impressed by the heroic asceticism of the local figure Arnulf of Villiers, may have embellished

Beatrice's ascetic feats. Amy Hollywood, *Soul as Virgin Wife*, pp. 29–32, similarly questions the accuracy of reports of Beatrice's harsh self-mortifications. See Chapter 7 of the present volume for a fuller discussion of the problems in trying to determine what is to be taken literally and what metaphorically when employing hagiographical texts as source material.

20 *Vita*, Bk. I, Ch. 2, p. 17.
21 *Vita*, Bk. I, Ch. 2, p. 18.
22 *Vita*, Bk. I, Ch. 2, p. 18. The chaplain places this unusual declaration within the framework of the topos based upon Matthew 10:37: "Anyone who loves his father or mother more than me is not worthy of me." However, the observation may also reflect Christine's view that Beatrice did not love her parents. Moreover, as the chaplain reports in *Vita*, Bk. I, Ch. 3, p. 20, Beatrice admitted in her own writings that the love she gave to the Beguine sisters at Zoutleeuw far exceeded any affection that she had ever given to her parents.
23 *Vita*, Bk. I, Ch. 3, p. 19. Whether this report of Beatrice's feat of memorization is to be treated as topos is problematic. Indeed, it is clear that children in the West until rather recent times were encouraged to prodigious feats of memory, and success in this area was not only widely accepted as evidence for personal discipline, but somewhat less accurately as an index of intelligence.
24 *Vita*, Bk. I, Ch. 3, p. 21.
25 See Stanley Jackson, "Acedia: The Sin and its Relationship to Sorrow and Melancholia in Medieval Times," *Bulletin of the History of Medicine*, 1986, 55: 172–85. Also, Stanley Jackson, *Melancholia and Depression*, New Haven, Yale University Press, 1986.
26 *Vita*, Bk. I, Ch. 3, p. 21.
27 *Vita*, Bk. I, Ch. 3, p. 22.
28 *Vita*, Bk. I, Ch. 4, p. 23.
29 *Vita*, Bk. I, Ch. 4, p. 23.
30 *Vita*, Bk. I, Ch. 4, p. 24.
31 *Vita*, Bk. I, Ch. 4, pp. 24–5.
32 *Vita*, Bk. I, Ch. 4, pp. 26–7.
33 *Vita*, Bk. I, Ch. 4, p. 28.
34 *Vita*, Bk. I, Ch. 5, p. 30.
35 *Vita*, Bk. I, Ch. 5, p. 31.
36 *Vita*, Bk. I, Ch. 5, p. 32.
37 *Vita*, Bk. I, Ch. 5, pp. 31–2. There is considerable controversy whether there is evidence from medieval source material of recognition of a distinct phase of life that we today designate as adolescence. Although moderns in general tend to view the existence of a developmental phase of adolescence as so obvious as to be incontrovertible, others claim that such assumptions are merely examples of Western ethnocentric thinking. See, for this latter viewpoint, James A. Schultz, "Medieval Adolescence: The Claims of History and the Silence of German Narrative," *Speculum*, 1991, 66: 519–39. Nevertheless, the *Vita* itself (Ch. 34, line 10) uses the Latin term for adolescence regularly in describing Beatrice. For example, the phrase "per omne fere tempus adolescentie" is used in describing the duration of her harsh penitential practices.
38 There is no particular evidence linking Beatrice's episodes of fever to malaria, nor is there evidence of malarial epidemics in those years. See Arturo Castiglioni, *A History of Medicine*, New York, Alfred Knopf, 1947, pp. 638–9; also Noel Poynter, *Medicine and Man*, Harmondsworth, Penguin, 1973. For the effects of malnutrition on resistance to infection, see Ann G. Carmichael, "Infection, Hidden Hunger, and History," *Journal of Interdisciplinary History*, 1983, 14: 249–64.
39 *Vita*, Bk. I, Ch. 6, pp. 34–5.
40 *Vita*, Bk. I, Ch. 7, pp. 38–9.
41 *Vita*, Bk. I, Ch.7, pp. 36–7.

42 *Vita*, Bk. I, Ch. 7, p. 40.
43 The monastery of Molesme, from which the Cistercian reform took shape, was established in 1075. St. Bernard's lifetime was 1090–1153. The issues relating to harsh asceticism versus contemplative mysticism each had their strong advocates and were still unsettled during Beatrice's lifetime. See B. Lackner, *The Eleventh-Century Background of Citeaux*, Washington, DC, Cistercian Publications, 1972, pp. 217–74. See also De Ganck, *Beatrice of Nazareth in her Context*, pp. 1–22; McGinn devotes half of his second volume of a history of Western Christian mysticism to the development of the Cistercian order. See, B. McGinn, *The Growth of Mysticism*, New York, Crossroad, 1994, pp. 149–323.
44 *Vita*, Bk. I, Ch. 8, p. 43.
45 *Vita*, Bk. I, Ch. 9, pp. 45–7.
46 *Vita*, Bk. I, Ch. 9, p. 48 devotes but one paragraph to this happy year.
47 *Vita*, Bk. I, Ch. 9, p. 48; Ch. 10, p. 49.
48 See Roger de Ganck, "Chronological Data in the Lives of Ida of Nivelles and Beatrice of Nazareth," *Ons Geestelijk Erf*, 1983, 57: 14–29.
49 *Vita*, Bk. I, Ch. 10, p. 53.
50 Ibid.
51 Ibid.
52 *Vita*, Bk. I, Ch. 11, p. 54.
53 *Vita*, Bk. I, Ch. 11, p. 56.
54 *Vita*, Bk. I, Ch. 62, p. 79.
55 *Vita*, Bk. I, Ch. 92, p. 117.
56 See J. Kroll and R. De Ganck, "The Adolescence of a Thirteenth Century Visionary Nun," *Psychological Medicine*, 1986, 16: 745–56; and by the same authors, "Beatrice of Nazareth: Psychiatric Perspectives on a Medieval Mystic," *Cistercian Studies*, 1989, 24: 301–23, for a discussion of problems involved in applying modern diagnostic concepts to persons of other cultures and eras.

11 BEATRICE OF ORNACIEUX

1 *The Life of the Virgin Saint Beatrice of Ornacieux*, by Margaret Oingt, trans. Renate Blumenfeld-Kosinski, Newburyport, MA, Focus Information Group, 1990. *Les Oeuvres de Marguerite d'Oingt*, publiees par Antonin Duraffour, Pierre Gardette, and Paulette Durdilly, Paris, Societe d'Edition "Les Belles Lettres," 1965.
2 *Life of Beatrice*, Ch. 1, p. 48.
3 *Life of Beatrice*, Ch. 1, p. 49.
4 Ibid.
5 *Life of Beatrice*, Ch. 2, p. 50.
6 *Life of Beatrice*, Ch. 3, p. 51.
7 Ibid.

12 HENRY SUSO

1 William James (1958 [1902]) *The Varieties of Religious Experience*, New York: New American Library, p. 241. It should be emphasized that the term "psychopathic" was employed in James's times merely to signify an abnormal personality and had no connotations of today's sense of psychopath as a sociopathic or criminal personality.
2 Henry Suso (1989) *The Exemplar, with Two German Sermons*, ed. Frank Tobin, New York: Paulist Press. All textual references will be to this volume, which include *The Life of the Servant* (Suso's "autobiography"), the *Little Book of Eternal Wisdom*, the *Little Book of Truth*, the *Little Book of Letters*, and two sermons. Tobin's introduction provides an excellent discussion of Suso's life and works.

NOTES

3. Suso, *Little Book of Truth*, Ch. 7, p. 329.
4. Tobin, Introduction, pp. 38–44 to *The Exemplar*. See also, for further discussion of the authorship of *The Life of the Servant*, E. Colledge and J.C. Marler (1984) "'Mystical' Pictures in the Suso Exemplar, MS Strasbourg 2929," *Archivum fratrum praedicatorum*, 54: 292–354.
5. *Life of the Servant*, p. 100.
6. *Life of the Servant*, p. 167. This pattern conforms to the topos of many saints' lives of the devout mother and worldly, and therefore sinful, father. Nevertheless there is no reason to suspect that this is not accurate in the case of Suso.
7. *Life of the Servant*, p. 75.
8. Ibid.
9. Henry Suso is indexed in European literature and bibliographical websites, such as <www.brepolis.net>, as Heinrich Seuse.
10. *Life of the Servant*, p. 88.
11. Ibid., p. 167.
12. See the discussion of this point by Frank Tobin in his Introduction to his edited volume (*The Exemplar*) on Suso's work. A similar theme arose in the Life of Peter of Luxembourg (1369–1387), of a noble family, who was appointed bishop at age 15 and cardinal at 16. Peter too was given to very harsh austerities, but did not live long enough to see if his heroic asceticism would have given way to a more mature spirituality.
13. *Life of the Servant*, pp. 138–9.
14. Ibid., pp. 63–4.
15. Ibid., p. 64.
16. Ibid., p. 66.
17. Ibid., pp. 83–4.
18. Ibid., p. 68.
19. Ibid., pp. 70–1. Most modern discussion about the "body as text" speak about women's use of their bodies, but here is a literal example in a man of employing his body as text.
20. Ibid., p. 73.
21. Ibid., p. 76.
22. Ibid., p. 81.
23. Ibid., p. 85.
24. Ibid., p. 87.
25. See Chapter 4, on the physiology of pain, for an explanation of the phenomenon of hyperalgesia to pain caused by enlargement of the inflamed area surrounding the already damaged section of skin.
26. *Life of the Servant*, p. 89.
27. Ibid., p. 92.
28. Ibid., p. 97.
29. Ibid., p. 99.
30. Ibid., p. 111.
31. Ibid., pp. 153–4.
32. Ibid., p. 155.
33. Ibid., p. 157.
34. Ibid., p. 94.
35. Ibid., pp. 126–7.
36. Ibid., p. 172.
37. Ibid., pp. 172–3.
38. *Little Book of Eternal Wisdom*, pp. 214–15. Barbara Newman has commented on the merging and alternating gender roles of the initially feminine Sophia (Wisdom) and the masculine Jesus in the writing and thinking of Suso. See Barbara Newman (1990) "Some Mediaeval Theologians and the Sophia Tradition," *Downside Review*, 108: 111–30.

39 *The Life of the Servant*, p. 123.
40 Ibid., p. 130.
41 *Little Book of Truth*, pp. 329–30.
42 *The Life of the Servant*, p. 203.
43 Ibid., pp. 196–7.
44 Ursula King (2001) *Christian Mystics: Their Lives and Legacies Throughout the Ages*, Mahwah, NJ, Hidden Spring (Paulist Press), p. 113.
45 See R.K.C. Forman (ed.) (1990) *The Problem of Pure Consciousness*, New York, Oxford University Press; and our discussion of these issues in Chapter 3 of this volume.
46 Karl Jaspers (1963) *General Psychopathology*, trans. Hoenig and M. Hamilton, Manchester, Manchester University Press, pp. 439–43.
47 American Psychiatric Association (1994) *Diagnostic and Statistical Manual*, fourth edition, Washington, DC, American Psychiatric Press.
48 M. Jackson and K.W.M. Fulford (1997) "Spiritual Experience and Psychopathology," *Philosophy, Psychiatry, Psychology*, 4: 41–90.
49 Bernard Williams (1981) "Moral Luck," in B. Williams, *Moral Luck: Philosophical Papers 1973–1980*, Cambridge, Cambridge University Press, pp. 20–39.

13 MENTAL ILLNESS, HYSTERIA, AND MYSTICISM

1 Noel D. O'Donoghue, *Heaven in Ordinaire*, Springfield, IL, Templegate, p. 26.
2 See, for instance, A. Ellis, *The Case Against Religiosity*, New York: Institute for Rational-Emotive Therapy, 1983. For the opposing view, see A.E. Bergin, "Religiosity and Mental Health: A Critical Re-evaluation and Meta-analysis," *Professional Psychology*, 1983, 14: 170–84. See also H.G. Koenig and D.B. Larson, "Religion and Mental Health: Evidence for an Association," *International Review of Psychiatry*, 2001, 13: 67–78. For an interesting article that carries the debate right into Ellis', own waiting room, see P.W. Sharkey and H.N. Maloney, "Religiosity and Emotional Disturbance: A Test of Ellis's Thesis in his own Counseling Center," *Psychotherapy*, 1986, 23: 640–1.
3 The best compendium of religious research instruments is P.C. Hill and R.W. Hood Jr., *Measures of Religiosity*, Birmingham, AL, Religious Education Press, 1999.
4 H. Newton Maloney, "The Clinical Assessment of Optimal Religious Functioning," *Review of Religious Research*, 1988, 30: 3–17.
5 Vicky Genia, "The Spiritual Experience Index: Revision and Reformulation," *Review of Religious Research*, 1997, 39: 344–61.
6 Gordon W. Allport, *The Individual and His Religion*, New York, Macmillan, 1950. See also, Gordon W. Allport and J. Michael Ross, "Personal Religious Orientation and Prejudice," *Journal of Personality and Social Psychology*, 1967, 5: 432–43. The religion referred to in most intrinsic-extrinsic studies is organized American Christianity.
7 Dean R. Hoge, "A Validated Intrinsic Religious Motivation Scale," *Journal for the Scientific Study of Religion*, 1972, 11: 369–76.
8 Unpublished data; as background, see Jerome Kroll, Elizabeth Egan, Paul Erickson, Kathleen Carey, and Myles Johnson, "Moral Conflict, Religiosty, and Neuroticism in an Outpatient Sample," *Journal of Nervous and Mental Disease*, 2004, 192: 682–8.
9 See Allen Bergin, "Values and Religious Issues in Psychotherapy and Mental Health," *American Psychologist*, 1991, 46: 394–403. An edited volume by John Schumaker, *Religion and Mental Health*, Oxford, Oxford University Press, 1992, provides an excellent review of research methodology and findings. See also Jerome Kroll, "Religion and Psychiatry," *Current Opinion in Psychiatry*, 1998, 11: 335–9.
10 Harold Koenig, Linda George, and Bercedis Peterson, "Religiosity and Remission of Depression in Medically Ill Older Patients," *American Journal of Psychiatry*, 1998, 15: 536–42.

11 Kenneth Kendler, Charles Gardner, and Carol Prescott, "Religion, Psychopathology, and Substance Use and Abuse: A Multimeasure, Genetic-Epidemiologic Study," *American Journal of Psychiatry*, 1997, 154: 322–29.
12 K.S. Kendler, X-Q. Liu, C.O. Gardner, M.E. McCullough, D. Larson and C.A. Prescott, "Dimensions of Religiosity and their Relationship to Lifetime Psychiatric and Substance Use Disorders," *American Journal of Psychiatry*, 2003, 160: 495–503. See also note 8 above.
13 Leslie Francis and T.H. Thomas, "Are Charismatic Ministers Less Stable? A Study among Male Anglican Ministers," *Review of Religious Research*, 1997, 39: 61–9.
14 For a discussion of essentialism, see Nicholas Haslam, "Psychiatric Categories as Natural Kinds: Essentialist Thinking about Mental Disorders," *Social Research*, 2000, 67: 1,031–58.
15 The transcultural literature is voluminous. For a review, see Martin Roth and Jerome Kroll, *The Reality of Mental Illness*, Cambridge, Cambridge University Press, 1986, pp. 40–4. See also H.B.M. Murphy, *Comparative Psychiatry*, Berlin, Springer, 1982; A.J. Marsella, R.G. Tharp, and T.J. Ciborowski (eds.) *Perspectives in Cross-Cultural Psychology*, New York, Academic Press, 1979. The classic studies of "mental illnesses" in societies virtually untouched by Western psychiatry are Jane Murphy, "Psychiatric Labeling in Cross-Cultural Perspective," *Science*, 1976: 191, 1,018–28, and Joseph Westermeyer and Ronald Wintrob, "'Folk' Explanations of Mental Illness in Rural Laos," *American Journal of Psychiatry*, 1979, 136: 901–5.
16 The revised edition of the 1980 *Diagnostic and Statistical Manual* (*DSM-III-R*, Washington, DC, American Psychiatric Association, 1987) placed in an appendix a list of proposed diagnostic categories needing further study. Among the proposals was one for "Sadistic Personality Disorder" which, in essence, would recast a "pattern of cruel, demeaning, and aggressive behavior" (DSM-III-R, p. 369–71) as a psychiatric illness. The storm of protest from various quarters, especially women's interest groups, that such a designation would serve as a psychiatric excuse for domestic violence directed primarily against women effectively removed this category from the subsequent revision (DSM-IV, 1994).
17 Paul R. McHugh, "How Psychiatry Lost its Way," *Commentary*, 1999, 108: 32–8.
18 See David Healy, *The Antidepressant Era*, Cambridge, MA, Harvard University Press, 1998, in which the author argues that the pharmaceutical industry and the psychiatric profession joined forces to define depression in disease terms that vastly increased its prevalence, and then defined antidepressant medications as the mandated treatment.
19 See Anthony J. Marsella, "Sociocultural Foundations of Psychopathology: An Historical Overview of Concepts, Events, and Pioneers Prior to 1970," *Transcultural Psychiatric Research Review*, 1993, 30: 97–142, for a succinct review and comprehensive bibliography of cultural theories of abnormal behavior.
20 Jackson, M. and Fulford, K.W.M., "Spiritual Experience and Psychopathology," *Philosophy, Psychiatry, Psychology*, 1997, 4: 41–90.
21 Thomas de Cantimpre, *The Life of Christina of Saint-Trond*, trans. Margot King, Saskatoon, Peregrina Press, 1986, pp. 4–9.
22 S. Fanning, *Mystics of the Christian Tradition*, London, Routledge, 2001, pp. 96–8.
23 B. McGinn, *The Flowering of Mysticism*, New York, Crossroad, 1998, pp. 160–2; quote is p. 160.
24 A. Hollywood, *The Soul as Virgin Wife*, Notre Dame, University of Notre Dame Press, 1995, pp. 45–6; footnote p. 294.
25 See Carol Gilligan (1982) *In a Different Voice*, Cambridge, MA, Harvard University Press. Gilligan's work itself on gender differences in moral development has been challenged for poor scientific methodology by many child development specialists. See Lawrence Walker, "Sex Differences in the Development of Moral Reasoning: A Critical

Review," *Child Development*, 1984, 55: 681; see also Christina H. Sommers, "Pathological Social Science: Carol Gilligan and the Incredible Shrinking Girl," in *The Flight from Science and Reason*, Annals of the New York Academy of Science, Vol. 775, 1996, pp. 369–81.

26 Lawrence Kohlberg, *The Psychology of Moral Development*, San Francisco, Harper & Row, 1984.

27 Hollywood, *Soul as Virgin Wife*, p. 294.

28 For a discussion about the "illness" of Margery Kempe, see Phyllis Freeman, Carley Rees Bogarad, and Diane Sholomskas, "Margery Kempe, a New Theory: The Inadequacy of Hysteria and Postpartum Psychosis as Diagnostic Categories," *History of Psychiatry*, 1990, 1: 169–90.

29 Karl Jaspers, *General Psychpathology*, trans. J. Hoenig and Marian Hamilton, Manchester, Manchester University Press, 1913/1963, p. 439.

30 See, for a rich discussion on the enduring debates about hysteria, Phillip Slavney, *Perspectives on "Hysteria,"* Baltimore, Johns Hopkins University Press, 1990.

31 Janet Beizer, *Ventriloquized Bodies: Narratives of Hysteria in Nineteenth-Century France*, Ithaca, Cornell University Press, 1994.

32 See Cristina Mazzoni, *Saint Hysteria*, Ithaca, Cornell University Press, 1996, for an excellent review and analysis of medical/psychiatric confounding of spirituality and hysteria in women, especially in late nineteenth-century European writings.

33 Herbert Moller, "The Social Causation of Affective Mysticism," *Journal of Social History*, 1971, 4: 305–38.

34 See Kenneth H. Craik, "Assessing the Personalities of Historical Figures," in, *Psychology and Historical Interpretation*, William M. Runyan (ed.), New York, Oxford University Press, 1988, pp. 196–218, for a review of methodological issues in psychohistory. David Stannard, *Shrinking History: On Freud and the Failure of Psychohistory*, Oxford, Oxford University Press, 1980, and Frederick Crews, *Skeptical Engagements*, New York, Oxford University Press, 1986, provide critical assessments of the use of Freudian theory and psychoanalytic methods of reasoning in approaching history.

35 Mazzoni, *Saint Hysteria*, p. 191.

36 Jaspers, *General Psychopathology*, p. 443. To give full justice to Jaspers, however, he earlier comments that it is impossible for any one individual to be sufficiently characterized by a single type, and discusses his uneasiness regarding attempts to diagnose personality, as opposed to diagnosing illness: "But in simple human terms, to classify and track down someone's personality implies a categorization which, if we look at it closely, is insulting and makes any further communication impossible" (p. 438).

37 *Lives of the Desert Fathers*, trans. Norman Russell, Kalamazoo, MI, Cistercian Publications, 1981, Ch. VIII, p. 78.

38 *The Cloud of Unknowing*, ed. and trans., Clifton Wolters, London, Penguin, 1978, Ch. 52, p. 122.

39 *Cloud of Unknowing*, Ch. 53, p. 123.

40 *The Book of the Blessed Angela of Foligno*, trans. Paul Lachance, Mahwah, NJ, Paulist Press, 1993, p. 141.

41 Ibid., p. 142.

42 Ibid., p. 131.

43 Ibid., p. 198.

44 Ibid., p. 163.

45 *Giles of Assisi*, trans. Walter Seton, Manchester, Manchester University Press, 1918, p. 71.

46 See C. Stewart, *Cassian the Monk*, New York, Oxford University Press, 1998, pp. 116–17, for a thoughtful discussion on ecstasy and ecstatic mysticism. Stewart points out that the ecstatic trances of Teresa of Avila have by now been accepted as the prototype of mysticism, with the result that earlier mystics of the contemplative variety

have been overlooked. See also, *The Problem of Pure Consciousness*, ed. Robert K.C. Forman, New York, Oxford, 1990.

47 See McGinn, *Flowering of Mysticism*, p. 30, for a discussion of the imagination in this regard.

48 R.C. Cloninger, D. Svtakic, and T. Przybeck, "Psychobiological Model of Temperament and Character," *Archives of General Psychiatry*, 1993, 50: 975–90.

49 In an earlier paper, we compared the hallucinations of 23 psychiatric patients with predominantly religious themes with descriptions of visions from medieval sources. None of the medieval visionaries was identified as mentally ill. See, Jerome Kroll and Bernard Bachrach, "Medieval Visions and Contemporary Hallucinations," *Psychological Medicine*, 1982, 12: 709–21; see also, by the same authors, "Visions and Psychopathology in the Middle Ages," *Journal of Nervous and Mental Disease*, 1982, 170: 41–9.

50 *Lives of the Desert Fathers*; see also Athanasius, *Life of Antony* and *The Letter to Marcellinus*, trans. Robert Gregg, New York: Paulist Press, 1980; John of Ephesus, *Lives of the Eastern Saints*, ed. and trans. E.W. Brooks, *Patrologia Orientalis*, 17–19, Paris, 1923–1925; Susan Ashbrook Harvey, *Asceticism and Society in Crisis*, Berkeley, University of California Press, 1991.

51 See B. McGinn, *The Foundations of Mysticism*, New York, Crossroad, 1991, pp. 131–2.

52 See Joseph H. Lynch, *The Medieval Church*, London, Longman, 1992, pp. 186–92.

53 The last chapter of *The Rule of St. Benedict*, entitled "All perfection is not herein attained," reminds the reader that, through observance of the Rule, "we may know we have made some progress in pursuit of virtue and the commencement of a monastic life." Benedict tells those who are in a hurry for perfection to read the works of the Holy Fathers. But for the rest, "if you wish to follow the path to God, make use of this little Rule for beginners." *The Rule of St. Benedict*, trans. Anthony Meisel and M.L. del Mastro, New York, Doubleday, 1975. See also Lynch, *The Medieval Church*, pp. 132–5, for a discussion of renewed interest in the harsher asceticism of the desert fathers. See also R. Markus, *The End of Ancient Christianity*, Cambridge, Cambridge University Press, 1990, pp. 181–97.

54 See Alan Watts, *The Way of Zen*, New York, New American Library, 1957; Thomas Merton, *Mystics and Zen Masters*, New York, Farrar, Straus, & Giroux, 1961. See also Merton's correspondence regarding the positive features of Zen, in, Thomas Merton, *The Hidden Ground of Love: Letters*, ed. William Shannon, New York, Farrar, Straus, & Giroux, 1985, pp. 439–43.

55 See Raymond T. Gawronski, "Why Orthodox Catholics Look to Zen," *New Oxford Review*, 1993, 60(6): 13–16. See also Cheslyn Jones, Geoffrey Wainwright, and Edward Yarnold (eds.) *The Study of Spirituality*, New York, Oxford University Press, 1986, who comment in their introduction (p. xxiii) that many today are traveling as far as India in their quest for a technique of meditation "because they are unaware that the Christian tradition, at least in its Anglo-Saxon pattern, contains anything like what they are looking for."

56 William Johnston, *Mystical Theology*, London, Harper Collins, 1995, pp. 120–36.

57 Johnston, *Mystical Theology*, p. 122.

14 CONCLUSION

1 Similar to the Introduction, we have tried to avoid notes in this chapter unless absolutely necessary, such as citation for a specific text. Full references are in the notes to each chapter.

2 Suso, *Life of the Servant*, pp. 189–90 (see Chapter 12, note 2 above).

3 De Ganck, *Life of Beatrice of Nazareth*, p. 243 (see Chapter 10, note 1 above).

NOTES

APPENDIX: STATISTICAL ANALYSES

1 In the Chi-square statistical analyses that follow, degrees of freedom (df) = 2 in all cases.
2 Rudolph Bell, *Holy Anorexia*, Chicago, University of Chicago Press, 1985.
3 Carolyn Bynum, *Holy Feast and Holy Fast*, Berkeley, University of California Press, 1987.
4 *Paphnutius, Histories of the Monks of Upper Egypt*, trans. Tim Vivian, Kalamazoo, Cistercian Publications, 1993; see also, Peter Brown, *The Body and Society*, New York, Columbia University Press, 1988, pp. 218–23.

BIBLIOGRAPHY

Acta Sanctorum (1863–1940) third edition, Antwerp–Brussels–Paris.

Akil, H., Watson, S., Young, E., Lewis, M., Khachaturian, H., and Walker, J.M. (1984) "Endogenous Opioids: Biology and Function," *Annual Review of Neuroscience*, 7: 223–55.

Allport, G.W. (1950) *The Individual and His Religion*, New York: Macmillan.

Allport, G.W. and Ross, J.M. (1967) "Personal Religious Orientation and Prejudice," *Journal of Personality and Social Psychology*, 5: 432–43.

American Psychiatric Association (1994) *Diagnostic and Statistical Manual*, fourth edition, Washington, DC: American Psychiatric Press.

Anand, B.K., Chhina, G.S., and Singh, B. (1961) "Some Aspects of Electroencephalographic Studies in Yogis," *Electroencephalography and Clinical Neurophysiology*, 13: 452–6.

Angela of Foligno (1993) *The Book of the Blessed Angela of Foligno*, trans. Paul Lachance, Mahwah, NJ: Paulist Press.

Anonymous (1969) "Life of St. Cuthbert" in Bertram Colgrave, trans. & ed., *Two Lives of St. Cuthbert*, New York: Greenwood.

Ardo (1979) *The Emperor's Monk: Contemporary Life of Benedict of Aniane*, trans. Allen Cabaniss, Ilfracombe, Devon: Arthur Stockwell.

Armstrong, D.M and Malcolm, N. (1984) *Consciousness and Causality: A Debate on the Nature of Mind*, Oxford: Basil Blackwell.

Aronen, E.T., Paavonen, E.J., Fjallberg, M., Soininen, M., and Torronen, J. (2000) "Sleep and Psychiatric Symptoms in School-age Children," *Journal of the American Academy of Child and Adolescent Psychiatry*, 39: 502–8.

Athanasius, *Life of Antony* and *The Letter to Marcellinus* (1980) trans. Robert Gregg, New York: Paulist Press.

Augustine (1961) *Confessions*, New York: Penguin.

Austin, J.H. (1998) *Zen and the Brain*, Cambridge, MA: MIT Press.

Babkoff, H., Sing, H., Thorne, D., Genser, S., and Hegge, F. (1989) "Perceptual Distortions and Hallucinations Reported During the Course of Sleep Deprivation," *Perceptual and Motor Skills*, 68: 787–98.

Bachrach, B. (1995) *Anatomy of a Small War*, Berkeley: University of California Press.

Barclay, C.R. (1986) "Schematization of Autobiographical Memory", in D.C. Rubin (ed.) *Autobiographical Memory*, New York: Cambridge University Press.

Bargh, J.A. and Chartrand, T. (1999) "The Unbearable Automaticity of Being," *American Psychologist*, 54: 462–79.

Baring-Gould, S. (1916) *The Lives of the Saints*, 16 vols., London.
Baudonivia, *Vita Radegunde*, Bruno Krush (ed.) MGH, SRM, 2: 358–405.
Baumeister, R.F. (1991) *Escaping the Self*, New York: Basic Books.
Beatrice of Nazareth, Life (1991) trans. and ed. Roger De Ganck, Kalamazoo, MI: Cistercian Publications.
Beatrijs of Nazareth (1986) "There are Seven Manners of Loving," trans. Eric Colledge, in Elizabeth A. Petroff (ed.) *Medieval Women's Visionary Literature*, New York: Oxford University Press, pp. 200–6.
Beckwith, S. (1986) "A Very Material Mysticism: The Medieval Mysticism of Margery Kempe," in David Aers (ed.) *Medieval Literature: Criticism, Ideology and History*, New York: St. Martin's Press, pp. 34–57.
Beizer, J. (1994) *Ventriloquized Bodies: Narratives of Hysteria in Nineteenth-Century France*, Ithaca: Cornell University Press.
Belenky, G.L. (1979) "Unusual Visual Experiences Reported by Subjects in the British Army Study of Sustained Operations," *Military Medicine*, 144: 695–6.
Bell, R. (1985) *Holy Anorexia*, Chicago: University of Chicago Press.
Bergin, A.E. (1983) "Religiosity and Mental Health: A Critical Re-evaluation and Meta-analysis," *Professional Psychology*, 14: 170–84.
Bergin, A.E. (1991) "Values and Religious Issues in Psychotherapy and Mental Health," *American Psychologist*, 46: 394–403.
Berlin, I. (1993) *The Hedgehog and Fox*, Chicago: Ivan Dee.
Berlioz, J. (1994), *L'Atelier du Medieviste*, Turnhout: Brepols.
Bibliotheca Sanctorum, 12 vols. (1960–1970) Pontifica Universita Lateranse, Instituto Giovanni XXIII, Rome: Città Nuova.
Biddick, K. (1993) "Genders, Bodies, Borders," *Speculum*, 68: 389–418.
Bolton, B. (1985) "Via Ascetica: A Papal Quandary," *Studies in Church History*, 22: 161–91.
Bonnet, M.H. and Arand, D.L. (2003) "Clinical Effects of Sleep Fragmentation Versus Sleep Deprivation," *Sleep Medicine Reviews*, 7: 297–310.
Borg, J., Andree, B., Soderstrom, H., and Farde, L. (2003) "The Serotonin System and Spiritual Experiences," *American Journal of Psychiatry*, 160: 1,965–9.
Born, J. and Fehm, H.L. (1991) "Interactions between the Hypothalamus–Pituitary–Adrenal System and Sleep in Humans," in J.H. Peter, T. Penzel, T. Podszus, and P. von Wichert (eds.) *Sleep and Health Risk*, Berlin: Springer, pp. 503–11.
Børresen, K.E. (1995) "Women's Studies of the Christian Tradition: New Perspectives," in Ursula King (ed.) *Religion and Gender*, Oxford: Blackwell, pp. 245–55.
Bouyer, L. (1955) "Asceticism in the Patristic Period," in Walter Mitchell, ed. and trans., *Christian Asceticism and Modern Man*, London: Blackfriars, pp. 15–29.
Bower, G. (1990) "Awareness, the Unconscious and Repression: An Experimental Psychologist's Perspective," in Jerome L. Singer (ed.) *Repression and Dissociation*, Chicago: University of Chicago Press.
Bowker, J. (1970) *Problems of Suffering in Religions of the World*, Cambridge: Cambridge University Press.
Brewin, C., Andrews, B., and Gotlib, I. (1993) "Psychopathology and Early Experience: A Reappraisal of Retrospective Reports," *Psychological Bulletin*, 113: 82–98.
Broderick, J.F. (1956) "A Census of the Saints (993–1955)," *American Ecclesiastical Review*, 135: 87–115.
Brose, W.G. and Spiegel, D. (1992) "Neuropsychiatric Aspects of Pain Management," in

Stuart Yudofsky and Robert Hales (eds.) *Textbook of Neuropsychiatry*, Washington: American Psychiatric Press, pp. 245–75.

Brown, J.E. (1971) *The Gift of the Sacred Pipe*, Norman: University of Oklahoma Press.

Brown, P. (1988) *The Body and Society*, New York: Columbia University Press.

Brown, W.D., Finn, P., Desautel, C., and Mezzanotte, W. (1996) "Adolescence, Sleepiness, and Driving," *Sleep Research*, 25: 459.

Butler's Lives of the Saints (1956), edited, revised, and supplemented by Herbert Thurston and Donald Attwater, 4 vols., London: Burns & Oates.

Bynum, C.W. (1987) *Holy Feast and Holy Fast*, Berkeley: University of California Press.

Bynum, W.F., Browne, E.J., and Porter, R. (1985) *Dictionary of the History of Science*, Princeton: Princeton University Press.

Carmichael, A.G. (1983) "Infection, Hidden Hunger, and History," *Journal of Interdisciplinary History*, 14: 249–64.

Carskadon, M.A. and Dement, W. (1987) "Sleepiness in the Normal Adolescent," in Christian Guilleminault (ed.) *Sleep and its Disorders in Children*, New York: Raven Press, pp. 53–66.

Carskadon, M.A., Orav, E.J., and Dement, W. (1983) "Evolution of Sleep and Daytime Sleepiness in Adolescents," in Christian Guilleminault and Elio Lugaresi (eds.) *Sleep/Wake Disorders: Natural History, Epidemiology, and Long-Term Evolution*, New York: Raven Press, pp. 201–16.

Carskadon, M.A., Vieira, C., and Acerbo, C. (1993) "Association between Puberty and Delayed Sleep Preference," *Sleep*, 16: 258–62.

Carton, S.M. (1984) "Beatrice of Nazareth: The Seven Steps of Love," *Cistercian Studies*, 19: 31–42.

Cassian, J. (1985) *Conferences*, New York: Paulist Press.

Castiglioni, A. (1947) *A History of Medicine*, New York: Alfred Knopf.

Ceci, S. and Bruck, M. (1993) "Suggestibility of the Child Witness: A Historical Review and Synthesis," *Psychological Bulletin*, 113: 403–39.

Chadwick, H. (1985) "The Ascetic Ideal in the History of the Church," *Studies in Church History*, 22: 1–23.

Chadwick, O. (1958) *Western Asceticism*, Philadelphia: Westminster.

Chapman, C.R. (1980) "Pain and Perception: Comparison of Sensory Decision Theory and Evoked Potential Methods," in John J. Bonica (ed.) *Pain*, New York: Raven Press.

Chapman, C.R. (1986) "Pain, Perception, and Illusion," in R.A. Sternbach (ed.) *Psychology of Pain*, New York: Raven Press, pp. 156–8.

Clark, W.H. (1970) "The Psychodelics and Religion," in B. Aaronson and H. Osmond (eds.) *Psychodelics: The Uses and Implications of Hallucinogenic Drugs*, New York: Doubleday, pp. 182–95.

Cloninger, R.C., Svrakic, D., and Przybeck, T. (1993) "A Psychobiological Model of Temperament and Character," *Archives of General Psychiatry*, 50: 975–90.

Coan, R.W. (1987) *Human Consciousness and Its Evolution: A Multidemensional View*, Westport, CT: Greenwood.

Cohen, D.B. (1980) "The Cognitive Activity of Sleep," *Progress in Brain Research*, 53: 307–24.

Cohen, J., Berliner, L., and Mannarino, A. (2003) "Psychosocial and Pharmacological Interventions for Child Crime Victims," *Journal of Traumatic Stress*, 16: 175–86.

Cohn, N. (1970) *The Pursuit of the Millennium*, New York: Oxford University Press.

Colledge, E. and Marler, J.C. (1984) "'Mystical' Pictures in the Suso Exemplar, MS Strasbourg 2929," *Archivum fratrum praedicatorum*, 54: 292–354.

Colt, E.W., Wardlaw, S.L., and Frantz, A.G. (1981) "The Effect of Running on ß-endorphins," *Life Sciences*, 28: 1,637–40.

Constable, G. (1966) *The Reformation of the Twelfth Century*, Cambridge: Cambridge University Press.

Constable, G. (1992) "Moderation and Restraint in Ascetic Practices," in Haijo Jan Westra (ed.) *From Athens to Chartres: Neoplatonism and Medieval Thought*, Leiden: E.J. Brill, pp. 315–27.

Cortes-Gallegos, V., Catenada, G., Alonso, R., Sojo, I., Carranco, A., Cervantes, C., and Parra, A. (1983) "Sleep Deprivation Reduces Circulatory Andogens in Healthy Man," *Archives of Andrology*, 10: 33–7.

Craik, K.H. (1988) "Assessing the Personalities of Historical Figures," in William M. Runyan (ed.) *Psychology and Historical Interpretation*, New York: Oxford University Press, pp. 196–218.

Crews, F. (1986) *Skeptical Engagements*, New York: Oxford University Press.

Csikszentmihalyi, M. (1990) *Flow: The Psychology of Optimal Experience*, New York: Harper & Row.

Czeisler, C., Moore-Ede, M., and Coleman, R. (1983) "Resetting Circadian Clocks: Applications to Sleep Disorders Medicine and Occupational Health," in Christian Guilleminault and Elio Lugaresi (eds.) *Sleep/Wake Disorders: Natural History, Epidemiology, and Long-Term Evolution*, New York: Raven Press, pp. 243–60.

d'Aquili, E. and Newberg, A.B. (1999) *The Mystical Mind: Probing the Biology of Mystical Experience*, Minneapolis: Fortress Press.

Dalai Lama (2002) *How to Practice: The Way to a Meaningful Life*, New York: Pocket Books.

De Ganck, R. (1983) "Chronological Data in the Lives of Ida of Nivelles and Beatrice of Nazareth," *Ons Geestelijk Erf*, 57: 14–29.

De Ganck, R. (1988) "The Biographer of Beatrice of Nazareth," *Cistercian Studies*, 22: 319–29.

De Ganck, R. (1991) Vol. I, *The Life of Beatrice of Nazareth*; Vol. II, *Beatrice of Nazareth in her Context*; Vol. III, *Towards Unification with God*, Kalamazoo: Cistercian Publications.

De Rios, M.B. (1989) "Power and Hallucingenic States of Consciousness among the Moche," in Colleen A. Ward (ed.) *Altered States of Consciousness and Mental Health: A Cross-Cultural Perspective*, Newbury Park, CA: Sage Publications, pp. 285–99.

de Waal, E. (1995) *A Life-Giving Way: A Commentary on the Rule of St. Benedict*, Collegeville, MN: Liturgical Press.

de Wilde, E., Kienhorst, I., Diekstra, R., and Wolters, W. (1992) "The Relationship between Adolescent Suicidal Behavior and Life Events in Childhood and Adolescence," *American Journal of Psychiatry*, 149: 45–51.

de Zwaan, M. and Mitchell, J. (1992) "Opioid Antagonists and Feeding in Humans: A Review of the Literature," *Journal of Clinical Pharmacology*, 32: 1,060–72.

Dehaene, S. and Naccache, L. (2001) "Towards a Cognitive Neuroscience of Consciousness: Basic Evidence and a Workspace Framework," *Cognition*, 79: 1–37.

Delatte, D.P. (1921) *The Rule of St. Benedict: A Commentary*, London: Burns, Oates & Washbourne.

Delehaye, H. (1939) *Analecta Bollandiana*, 57.

BIBLIOGRAPHY

Delehaye, H. (1962) *The Legends of the Saints*, trans. Donald Attwater, New York: Fordham.
Delooz, P. (1969) *Sociologie et canonisations*. Collection scientifique de la Faculté de Droit de l'Université de Liège, no. 30, Liège.
Delooz, P. (1983) "Towards a Sociological Study of Canonized Sainthood in the Catholic Church," in Stephen Wilson (ed.) *Saints and their Cults: Studies in Religious Sociology, Folklore, and History*, Cambridge: Cambridge University Press.
Dement, W. (1960) "The Effect of Dream Deprivation," *Science*, 131: 1705–7.
Dennett, D.C. (1991) *Consciousness Explained*, Boston: Little, Brown.
Dennett, D.C. (2002) "How Could I Be Wrong? How Wrong Could I Be?" *Journal of Consciousness Studies*, 9: 13–16.
Dinges, D.F., Pack, F., Williams, K., Gillen, K.A., Powell, J.W., Ott, G.E., Aptowicz, C., and Pack, A.I. (1997) "Cumulative Sleepiness, Mood Disturbance, and Psychomotor Vigilance Performance Decrements During a Week of Sleep Restricted to 4–5 Hours per Night," *Sleep*, 20: 267–77.
Dinzelbacher, P. (1987) "The Beginnings of Mysticism Experienced in Twelfth Century England," in Marion Glasscoe (ed.) *The Medieval Mystical Tradition in England: Exeter Symposium IV*, Woodbridge, Suffolk: Boydell & Brewer.
Dunbar, A.B.C. (1904–1905) *A Dictionary of Saintly Women*, 2 vols., London: G. Bell & Sons.
Eccleston, C. and Crombez, G. (1999) "Pain Demands Attention: A Cognitive-Affective Model of the Interruptive Function of Pain," *Psychological Bulletin*, 125: 356–66.
Eliade, M. (ed.) (1987) *Encyclopedia of Religion*, Vo. 1, New York: Macmillan.
Ellis, A. (1983) *The Case Against Religiosity*, New York: Institute for Rational-Emotive Therapy.
Fabian, W. Jr. and Fishkin, S. (1991) "Psychological Absorption: Affect Investment in Marijuana Intoxication," *Journal of Nervous and Mental Disease*, 179: 39–43.
Falloon, B. and Horwath, E. (1993) "Asceticism: Creative Spiritual Practice or Pathological Pursuit," *Psychiatry*, 56: 310–20 (with commentary by William Meissner).
Fanning, S. (2001) *Mystics of the Christian Tradition*, London: Routledge.
Farber, I.B. and Churchland, P.S. (1995) "Consciousness and the Neurosciences: Philosophical and Theoretical Issues," in Michael Gazzaniga (ed.) *The Cognitive Neurosciences*, Cambridge, MA: MIT Press.
Farmer, D.H. (1987) *The Oxford Dictionary of Saints*, second edition, Oxford: Oxford University Press.
Favazza, A. (1995) *Bodies Under Siege*, second edition, Baltimore: Johns Hopkins University Press.
Felix's *Life of Saint Guthlac* (1956) trans. Bertram Colgrave, Cambridge: Cambridge University Press.
Fenwick, P. (1996) "The Neurophysiology of Religious Experience," in Dinesh Bhugra (ed.) *Psychiatry and Religion: Context, Consensus, and Controversies*, London: Routledge.
Fernandez, E. and Turk, D.C. (1992) "Sensory and Affective Components of Pain: Separation and Synthesis," *Psychological Bulletin*, 112: 205–17.
Fichter, M.M. and Pirke, K.-M. (1989) " Disturbances of Reproductive Function in Eating Disorders," in K.M. Pirke, W. Wuttke, and U. Schweiger (eds.) *The Menstrual Cycle and its Disorders*, Berlin: Springer, pp. 179–88.
Fichter, M.M. and Pirke, K.-M. (1990) "Psychobiology of Human Starvation," in Helmut Remschmidt and Martin H. Schmidt (eds.) *Anorexia Nervosa*, Toronto: Hogrefe & Huber, pp. 13–29.

Fields, H., Heinricher, M., and Mason, P. (1991) "Neurotransmitters in Nociceptive Modulatory Circuits," *Annual Review of Neuroscience*, 14: 219–45.
Fish's Clinical Psychopathology (1974) ed. M. Hamilton, Bristol: John Wright.
Flynn, M. (1996) "The Spiritual Uses of Pain in Spanish Mysticism," *Journal of the American Academy of Religion*, 54: 257–78.
Folz, R. (1894) *Les saints rois du Moyen Age en Occident*, Brussels.
Forman, R.K.C. (ed.) (1990) *The Problem of Pure Consciousness*, New York: Oxford University Press.
Forman, R.K.C. (1998) "What Does Mysticism Have to Teach Us about Consciousness?" *Journal of Consciousness Studies*, 5: 188–201.
Fortunatus, V. "De excidio Thoringae," Bruno Krush (ed.) MGH, AA, I: 271–5.
Fortunatus (1991) "Life of the Holy Radegund," in Jo Ann McNamara and John Halborg (eds.) *Sainted Women of the Dark Ages*, Durham, NC: Duke University Press, pp. 60–105 (MGH, SRM, II: 358–405).
Foulkes, D. (1996) "Dream Research: 1953–1993," *Sleep*, 19: 609–24.
Francis, L. and Thomas, T.H. (1997) "Are Charismatic Ministers Less Stable? A Study among Male Anglican Ministers," *Review of Religious Research*, 39: 61–9.
Frank, H., Cannon, J.T., Lewis, J.W., and Liebeskind, J.C. (1986) "Neural and Neurochemical Mechanisms of Pain Inhibition," in R.A. Sternbach (ed.) *Psychology of Pain*, New York: Raven Press, pp. 25–39.
Freeman, P., Bogarad, C.R., and Sholomskas, D. (1990) "Margery Kempe, A New Theory: The Inadequacy of Hysteria and Postpartum Psychosis as Diagnostic Categories," *History of Psychiatry*, 1: 169–90.
Gajano, S.B. (1976) *Agiografia altomedioevale*, Bologna: Mulino.
Gawronski, R.T. (1993) "Why Orthodox Catholics Look to Zen," *New Oxford Review*, 60(6): 13–16.
Genia, V. (1997) "The Spiritual Experience Index: Revision and Reformulation," *Review of Religious Research*, 39: 344–61.
George, K. and George, C. (1955) "Roman Catholic Sainthood and Social Status: A Statistical and Analytical Study," *Journal of Religion* 35: 85–98.
Gertrude the Great of Helfta (1989) *Spiritual Exercises*, trans. Gertrude Jaron Lewis and Jack Lewis, Kalamazoo, MI: Cistercian Publications.
Gherardesca of Pisa (1992) "Blessed Life," trans. Elizabeth Petroff, *Vox Benedictina*, 9: 227–85.
Giles of Assisi (1918) *Life*, trans. Walter Seton, Manchester: Manchester University Press.
Gilligan, C. (1982) *In a Different Voice: Psychological Theory and Women's Development*, Cambridge, MA: Harvard University Press.
Gimello, R. (1983) "Mysticism in Its Context," in Steven T. Katz (ed.) *Mysticism and Religious Traditions*, Oxford: Oxford University Press, pp. 61–88.
Goldstein, J. (1994) *Insight Meditation*, Boston: Shambhala.
Gombrich, E. (1972) *The Story of Art*, New York: Phaidon.
Goodich, M. (1982) *Vita Perfecta: The Ideal of Sainthood in the Thirteenth Century*, Stuttgart: Anton Hiersemann.
Graffin, N.F., Ray, W.J., and Lundy, R. (1995) "EEG Concomitants of Hypnosis and Hypnotic Susceptibility," *Journal of Abnormal Psychology*, 104: 123–31.
Green, C. and McCreery, C. (1994) *Lucid Dreaming: The Paradox of Consciousness during Sleep*, London: Routledge.

Gregory of Tours (1974) *The History of the Franks*, ed. and trans. Lewis Thorpe, Harmondsworth: Penguin.
Guerin, P. (1882–1888) *Les petites Bollandistes*, 17 vols., third revised edition, Paris.
Halligan, S.L., Michael, T., and Clark, D.M. (2003) "Posttraumatic Stress Disorder Following Assault: The Role of Cognitive Processing, Trauma Memory, and Appraisals," *Journal of Consulting and Clinical Psychology*, 71: 419–31.
Harris, S., Morley, S., and Barton, S.B. (2003) "Role Loss and Emotional Adjustment in Chronic Pain," *Pain*, 105: 363–370.
Hartmann, E. (1991) *Boundaries in the Mind*, New York: Basic Books.
Harvey, S.A. (1991) *Asceticism and Society in Crisis*, Berkeley: University of California Press.
Haslam, N. (2000) "Psychiatric Categories as Natural Kinds: Essentialist Thinking about Mental Disorders," *Social Research*, 67: 1,031–58.
Healy, D. (1998) *The Antidepressant Era*, Cambridge, MA: Harvard University Press.
Heim, C., Meinlschmidt, G., and Nemeroff, C. (2003) "Neurobiology of Early-Life Stress," *Psychiatric Annals*, 33: 18–26.
Hennevin, E. and Hars, B. (1985) "Post-learning Paradoxical Sleep: A Critical Period when New Memory is Activated?" in B.E. Will, P. Schmitt, and J.C. Dalrymple-Alford (eds.) *Brain Plasticity, Learning and Memory: Advances in Behavioral Biology*, New York: Plenum, pp. 193–203.
Henry Suso (1989) *The Exemplar, with Two German Sermons*, ed. Frank Tobin, New York: Paulist Press.
Herman, J. (1991) *Trauma and Recovery*, New York: Basic Books.
Hilgard, E. (1965) *Hypnotic Susceptibility*, New York: Harcourt, Brace, and World.
Hilgard, E. (1985) *Divided Consciousness*, New York: Wiley.
Hilgard, E. (1991) "Suggestibility and Suggestions as Related to Hypnosis," in John F. Schumaker (ed.) *Human Suggestibility: Advances in Theory, Research, and Application*, New York: Routledge, pp. 37–58.
Hilgard, E. and Hilgard, J. (1975) *Hypnosis in the Relief of Pain*, San Francisco: William Kaufman.
Hill, P.C. and Hood, R.W. Jr. (1999) *Measures of Religiosity*, Birmingham, AL: Religious Education Press.
Hobson, J.A. (1988) *The Dreaming Brain*, New York: Basic Books.
Hoge, D.R. (1972) "A Validated Intrinsic Religious Motivation Scale," *Journal for the Scientific Study of Religion*, 11: 369–76.
Hollywood, A. (1995) *The Soul as Virgin Wife*, Notre Dame, IN: University of Notre Dame Press.
Holweck, F.G. (1924) *A Biographical Dictionary of Saints*, St. Louis: Herder.
Horne, J.A. (1978) "A Review of the Biological Effects of Total Sleep Deprivation in Man," *Biological Psychiatry*, 7: 55–102.
Horne, J. (1988) *Why We Sleep*, Oxford: Oxford University Press.
Horowitz, M.J. (1987) *States of Mind: Configurational Analysis of Individual Psychology*, New York: Plenum.
Hoyt, I., Nadon, R., Register, P., Chorny, J., Fleeson, W., Grigorian, E., Otto, L., and Kihlstrom, J. (1989) "Daydreaming, Absorption, and Hypnotizability," *International Journal of Clinical and Experimental Hypnosis*, 37: 332–42.
Huxley, A. (1954) *The Doors of Perception*, London: Chatto & Windus.
Ida of Louvain (1990) *Life*, trans. Martinus Cawley, Lafayette, OR: Guadalupe Translations.
Irenaeus of Lyons (1992) *Against the Heresies*, New York: Paulist Press.

Iversen, S.D. (1983) "Brain Endorphins and Reward Function: Some Thoughts and Speculations," in James E. Smith and John D. Lane (eds.) *The Neurobiology of Opiate Reward Processes*, Amsterdam: Elsevier, pp. 439–68.
Jackson, M. and Fulford, K.W.M. (1997) "Spiritual Experience and Psychopathology," *Philosophy, Psychiatry, Psychology*, 4: 41–90.
Jackson, S. (1986) "Acedia: The Sin and its Relationship to Sorrow and Melancholia in Medieval Times," *Bulletin of the History of Medicine*, 55: 172–85.
Jackson, S. (1986) *Melancholia and Depression*, New Haven: Yale University Press.
Jacques de Vitry (1986) *The Life of Marie d'Oignies*, trans. Margot King, Saskatoon: Peregrina.
James, W. (1958 [1902]) *The Varieties of Religious Experience*, New York: New American Library.
Jaspers, K. (1963) *General Psychopathology*, trans. J. Hoenig and Marian Hamilton, Manchester: Manchester University Press.
Jerison, H. (1991) *Brain Size and the Evolution of Mind*, New York: American Museum of Natural History.
Jilek, W.G. (1989) "Therapeutic Use of Altered States of Consciousness in Contemporary North American Indian Dance Ceremonials," in Colleen A. Ward (ed.) *Altered States of Consciousness and Mental Health*, Newbury Park, CA: Sage, pp. 167–85.
John of Ephesus (1923–1925) *Lives of the Eastern Saints*, ed. and trans E.W. Brooks, *Patrologia Orientalis*, 17–19, Paris.
John, E.R. (1976) "A Model of Consciousness," in Gary E. Schwartz and David Shapiro (eds.) *Consciousness and Self-Regulation*, New York: Plenum, pp. 1–50.
Johnson, M.H., Breakwell, G., Douglas, W., and Humphries, S. (1998) "The Effects of Imagery and Sensory Detection Distractors on Different Measures of Pain: How Does Distraction Work?" *British Journal of Clinical Psychology*, 37: 141–54.
Johnston, W. (1995) *Mystical Theology*, London: Harper Collins.
Jones, C., Wainwright, G., and Yarnold, E. (eds.) (1986) *The Study of Spirituality*, New York: Oxford University Press.
Jones, R.H. (1993) *Mysticism Examined: Philosophical Inquiries into Mysticism*, Albany: State University of New York Press.
Juliana of Mont Cornillon, Life (no year) trans. Barbara Newman, Toronto: Peregrina.
Kalendars of Scottish Saints (1872) ed. A.P. Forbes, Edinburgh.
Kamiya, J. (1972) "Operant Control of the EEG Alpha Rhythm and Some of its Reported Effects on Consciousness," in Charles T. Tart (ed.) *Altered States of Consciousness*, Garden City, NY: Doubleday, pp. 519–29.
Karni, A., Tanne, D., Rubenstein, B., Askenasy, J., and Sagi, D. (1994) "Dependence on REM Sleep of Overnight Improvement of a Perceptual Skill," *Science*, 265: 679–82.
Katz, S.T. (1978) "Language, Epistemology, and Mysticism," in S.T. Katz (ed.) *Mysticism and Philosophical Analysis*, New York: Oxford University Press, pp. 22–74.
Kemp, E.W. (1948) *Canonization and Authority in the Western Church*, London: Oxford University Press.
Kendler, K., Gardner, C., and Prescott, C. (1997) "Religion, Psychopathology, and Substance Use and Abuse: A Multimeasure, Genetic-epidemiologic Study," *American Journal of Psychiatry*, 154: 322–9.
Kendler, K.S., Liu, X-Q., Gardner, C.O., McCullough, M.E., Larson, D., and Prescott, C.A. (2003) "Dimensions of Religiosity and their Relationship to Lifetime Psychiatric and Substance Use Disorders," *American Journal of Psychiatry*, 160: 495–503.

Keys, A., Brozek, J., Henschel, A., Mickelsen, O., and Taylor, H. (1950) *The Biology of Human Starvation*, 2 vols., Minneapolis: University of Minnesota Press.

Kieckhefer, R. (1984) *Unquiet Souls*, Chicago: University of Chicago Press.

Kihlstrom, J.F. (1987) "What this Discipline Needs is a Good Ten-cent Taxonomy of Consciousness," *Canadian Psychology*, 28: 116–18.

King, U. (2001) *Christian Mystics: Their Lives and Legacies Throughout the Ages*, Mahwah, NJ: Hidden Spring (Paulist Press).

Kissin, B. (1986) *Conscious and Unconscious Programs in the Brain*, New York: Plenum.

Klein, D.B. (1986) *The Concept of Consciousness*, Lincoln: University of Nebraska Press.

Kleinman, A. (1982) "Neurasthenia and Depression: A Study of Somatization and Culture in China," *Culture, Medicine, and Psychiatry*, 6: 117–90.

Knowles, D. (1963) *Great Historical Enterprises: Problems in Monastic History*, London: Nelson.

Koenig, H.G. and Larson, D.B. (2001) "Religion and Mental Health: Evidence for an Association," *International Review of Psychiatry*, 13: 67–78.

Koenig, H.G, George, L., and Peterson, B. (1998) "Religiosity and Remission of Depression in Medically Ill Older Patients," *American Journal of Psychiatry*, 15: 536–42.

Kohlberg, L. (1984) *The Psychology of Moral Development*, San Francisco: Harper & Row.

Koslowsky, M. and Babkoff, H. (1992) "Meta-analysis of the Relationship between Total Sleep Deprivation and Performance," *Chronobiology International*, 9: 132–6.

Kroger, W. (1977) *Clinical and Experimental Hypnosis*, second edition, Philadelphia: Lippincott.

Kroll, J. (1988) *The Challenge of the Borderline Patient*, New York: W.W. Norton.

Kroll, J. (1993) *PTSD/Borderlines in Therapy*, New York: W.W. Norton.

Kroll, J. (1998) "Religion and Psychiatry," *Current Opinion in Psychiatry*, 11: 335–39.

Kroll, J. (2003) "Posttraumatic Symptoms and the Complexity of Responses to Trauma," *Journal of the American Medical Association*, 290: 667–70.

Kroll, J. and Bachrach, B. (1982) "Medieval Visions and Contemporary Hallucinations," *Psychological Medicine*, 12: 709–21.

Kroll, J. and Bachrach, B. (1982) "Visions and Psychopathology in the Middle Ages," *Journal of Nervous and Mental Disease*, 170: 41–9.

Kroll, J. and Bachrach, B. (1986) "Sin and the Etiology of Disease in Pre-Crusade Europe," *Journal of the History of Medicine*, 41: 395–414.

Kroll, J. and Bachrach, B. (1993) "Justin's Madness: Weak-mindedness or Organic Psychosis?" *Journal of the History of Medicine*, 48: 40–67.

Kroll, J. and De Ganck, R. (1986) "The Adolescence of a Thirteenth Century Visionary Nun," *Psychological Medicine*, 16: 745–56.

Kroll, J. and De Ganck, R. (1989) "Beatrice of Nazareth: Psychiatric Perspectives on a Medieval Mystic," *Cistercian Studies*, 24: 301–23.

Kroll, J., Egan, E., Erickson, P., Carey, K., and Johnson, M. (2004) "Moral conflict, religiosity, and neuroticism in an outpatient sample," *Journal of Nervous and Mental Disease*, 192: 682–8.

Kroll, J., Habenicht, M., Mackenzie, T., Yang, M., Chan, S., Vang, T., Nguyen, T., Ly, M., Phommasouvanh, B., Nguyen, H., Vang, Y., Souvannasoth, L., and Cabugao, R. (1989) "Depression and Posttraumatic Stress Disorder in Southeast Asian Refugees," *American Journal of Psychiatry*, 146: 1,592–7.

LaBerge, S. (1992) "Physiological Studies of Lucid Dreaming," in J.S. Antrobus and M. Bertini (eds.) *The Neuropsychology of Sleep and Dreaming*, Hillsdale, NJ: Lawrence Erlbaum, pp. 289–303.

Lackner, B. (1972) *The Eleventh-Century Background of Citeaux*, Washington, DC: Cistercian Publications.

Lakoff G (1987) *Women, Fire, and Dangerous Things*, Chicago: University of Chicago Press.

Lakoff, G. and Johnson, M. (1986) *Metaphors We Live By*, Chicago: University of Chicago Press.

Laor, N., Wolmer, L., Kora, M., Yucel, D., Spirman, S., and Yazgan, Y. (2002) "Posttraumatic, Dissociative, and Grief Symptoms in Turkish Children Exposed to the 1999 Earthquakes," *Journal of Nervous and Mental Disease*, 190: 824–32.

Laughlin, C.D., McManus, J., and d'Aquili, E. (1990) *Brain, Symbol & Experience: Toward a Neurophenomenology of Human Consciousness*, Boston: Shambhala.

Lawrence, C.H. (1989) *Medieval Monasticism*, second edition, London: Longman.

Lindworsky, J. (1936) *The Psychology of Asceticism*, trans. Emil Heiring, London: H.W. Edwards.

Lives of the Desert Fathers (1981) trans. Norman Russell, Kalamazoo, MI: Cistercian Publications.

Lloyd, D. (2002) "Functional MRI and the Study of Human Consciousness," *Journal of Cognitive Neuroscience*, 14: 818–31.

Lochrie, K. (1991) *Margery Kempe and Translations of the Flesh*, Philadelphia: University of Pennsylvania Press.

Locke, J. (1939) "An Essay Concerning Human Understanding," in E.A. Burtt (ed.) *The English Philosophers from Bacon to Mill*, New York: Random House.

Ludwig, A.M. (1966) "Altered States of Consciousness," *Archives of General Psychiatry*, 15: 225–34.

Lutgard of Aywieres: Life (1987) by Thomas de Cantimpre, trans. Margot King, Saskatoon: Peregrina.

Lynch, J.H. (1973) "The Cistercians and Underage Novices," *Citeaux*, 24: 283–97.

Lynch, J.H. (1992) *The Medieval Church*, London: Longman.

McCormick, L., Nielsen, T., Ptito, M., Hassainia, F., Ptito, A., Villemure, J.-G., Vera, C., and Montplaisir, J. (1997) "REM Sleep Dream Mentation in Right Hemispherectomized Patients," *Neuropsychologia*, 35: 695–791.

McDonnell, E. (1954) *The Beguines and Beghards in Medieval Culture, with Special Emphasis on the Belgian Scene*, New Brunswick, NJ: Rutgers University Press.

McGinn, B. (1991) *The Foundations of Mysticism*, New York: Crossroad.

McGinn, B. (1994) *The Growth of Mysticism*, New York: Crossroad.

McGinn, B. (1998) *The Flowering of Mysticism*, New York: Crossroad.

McHugh, P.R. (1999) "How Psychiatry Lost its Way," *Commentary*, 108: 32–8.

McKitterick, R. (1977) *The Frankish Church and the Carolingian Reforms, 789–895*, London: Royal Historical Society.

MacLean, P. (1990) *The Triune Brain in Evolution*, New York: Plenum.

McNamara, J. and Halborg, J. (eds.) (1992) *Sainted Women of the Dark Ages*, Durham, NC: Duke University Press.

Malinowsky-Rummell, R. and Hansen, D. (1993) "Long-term Consequences of Childhood Physical Abuse," *Psychological Bulletin*, 114: 68–79.

Malmquist, C. (1986) "Children who Witness Parental Murder: Posttraumatic Aspects," *Journal of the American Academy of Child Psychiatry*, 25: 320–5.

Maloney, H.N. (1988) "The Clinical Assessment of Optimal Religious Functioning," *Review of Religious Research*, 30: 3–17.

Mandler, G. (1979) "Thought Processes, Consciousness, and Stress," in V. Hamilton and D.M. Warburton (eds.) *Human Stress and Cognition*, Chichester: John Wiley, pp. 179–201.

Margaret Oingt (1990) *The Life of the Virgin Saint Beatrice of Ornacieux*, trans. Renate Blumenfeld-Kosinski, Newburyport, MA: Focus Information Group.

Margaret of Ypres: Life (1990) by Thomas de Cantimpre, trans. Margot King, Toronto: Peregrina Press.

Marguerite d'Oingt (1965) *Les Oeuvres*, Publiees par Antonin Duraffour, Pierre Gardette, and Paulette Durdilly, Paris: Societe d'Edition "Les Belles Lettres."

Marie d'Oignies: Life (1986) by Jacques de Vitry, trans. Margot King, Saskatoon: Peregrina Press.

Markus, R. (1990) *The End of Ancient Christianity*, Cambridge: Cambridge University Press.

Marsella, A.J. (1993) "Sociocultural Foundations of Psychopathology: An Historical Overview of Concepts, Events, and Pioneers Prior to 1970," *Transcultural Psychiatric Research Review*, 30: 97–142.

Marsella, A.J., Tharp, R.G., and Ciborowski, T.J. (eds.) (1979) *Perspectives in Cross-Cultural Psychology*, New York: Academic Press.

Martyrologium Romanum (1949) Torino.

Mazzoni, C. (1996) *Saint Hysteria*, Ithaca: Cornell University Press.

Meagher, P.K., O'Brien, T.C., and Aherne, C.M. (eds.) (1979) *Encyclopedic Dictionary of Religion*, Washington, DC: Sisters of St. Joseph of Philadelphia.

Melzack, R. (1986) "Neurophysiological Foundations of Pain," in R.A. Sternbach (ed.) *The Psychology of Pain*, second edition, New York: Raven Press.

Merton, T. (1949) *The Waters of Siloe*, New York: Harcourt Brace Jovanovich.

Merton, T. (1961) *Mystics and Zen Masters*, New York: Farrar, Straus, & Giroux.

Merton, T. (1985) *The Hidden Ground of Love: Letters*, ed. William Shannon, New York: Farrar, Straus, & Giroux.

Midgley, M. (1996) "One World, but a Big One," *Journal of Consciousness Studies*, 3: 500–14.

Miller, G.A. (1956) "The Magical Number Seven, Plus or Minus Two: Some Limits on Our Capacity for Processing Information," *Psychological Review*, 63: 81–97.

Mindell J.A., Owens, J.A., and Carskadon, M.A. (1999) "Developmental Features of Sleep," *Child and Adolescent Psychiatric Clinics of North America*, 8: 695–725.

Mitchell, J., Laine, D., Morley, J., and Levine, A. (1986) "Naloxone but not CCK-8 May Attenuate Binge-eating in Patients with Bulimia," *Biological Psychiatry*, 21: 1,399–406.

Moller, H. (1971) "The Social Causation of Affective Mysticism," *Journal of Social History*, 4: 305–38.

Mullaney, D.J., Kripke, D.F., Fleck, P.A., and Johnson, L.C. (1983) "Sleep and Nap Effects on Continuous Sustained Performance," *Psychophysiology*, 20: 643–51.

Mullen, P., Martin, J., Anderson, J., Romans, S., and Herbison, G.P. (1993) "Childhood Sexual Abuse and Mental Health in Adult Life," *British Journal of Psychiatry*, 163: 721–32.

Murdock, G. and White, D. (1969) "Standard Cross-cultural Sample," *Ethnology*, 8: 329–69.

Murdoch, I. (1999) *Existentialists and Mystics*, Harmondsworth: Penguin Books.
Murphy, H.B.M. (1982) *Comparative Psychiatry*, Berlin: Springer.
Murphy, J. (1976) "Psychiatric Labeling in Cross-cultural Perspective," *Science*, 191: 1,018–28.
Murphy, M. and Donovon, S. (1997) *The Physical and Psychological Effects of Meditation: A Review of Contemporary Research with a Comprehensive Bibliography 1931–1996*, second edition, Sausalito, CA: Institute of Noetic Sciences.
Nagel, T. (1986) *The View from Nowhere*, New York: Oxford University Press.
Natsoulas, T. (1978) "Consciousness," *American Psychologist*, 33: 906–14.
New Oxford Annotated Bible (1991) ed. Bruce Metzger and Roland Murphy, New York: Oxford University Press.
Newman, B. (1990) "Some Mediaeval Theologians and the Sophia Tradition," *Downside Review*, 108: 111–30.
Nigg, W. (1972) *Warriors of God*, New York: Knopf.
O'Donoghue, N.D. (1979) "Vocation," in Noel D. O'Donoghue, *Heaven in Ordinaire: Some Radical Considerations*, Springfield, IL: Templegate.
O'Hanlon, J. (1875–1913) *Lives of the Irish Saints*, 10 vols., Dublin.
Onen, S.H., Alloui, A., Gross, A., and Eschallier, A. (2001) "The Effects of Total Sleep Deprivation, Selective Sleep Interruption and Sleep Recovery on Pain Tolerance Thresholds in Healthy Subjects," *Journal of Sleep Research*, 10: 35–42.
Pagels, E. (1979) *The Gnostic Gospels*, New York: Random House.
Pagels, E. (2003) *Beyond Belief: The Secret Gospel of Thomas*, New York: Random House.
Paphnutius (1993) *Histories of the Monks of Upper Egypt*, trans. Tim Vivian, Kalamazoo, MI: Cistercian Publications.
Parkes, J.D. (1985) *Sleep and its Disorders*, Philadelphia: Saunders.
Pearson, K.L. (1997) "Nutrition and the Early-medieval Diet," *Speculum*, 72: 1–32.
Pekula, R., Wegner, C., and Levine, R. (1985) "Individual Differences in Phenomenological Experience: States of Consciousness as a Function of Absorption," *Journal of Personality and Social Psychology*, 48: 125–32.
Petroff, E. (1986) *Medieval Women's Visionary Literature*, New York: Oxford University Press.
Petroff, E. (1994) *Body and Soul*, New York: Oxford University Press.
Petrus de Natalibus (1513) *Catalogus sanctorum et gestarum eorum ex diversis volumnibus collectus*, ed. Antonio Verlo, Strasbourg.
Pilcher, J.J. and Huffcutt, A.I. (1996) "Effects of Sleep Deprivation on Performance: A Meta-analysis," *Sleep*, 19: 318–26.
Pomeroy, C. and Mitchell, J.E. (1989) "Medical Complications and Management of Eating Disorders," *Psychiatric Annals*, 19: 488–93.
Potter, N.N. (2003) "Commodity/Body/Sign: Borderline Personality Disorder and the Signification of Self-Injurious Behavior," *Philosophy, Psychiatry, Psychology*, 10: 1–16.
Powers, W.K. (1975) *Oglala Religion*, Lincoln: University of Nebraska Press.
Poynter, N. (1973) *Medicine and Man*, Harmondsworth: Penguin.
Pribram, K.H. (1977) "Some Observations on the Organization of Studies of Mind, Brain, and Behavior," in N. Zinberg (ed.) *Alternate States of Consciousness*, New York: Free Press, pp. 220–9.
Price, D. (1988) *Psychological and Neural Mechanisms of Pain*, New York: Raven Press.
Prigge, N. and Kessler, G. (1990) "Is Mystical Experience Everywhere the Same?" in R.K.C.

Forman (ed.) *The Problem of Pure Consciousness*, New York: Oxford University Press, pp. 269–87.
Proudfoot, W. (1985) *Religious Experience*, Berkeley: University of California Press.
Proust, M. (1992) *Swann's Way*, Vol. I of *In Search of Lost Time*, trans. C.K. Scott Moncrieff and Terence Kilmartin, New York: Modern Library.
Purves, D. (1992) Book Review of David Dennett, "Consciousness Explained," *Science*, 257: 1,291–2.
Putnam, F.W., Zahn, T.P., and Post, R.M. (1990) "Differential Autonomic Nervous System Activity in Multiple Personality Disorder," *Psychiatry Research*, 31: 251–60.
Ramamurthi, B. (1995) "The Fourth State of Consciousness: The Thuriya Avastha," *Psychiatry and Clinical Neurosciences*, 49: 107–10.
Ramsey, W., Stich, S., and Garon, J. (1993) "Connectionism, Eliminativism, and the Future of Folk Psychology," in Scott Christensen and Dale Turner (eds.) *Folk Psychology and the Philosophy of Mind*, Hillsdale, NJ: Lawrence Erlbaum, pp. 315–39.
Remschmidt, H. and Schmidt, M.H. (eds.) (1990) *Anorexia Nervosa*, Toronto: Hogrefe & Huber.
Reypens, L. (ed.) (1964) *Vita Beatricis: De Autobiografie van de Z. Beatrijs van Tienen O. Cist.*, 1200–1268, Antwerp: Uitgave Van Het Ruusbroec-Genootschap.
Reypens, L. and Van Mierlo, J. (1926) *Beatrijs van Nazareth: Seven Manieren van Minne*, Leuven.
Rhue, J. and Lynn, S.J. (1989) "Fantasy Proneness, Hypnotizability, and Absorption – A Re-examination," *International Journal of Clinical and Experimental Hypnosis*, 37: 100–6.
Richard of St. Victor (1983) *The Twelve Patriarchs* (also called *Benjamin Minor*), trans. Patrick Grant, *Literature of Mysticism in Western Tradition*, New York: St. Martin's Press.
Riehle, W. (1981) *The Middle English Mystics*, London: Routledge & Kegan Paul.
Rorty, R. (1979) *Philosophy and the Mirror of Nature*, Princeton: Princeton University Press.
Ross, J.J. (1965) "Neurological Findings after Prolonged Sleep Deprivation," *Archives of Neurology*, 12: 399–403.
Ross, M. and Conway, M. (1996) "Remembering One's Own Past: The Construction of Personal Histories," in R.M. Sorrentino and E.T. Higgins (eds.) *Handbook of Motivation and Cognition: Foundations of Social Behavior*, New York: Wiley.
Roth, A., Ostroff, R. and Hoffman, R. (1996) "Naltrexone as a Treatment for Repetitive Self-injurious Behavior: An Open-label Trial," *Journal of Clinical Psychiatry*, 57: 233–7.
Roth, M. and Kroll, J. (1986) *The Reality of Mental Illness*, Cambridge: Cambridge University Press.
Rothman, T. (1972) "De Laguna's Commentaries on Hallucinogenic Drugs and Witchcraft in Dioscorides' Materia Medica," *Journal of the History of Medicine*, 46: 562–7.
Rousseau, P. (1978) *Ascetics, Authority, and the Church in the Age of Jerome and Cassian*, Oxford: Oxford University Press.
Rule of St. Benedict (1975) trans. Anthony Meisel and M.L. del Mastro, New York: Doubleday.
Rule of St. Benedict (1982) Collegeville, MN: Liturgical Press.
Russ, M., Roth, S., Kakuma, T., Harrison, K., and Hull, J. (1994) "Pain Perception in Self-injurious Borderline Patients: Naloxone Effects," *Biological Psychiatry*, 35: 207–9.

Rusticula, or Marcia, Abbess of Arles: Life (1992) in Jo Ann McNamara and John Halborg (eds. and trans.), *Sainted Women of the Dark Ages*, Durham: Duke University Press, Chapter 7.

St. Augustine's Abbey at Ramsgate (1947) *The Book of Saints: A Dictionary of Servants of God Canonized by the Catholic Church*, fourth edition, New York: Macmillan.

Sanchez-Bernardos, M.L. and Avia, M.D. (2004) "Personality Correlates of Phantasy Proneness among Adolescents," *Personality and Individual Differences*, 37: 1,069–79.

Sandman, S. (1991) "The Opiate Hypothesis in Autism and Self-injury," *Journal of Child and Adolescence Psychopharmacology*, 1: 237–48.

Savage, A. and Watson, N. (trans. & eds.) (1991) *Anchoritic Spirituality: Ancrene Wisse and Associated Works*, New York: Paulist Press.

Scarry, E. (1985) *The Body in Pain*, New York: Oxford University Press.

Schredl, M. and Erlacher, D. (2004) "Lucid Dreaming Frequency and Personality," *Personality and Individual Differences*, 37: 1,463–73.

Schulenburg, J.T. (1978) "Sexism and the Celestial Gynaeceum, from 500 to 1200," *Journal of Medieval History*, 4: 117–33.

Schulenburg, J.T. (1998) *Forgetful of Their Sex: Female Sanctity and Society, ca. 500–1100*, Chicago: University of Chicago Press.

Schultz, J.A. (1991) "Medieval Adolescence: The Claims of History and the Silence of German Narrative," *Speculum*, 66: 519–39.

Schumaker, J. (1992) *Religion and Mental Health*, Oxford: Oxford University Press.

Sharkey, P.W. and Maloney, H.N. (1986) "Religiosity and Emotional Disturbance: A Test of Ellis's Thesis in His Own Counseling Center," *Psychotherapy*, 23: 640–1.

Simeon, D. and Abugel, J. (2004) *Feeling Unreal: Depersonalization Disorder and the Loss of Self*, New York, Oxford University Press.

Simoen, D., Gross, S., Guralnik, O., Stein, D., Schmeidler, J., and Hollander, E. (1997) "Feeling Unreal: 30 Cases of DSM-III-R Depersonalisation Disorder," *American Journal of Psychiatry*, 154: 1,107–13.

Singer, J.L. (1977) "Ongoing Thought: The Normative Baseline for Alternate States of Consciousness," in N. Zinberg (ed.) *Alternate States of Consciousness*, New York: Free Press, pp. 89–120.

Slavney, P. (1990) *Perspectives on "Hysteria,"* Baltimore: Johns Hopkins University Press.

Smith, C. (1993) "REM Sleep and Learning: Some Recent Findings," in A. Moffit, M. Kramer, and R. Hoffman (eds.) *The Functions of Dreaming*, Albany: State University of New York Press.

Smith, C. (1995) "Sleep States and Memory Processes," *Behavioral Brain Research*, 69: 137–45.

Smith, H. (1964) "Do Drugs Have Religious Import?" *Journal of Philosophy*, 61: 517–30.

Smith, H. (2000) *Cleansing the Doors of Perception: The Religious Significance of Entheogenic Plants and Chemicals*, Boulder, CO: Sentient Publications.

Smolensky, P. (1988) "On the Proper Treatment of Connectionism," *Behavioral and Brain Sciences*, 11: 1–74.

Sommers, C.H. (1996) "Pathological Social Science: Carol Gilligan and the Incredible Shrinking Girl," in *The Flight from Science and Reason, Annals of the New York Academy of Science*, 775: 369–81.

Sorokin, P.A. (1950) *Altruistic Love: A Study of American "Good Neighbors" and Christian Saints*, Boston: Beacon.

Spanos, N.P. (1986) "Hypnotic Behavior: A Social-psychological Interpretation of Amnesia, Analgesia, and 'Trance Logic'," *Behavioral and Brain Sciences*, 9: 449–566.
Spiegel, D., Bierre, P., and Rootenberg, J. (1989) "Hypnotic Alteration of Somatosensory Perception," *American Journal of Psychiatry*, 146: 749–54.
Staal, F. (1975) *Exploring Mysticism*, Berkeley: University of California Press.
Stace, W.T. (1960) *Mysticism and Philosophy*, London: Macmillan.
Stannard, D. (1980) *Shrinking History: On Freud and the Failure of Psychohistory*, Oxford: Oxford University Press.
Stewart, C. (1998) *Cassian the Monk*, New York: Oxford University Press.
Sullivan, M. (1996) "Key Concepts: Pain," *Philosophy, Psychiatry, Psychology*, 2: 278–80.
Szmukler, G.I. and Tantam, D. (1984) "Anorexia Nervosa: Starvation Dependence," *British Journal of Medical Psychology*, 57: 303–10.
Tart, C.T. (1977) "Putting the Pieces Together: A Conceptual Framework for Understanding Discrete States of Consciousness," in N. Zinberg (ed.) *Alternate States of Consciousness*, New York: Free Press, pp. 158–219.
Tellegen, A. and Atkinson, G. (1974) "Openness to Absorbing and Self-altering Experiences ('Absorption'), A Trait Related to Hypnotic Susceptibility," *Journal of Abnormal Psychology*, 83: 268–77.
Terr, L. (1991) "Childhood Traumas: An Outline and Overview," *American Journal of Psychiatry*, 148: 10–20.
The Cloud of Unknowing (1978) ed. and trans. Clifton Wolters, London: Penguin.
Thomas de Cantimpre (1986) *The Life of Christina of Saint-Trond*, trans. Margot King, Saskatoon: Peregrina Press.
Tymoczko, D. (1996) "The Nitrous Oxide Philosopher," *Atlantic Monthly*, May, pp. 93–101.
Van Caenegem, R.C. and Ganshof, F.L. (1962) *Kurze Quellenkunde des Westeuropischen Mittelalters*, Gottingen: Vandenhoeck & Ruprecht.
Van der Kolk, B., Perry, J.C., and Herman, J. (1991) "Childhood Origins of Self-destructive Behavior," *American Journal of Psychiatry*, 148: 1,665–71.
Van Deth, R. and Vandereycken, W. (1991) "Was Nervous Consumption a Precursor of Anorexia Nervosa?" *Journal of the History of Medicine*, 46: 3–19.
Vandereycken, W. and Lowenkopf, E.L. (1990) "Anorexia Nervosa in 19th Century America," *Journal of Nervous and Mental Disease*, 178: 531–35.
Vandereycken, W. and van Deth, R. (1994) *From Fasting Saints to Anorexic Girls*, New York: New York University Press.
Vauchez, A. (1993) *The Laity in the Middle Ages: Religious Beliefs and Devotional Practices*, Notre Dame, IN: University of Notre Dame Press.
Vekeman, H. (1972) "Vita Beatricis en Seuen manniern van Minne: Een Vergelijk Studie," *Ons Geestelijk Erf*, 46: 3–54.
Vies des saints et des bienheureux selon l'ordre du calendrier (1935–1959) eds. Jules Baudot and Leon Chausesin, 13 vols., Paris.
Vogel, G.W. (1975) "A Review of REM Sleep Deprivation," *Archives of General Psychiatry*, 32: 749–61.
Walker, L. (1984) "Sex Differences in the Development of Moral Reasoning: A Critical Review," *Child Development*, 55: 681.
Watson, N. (1987) "The Methods and Objectives of Thirteenth Century Anchoritic Devotion," in Marion Glasscoe (ed.) *The Medieval Mystical Tradition in England: Exeter Symposium IV*, Woodbridge, Suffolk: Boydell & Brewer.

Watts, A. (1957) *The Way of Zen*, New York: New American Library.
Webb, W.B. (1985) "A Further Analysis of Age and Sleep Deprivation Effects," *Psychophysiology*, 22: 156–61.
Wegner, D.M. and Wheatley, T. (1999) "Apparent Mental Causation: Sources of the Experience of Will," *American Psychologist*, 54: 480–92.
Weil, S. (1987 [1963]) *Gravity and Grace*, trans. Gustave Thibon, London: Routledge.
Weinstein, D. and Bell, R. (1982) *Saints and Society, Christendom, 1000–1700*, Chicago: University of Chicago Press.
Wessley, S. (1994) "Neurasthenia and Chronic Fatigue: Theory and Practice in Britain and America," *Transcultural Psychiatric Research Review*, 31: 173–209.
West, L.J., Jantzen, H.H., Lester, B.K., and Corneilson, F.S. (1962) "The Psychosis of Sleep Deprivation," *Annals of the New York Academy of Sciences*, 96: 66–70.
West, M.A. (1980) "Meditation and the EEG," *Psychological Medicine*, 10: 369–75.
Westermeyer, J. and Wintrob, R. (1979) "'Folk' Explanations of Mental Illness in Rural Laos," *American Journal of Psychiatry*, 136: 901–5.
Whang, E.E., Perez, A., Ito, H., Mello, M.M., Ashley, S.W., and Zinner, M.J. (2003) "Work Hours Reform: Perceptions and Desires of Contemporary Surgical Residents," *Journal of the American College of Surgeons*, 197: 624–30.
Wilkinson, R.T. (1965) "Sleep Deprivation," in O.G. Edholm and A.L. Bacharach (eds.) *Physiology of Survival*, London: Academic Press, pp. 399–430.
Williams, B. (1981) "Moral Luck," in B. Williams, *Moral Luck: Philosophical Papers 1973–1980*, Cambridge: Cambridge University Press.
Williams, H., Morris, G., and Lubin, A. (1958) "Illusions, Hallucinations and Sleep Loss," in L.J. West (ed.) *Hallucinations*, New York: Grune & Stratton, pp. 158–65.
Winkelman, M. (1992) *Shamans, Priests and Witches: A Cross-Cultural Study of Magico-Religious Practitioners*, Tempe: Arizona State University Anthropological Research Papers, No. 44.
Winkelman, M. (2000) *Shamanism: The Neural Ecology of Consciousness and Healing*, Westport, CT: Greenwood.
Wise, R.A. (1983) "Brain Neuronal Systems Mediating Reward Processes," in J.E. Smith and J.D. Lane (eds.) *The Neurobiology of Opiate Reward Processes*, Amsterdam: Elsevier, pp. 405–37.
Wolfson, A.R. and Carskadon, M.A. (1996) "Early School Start Times Affect Sleep and Daytime Functioning in Adolescents," *Sleep Research*, 25: 117.
Wolfson, A.R. and Carskadon, M.A. (1998) "Sleep Schedules and Daytime Functioning in Adolescents," *Child Development*, 69: 875–87.
Yates, A., Leehey, K., and Shisslak, C.M. (1983) "Running: An Analogue of Anorexia?" *New England Journal of Medicine*, 308: 251–5.
Zaehner, R.C. (1957) *Mysticism Sacred and Profane*, Oxford: Clarendon Press.

INDEX

Note: page numbers in italics refer to illustrations or tables

abnormality/religiosity 190–1, 199
absorption, altered states of consciousness 3, 42–3, 58, 59–60, 64, 196
acedia 151
Acta Sanctorum 92, 93, 99
Adalbert 107
addictions 28, 71
Adelheid of Vilich 98
adolescence 163, 164, 240n37; *see also* age factors
Aelred of Rievaulx 21
age factors 76, 78, 82
Ahab 24
Ailred of Rievaulx 118
Akil, H. 74
Alaric 100
alcohol 2, 3–4, 30, 59–60, 64
Allport, Gordon 184–5
Amalfred 136–8
Amelberge *106, 197*
amenorrhea 87
Ammon 74
analgesia 28
anchoresses 22
Ancrene Wisse 22
anesthesia 28
Angela of Foligno 52, 121, 194–6
Anglican clergy sample study 186–7
anorexia nervosa 5, 22, 87, 188
Anthony, Saint 54
anti-abortionists 188
Apollo, desert father 74, 193
apophatic tradition 51, 63, 74, 111, 178, 198, 201
Archilochus 58
Arnulf of Villiers 103, 111, 239–40n19

asceticism 17, *17*, 18–21; adolescents 164, 240n37; Beatrice of Nazareth 103, 121, 160; biological approach 7–8; Church 143–4; consciousness, altered states 28–9; cultural factors 36, 127; Eastern 219n7; ecstasy 65; gender factors 115–16, 127–8; hagiography 62; holiness 101; motivation 17, 62; and mysticism 7, 48, 110, 119–28, 203, 206, 217–18, 236n24, 236n25; neurophysiology 28–9; physiology of 10–11, 27–8; privately performed 25–6; psychology 10–11, 25–6; publicly performed 23–5, 74; Radegund 130, 132–3, 140–1; as rebellion 125; reductionism 29–30; ritual 153; spirituality 125; union with God 181; *see also* fasting; laceration of flesh; sleep deprivation
ascetics 1, 2, 5–6, 207; carnal desires 48; cultural factors 208; deviants 4; female 6, 22; mystical experience 48; pain 68; psychological approach 5; sanity 35; self-injurious behavior 3, 7, 61–2; time frame *213*
athletes 164
Attwater, D.:*see* Butler's *Lives of the Saints*
Augustine, Saint 50, 168, 199–200
Avignon papacy 124

Baal priests 24
Babylas *73*
Babylonian captivity 125
Bachrach, B. 114
Balthild of Neustria 98
Baring-Gould, Sabine 94

264

Basil 22
Bathilde *109*
Baudonivia 129, 132, 140, 143
Baudot, Jules 94, 96, 99
Beatrice of Nazareth 98; asceticism 103, 121, 160; biographer 111, 147–50; childhood 150–2; depression 151, 160, 199, 205; diary 148, 150; ecstatic state 158, 159; family background 146–7; feigning madness 23, 205; God's grace 158; Maagdendaal 147; novitiate 146–7, 152–3, 156–7; pain 68; Rameya 147, 157–8; religious community's response 155–6; scriptorium 147, 148, 157; self-injurious behavior 154–6, 240n19; *Seven Manieren van Minne* 52, 54, 149, 160, 239n13, 239n14; sleep avoidance 81–2; sloth 159; spiritual development 13, 157, 160, 181, 207; *vitae* 39–40, 68–9, 149, 205
Beatrice of Ornacieux: burning the flesh 161–2, 163; carnal desires 160, 162; devil 161–2; grace 162–3; spiritual development 13, 161–4, 181; vision 162
Becket, Thomas 107
Bede, Venerable 100
Beizer, Janet 191
Belgian women mystics 98
Bell, Rudolph: asceticism 212; fasting 22, 22, 220n18; and Weinstein 96, 97, 99, 113, *114*, 123, 206; women saints 99, 113, *114*, 123
Benedict, Saint: *The* Rule of St Benedict 61, 79, 200, 246n53
Benedict of Aniane 1, 18–19, 58
Benedict of Nursia 18, 22, 49, 105
Benedictine Ramsgate scholars 93–4
Berlin, Isaiah 58
Bernard of Clairvaux 22, 57, 192–3, 204, 241n43
Bernard the Penitent 21
Berthar 129
beta-encephalin 69
beta-endorphin 72
Beutler, Madgalena, of Freiberg 98
Bibliotheca Sanctorum 94, 96
biofeedback 42–3
biographers 59, 111, 147–50
Biographical Dictionary 94
biological approach 7–8, 204
Black Plague 124

blasphemy 160, 163
Bloemardine of Brussels 98
Bloemendaal 146, 152, 156, 157–8
blood chemistry 70
blood pressure reduction 44
blood sugar levels 27, 30
bodily urges *see* carnal desires
body as text 170, 242n19
Bolland, John 92
Bollandists 97
Boniface 54, 107
Borderline Personality Disorder 5, 71
Børresen, Kari 103
Bouyer, L. 107
brain: alcohol 30; consciousness, altered states 27, 43–4; hominid 70; imagery 45; pain 71–2, 74; reptilian 70; reward centers 69–71; right/left dominance 46; serotonin 226n73
Branch Davidian cult 188
breathing 70
bridal mysticism 63, 192–3
Broderick, J.F. 94
Bruno of La Chartreuse 22
Buddhism 2, 63, 200, 204
bulimics 71, 188
burning the flesh 19, 112, 141–3, 161–2, 163
Butler, Alban: *Lives of the Saints* 94, 97; as database 12, 91, 99, 104, 112–13; saints 96, 203
Bynum, C. W. 22, 212

cardiovascular competence 44
caring for sick 140
carnal desires: ascetics 48; Beatrice of Ornacieux 160, 162; closeness to God 17; Isaac 49; self-injurious behavior 48; starvation 22, 86–7; Suso 167–8
Carolingian saints 94
Carskadon, M.A. 78
Carthusian monasteries 163
Cassian, John: communal worship 200; *Conferences* 49–50; consciousness, altered states 120; meditation 2, 48–9, 60; sleep 79
Catherine of Siena 1
celibacy 105, 209–10
Celtic saints 21
central nervous system 28, 40, 66, 71–2
cerebral cortex 71
chain-wrapping 21, *24*, 143, 238n33
chanting 30, 34

INDEX

Charcot, Jean Martin 192
charity 105, 110, 133, 196, 203, 205, 209
Charlemagne 1, 19
chastity 225n42
child development 244–5n25
childhood trauma 4, 133–4, 142, 144, 237n16
Chilperic 130
Chlodovald 108
Chramm 132
Christianity: alcohol/drug-induced states 3; class 60; exemplars 1; forgiveness 143; Franks 130; religious experience 100–1; Roman Empire 100, 107; salvation 136; Saul 50; self-injurious behavior 6; Western medieval 1, 2, 10, 51, 60, 73–4; women 123–4; *see also* missionaries
Christina Mirabilis 1, 59, 182, 189–90
Christina of Markyate 98, 118
Christina of St. Trond 189
Christina the Astonishing *see* Christina Mirabilis
Christine, sister of Beatrice of Nazareth 149, 150
Christopher, Saint 93
Chrysostom, Saint John 22, 60
Church 200; asceticism 143–4; disapproval 21, 22; hierarchy 6; institutions 209; moral authority 125; reform 10; self-injurious behavior 24–5; state 182; women's role 124
Church fathers 22
Churchland, Patricia 37
circadian cycle 21, 40, 75, 77
Cistercian Order 80, 108, 146, 153
class factors 60, 209, 210, 211, 212
climate change 125
Cloninger, R. C. 64
Clothar I 129, 130–1, 132, 133–4, 139, 145
Clotild 130, 133
Cloud, Saint 108, 210–11, 235n7
The Cloud of Unknowing 193–4, 201
Clovis 130
cocaine 59
cognitive neuroscience 45, 65
cognitive psychology 228n6
cold, extremes of 21, 130, 139, 153, 155, 162
Colette, Sainte *20*, 21
Cometa *73*
community/individual 61

consciousness 7, 9, 37–8; apophatic tradition 51, 63, 74, 111, 178; Eastern view 37–8; focal attention 66–7; information chunking 67; metaphor 37; mystics 55; neuropsychology 38; sleep 40, 57; transcendence 1–2; *see also* stream of consciousness
consciousness, altered states 2–3; asceticism 28–9; biological view 204; brain physiology 27, 43–4; Cassian 120; divine presence 55; fasting 3, 10, 205; individual differences 3, 64; induction techniques 36, 59–62; Ludwig 38; meditation 200; mystical experience 110; pain 74, 221n35; personality traits 64; physiological changes 10; psychological analysis 6; quality of experience 198–9; self-injurious behavior 2, 7, 9–10, 28; silence 204; sleep deprivation 10, 31; Suso 170; valued by society 64–5; visions 110; *see also* hypnotic states; trance states
consciousness-altering substances 48
conservatism 56
Constable, Giles 22, 98
Constantine, Emperor 100
Constantinople 100
contemptus mundi 2, 10
conversion 50, 54
corticosteroids 72–3
cross, wooden 172
Csikszentmihalyi, Mihaly 65
cultural factors 86; anorexia nervosa 87; asceticism 36, 127; ascetics 208; depression 118; discipline 201; mysticism 201, 203–4; mystics 208; religiosity 184–5; sacrifice 201; self-injurious behavior 25, 123; vision 86
Cuthbert 106–7

Dalai Lama 37–8
Daniel, missionary 107
Daniel the Stylite 21
databases 91–6, 113–15
daydreaming 57, 58
De Ganck, R. 103, 111, 239–40n19
Delatte, Paul 79
Delehaye, Hippolyte 97
Delooz, Pierre 96–7, 98
demonic hordes *85*, 86
Dennett, David 37

266

depersonalization 9, 41
depression 187, 244n18; Beatrice of Nazareth 151, 160, 199, 205; cultural factors 118; pain 72; religiosity 185–6
derealization state 41
dervish, whirling 61
desert fathers 34–5, 73–4, 168, 216
detachment: asceticism 17; suffering 176–7; Suso 166, 173, 174, 176, 177, 201
deviants 4, 189
devil 17, 161–2
Dinzelbacher, Peter 118
Dionysius Exiguous 100
discipline 22, 34–5, 170, 201
discipline (whip) 21, *73*, 171, 172
dissociative episodes 4, 9
divine presence 55; *see also* union with God
Dominicus Loricatus 24
Donovon, Steven 44
dowries 161
dream states 40, 76–7, 112
drivenness 145, 164, 183, 189
drug use 2, 9, 31, 59–60, 64; *see also* psychedelic drugs
drumming 2, 30, 61
Dunbar, Agnes: *A Dictionary of Saintly Women* 94

earthbound individuals 3, 59
Eastern Orthodoxy 2, 60
Ebner, Christine 98
Ebner, Margarete 98
ecclesiastic position 211
Eckhart, Meister 98, 201
ecstasy: asceticism 65; Beatrice of Nazareth 158, 159; divine presence 55; gender factors 110; Giles of Assisi 196; inauthenticity 197–8; Margaret of Ypres 43; neurophysiology 45; Suso 169; Teresa of Avila 245–6n46; visions 19
Edmund of Eynsham 118
electroencephalographic patterns 45–6, 75
Eliade, Mircea 17
Elijah 24
Elizabeth of Reute 98
Elizabeth of Spalbeck 98
encephalins 72
endorphins 27, 69, 71, 72, 74
English saints 94
Enlightenment 184

erotic imagery 192–3
esoteric religions 60
euphoria 70–1
Eustadiola of Bourges 98
Evagrius 60
Eve of St Martin 98
evolution, bodily 70, 229n11
exaggeration 193, 198, 204
Eysenck Personality Questionnaire 186

familicide 132, 210
famine 83, 124–5
fanatics 188, 190–1
Fanning, S. 190
Farber, Ilya 37
Farmer, David 94
fasting 2; Beatrice of Nazareth 155; Bell 22, 220n18; consciousness, altered states 3, 10, 205; data 123; desert fathers 216; gender factors 214, 218; Guthlac, the warrior 85–6; liturgical 21; Minnesota group 83–4; monastic 83; mysticism 213, 216–17; nutrition 83–4; physiology 27; as protest 22, 87; psychology 84, 207; Radegund 130, 132, 139; as self-injurious behavior 19, 34, 74, 112; women 22, 123–4, 125
femininity 192, 198
feminist critical theorists 63, 94, 102, 202, 207
Fish, Frank 37
flagellants 25, 193
flash-backs 48, 135
Flemish mystics 63, 146
Flora of Beaulieu 1
flow experiences 65, 164
forgiveness 143, 174
Forman, Robert 41–2, 51, 204
Fortunatus, Venantius 129, 134–5, 141–2, 143, 238n32
Foucault, Michel 125
fox/hedgehog modes 58
Francis, Leslie 186
Francis of Assisi 1, 52, 121
Franciscan order 96–7
Franks 129, 130, 138, 142
Fredegund 130, 237n9
Freud, Sigmund 191–2
fringe movements 188
Fulford, K.W.M. 179–80

Gall, missions 54
Gandhi, M. 25

Gawronski, Raymond 200
gender factors: asceticism 115–16, 127–8; child development 244–5n25; ecstasy 110; fasting 214, 218; hagiography 11; holy persons 94, 98, 113–15, 124, 209, 211; hysteria 192; justice 236n31; male domination 6, 123; mysticism 119–20; self-injurious behavior 123; sleep deprivation 125, 214–15; sleep requirements 76, 78; thick-/thin-boundaried people 58; time frame 122; *see also* men; women
Genia, Vicky 184
genius 189
Genovefa, Life of 63
genuflection 21, 153, 154
Geoffrey of St. Thierry 98
George, Charles 96
George, Katherine 96
George, Saint 93
Gerald of Salles 98
Gerard of St. Albinus 98
Germanus, Saint 63
Gertrude of Helfta 33–4, 63, 201
gesta (deeds) 99
Gherardesca of Pisa 29, 41–2, 52, 98
Giles of Assisi 1, 58, 196
Gilligan, Carol 190, 244–5n25
Glodesind of Metz 98
gluttony 225n42
Gnosticism 61
God: intercession 34, 34; loving 205–6; personal closeness 60, 65, 73, 109–10, 125–6, 164, 201; presence of 55, 62; Suso 171, 172–3, 175, 177–8; *see also* grace of God; union with God
Good Friday study 31–2
good works *see* charity
Goodich, Michael 95, 97, 99, 115, 206
grace of God 33–6; Beatrice of Nazareth 158; Beatrice of Ornacieux 162–3; mystical state 3, 29–30; transcendence 31, 50
Graffin, N. F. 46
Gregory of Tours 22, 129, 130–1, 143, 235n7, 237n9
growth hormone 77
Gudule 197
Guerin, P.: *Les petites Bollandistes* 94
Guigo of La Chartreuse 98
guilt, survivors 134, 136
Guthlac, the warrior 51–2, 85–6, 232n6

Hadewyjch of Antwerp 98
hagiographers, male 102–3, 113, 149–50
hagiography 11, 19, 62, 102, 127
hairshirts 21; Radegund 130, 132, 142; Rusticula 19; Suso 171
Hale-Bopp comet suicides 179
hallucinogens 4
Hartmann, Ernest 58, 64; thin/thick boundaried people 55–7
heart teachings 63
hedgehog/fox modes 58
Helle, Abba 74
Henry, spiritual advisor 23
Henskens, Godefroid 92
heresy 61, 98
Herman, Judith 144
Hermanfrid 129, 138
hermits 52, 107
hibernation 40
Hildegard of Bingen 1
Hilgard, Ernest 42
Hinduism 25, 200, 204
historiography 101
history, statistical methods 232n1
holiness 212, 234n2; asceticism 101; charity 203, 205, 209; eccentricity 190; feminization 110; pathways to 12, 105, 205; saints 105–7; self-injurious behavior 3; socio-political factors 108–10; visions 93
Hollywood, Amy 102, 103, 149–50, 190, 240n19
Holweck, F.G. 93–4
holy persons: class 209; databases 91–6, 113–15; enclaustration 124; gender 94, 98, 113–15, 124, 209, 211; mental stability 182; personality 204; *see also* ascetics; mystics; saints
Honorius, Emperor 100
Honorius III, Pope 108
household gods 238n21
Huffcutt, M. 76
Hume, David 37
humor 175–6
Hundred Years War 125
Hungary *81*
hunger strikes 25
Huxley, Aldous 201; *The* Doors of Perception 32
hyperalgesia 67–8, 242n25
hypermotility 61
hypersensitivity 68
hyperventilation 61, 70

hypnagogic reveries 77
hypnotic states 40–2; hidden observer construct 224n26; neurophysiological approach 44–5; pain 28, 72; as voluntary response strategy 229n18
hypnotizability 42–4, 46, 58
hysteria 182; abnormality 190–1; Angela of Foligno 194–6; diagnoses 183; exaggeration 193, 198, 204; gender factors 192; mysticism 196; personality 193; sexual frustration 192–3; suggestibility 191, 193, 196–7, 204; thin-boundaried people 198

Ida of Leau 98
Ida of Louvain 50–1
Ida of Nivelles 98, 158
Ignatius Loyola 4, 200
imitatio Christi 10
individual/community 61
individual differences: absorption 59–60; consciousness, altered states 3, 64; sleep requirements 27; statistical deviations 80; susceptibility to drugs 59–60
induction techniques 31, 36, 59–62
inertia 136
information chunking 67
Innocent III 34, 220n15
Irenaeus, Bishop 61
Irish Catholics 25
Irish saints 94
Isaac, desert father 49, 51
Islam 54, 125
isolation 2, 61, 86, 106–7, 136–8
Italian saints 95, 96–7, 99

Jackson, M. 179–80
James, William 55, 165, 170, 241n1
Jaspers, Karl 178–9, 193, 194, 245n36
Jesuits 201
Jesus Christ: as heavenly bridegroom 63; ridiculed 23; suffering *106*, 176
Joan of Arc 57, 210
John, desert father 26
John, King of England 34
John of Lycopolis 74
John of the Cross 4, 200
Johns, E. Roy 38
Johnson, M. 62
Johnston, William 200–1
Jones, Richard 51
Jonestown suicides 188

Julian of Norwich 1, 201
Juliana of Mont Cornillon 1, 107–8
justice 236n31

Kalendars of Scottish Saints 94
Kempe, Margery 201
Kendler, Kenneth 186
Kentigern of Strathclyde, Saint 21
Kevin, Saint 21
Keys, Ancel 83–4
kinetic stimulation 61
King, Ursula 178
1 Kings 24
knowledge acquisiton 58
Koenig, Harold 185
Kohlberg, Lawrence 190
Kroll, J. 114

laceration of flesh 34, 66, 112, 122, 123, 205, *213*, 216; Beatrice of Nazareth 154–5; hagiography 7, 19; neural networks 26; psychological effects 207; Radegund 141; Suso 171–2; women 124, 125
Ladislaus, King *81*
Lakoff, G. 62
Langton, Stephen 34
language factors 62–3, 66, 206
Leary, Timothy 32
Lenten exercises 141, 170–1
lepers 196
The Lives of the Desert Fathers 74
Locke, John 47
love of God 205–6
LSD 59
lucid dreams 40
Ludwig, Arnold 38–40
Luke's Gospel 62
Lutgard of Aywieres 34, 51, 58
Lutgard of Tongeren 98

Maagdendaal 147
McGinn, Bernard 55, 103–4, 112, 190, 199
McNamara, Jo Ann 94, 98
male domination 6, 123
Malmquist, Carl 134
malnutrition 83, 84
Mandler, G. 66–7
manic depression 187
mantras 48, 61
Margaret of Cortona 52, *53*
Margaret of Oingt 161

INDEX

Margaret of Ypres 19, 43, 98
Marguerite d'Oingt 98
Marie d'Oignies 21, 59, 102
marijuana 59, 60
Markus, Robert 61
married life 140
Martha—Mary story 62
martyrdom 54, 105, 107–8, 138, 143, 175
masochism 165
Matthew's Gospel 100
Mazzoni, Christina 192
meditation: absorption 42; Cassian 2, 48–9, 60; consciousness, altered states 200; Eastern traditions 4, 200; EEG patterns 45–6; neurophysiology 44–5; prayer 2, 33–4, 61; techniques 4; trance states 60–1
melancholia 136; *see also* depression
men: celibacy 105, 209–10; hagiographers 102–3, 149–50; male domination 6, 123; married life 140; mystics 127; patriarchy 22; saints 126–7
mental clutter: escape from 2, 163; mysticism 48–9; reduction 39, 47–8, 63–4, 63–4
mental illness: diagnoses 183; religiosity 183–4, 183–7, 186; self-injurious behavior 7–8, 25–6, 203; Suso 178, 182, 199
mental state 35–6, 80, 182, 223n4
Merovingians: familiacide 132; Franks 129; queens 130; saints 94, 96, 101–2, 108–9, 130; social conditions 144; Thuringian royal house 135; vengeance 133
Merton, Thomas 80
mescalin 31, 32
metaphor 37, 62–3, 192, 227n89
microsleep 81
Middle Ages as concept 10–11, 84, 122–3, 207
Milan Edict 107
Miller, G.A. 228n6
mind—body dichotomy 29–30
mineral deficiencies 84
Minnesota group 83–4, 86
miracles 93, 105
missionaries 54, 107
mobility restrictions 21, 25–6, 61, 172
modern culture 201
Moller, Herbert 192
monasteries 11, 79–81, 83, 110

Morocco 107
mortification of the flesh: asceticism 1, 3; Beatrice of Nazareth 156; motivation 5–6; pathway to God 188; physiology 10, 27; Suso 165; *see also* laceration of flesh
Moses, desert ascetic 49, 51
murder 188
Murdoch, Iris 236n32
Murdock, G. 60
Murphy, Michael 44
musicians 164
mystical experience 42, 51, 110–11, 228n99; authenticity 29–30, 31–3; biological explanations 204; grace 3, 29–30
mysticism 117–19; affective 126, 196, 198; apophatic 198, 201; asceticism 7, 48, 110, 119–28, 203, 206, 217–18, 236n25; biological approach 7–8; cultural factors 201, 203–4; erotic imagery 192; fasting 213, 216–17; hagiography 127; hysteria 196; mental clutter 48–9; metaphor 227n89; psychedelic drugs 32; psychological traits 55–7, 182, 186; self-injurious behavior 217; speculative 198; union with God 32; Zaehner 32
mystics 1, 207, 235n13; administrative powers 57; biographers 59; Cistercians 153; consciousness 55; cultural factors 208; Eastern 204; Flemish 63, 146; gender factors 119–20, 127; Rhineland 63, 98, 190, 200; thin-boundaried people 57–8; women 63, 87, 98, 110, 117, 149–50; *see also* holy persons

Natali, Pietro: *Catalogus sanctorum* 92
Nathalan 21
Nazareth religious community 147, 148; *see also* Beatrice of Nazareth
Neot, Saint 21
nerve synapses 69
neural networks 28, 71, 72
neuroendocrine functions 86–7
neurophysiological approach 6, 28–9, 44–5
neuropsychology 38
neuroticism scales 186
neurotransmitters 69, 70, 71–2, 187
New Oxford Review 200
Newman, Barbara 242n38

Nicetas of Pereaslav 21
Nicosa 73
nicotinic acid 31–2
Nigg, Walter 54
nociceptive system *see* pain
non-attachment 48; *see also* detachment
novelty seeking 56
nutritional requirements 83–4

Odile 56
O'Donoghue, Noel 17, 183
Oedipal complex 192
O'Hanlon, J. 94, 95
openness 3, 64, 126, 184, 196, 226n73
opiate peptides 69, 70
opiates, endogenous 69–71, 72, 72–3
Or, Abba 74
Origen 60
other-worldliness 1, 57–8
Otloh of St. Emmeram 98
Otto IV 34
out-of-body experiences 41

paganism 135, 136
Pagels, Elaine 61
pain: acute/chronic 67–9; ascetics 68; avoidance 70, 201, 203; brain 71–2, 74; consciousness, altered states 73–4, 221n35; depression 72; hyperalgesia 242n25; hypnotic states 28, 72; mental state 35–6; redemptive power 72; self-imposed 21; sleep deprivation 67, 80; stream of consciousness 66; in teeth 27
pain control 44
papacy 124, 125
Paphnutius 74
Paradiso, Domenica Dal 98
paranoid people 191
patriarchy 22
Pearson, Kathy 84
penance 17, 171, 190
penitence 35
periodization 99, 100
Perpetua, Saint 98
personality: consciousness, altered states 64; holy persons 204; hysteria 193; mixtures 58; multiple 221n33; religiosity 184; saintliness 204–5; saints 199; starvation 86; thin-/thick-boundaries 55–7
personality disorder 5, 71, 170, 178–9, 244n16

Peter, Saint 100
Peter of Alcantara 183
Peter of Luxembourg 1, 111, 242n12
Peter of Ruffia 107
Petroff, Elizabeth 94, 98, 125
phantasy-proneness 42, 58
pharmaceutical industry 187, 244n18
Philip Augustus, King of France 34
phylogenetic development 40
physical performance 189
physiological changes: asceticism 10–11, 27–8; consciousness, altered states 10; fasting 27; psychological state 6; self-injurious behavior 4–5, 206; sleep deprivation 205
Pilcher, J.J. 76
pillar sitting:*see* stylites
Pityron 74
Plains Indians 24–5
plant medicinals 3
Poitiers convent 132, 140
political protests 25
Poor Clares 21
Porete, Marguerite 98
post-traumatic stress responses 4, 48, 133–4
power/spirituality 125
prayer: meditation 2, 33–4, 61; sleep avoidance 75, 81–2, 130, 132, 152, 153; sleep deprivation 75, 79
pride 22, 35
propitiation 23
Proudfoot, Wayne 30, 31
Proust, Marcel 57
psilocybin ingestion 31
psychedelic drugs 31, 32, 33–4, 60, 226n77
psychiatry 182, 187–9, 244n18
psychodynamic theory 206
psychology: asceticism 10–11, 25–6; ascetics 5; consciousness, altered states 6; fasting 84, 207; laceration 207; mysticism 55–7, 182, 186; physiological changes 6; Radegund 133, 140, 145; sleep deprivation 205, 207; trance states 6; transcendence 55–7
psychopathology 5, 165, 179–80, 198, 241n1
psychosexual developmental stages 191–2
publicity-seeking 22, 35
puncturing the flesh 19, 68; *see also* laceration of flesh

purgatory 190
Purves, Dale 37

queen saints 130

Rabin, Y. 188
Radegund: asceticism 130, 132–3, 140–1; burning the flesh 112, 141–3; caring for sick 140; charity 133; childhood trauma 133–4, 142, 144; Clothar 130–1, 132, 139–40, 145; cold, extremes of 130, 139; drivenness 145, 164; family background 13, 129–30; fasting 130, 132, 139; hairshirts 130, 132, 142; household gods 238n21; isolation 136–8; laceration of flesh 141; martyrdom 138, 143; murder of brother 130–1, 132, 137–8; prayer vigils 130; psychological conflict 133, 140, 145; religiosity 138–9; at Saix 131, 132, 140; self-injurious behavior 132–3, 142, 144; suicide plans 132, 140, 141; as survivor 134, 136; *The* Thuringian War 129, 131, 134–5, 136–7, 142; *see also* Fortunatus
Rameya 147, 157–8
reality concepts 54, 65
reclusives 62; *see also* isolation
reductionism 29–30, 222n37
relaxation states 44
religiosity: abnormality 190–1, 199; behavior 184; culture 184–5; depression 185–6; good works 203; intrinsic/extrinsic 185; mental illness 183–7; personality 184; Radegund 138–9
religious experience 31, 100–1, 179–80
religious services 59, 79
renunciation of flesh 17, 21, 35, 73–4
repression 144
reproduction 70, 229n11
reward centers 69–71
Rhineland mystics 63, 98, 190, 200
Richalm of Schonthal 98
Richard of St. Victor 62
ridicule 1, 21, 23, 58
risk-taking 56
rites of passage 163
ritual 24–5, 135, 153
Robert of Arbrissel 22
Roman Empire 100, 107
Roman Martyrology 94

Romans, Book of 50
Rome, sacked 100
Rusticula of Arles 19, 98

sacrifice 17, 23, 105, 201
Sadistic Personality Disorder 244n16
saintliness 130, 204–5
saints 93–4, 206–7; biographies 99; Carolingian 94; Celtic 21; class 210, *211*, 212, 213; ecclesiastical status *210*; holiness 105–7; Italian 99; men 126–7; Merovingian 94, 96, 101–2, 108–9, 130; as models 51–2; mystics/ascetics 203; national groups 94, 95, 96–7, 99; personality 199; royal 95, 130; sleep deprivation 214–15; spirituality 190; statistical study 207; time frame *212*, *213*; women 94, 96, 102–3, 113–15, 116, 117; *see also* hagiography; holy persons
salvation 136, 199
Saul of Tarsus 50
Scarry, Elaine 66
schizophrenia diagnosis 26, 178, 187
Scholastica 105
Schulenburg, Jane 94–8, 113, *114*, 123, 206
scourging 29, 41–2, 170
scriptoria 92, 147, 148
seclusion *see* isolation
self, non-physical 30
self-consciousness 9, 38
self-immolation 25
self-injurious behavior 4–5, 5, 74; ascetics 3, 7, 61–2; Beatrice of Nazareth 154–6, 240n19; Borderline Personality Disorder 71; carnal desires 48; Christianity 6, 21, 22; Church 24–5; closeness to God 73; conditioning effects 28; consciousness, altered states 2, 7, 9–10, 28; covert 68–9; cultural factors 25, 123, 222n40; excessive 22, 112; gender factors 123; Hinduism 25; holiness 3; intercession of God 34; as mental illness 7–8, 25–6, 203; mysticism 217; penitence 35; physiological approach 4–5, 206; Radegund 132–3, 142, 144; ritual 24–5; sacrifice 23; sexual abuse 4; spirituality 112; Suso 171, 172; synaptic pathways 28; union with God 21; *vitae* 102; *see also* asceticism; burning the flesh; fasting; laceration of

flesh; mortification of flesh; sleep deprivation
self-reflectivity 47
sensory deprivation 61
sensory inputs 66
serotonin 226n73
sexual abuse 4
sexual desire *see* carnal desire
sexual frustration 192–3
sexuality 163
shamanism 60
shrines of saints 93
Simeon Stylites, the elder 1, 21
Simeon Stylites, the younger 1
simony 24, 168
sin 35
Singer, Jerome 47
sleep 11, 40, 57, 75–7, 79–81
sleep avoidance 81–2, 130, 132, 152, 153
sleep deprivation 2, 3, 7, 21, 27, 36, 112, 122, 213; behavior 75–6; consciousness, altered states 10, 31; gender factors 125, 214–15; mental state 80; monasteries 11; pain 67, 80; partial 76, 78–9; physiology 205; prayer 75, 79; psychological effects 205, 207; Rusticula 19; saints 214–15; techniques 81, 82; total 77, 230n11
sleep fragmentation 76, 79
sleep requirements: age factors 76, 78, 82; gender factors 76, 78; individual differences 27
slimming 188
sloth 159
Smith, Huston 31, 32
social protest 126, 205
socially disruptive behavior 187
socio-political factors 108–10
solitary contemplation 61, 106–7; *see also* isolation
Song of Songs 63, 153, 204
Sorokin, Pitirim 96, 97
Spanos, Nicholas 44
spiritual development 54–5; Beatrice of Nazareth 13, 157, 160, 181, 207; Beatrice of Ornacieux 13, 161–4, 181; Suso 166, 174–5, 181, 207
spiritual directors 22, 23, 25, 43
Spiritual Experience Index 184
spirituality 184; abnormality 199; asceticism 125; Eastern 200; power 125; Rhinelands 190; saints 190;

self-injurious behavior 112; training for 189; women 102, 127
sports excesses 71
Staal, F. 204
Stace, W.T. 204
Stagel, Elsbeth 98, 166, 168, 173, 178
standing motionless 21, 25–6
starvation 122; carnal desire 22, 86–7; famine 83; neuroendocrine functions 86–7; personality 86; psychological changes 7, 36, 86, 220n18; women mystics 87; *see also* fasting
statistical methods 11–12, 80, 207, 232n1
Stephen of Hungary 81
stream of consciousness 47, 48, 64, 66
stylites 1, 21, 107
subjectivity/language 206
subjugation of will 188
suffering: body/soul 150; detachment from the world 176–7; Jesus Christ 106, 176; as penance 190; Suso 169; symbolic meaning 27; thin-boundaried people 56–7; *see also* pain
suggestibility 126; absorption 196; children 237–8n20; consciousness, altered states 3, 43–4; hysteria 191, 193, 196–7, 204; mystics 198
suicides 179, 188; planned 132, 140, 141
Sun Dance 24–5
survivor's guilt 134, 136
Suso, Henry 13, 24, 121; autobiography 166; carnal desires 167–8; consciousness, altered states 170; detachment 166, 173, 174, 176, 177, 201; Dominican monastery 168; ecstasy 169; *The Exemplar* 166; exhibitionism 205; family background 167–8; God 171, 172–3, 175, 177–8; humor 175–6; laceration of flesh 171–2; Lenten exercises 170–1; *The Life of the Servant* 166, 168, 175, 178; *The Little Book of Eternal Wisdom* 176; *Little Book of Truth* 165, 177; martyrdom 175; masochism 165; mental illness 178, 182, 199; mortification of the flesh 165; personality 199; psychopathology 165; self-centredness 173–4, 175; self-injurious behavior 171, 172; sister 173–4, 204–5; spiritual development 166, 174–5, 181, 207; suffering 169; as victim 180; vocation 169; *see also* James

synaptic pathways 28
Szmukler, G.I. 87

Tantam, D. 87
Tart, Charles 38–9
Tellegen, A. 64
temptation 63
Teresa of Avila 57, 201, 245–6n46
Theodosian II 100
Theudebert 133
Theuderic I 129
thick-boundaried people 3, 55–7, 58, 64–5
thin-boundaried people 55–8, 64, 198
Thomas, T. Hugh 186
Thomas de Cantimpre 19
thorn-wraps 21, 68–9, 154
thought-deflection techniques 28
Thuringian royal house 129, 135, 138, 142
Thurston, H.:*see* Butler's *Lives of the Saints*
Tobin, Frank 166
Toleration Edict 100
tooth pain 27
tortures 21, 172
trance induction 61–2, 120; adolescence 164; alcohol/drugs 3–4; emotion 126; meditation 60–1; psychedelic drugs 226n77; religious ceremonies 59; scourging 29
trance states 1, 6, 40–2, 43
transcendence: canonical teachings 61; consciousness 1–2; divine 33; grace of God 31, 50; hallucinogens 4; induction techniques 36; metaphor 62–3; openness 3, 64; psychological traits 55–7; vocabulary 62
trauma 144; *see also* childhood trauma
Truth 191
twin studies 186

union with Absolute 204
union with God: asceticism 181; hagiography 112; metaphor 192; mysticism 32; pathways 2, 109–10, 166; salvation 199; self-injurious behavior 21; Suso 177–8

urinary system 70

Van Deth, R. 87
Vandereycken, W. 87
Vauchez, A. 110
Vianney, John 183
virginity 210
visions: Beatrice of Ornacieux 162; consciousness, altered states 110; cultural factors 86; in dreams 112; ecstasy 19; Forman 51; Gherardesca 41–2; holiness 93; McGinn 103–4; Odile 56
vitae 92–3, 101, 102
de Vitry, Jacques 59, 102
vocation 17, 52, 54, 125, 169
voices, supernatural 29
vulnerability 188–9

Watson, Nicholas 110
Weil, Simone 51, 112
Weinstein, Donald 96, 97, 99, 113, *114*, 123, 206
West, Michael 45–6, 46
whipping 153–4; *see also* laceration of flesh; scourging
whirling 2, 61
White, D. 60
William of Bourges 108
Williams, Bernard 180
Winkelman, Michael 60
Witger, Count *197*
women: celibacy 105, 209–10; Christianity 123–4; church reform 124; fasting 22, 123–4, 125; married life 140; mystics 63, 87, 98, 110, 117, 149–50; saints 94, 96, 102–3, 113–15, 116, 117; spirituality 102, 127; virginity 210; *see also* gender factors
worship, communal 200

Zaehner, R.C. 32, 204
zealots 189
Zen Buddhism 200–1
Zoerard *81*

eBooks – at www.eBookstore.tandf.co.uk

A library at your fingertips!

eBooks are electronic versions of printed books. You can store them on your PC/laptop or browse them online.

They have advantages for anyone needing rapid access to a wide variety of published, copyright information.

eBooks can help your research by enabling you to bookmark chapters, annotate text and use instant searches to find specific words or phrases. Several eBook files would fit on even a small laptop or PDA.

NEW: Save money by eSubscribing: cheap, online access to any eBook for as long as you need it.

Annual subscription packages

We now offer special low-cost bulk subscriptions to packages of eBooks in certain subject areas. These are available to libraries or to individuals.

For more information please contact webmaster.ebooks@tandf.co.uk

We're continually developing the eBook concept, so keep up to date by visiting the website.

www.eBookstore.tandf.co.uk